## Praise for *Canadian Communication Policy and Law*

"Canada's rapidly-changing communications system requires thoughtful analysis of both long-standing and emergent issues, from intellectual property law to telecommunications policy. Synthesizing decades of research and legal precedent, Dr. Bannerman unpacks core debates from various theoretical and normative standpoints, paying close attention to power relations and systemic bias, and offering readers a framework to engage in policy research. This is a valuable resource that connects communications policies with the lived experiences of the diverse individuals and groups who make up Canadian society."

—Rob McMahon, Communications and Technology, University of Alberta

"This work is immensely valuable in many respects—it offers an engaging introduction to a wide range of theoretical approaches that are made accessible through clear prose and compelling real-world examples. Unlike many introductory texts, which present perspectives on law and policy in a neutral fashion, this work offers a vigorous critique of Canada's legal and regulatory communications framework—a regime that, while neutral in its face, serves to reinforce inequity and preserve the status quo."

—Lisa Taylor, JD, LLM, School of Journalism, Ryerson University

"Sara Bannerman offers a unique primer on a range of Canadian policy and legal issues pertaining to media and communications; its expansive scope is unparalleled. What especially stands out about this book is its attention to the underlying power structures that shape policy and law, as well as its innovative approach to guiding readers through the process of legal research. This text is essential for anyone interested in how Canadian media and communications are shaped by law and policy."

—Tamara Shepherd, Communication, Media and Film, University of Calgary

# CANADIAN COMMUNICATION POLICY *and* LAW

# CANADIAN COMMUNICATION POLICY *and* LAW

*Sara Bannerman*

CANADIAN
SCHOLARS

Toronto | Vancouver

Canadian Communication Policy and Law
Sara Bannerman

First published in 2020 by
**Canadian Scholars, an imprint of CSP Books Inc.**
425 Adelaide Street West, Suite 200
Toronto, Ontario
M5V 3C1

**www.canadianscholars.ca**

**Library and Archives Canada Cataloguing in Publication**

Title: Canadian communication policy and law / Sara Bannerman.
Names: Bannerman, Sara, 1975- author.
Description: Includes bibliographical references and index.
Identifiers: Canadiana (print) 2020018332X | Canadiana (ebook) 20200183346 |
    ISBN 9781773381725 (softcover) | ISBN 9781773381732 (PDF) |
    ISBN 9781773381749 (EPUB)
Subjects: LCSH: Communication policy—Canada—Textbooks. | LCSH: Mass media—
    Law and legislation—Canada—Textbooks. | LCGFT: Textbooks.
Classification: LCC KE2460 .B36 2020 | LCC KF2750 .B36 2020 kfmod |
    DDC 343.7109/9—dc23

Page layout: S4Carlisle Publishing Services
Cover design: Rafael Chimicatti

Printed and bound in Ontario, Canada

Canadä

# CONTENTS

# INTRODUCTION

This book asks, "Whom does Canadian communication policy and law serve?" This question is political; the answer depends on the vantage point of the person or group responding to the question and on the values and experiences that inform their point of view. What, and who, do we primarily think of when we answer that question? What experiences inform our answer? What advantages and disadvantages have we experienced? Communication policy does not serve everyone equally. Depending on our experiences and insights, we might answer the question in different ways.[1]

This book draws on a set of theories—concepts and hypotheses—that highlight different standpoints within communication policy and law. The theories chosen are intended to cover a broad range of perspectives, though they will undoubtedly do so only partially and imperfectly. Each **theory** can be drawn on to answer the question "Whom does Canadian communication policy and law serve?" in some way. Some of these theories highlight the standpoints of those who experience systemic and institutional bias and discrimination as these play out in communication policy and law.

Communication policy and law raises many questions, including: Is the availability of violent, racist, or misogynist content on the internet a problem that should be addressed by greater regulation? Is the regulation of internet content a threat to freedom of expression? In an age of sharing, is privacy still important? Are government mass surveillance programs legal and constitutional? Doesn't "owning" a word or phrase infringe on freedom of expression? Is it important that programming available on television, radio, cable, satellite, and online streaming services is Canadian? If so, what policies best serve that goal? Many of these questions are political; different people's answers to these questions may conflict or vary depending, in many cases, on the standpoint, values, and priorities of the answerer.

Chapter 1 introduces the concepts of *law, policy, government*, and *state*. It gives an overview of the theories drawn on in the chapters that follow. It begins with **pluralism**, a theory that sees Western law, policy, and government as serving, to some extent, the public interest by balancing the interests of various groups. The chapter then moves to examine theories that are more skeptical of law, policy, and government: **bureaucratic theory**, neoliberalism, and libertarian theory. These theories tend to be critical of large government bureaucracies and strong regulation. The chapter then examines theories that are often critical of law, policy, and government on different grounds. Critical political economy, feminist and queer studies, critical race theory, critical disability theory, and Indigenous and postcolonial theories highlight the ways in which government serves the privileged, often failing to serve—and sometimes acting to oppress—working-class people, the poor, citizens, and consumers; women, queer, trans, and gender non-conforming people; people with disabilities; people who are **racialized;** and Indigenous peoples. It also examines the role of private companies, networks, and technologies in regulation and governance.

Chapter 2 introduces the Canadian legal system. It gives an overview of the common law and civil law systems, public and private law, the branches of government, and the place of Indigenous law within the Canadian legal system. It also introduces the concepts of judicial precedent and judicial review.

Chapters 3 to 12 can be read in any order. The first half of each chapter introduces a law or policy area under discussion. The second half of each chapter returns to our question: "Whom does Canadian communication policy serve?" These discussions draw on the theories introduced in Chapter 2.

Chapter 3, "Freedom of Expression and Censorship," introduces the rights of freedom of expression and the press, as well as the limits placed on those rights in Canada. It discusses the breadth of freedom of expression, and discusses the applicability of freedom of "the press" to new media. Second, the chapter discusses limits on freedom of expression. It examines some of these limits, including those placed by laws prohibiting child pornography; obscenity; hate speech; and violent, bullying, or harassing speech. It also addresses the role of private companies in regulating speech, focusing on the actions of search engines in delisting search results. The second half of the chapter asks, "Whom do laws relating to speech serve?", drawing on the liberal and critical theories introduced in Chapter 1.

Chapter 4, "Defamation," discusses defamation law in Canada by first introducing basic concepts and principles in defamation law, including the elements of defamation and defences to defamation suits. It discusses criminal defamation law, as well as strategic lawsuits against public participation (SLAPP) suits that can be used by individuals or companies seeking to chill criticism. The second half of the chapter asks, "Whom does defamation law serve?", drawing on the theories introduced in Chapter 1.

Chapter 5, "Privacy," reviews privacy law in Canada, defining the right to privacy, discussing the history of privacy regulation, and reviewing both privacy legislation and common law torts of privacy. It discusses privacy in the context of new technologies and the internet, including the emerging European "right to be forgotten" and its applicability in Canada. The second half of the chapter asks, "Whom does privacy law serve?", drawing on the theories introduced in Chapter 1.

Chapter 6, "Government Surveillance," defines surveillance and lawful access, and introduces the history of government surveillance in Canada, the *Criminal Code* provisions that apply to the interception of private communications, and mass surveillance programs that operate in Canada and internationally. The second half of the chapter then asks, "Whom does government surveillance serve?"

Chapter 7, "Intellectual Property," introduces the main categories of intellectual property and the key concepts used in each. It then asks, "Does intellectual property provide equal benefits to all?"

Chapter 8, "Telecommunication Regulation," starts by defining telecommunications and discussing the history of telecommunications regulation in Canada. It reviews the major forms of telecommunications regulation, from basic service and price regulation to the regulation of spectrum and foreign ownership of telecommunications services. In the second half, it asks, "Whom does Canadian telecommunications policy serve?"

Chapter 9, "Broadcasting Regulation," defines broadcasting and introduces broadcasting regulation. It reviews the major justifications for broadcasting regulation in Canada. It discusses the Canadian Radio-television and Telecommunications Commission (CRTC)'s role in regulating broadcasters, broadcast distribution undertakings, and programming undertakings. Following an overview of the history of broadcasting regulation in Canada, it discusses various types of broadcasting policy: media ownership regulation, and policies on content, representation, and accessibility. In the second half, it asks, "Whom does broadcasting regulation serve?

Chapter 10, "Internet Regulation," discusses the roles that government, non-governmental organizations (NGOs), and private companies play in governing the internet. The first section discusses the CRTC and the government's roles in regulating the internet. The second section discusses the roles that NGOs play in administering the architecture of the internet. The third section discusses the ways in which private corporations like Facebook and Google regulate the internet. Finally, the chapter asks, "Whom does internet regulation serve?", drawing on the theories introduced in Chapter 1.

Chapter 11, "Access to Information," introduces the right of access to information and related institutions in Canada. It reviews the process for requesting information under access to information law. In the second half, it asks, "Whom does access to information law serve?"

Chapter 12 gives an overview of legal and policy research and citation. It discusses key sources of legal and policy documents and how such documents can be accessed. It gives an overview of how to access and read judicial decisions— how to identify unanimous, majority, plurality, concurring, and dissenting opinions; and how to locate related decisions that may indicate whether a judicial decision is still current. This chapter also describes how to cite legal documents and jurisprudence in Canada, drawing on the standard guide to legal citation in Canada: the *Canadian Guide to Uniform Legal Citation*, known as the *McGill Guide* for short. It covers the citation of legislation, the Canadian Constitution and the *Canadian Charter of Rights and Freedoms*, jurisprudence, and law review articles, describing the standard citation formats for these items, with examples. This chapter can be used as a handy reference.

The concluding chapter sums up the main arguments of the book. Too often, this book argues, communications policy and law serve those who are already privileged, failing to serve those who are underrepresented and oppressed. At the same time, there are many instances where communications policy and law has enabled and supported those fighting for representation and equality. Communications policy and law are ultimately tied to broader forces and broader struggles for equality.

Key terms are bolded on first use. Definitions can be found in the glossary.

None of what is written in this book should be taken or relied on as legal advice. The author is a communications scholar and not a lawyer. If you require legal advice, be sure to consult a lawyer.

## COMMUNICATIONS GOVERNANCE NEWSLETTER

Students who are interested in following current news and events related to communications policy and law may subscribe to McMaster University's Communications Governance Observatory's *Communications Governance Newsletter*, available at http://cgo.mcmaster.ca/newsletter/.

## ACKNOWLEDGEMENTS

First, I would like to thank my students; it is they who inspired and encouraged me to write this book. I would like to thank those who have generously reviewed portions of this manuscript: Mary Caldbick, Julia Kalinina, Normand Landry, Michèle Martin, Fenwick McKelvey, Rob McMahon, Bruce Ryder, Leslie Regan Shade, Tamara Shepherd, Julia Szwarc, Lisa Taylor, Stanley Tromp, and the students of my class Communication Policy and Law in Winter 2019. I am enormously thankful for your insights and suggestions. Any errors are entirely my own. I would like to thank the Research Assistants who worked tirelessly on this project: Emmanuel Appiah, Brittany Green, Todd Harris, Nic Lazzarato, Timon Moolman, Charnjot Shokar, Ian Steinberg, and Coralie Zaza. Their hard work and patient research was important to putting this text together. As well, I would like to thank the editors at CSPI, including Emma Melnyk and Natalie Garriga, as well as Ashley Rayner, for their work with me on this book. I am thankful to McMaster University, my department and colleagues, my dean and faculty, and the Canada Research Chairs program for supporting my work and making this project possible. Finally, I would like to thank my family and friends, particularly my partner, Mary Caldbick; my mother, Deborah Bannerman; my step-father, Dennis Souder; and my sister, Molly Bannerman, for their support, encouragement, and patience as I worked on this project.

## NOTE

1.  Sandra Harding, "Rethinking Standpoint Epistemology: What Is 'Strong Objectivity?'", *The Centennial Review* 36, no. 3 (1992): 437–70; Donna Haraway, "Situated Knowledges: The Science Question in Feminism and the Privilege of Partial Perspective," *Feminist Studies* 14, no. 3 (1988): 575–99; Donna Jeanne Haraway, *The Haraway Reader* (London: Routledge, 2003); Nancy Hartsock, *The Feminist Standpoint Revisited and Other Essays* (New York: Basic Books, 1999); Sandra Harding, *The Feminist Standpoint Theory Reader: Intellectual and Political Controversies* (London: Routledge, 2003); Elizabeth Hirsh, Gary A. Olson, and Sandra Harding, "Starting from Marginalized Lives: A Conversation with Sandra Harding," *JAC* 15, no. 2 (1995): 193–225.

# 1 Whom Do Law and Policy Serve?

## INTRODUCTION

Whom do law, the legislators who make law, policy, and the bureaucracy of government serve? The answer to this question may seem obvious: Governments and the laws they make are meant to serve the public. Governments are composed, in part, of politicians elected by members of the public who represent the public and who make laws and policies on behalf of the public. They are staffed with public servants whose role it is to serve the public, as the words *public servant* imply.

However, law and government often fail or fall short of this ideal. In many cases, they prioritize the interests of particular groups, failing to serve—or acting to oppress—others. What is *the public interest*? For that matter, who is *the public* and what matters concern the public? What qualifies as an issue of public concern as opposed to a private matter? These are not easy questions.[1]

Law and government are often critiqued as serving an educated elite, big business, privileged classes, the able-bodied, the white majority, settler populations, and **cisgender** straight men over others. Furthermore, law and government can sometimes be critiqued for failing to serve any public at all; rather, government can work to serve itself. Lawmakers, politicians, and bureaucrats are sometimes criticized for serving the legal systems and bureaucracies of which they are a part. In other words, lawmakers and those in government at times, often unwittingly, work to serve themselves or the institutions they work for rather than the public more generally.

In short, we might see law and government as serving: (1) the public at large; (2) particular groups within the public; or (3) government and lawmakers themselves. Different bodies of theoretical work focus our attention on one or more of these facts.

This chapter will ask the following questions: Whom does the government serve? In whose interests does the government work? What groups are involved, or should be involved, in law and policymaking? After addressing the questions "What is law?" and "What is policy?", this chapter will review a number of theories about whom government serves and which groups are involved in law and policymaking processes.

## WHAT IS GOVERNMENT? WHAT IS THE STATE?

The words *government* and *the state* are sometimes used interchangeably. However, the terms have slightly different meanings. **Government** means the people and bureaucratic entities that fulfill and carry out the functions of the state. Governments change with elections, and bureaucracies evolve and change, but the **state** is a more abstract legal and political concept that signifies the political entity from which government derives its authority, the unit of politics recognized at the international level, and the abstract notion of the country or nation as a sovereign political power.[2]

It is important to recognize that when the words *government* or *the state* are used, they often reference Western conceptualizations of government and states. These concepts of *state* and *government,* as we use them here, arose at a historical and political moment tied to imperialism and colonialism. They are concepts that have rendered invisible other forms of political order, including Indigenous political orders.[3]

## WHAT IS POLICY? WHAT IS LAW?

What is **policy**? Whereas laws are enacted by a legislature and made or interpreted by a judiciary, policies can be made by political parties, bureaucrats, or other governance bodies. High-level policies set out the priorities and intentions of governments and are sometimes carried out through legislative change. For example, the Liberal Party of Canada committed to a policy of greater transparency and open government as a part of its policy platform during the 2015 federal election.[4] "Greater transparency" and "open government" are broad, abstract concepts. The party promised to enact these broad policies by, among other things, changing access-to-information laws to make government information more accessible to citizens (see Chapter 11). Lower-level policies might direct the everyday actions of government bureaucrats, determining routine actions such as the standard layout of government websites.[5] Policies can be formal and set out in writing as the result of a decision-making process, or they can be informal.

They can be the result of a single policy direction, or they can be the result of a series of actions and decisions.[6]

The question "What is **law**?" has a simple answer, but also gives rise to complex political and philosophical debates. The simple answer is that law is "the body of rules, whether proceeding from formal enactment or from custom, which a particular state or community recognizes as binding on its members or subjects."[7] Laws are generally set and enforced by the state. They are contained in legislative statutes, administrative rules, and court decisions.[8]

The question "What is law?" is also a political question, because defining *law* confers authority and legitimacy on some rules, customs, and institutions while denying such authority and legitimacy to others. It is important to remember that many of the concepts of law that are dominant in Canada are Western notions that have historical roots in the dominance of the Western state and legal systems; they are connected with imperialism and colonialism that ignored or obliterated other forms of law. When we speak of *law* in the West, we are usually focused on legal systems in which legal professionals and state institutions are central. This conception of law is different from legal orders that are centred not in state institutions but in religious, spiritual, political, or economic systems.[9] Canon law, Sharia law, and Indigenous law are all examples legal traditions that are not state-based, though they may be, in some cases and to varying extents, influential on, recognized by, or adopted by state institutions.

More complicated answers to the question also play out in the domain of legal philosophy, where different schools of thought consider questions about where law comes from, what laws are valid, and why. Law is, after all, just one set of norms that guide our behaviour; there are also systems of morality, convention, religion, and etiquette. What gives law its special force among these normative systems? Is law dependent on or separate from morality, convention, and religion?[10] Different approaches in legal philosophy answer these questions in different ways.

## Natural Law Theory

Some thinkers understand the authority of law as being derived from its moral merit. According to "natural law" theories of law, law is only really law when it corresponds with moral standards; law that is immoral is not law, or, at least, is not law in the full sense.[11] Thomas Aquinas and William Blackstone both argued that immoral laws are not law. Viewing morality as part of the laws of nature, Aquinas, a thirteenth-century Italian philosopher, argued that "if at any point [human law conflicts with] the law of nature, it is no longer a law but a perversion of law."[12] Similarly, the English jurist William Blackstone commented that the "law of nature, being [...] dictated by God himself, is of course superior in obligation to any other."[13] Other natural law legal theorists argue that immoral laws are law, and thus legally binding, but are defective; they are not law "in the fullest sense." Still others, including Ronald Dworkin, note that it is often necessary for judges to use moral principles when they interpret the law in particular cases.[14] Dworkin's approach is called **legal interpretivism**.[15]

## Positivist Legal Philosophy

Positivist legal philosophers, unlike natural law legal theorists, draw a strong distinction between law and morality. Law is whatever is *posited* (ordered, decided, practised, or tolerated).[16] Whatever law is produced by lawmakers—whether right or wrong, just or unjust, sensible or lacking in sense—is the law.[17] Law, in this view, is produced by humans; it does not have a divine origin, nor does it have origins in the laws of nature.[18] The question of whether a law should be followed is considered by positivists to be a separate question of morality and judgment.[19] Prominent legal positivists include Thomas Hobbes, David Hume, John Austin, H.L.A. Hart, and Jeremy Bentham.

Thomas R. Dye's definition of public policy as "whatever governments choose to do or not to do" reflects the stance of legal positivists to some degree.[20] Critics of both this definition and of the legal positivist stance argue it is more important to analyze effectiveness, and the power relations that law and policy set in place, than it is to acknowledge that law and policy are defined by lawmakers and policymakers.[21]

Positivist legal philosophy has been criticized for taking a narrow approach in its understanding of what constitutes a source of law, acknowledging some sources of law and not others in a culturally biased way. The recognition of Western legal systems and norms and the non-recognition of non-Western and Indigenous legal systems and institutions perpetuates colonialism, subordinating and contributing to the elimination of Indigenous peoples' legal systems and institutions, while requiring conformity to Western norms.[22]

## Indigenous Legal Systems and Legal Pluralism: Canada's Truth and Reconciliation Commission

In Canada, the non-recognition of existing Indigenous legal traditions and Indigenous law by the settler state is based in positivist legal philosophy that recognizes state-based laws and legal institutions as either the only sources of law or as the highest forms of law—a hierarchy that places the Canadian Constitution at the top of the legal hierarchy, federal and provincial laws below that and, at the bottom of the hierarchy, customary law such as Indigenous legal traditions—if Indigenous law is recognized as law at all.[23] This subordination and erasure of Indigenous law in Canada is a central tool of colonialism that has damaged the governance systems of Indigenous nations.[24]

Canada's **Truth and Reconciliation Commission** (TRC) recognized that, throughout Canada's history, Canadian governments have worked to eliminate Indigenous governments, as well as the Treaties and legal relationships that were established between Canada and First Nations.[25] The TRC was established in 2008 and concluded in 2015. Its mission was to document the experiences of Indigenous peoples who were taken from their families and placed in the Canadian residential school system as a part of a policy of assimilation that aimed to "cause Aboriginal peoples to cease to exist as distinct legal, social, cultural, religious, and racial entities in Canada."[26] It recognized that Indigenous peoples in Canada often see Canada's legal system as "diametrically opposed to their interests" because of Canadian laws and institutions that have aimed to eliminate Indigenous institutions and culture, that still fail to protect Indigenous peoples, and that continue to fail to recognize Indigenous legal traditions.[27] Canadian law, the TRC noted, "has been, and continues to be, a significant obstacle to reconciliation."[28]

The TRC issued 94 calls to action aimed at advancing processes of reconciliation. Among these, the TRC called on the Government of Canada to:

> Reconcile Aboriginal and Crown constitutional and legal orders to ensure that Aboriginal peoples are full partners in Confederation, including the recognition and integration of Indigenous laws and legal traditions in negotiation and implementation processes involving Treaties, land claims, and other constructive agreements.[29]

This call to action reflects Article 40 of the *United Nations Declaration on the Rights of Indigenous Peoples* (UNDRIP), which recognizes the rights of Indigenous peoples to decisions that "give due consideration to the customs, traditions, rules and legal systems of the indigenous peoples concerned."[30]

The TRC suggested that Indigenous peoples should take a lead role, becoming "the law's architects and interpreters where it applies to their collective rights and interests."[31] The TRC therefore called on the federal government to fund

Indigenous law institutes to further the goals of understanding and renewing Indigenous legal traditions.[32]

**Legal pluralism** calls for the recognition of a greater multiplicity of legal sources and norms.[33] The TRC's and UNDRIP's calls for the recognition and integration of Indigenous laws and legal traditions are consistent with legal pluralists' calls for recognition of multiple sources of law. Even as Canadian courts have failed to recognize Indigenous rights and have subordinated Indigenous law, the Supreme Court of Canada has also recognized that Indigenous peoples' legal traditions exist and survive.[34]

Alongside the legal philosophies just described, which inquire about the origins and legitimacy of law, there are numerous political and sociological theories about whom law and policy serve.

## WHOM DO LAW AND GOVERNMENT SERVE?

The question "Whom do law and government serve?" always has multiple answers. Law and government may, in many cases, make the lives of many citizens better. At the same time, law and government might serve the interests of some citizens better than they serve the interests of others, with programs and services focusing on some groups over others. For example, government may set privacy laws that permit businesses to run smoothly while failing to protect the privacy of individuals. Laws and policies might make some citizens' lives better, while making others' lives worse, creating inconveniences or injustices. For example, regulators might grant broadcasting licences to some businesses, while limiting the granting of such licences to organizations serving minority communities. Intellectual property laws may protect copyright owners while making life more difficult or costly for those who wish to use samples of music in a new remix or who wish to copy works in course packs.

Law and policy can be influenced by the lobbying of corporations that may have a common interest in making money, but which often have conflicting interests among themselves. For example, new technology companies like internet service providers may have very different interests from older technologies companies like broadcasters.

Laws and policies can be influenced by the interests of government bureaucrats who seek to expand or retain their own power. Here, too, different government agencies may have differing political visions or different stakes in the game. For example, the Department of Global Affairs may view Canada's intellectual property laws with an emphasis on how they will affect Canada's relationships with other countries, while the Department of Innovation, Science and Economic Development may focus on how intellectual property laws affect Canadian businesses. Laws and policies are influenced by the interests of politicians and lawmakers who seek to win votes and power (each serving different publics, parties, and interests). For example, in 2018, there was a bitter dispute between Alberta and British Columbia over the expansion of the Trans Mountain oil pipeline. The NDP government of Alberta sought to serve the economic and political interests of the oil industry and Albertans affected by it by supporting the expansion project. Meanwhile, British Columbia also had an NDP government but opposed the pipeline expansion project in efforts to meet environmental concerns and respect Indigenous peoples' land rights.[35]

Technologies and technology designers also play a role in the construction of law and policy, setting their own private forms of regulation in software code and the terms of use associated with it. Whatever legal, political, or technological settlement is reached may serve some interests better than others. For example, film companies may install digital locks on DVDs to prevent copying—even copying that may otherwise be perfectly legal.

Theories of law and bureaucracy give us the tools to think in a big-picture sense about whom law and policy serve. Major thinkers have theorized that law and government primarily serve not the public, but legal institutions and bureaucracies. Others have argued that law and government primarily serve particular groups of people, such as a ruling or capitalist class or particular elites. Some thinkers now argue that software code matters more in our daily lives than legal code, since technologies influence what can be done in our digital lives and have enormous power in regulating our actions. Still other theorists argue that, while imperfect, law and government do broadly serve the various publics they are meant to serve.

## The Public Interest?

One of the most common notions about law and policy is that they exist to serve the public interest. However, many of the theories discussed in this chapter challenge this notion. The *public interest* is a nebulous and highly contested concept; everyone has a different idea of what "the public interest" is. As a result, we are confronted with a problem: *Which* public interest does government serve?

### Pluralism

Some political scientists observe that a key element of democracy is civil society, a set of diverse groups formed around private and public interests that vie to have their voices heard in the public sphere or political arena.[36] According to pluralist theory, democracy exists if conflict is institutionalized through political processes that allow competing civil society groups' voices to challenge each other and those in power.[37] In a pluralist democracy, political power is diffused among various economic, cultural, professional, and social groups who must, to some extent, tolerate and accommodate each other.[38] Such groups provide checks and balances to each other, making it difficult or impossible for any one person or group to fully control political processes. Ordinary citizens possess a reserve of political power that is not always used, but can be called upon when those in power take policy measures to which they object.[39] Governments and legislators conduct a balancing act, attempting to find solutions to satisfy all, or most, groups. There are many participants in the process, and no single group dominates.[40]

While no single group dominates, some groups have more power than others because they are better organized and/or have access to more resources. Several factors influence groups' ability to influence policymaking and law-making processes. Money is an important one; well-resourced groups can more effectively communicate their message to legislators and governments. Determination is another; if a group is very committed to, and willing to spend time organizing on, a particular issue, that group is more likely to succeed.[41] If no such group exists—because those concerned about an issue feel demoralized or powerless due to a lack of resources, geographic diffusion, or other barriers to participation and organizing—that issue is less likely to be solved via law and policymaking.[42]

The size and multiple agencies of government mean that even though money matters, multiple parties have access to government because there are many access points. The **bureaucracy** of government is composed of various rival departments and agencies that ensure no single group can dominate overall. Government agencies sometimes provide support to groups trying to influence policy.[43]

The film industry provides an example where various groups vie for funding. Filmmakers compete with other artistic and cultural organizations, and those same organizations in turn compete with groups seeking funding for other priorities such as health or agriculture. All of these compete with voices calling for lower taxes and smaller government. Various government departments also compete with each other; the Department of Canadian Heritage competes with other government departments seeking funding. A large government provides many points at which a group might try to influence policy.

Critics of pluralist theory argue the pluralist vision of politics overemphasizes the equality and potential influence of groups and underemphasizes the power of business owners and owners of **capital**. They argue that the pluralist view misrepresents what is actually a highly imbalanced system as being balanced, with all (or most) groups having equal influence. Critics suggest owners of capital have undue influence and are able to set the terms of the debate and the limits of possibility within which other groups, including the state, must act.

## Bureaucracy and Bureaucrats?

While pluralists argue that law and government emerge out of a contest between competing voices that generally results in laws and policies to serve the public, other theories focus on the ways in which law and policy tend to serve government and lawmakers. German sociologist Max Weber (1864–1920) was a prominent observer of the role of bureaucracy in government.

### Bureaucratic Theory

Weber argued that mass administration and mass democracy require bureaucracies—hierarchical organizations whose officials have fixed duties, which they carry out in a professional and impersonal manner based on rules and technical expertise, using standardized processes and written documents.[44] Modern legal and bureaucratic systems, Weber observed, divide workers and bureaucrats into specializations, requiring taxation to support a large number of officials.

Some observers argue that government bureaucrats, who have technical expert knowledge, can threaten democracy because politicians, who have limited time and technical knowledge, are forced to rely on them for advice. This can undermine democratic institutions, leading to political regimes that resist change due to the relative permanence and power of bureaucrats. The dominant classes—those who are most economically and socially advantaged—secure their power by using and expanding bureaucracy to provide security to middle-class intellectuals and bureaucrats.[45]

According to Weber, bureaucracy can carry out the impersonal exercise of authority in a uniform manner, justified by the idea that such impersonal exercise of power ensures "equality before the law."[46] However, bureaucracy can become a "shell of bondage" or an "iron cage" that reduces workers to cogs in a bureaucratic machine,[47] paralyzes economic initiative,[48] and makes politicians and citizens subservient to the bureaucracy that is supposed to govern them.[49] This has been called the **iron law of oligarchy** (**oligarchy**: rule by a few): the tendency that power becomes concentrated at the top in a bureaucracy.[50]

Weber's view of the law was similar; law, like bureaucracy, can create an "iron cage." While it purports to be a system that promotes freedom by enforcing rules representing the will of citizens, law can also play a more negative role. Law facilitates the subjection of workers to the will of factory owners, locking them "all the more tightly into the numbing discipline of the factory" using a set of rules that is specialized, technical, and inaccessible to the average person.[51]

We can see this in the administration of government tax credits and funding for the Canadian film industry, which makes a large bureaucracy necessary. Impersonal principles govern decisions about who is eligible for tax credits, where funding goes, and what qualifies as "Canadian content" for radio airplay. These rules can sometimes become so bureaucratic that they appear not to make sense. The 1992 hit song "(Everything I Do) I Do It for You" by Canadian rock star Bryan Adams famously did not meet the bureaucratic criteria to be "**Canadian content**" because Adams's co-writer was not Canadian.[52]

### Neoliberalism

**Neoliberal** theory posits that "human well-being can best be advanced by liberating individual entrepreneurial freedoms and skills within an institutional framework characterized by strong property rights, free markets and free trade."[53] Neoliberal proponents emphasize the limited role of the state; the state must guarantee the integrity of monetary and financial systems and ensure that legal and security institutions are in place to allow markets to operate. States may also work to create markets.[54] In neoliberal theory, states should not stray far beyond these basic functions, because "the state cannot possibly possess enough information to second-guess market signals (prices) and because powerful interest groups will inevitably distort and bias state interventions (particularly in democracies) for their own benefit."[55]

Neoliberal thought became dominant in the 1980s, following the decline of Keynesian economics in the 1970s and the collapse of communist countries in the 1980s.[56] It has been a driving force in opening up international markets for trade and, as such, has been associated with the rise of globalization.[57] It has been influential in guiding the operations of international institutions such as the International Monetary Fund (IMF), the World Bank, and the World Trade Organization (WTO).[58] In particular, neoliberalism has been influential in the trend toward the privatization of telecommunications services and in the global extension of intellectual property rights since the 1980s.

### *Libertarian Theory*

Libertarian theorists, too, question the efficacy of bureaucracy and law in serving the public interest when bureaucracy and law stray beyond basic functions. Libertarian theory takes as its main premise that every person has a right to maximum negative liberty—the right not to be interfered with. It understands people as having full self-ownership: the right to fully control, use, be compensated for the loss of, and to freely give, one's property and one's self.[59]

There are two versions of **libertarianism**, left-libertarianism and right-libertarianism. They differ in how they treat the appropriation or ownership of natural resources. The most prominent right-libertarian position is Lockean libertarianism, which considers individuals to have the right to appropriate natural resources—especially those natural resources they labour on—as long as they leave "enough and as good" for others.[60] Such thinking has been used to justify the appropriation of Indigenous lands by settlers.[61]

Left-libertarians permit the appropriation of natural resources, but they permit only the appropriation of one's per capita share (equal-share left-libertarianism), or only so much as leaves others sufficient amounts for an equal quality of life to the taker. That is, equal-share left-libertarianism acknowledges that individuals have different levels of needs and permits those with more needs to take a larger share of the natural resources.[62]

Libertarians advocate minimal state and legal intervention in individuals' affairs. They argue that bureaucracy and social planning destroy political and economic freedom. Libertarians oppose laws that promote safety (such as laws requiring individuals to wear seat belts), since such laws limit freedom. With the exception of left-libertarian requirements that payments be made to others for rights claimed over natural resources, libertarians largely oppose taxation policies that require individuals to pay for public works.[63] According to libertarians, taxation not only limits freedom but it is also wasteful because people (in this case bureaucrats and politicians) will never spend someone else's money as carefully as they would spend their own.[64]

Libertarians oppose the increasing levels of bureaucracy that planning requires, since bureaucracy ultimately wields enormous power over individual citizens' lives. Government programs and income redistribution tend to benefit the middle class rather than the poor. Bureaucrats themselves also benefit, and bureaucrats come to depend on this power and its expansion for career advancement. Governments do not work in "the public interest," because there is no public interest; libertarianism is a philosophy that views the world, and people's interests, in very individualized terms.[65]

Public funding for film, libertarians would likely argue, wears away at the political freedom of filmmakers by making them conform to bureaucratic standards. In this view, funding for film erodes the proper operation of market forces that reflect individual choices, thus permitting bureaucrats in charge of funding to wield enormous power. Money is not spent carefully, and taxpayers' money is wasted. Film funding does not serve "the public interest" from a libertarian perspective; it serves the private interests of politicians, bureaucrats, and/or filmmaking elites.

## The Privileged?

### *Critical Political Economy*

Political economists and Marxian scholars note that, fundamentally, Western law acts as the groundwork for capitalism. The law of contract, the legal basis of the modern corporation with limited liability, insurance law, banking law, and perhaps most importantly, the law of property, are basic pillars of the capitalist system.[66] These legal regimes have unequal social effects and are set up primarily to serve the interests of owners of corporations, insurance companies, banks, and property owners. At the same time, law is an arena of struggle, and subordinate groups make efforts to translate law to their interests, with some efforts—especially those that can be understood in terms of the rights that law grants—having more success than others.[67]

Marxian **political economy** and legal theory view government, legal systems, and culture industries in capitalist societies as serving to sustain a system that permits the owners of capital (i.e., money and assets that are used to make more money) to exploit workers and take the profits. Law and government, in this view, construct a property system that serves owners of capital and disenfranchises the poor, ensuring stability and a social order that sustains the conditions of capitalist production and exploitation. Capitalists' concerns dominate those of workers and the poor. In Marxian theory, bureaucracy and law—the state—is an instrument of the capitalist class. This is a structural necessity, because income and business taxes finance government; the state is therefore financially bound to support the order.[68]

Law not only sets up the basic pillars of capitalism but also legitimizes the fundamentally unjust capitalist economic order. In Marxian analysis, law serves an ideological function, legitimating the prevailing values of dominant classes. (**Ideology** is a frame of reference, or common sense, through which people view the world.[69]) Accorded a high level of respect and legitimacy, the law reinforces these values.[70] This frame of reference appears natural, normal, and right, though it is always contested.[71]

At the same time, some compromise must be formed between dominant and subordinated groups, in order to attain the assent of the subordinated to the overall system. The state and dominant class must perform vital social functions and act, to some extent, on behalf of society as a whole. Failure to do so would inspire resistance and require rule by brute force.[72]

The Marxian-influenced Frankfurt School emphasized the role that culture industries such as film, television, and popular music play in legitimating the capitalist system. The culture industries, according to Theodor Adorno and Max Horkheimer, serve to propagate the myths of success, escapism, and false happiness that prevent independent thinking and promote acceptance of capitalism, along with the subordination of people as employees.[73]

In some Marxian theory, bureaucracy creates processes of alienation—the estrangement of individuals from one another, from their work, and from their own humanity. Bureaucracy—whether governmental or non-governmental—is a social structure that oppresses people and separates them from the products of their work, turning social relationships into impersonal ones that facilitate the labour processes and permit the owners of capital to profit.[74]

Critical political economists study "the social relations, particularly the power relations, that mutually constitute the production, distribution and consumption of resources, including communication resources."[75] From this point of view, Canadian film funding and tax credits serve a primarily capitalist function; their purpose is to foster a film industry that will contribute to economic growth, to the direct benefit of owners of businesses involved in the film industry. To some extent, film tax credits and funding take money from regular Canadians and enrich owners of film companies, in many cases helping to make films that act as ideological voice boxes of the capitalist system.

On the other hand, tax credits and funding for film can be seen as progressive or socialist policies, to the extent that they promote the arts as part of a collective public endeavour, including, at times, films that are critical of the existing order. From this point of view, film tax credits and funding might be seen as a part of the compromise that sees bureaucracy serve a broader public, thus legitimating its own role, as it simultaneously enables, extends, and supports a capitalist system that critical political economists view as perpetuating inequality and injustice.

### Feminist and Queer Studies

In feminist and **queer theory**, the state has dual roles. On one hand, the state, including law, reproduces and reinforces power structures of patriarchy, sexism, cissexism, and heterosexism by focusing public policy on the needs of men and cisgender straight people, drawing on androcentric, heterosexist views of the world. The legal system and government have reproduced and reinforced patriarchal, heterosexist, and cissexist power structures, for example, by prohibiting women from voting and owning property; by failing to recognize rape within marriage as a criminal act until 1983;[76] by failing to adequately address the failures of the criminal justice system in matters of sexual assault;[77] by making homosexuality illegal in Canada until 1969;[78] and by failing to recognize sexual orientation and gender identity as prohibited grounds of discrimination until the 1990s[79] and 2017,[80] respectively, among innumerable other examples.

On the other hand, law and the state have played significant roles in addressing discrimination against women, lesbian, gay, bisexual, transgender, gender-non-conforming, and queer people.[81] Law and government can play a role in claims for recognition of such groups. For example, Canadian law now formally protects lesbian, gay, bisexual, and trans (**LGBT**) people from discrimination; homosexuality has been decriminalized; same-sex marriage is now recognized in Canada; and Canadian law now protects against discrimination based on gender expression or gender identity.[82] Law and government can also play a role in redistribution of income through tax dollars spent on social programs for women and sexual or gender minorities, or on taxation and welfare systems that create greater economic equality for such groups.[83]

Some feminists have argued the hierarchical bureaucracies that are part of government, along with bureaucracies more broadly (e.g., hierarchically organized private companies), serve as power structures that perpetuate patterns of dominance and subordination that oppress women (and men as well). Writing in 1984, Kathy Ferguson argued that, while a few women had meaningful and satisfying careers in bureaucratic organizations, women most often served in low-paying, low-level positions. She and other radical feminists argued that the path to liberation for women was not the stepping stones of education followed by a career in public administration; schools of public administration inculcate students into administrative discourse, training them in managerial skills while, at the same time, teaching techniques of discipline and control that work to subordinate women and men, helping to construct consensus about the acceptance and use of systems of domination.[84] For women to be liberated, Ferguson argued, bureaucratic modes of power must be confronted and alternative anti-hierarchical forms of organization must be adopted.

This view of feminist liberation contrasts with liberal **feminism**, which has concentrated on gaining access for women to higher-paying and higher-level positions within bureaucracies by ensuring equal recognition for men and women under the law.[85] Radical feminism does not reject affirmative action, but argues that in the absence of genuine societal equality, legal and policy provisions such as anti-discrimination and affirmative action are inadequate.[86]

Feminist theory and queer theory are useful in analyzing the ways that law and government contribute to patriarchy, heteropatriarchy, and the dominance of norms of gender identity and expression. They aim to dismantle patriarchal, heterosexist, and cissexist power structures.[87] As we shall see in the chapters to follow, they have critiqued and suggested alternatives to obscenity laws, defamation law, privacy structures, intellectual property law, and telecommunications and broadcast policies. Feminist scholars of communications policy and law have argued for greater representation of women among media and communications policymaking and for greater recognition of women's work in communications-related fields. Others have focused on creating alternative women-run media with non-hierarchical structures.

### Critical Race Theory

**Critical race theory, critical disability theory, Indigenous legal theory,** and **postcolonial analysis** focus on the ways that law and government have acted to oppress people of colour, people with disabilities, and Indigenous peoples, while supporting racialization, ableism, colonialism, and postcolonial forms of oppression. Critical race theorists argue that the law serves to maintain the status quo of white supremacy, correcting injustices that affect people of colour only when such a move also serves the interests of whites.[88]

Critical race theorists oppose the idea that law is neutral. They note that laws appear "neutral" to whites because whites do not experience or think of themselves as having a race. A legal system that was founded to serve white interests and maintain a system of white supremacy thus appears to whites not as a form of race discrimination but as neutral.[89]

Building on the earlier ideas of critical legal studies and legal realists, critical race theorists reject the idea that the law exists apart from the world, in its own realm. Instead, they see law as fundamentally influenced by the forces around it, including politics, economics, and social trends.

Critical race theorists critique the notion that the law is, or could be, colourblind. The false ideology of colourblindness is part of the ideology of liberalism, which views all people as equal. Viewing all people as equal often means ignoring historical, race-based, and other intersecting inequities. Race discrimination permeates laws and must be addressed directly by equity-promoting measures; pretending to enact "neutral" laws risks failing to address the realities of race-based inequity. "Colourblindness," critical race theorists argue, affirms non-discrimination on the surface, but fails to address historic and real forms of discrimination. For example, legal reforms, such as those granting civil and voting rights to African Americans and prohibiting segregation in schools in the United States, ended formal segregation but failed to end the forms of discrimination, segregation, and inequalities in economic and social opportunities that were experienced in the everyday lives of most African Americans.[90] Critical race theorists argue that judges should consider the social consequences of decisions, rather than simply following the original intent and letter of the law (the latter approach is called **legal formalism**). Critical race theorists have been strong supporters of affirmative action policies.

Critical race theorists adopted the method of storytelling as a key element of their work. Storytelling allows majoritarian views of the world, and experiences of the law, to be countered with the stories of racialized and marginalized people. Storytelling is seen as an empowering practice of consciousness-raising.[91] It can broaden the types of narratives that are acceptable in legal discourse and proceedings, challenging the idea that there is a single true and neutral narrative.[92]

### *Intersectional Analysis*
**Intersectional analysis** is a mode of analysis built out by critical race theorists and feminists.[93] It has been taken up by many policy and advocacy organizations, including the federal government.[94] It emphasizes the degree to which various forms of oppression are intertwined, such that forms of oppression cannot be analyzed individually. For example, we may note the ways in which laws pertaining to rape and sexual assault are inadequate—the ways in which they oppress, marginalize, and fail women. However, an analysis focusing only on gender would fail to take account of the ways that such laws *differently* marginalize and fail white women and women of colour.[95] Single-dimension analyses tend to focus on more privileged groups, while ignoring people who are subject to multiple forms of oppression.[96] For example, victims of hate speech may be targeted differently due to multiple identity categories: a white trans woman might be targeted differently from a trans woman of colour. When legal systems and courts fail to take into account multiple dimensions of oppression, they may address one dimension of oppression while allowing others to be strengthened.[97] To take another example, we can observe that failing to take intersecting identities seriously can cause groups of people to "disappear" from our analysis. Black women's organizations and Indigenous women's organizations, for example, are sometimes excluded from legal or policy processes on the premise that they represent neither

all women nor all Black or Indigenous people. Instead, male-dominated Black or Indigenous groups represent Black or Indigenous people, while women's groups dominated by white women represent women. The interests and views of Black and Indigenous women then "disappear" and are not heard and considered.[98]

Efforts to incorporate intersectional analysis and gender-based analysis plus (GBA+) can help to counter such problems. GBA+ has been adopted by the Canadian federal government. It is intended to "recognize that there are barriers to public participation in traditional government structures" and to incorporate the intersecting considerations of gender, sex, "mental or physical disability, race, national or ethnic origin, indigeneity, age, language and sexual orientation" to understand systemic barriers to government inclusion and accessibility during all stages of policymaking processes.[99]

### Critical Disability Theory

Critical disability theory builds on some of the same foundations as critical race theory; it questions the neutrality of the law and its ideological foundations, which see people as self-actualizing individuals rather than interconnected and actualized via social supports and structures that are unequally distributed. The law, while granting formal equality, fails to grant substantive equality and inclusion, especially to people with disabilities. It exists as part of a culture built around a hierarchy or bell curve in which the "normal" and most able are centred, while constructing others as "abnormal," lacking, or disabled.[100] "Normal" and "disability" are social constructions that law and policy often do little to counter.[101]

### Indigenous Legal Theory and Postcolonial Analysis

Postcolonial legal theorists have argued that Western legal systems have long served the neoimperial and white settlers' interests.[102] Rooted in Lockean property rights, Western legal systems justify the taking of property by white settlers, while failing to recognize Indigenous legal and governance systems. International law, as formulated by European positivist jurists, first "purported to expel the non-European world from the realm of legality" by failing to recognize "noncivilized" states as capable of producing law.[103] International law then "proceeded to enact the readmission of non-European states into international society" by defining "the terms and methods by which they were to be assimilated into the legal framework."[104] This re-entry took place "on terms that completely subordinated and crippled non-European societies."[105]

Postcolonial legal theorists note that legal concepts such as the **Doctrine of Discovery** and *terra nullius* are the foundations of colonialism. The Doctrine of Discovery was a legal doctrine that permitted the European colonization of lands, including those inhabited by Indigenous peoples, under the false premise that the lands were being newly discovered. Under the legal concept of *terra nullius*, lands that were "no man's land" could be seized by European colonial powers. By such colonial reasoning, Indigenous peoples did not own but merely occupied the lands on which they lived, because true ownership came from the agricultural working of the land.[106]

Indigenous legal theory has been influential on the TRC, which, as discussed above, calls for greater recognition and renewal of Indigenous law. The TRC calls on the federal government and others to "repudiate concepts used to justify European sovereignty over Indigenous lands and peoples such as the Doctrine of Discovery and *terra nullius*."[107]

Indigenous legal theorists work to combat the colonial myth that Indigenous peoples have no laws or are lawless, as this myth has historically been used by Western states and legal systems to subordinate Indigenous norms and peoples.[108] "The concept of Indigenous peoples as the 'lawless other,'" Hadley Friedland observes, "is an illogical myth that historically served to justify denials of Indigenous sovereignty over desired land by imperial cultures."[109]

### Governmentality and Networked Governance

While many classic theories of law take legislatures (and, in some cases, courts) as the only legitimate source(s) of law, and government as the only legitimate source of public policy, some scholars have noted that a vast array of other bodies are, in fact, in the business of setting law and policies—for better or for worse.

Are state bodies still the most significant source of law and governance? *Law, governance,* and *regulation* are all words for attempts to influence behaviour. The terms *governance* or **networked governance** reflect the idea that, today, private, public, and technological actors are *all three* involved in governing or regulating behaviour.

For example, in the domain of policing, police forces—state actors—govern. However, private security firms are more and more important in securing premises and computer networks. Technological actors, such as internet service providers (ISPs), are enrolled in regulating network security and granting access to police forces for police investigations. Computer security software is crucial in governing network security and the security of personal computers. Messages that call on individuals to adopt techniques of personal safety, such as not emailing credit card information and training in how to avoid phishing attacks, are also part of a network of governance that governs security, with private and technological actors playing a much broader and more powerful role than police forces alone.

This theoretical perspective is rooted partly in the influential writings of French historian Michel Foucault (1926–1984). Some of Foucault's most influential work was focused on the history of regimes of discipline and control. In examining the history of disciplinary or governance regimes, he sought to reveal the role not just of law and government, but the broader role of multiple types of actors and techniques in governance.[110] In much of his writing, he sought to focus not on law and state power, but on local power, or power "on the peripheries"— on "the techniques and tactics of domination," and on the power of discourse.[111] He examined the history of **governmentality**: the forms of knowledge and the mentalities associated with particular regimes of governance.[112]

Foucault, and many scholars to follow, also sought to examine the role of discourse—words in action or "intertwined habits of talk and action."[113] Policy and law can be examined not just in a legal and technocratic way; the words and concepts that are central to policy regimes also provide the mental and practical models through which policies and power are actualized.[114]

Marxian scholars and political economists focus on how power is held by the capitalist class, and feminist scholars note that power is held, to an inequitable degree, by cisgender men. Scholars who adopt a networked governance approach suggest that everybody, including both dominant and subordinate groups, is always trying to shift or translate events, networks, organizations, and people to make them work in their own interests, consciously or unconsciously. Power, rather than being "held" by individuals or offices, is created in networks of people, institutions, and technologies.[115] Power exists by virtue of networks, which is not to say it is equitably distributed; power in networks can concentrate powerfully at specific nodes or chokepoints,[116] but it always requires enrolling a chain of actors.

When there is a reduced role for the state and a heightened role for private actors and technologies, a "democratic deficit" or lack of public oversight can result. This is particularly true when private bodies take on roles formerly or traditionally done by government.

For example, in the domain of cultural funding, governments have played important roles. They fund and regulate cultural institutions such as public radio, and they provide direct funding through government cultural grants. However, private philanthropic or cultural organizations also fund the arts, and civic organizations such as churches and volunteer organizations often mount cultural productions. Technologies play an increasingly significant role in cultural funding as cultural producers turn to crowdfunding platforms to fund their projects.[117] This network of actors (including technological actors) helps to construct a discourse or mentality that regulates conduct in the field of culture. The governmentality of culture largely individualizes responsibility for cultural production to cultural producers and prioritizes commercial forms of culture over others.[118] There is, ultimately, little public oversight for many forms of cultural funding, since it takes place on a multiplicity of sites in which there is little transparency or accountability.

Some scholars, including some networked governance scholars, have argued that software code is now just as important, or perhaps more important, in governing communications than the laws and policies made by governments. Code is a crucial "node" in networked governance. Lawrence Lessig expressed this well in his book *Code*, where he argues "code is law."[119] He argues that the internet did not create, as some expected, a space of perfect freedom; rather, technologies are built by interested actors and could easily become "a perfect tool of control."[120] "Cyberspace," he argues, "demands a new understanding of how regulation works. It compels us to look beyond the traditional lawyer's scope—beyond laws, or even norms. It requires a broader account of 'regulation,' and most importantly, the recognition of a newly salient regulator ... Code." Technologies and code can enable that which is illegal and can make impossible actions that are undesirable by their creators, whether those actions are legal or illegal. Because of the democratic deficit this can create, Lessig argues for greater government—and civilian—oversight of technological governance.[121]

### Technology and Geography

While Lessig focused on technology as an increasingly significant regulator, it is often argued that governments act as a servant of technology, attempting to drive forward innovation and technological progress. Technologies themselves, and technological change, are often seen as drivers of law, policy, and regulation. For example, the rise of digital technologies such as smartphones and the internet are often seen as driving **convergence** between telecommunications and broadcasting, as phones (a telecommunications device) deliver broadcasting services. While this is a powerful logic, many communication scholars have argued that it is a myth. **Technological determinism** (the idea that the characteristics of technology are a primary driver of events and history) has been broadly criticized. Political economists of communication like Robert Babe, for example, point to the business interests that lie behind both convergence and deconvergence, and other regulatory changes.[122] It is people, politics, and economic and social systems that drive change, including technological change—not technology alone.

Communication policy is often tied to nationalist visions. **Technological nationalism** is a concept that connects Canadian nationalism with technologies of transportation, like railways, and technologies of communication, like broadcast networks—technologies that have been constructed in order to knit the country together and to resist the powerful North-South links that would otherwise bind Canada to the United States. Canadian political economist Harold Innis theorized that the possibilities of national community, and the strength of governments, are tied to governments' use of communication and transportation technologies that permit governance over space and across time.[123] Communication scholars like Robert Babe, on the other hand, have called technological nationalism a myth, noting that most communication technologies are constructed to link Canadian and American cities together. Thus, Canada exists *despite*, not because of, communication technologies.[124] Technological nationalism continues to influence thinking about Canadian communications policy, though perhaps less so than in the past.

Canadian communications scholar Darin Barney argues that a "New National Dream" for Canada has been formed, one that has reduced the scope of democratic politics. In technological societies, he notes, "the design, development and regulation of technology is often exempt from formal, democratic political judgment, left instead to the private interests and technical calculus of scientists, engineers, military and police agencies, major corporations, technocrats and consumers."[125] Under an "innovation agenda," the development of new technologies is prioritized, but not in the way that produced the state-led national projects of connecting Canada by rail or telephone. Instead, "the state's role as a regulator and redistributor of resources is reduced, and its role as a facilitator, sponsor and promoter of capital accumulation is enlarged."[126] Technological change is depoliticized, driven by private companies making choices over which citizens, and political and legal institutions, have little control. This occurs in a political climate where there is little room for crucial debate over what constitutes "the good life" now.[127]

## CONCLUSION

The descriptions provided here are very brief accounts of what are, in actual fact, large bodies of thought; each has been very influential on thinking about law and policy in many areas. None of these theories are merely academic; each is inspired by the real-life experiences, intuitions, and empirical research of many different thinkers. Each theory also accords a set of values; libertarian theory prizes individual freedom, while critical political economy emphasizes the inequities created through capitalist economic and social structures and the struggles to mitigate and overcome those inequities. Feminist and queer, critical race, critical disability, Indigenous, and postcolonial theories emphasize the inequities and oppressions constructed through gendered, racialized, and colonial relations, seeking ways to overcome them. Each theory provides a set of conceptual starting points for the analysis of communications policy and law.

All the theories described here arise from people's positions in life, people's varying frustrations with law and government, or from people's positive experiences or thoughts about law and government. Each one has a different vantage point, a different perspective, and each suggests a different approach to changing law and government. Pluralist theory suggests inclusion in policymaking processes; libertarian theory suggests the reduction of bureaucracy and regulation; Marxian and political economic theory suggests changes in the distribution of ownership and control; feminist analyses suggest various strategies for overcoming sexism and intersecting oppressions; critical race theory, Indigenous, and postcolonial analyses suggest addressing the deep, intersecting biases of the legal and governance systems; critical disability theory suggests building law and policy around broader conceptualizations of people's abilities; and networked governance suggests directing efforts toward change not only at the state, but also at private regulators and code. Each one presents a different account of people's dreams for the future, of what parts of our law and governance systems we ought to celebrate and those we should change, and of how we should work to change our world.

## FURTHER READING

Babe, Robert E. *Telecommunications in Canada: Technology, Industry, and Government.* Toronto: University of Toronto Press, 1990.

Borrows, John. *Recovering Canada: The Resurgence of Indigenous Law.* Toronto: University of Toronto Press, 2002.

Collins, Patricia Hill, and Sirma Bilge. *Intersectionality.* Hoboken, NJ: John Wiley & Sons, 2016.

Crenshaw, Kimberlé. "Mapping the Margins: Identity Politics, Intersectionality, and Violence against Women." *Stanford Law Review* 43, no. 6 (1991): 1241–99.

Dahl, Robert A. *Who Governs?: Democracy and Power in an American City,* 2nd ed. New Haven, CT: Yale University Press, 2005.

Flew, Terry. "Six Theories of Neoliberalism." *Thesis Eleven* 122, no. 1 (2014): 49–71.

Friedland, Hadley. "Reflective Frameworks: Methods for Accessing, Understanding and Applying Indigenous Laws." *Indigenous Law Journal* 11, no. 1 (2012): 1–40.

Harvey, David. *A Brief History of Neoliberalism*. Oxford: Oxford University Press, 2007.

Hunt, Alan. "Foucault's Expulsion of Law. Toward a Retrieval." *Law & Social Inquiry* 17, no. 1 (1992): 1–38.

———. "Marxist Theory of Law." In *A Companion to Philosophy of Law and Legal Theory*, edited by Dennis Patterson, 2nd ed., 350–60. Malden, MA: Blackwell, 2010.

Jones, Bernie D. "Critical Race Theory: New Strategies for Civil Rights in the New Millennium?" *Harvard Black Letter Law Journal* 18 (2002): 1–90.

Lessig, Lawrence. *Code*. Version 2.0. New York: Basic Books, 2006.

Lipset, Seymour Martin. "The Social Requisites of Democracy Revisited: 1993 Presidential Address." *American Sociological Review* 59, no. 1 (1994): 1–22.

Meehan, Eileen R., and Ellen Riordan, eds. *Sex & Money: Feminism and Political Economy in the Media*. Minneapolis: University of Minnesota Press, 2002.

Mosco, Vincent. *The Political Economy of Communication: Rethinking and Renewal*. 2nd ed. London: SAGE, 2009.

Sarikakis, Katharine, and Leslie Regan Shade, eds. *Feminist Interventions in International Communication: Minding the Gap*. Toronto: Rowman & Littlefield Publishers, 2007.

Vossen, Bas van der, and Peter Vallentyne. "Libertarianism." In *The Stanford Encyclopedia of Philosophy*, edited by Edward N. Zalta. Stanford, CA: Stanford University, 2018. https://plato.stanford.edu/archives/fall2018/entries/libertarianism/.

Weber, Max. *Economy and Society: An Outline of Interpretive Sociology*. Los Angeles: University of California Press, 1978.

# NOTES

1. See Walter Lippman, "The Phantom Public" (1925); John Dewey and Melvin L. Rogers, *The Public and Its Problems: An Essay in Political Inquiry* (University Park, PA: Penn State Press, 2012); and Nancy Fraser, "Rethinking the Public Sphere: A Contribution to the Critique of Actually Existing Democracy," *Social Text*, no. 25/26 (1990): 56–80.

2. "The body politic as organized for supreme civil rule and government; the political organization which is the basis of civil government. Hence: the supreme civil power or government of a country or nation; the group of people collectively engaged in exercising or administering this." See *OED Online*, s.v. "state, n.," accessed February 15, 2019; see also Edward Heath Robinson, "The Distinction between State and Government," *Geography Compass* 7, no. 8 (2013): 556–66.

3.  Val Napoleon, "Extinction by Number: Colonialism Made Easy," *Canadian Journal of Law & Society* 16, no. 1 (2001): 113–45; "*Delgamuukw*: A Legal Straightjacket for Oral Histories?" *Canadian Journal of Law & Society/La Revue Canadienne Droit et Société* 20, no. 2 (2005): 123–55.

4.  Liberal Party of Canada, "Real Change: A Fair and Open Government," August 2015, https://www.liberal.ca/wp-content/uploads/2015/08/a-fair-and-open-government.pdf.

5.  Treasury Board of Canada Secretariat, "Standard on Web Accessibility," August 2, 2011, http://www.tbs-sct.gc.ca/pol/doc-eng.aspx?id=23601.

6.  Kenneth Kernaghan and David Siegel, *Public Administration in Canada: A Text,* 4th ed. (Scarborough, ON: ITP Nelson, 1999), 130–33.

7.  *OED Online,* s.v. "law, n. 1," accessed February 15, 2019.

8.  Ashley Packard, *Digital Media Law,* 2nd ed. (Malden, MA: Wiley-Blackwell, 2013), 13.

9.  Napoleon, "Thinking about Indigenous Legal Orders."

10. Andrei Marmor and Alexander Sarch, "The Nature of Law," in *The Stanford Encyclopedia of Philosophy,* ed. Edward N. Zalta, Fall 2015, https://plato.stanford.edu/archives/fall2015/entries/lawphil-nature/.

11. Kenneth Einar Himma, "Natural Law," *Internet Encyclopedia of Philosophy* (n.d.), http://www.iep.utm.edu/natlaw/.

12. Thomas Aquinas, *On Law, Morality, and Politics,* eds. William P. Baumgarth and Richard J Regan, trans. Richard J. Regan (Indianapolis: Hackett Publishing, 1988), ST III, Q.95, A.II. As quoted in Himma.

13. William Blackstone, *Commentaries on the Laws of England: A Facsimile of the First Edition of 1765–1769, with an Introduction by Stanley N. Katz,* 4 vols. (Chicago: University of Chicago Press, 1979), 41. As quoted in Himma.

14. See Himma.

15. Nicos Stavropoulos, "Legal Interpretivism," October 14, 2003, https://plato.stanford.edu/archives/sum2014/entries/law-interpretivist/.

16. Leslie Green, "Legal Positivism," accessed October 2, 2018, https://plato.stanford.edu/archives/fall2009/entries/legal-positivism/.

17. Ibid.

18. Ibid.

19. Ibid.

20. Thomas R. Dye, *Understanding Public Policy,* 5th ed. (Englewood Cliffs, NJ: Prentice-Hall, 1992), 1.

21. John J. Prunty, "Signposts for a Critical Educational Policy Analysis," *Australian Journal of Education* 29, no. 2 (1985): 133–40.

22. Antony Anghie, "Finding the Peripheries: Sovereignty and Colonialism in Nineteenth-Century International Law," *Harvard International Law Journal* 40, no. 1 (1999): 1–80; Napoleon, "Delgamuukw."

23. John Borrows, *Canada's Indigenous Constitution* (Toronto: University of Toronto Press, 2010).

24. Borrows, 13; Val Napoleon, "Thinking about Indigenous Legal Orders," in *Dialogues on Human Rights and Legal Pluralism* (Dordrecht, Netherlands: Springer, 2013), 229–45.

25. Truth and Reconciliation Commission of Canada, "Honouring the Truth, Reconciling for the Future: Summary of the Final Report of the Truth and Reconciliation Commission of Canada" (Winnipeg: Truth and Reconciliation Commission of Canada, 2015), 1. In 1996, the Royal Commission on Aboriginal Peoples had urged a process of reconciliation, but its recommendations were, to a large extent, not implemented. Truth and Reconciliation Commission of Canada, 7; *Report of the Royal Commission on Aboriginal Peoples* (Ottawa: Canada Communication Group, 1996).

26. Truth and Reconciliation Commission of Canada, 1.

27. Ibid, 202.

28. Ibid.

29. Ibid, 199.

30. United Nations. *Declaration on the Rights of Indigenous Peoples*, A/RES/61/295, October 2, 2007, https://www.un.org/development/desa/indigenouspeoples/declaration-on-the-rights-of-indigenous-peoples.html. As quoted in Truth and Reconciliation Commission of Canada, 203.

31. Truth and Reconciliation Commission of Canada, 205.

32. Ibid., 207, Call to Action 50.

33. Sally Engle Merry, "Legal Pluralism," *Law and Society Review* 22, no. 5 (1988): 869–96.

34. Borrows, 11.

35. Globe Staff, "Trans Mountain, Trudeau and First Nations: A Guide to the Political Saga so Far," *The Globe and Mail*, April 18, 2018, https://www.theglobeandmail.com/politics/article-trans-mountain-kinder-morgan-pipeline-bc-alberta-explainer/.

36. Jürgen Habermas, *The Structural Transformation of the Public Sphere* (Cambridge, MA: MIT Press, 1989).

37. Seymour Martin Lipset, "The Social Requisites of Democracy Revisited: 1993 Presidential Address," *American Sociological Review* 59, no. 1 (1994): 12.

38. Ibid., 4.

39. Robert A. Dahl, *Who Governs?: Democracy and Power in an American City* (New Haven, CT: Yale University Press, 2005), 305–25.

40. Kernaghan and Siegel, 31–32.

41. Dahl.

42. Consumer groups, for example, are diffuse and can be difficult to organize. Peter Drahos, "Six Minutes to Midnight: Can Intellectual Property Save the World?" in *Emerging Challenges in Intellectual Property*, eds. Kathy Bowrey, Michael Handler, and Dianne Nicol (Oxford: Oxford University Press, 2011); Dahl.

43. Kernaghan and Siegel, 31–32.

44. Max Weber, *Economy and Society: An Outline of Interpretive Sociology* (Los Angeles: University of California Press, 1978), 956. Also see Paul Barker and Kenneth Kernaghan, *Public Administration in Canada* (Toronto: Thomson Nelson, 2008), 17–21.

45. Kernaghan and Siegel, *Public Administration in Canada*, 130–32.

46. Weber, 983. See also Kernaghan and Siegel, 30–31.

47. Gunther Roth, "Introduction," in *Economy and Society: An Outline of Interpretive Sociology*, by Max Weber (Los Angeles: University of California Press, 1978), lix.

48. Ibid., lviii.

49. Kernaghan and Siegel.

50. Robert Michels, *Political Parties: A Sociological Study of the Oligarchical Tendencies of Modern Democracy* (New York: Hearst's International Library Company, 1915).

51. David M. Trubek, "Max Weber's Tragic Modernism and the Study of Law in Society," *Law & Society Review* 20, no. 4 (1986): 591.

52. "Bryan Adams Not Canadian?" CBC Archives, accessed October 3, 2018, https://www.cbc.ca/archives/entry/bryan-adams-not-canadian.

53. David Harvey, *A Brief History of Neoliberalism* (Oxford: Oxford University Press, 2007), 2.

54. Ibid.

55. Ibid.

56. Terry Flew, "Six Theories of Neoliberalism," *Thesis Eleven* 122, no. 1 (2014): 49–71.

57. Ibid.

58. Ibid.

59. Bas van der Vossen and Peter Vallentyne, "Libertarianism," in *The Stanford Encyclopedia of Philosophy*, ed. Edward N. Zalta, Fall 2018, https://plato.stanford.edu/archives/fall2018/entries/libertarianism/.

60. John Locke, *Second Treatise of Government: An Essay Concerning the True Original, Extent and End of Civil Government*, ed. Richard H. Cox (Hoboken, NJ: John Wiley & Sons, 2014), chap. 5.

61. Barbara Arneil, "Trade, Plantations, and Property: John Locke and the Economic Defense of Colonialism," *Journal of the History of Ideas* 55, no. 4 (1994): 591–609.

62. van der Vossen and Vallentyne.

63. Ibid.

64. Kernaghan and Siegel, 34–36.

65. Ibid., 29.

66. Alan Hunt, "Marxist Theory of Law," in *A Companion to Philosophy of Law and Legal Theory*, ed. Dennis Patterson, 2nd ed. (Malden, MA: Blackwell, 2010), 357–58.

67. Ibid.

68. Kernaghan and Siegel, 34–36.

69. Hunt, 356–57.

70. Ibid.

71. Ibid.

72. Edward Greer, "Antonio Gramsci and Legal Hegemony," in *The Politics of Law: A Progressive Critique*, ed. David Kairys (New York: Pantheon Books, 1982), 304–8; Thomas R. Bates, "Gramsci and the Theory of Hegemony," *Journal of the History of Ideas* (1975): 351–66.

73. Max Horkheimer and Theodor W. Adorno, "The Culture Industry: Enlightenment as Mass Deception," in *Dialectic of Enlightenment: Philosophical Fragments*, ed. Gunzelin Schmid Noerr, trans. Edmund Jephcott (Stanford, CA: Stanford University Press, 2002), 94–136.

74. Kathy E. Ferguson, *The Feminist Case against Bureaucracy* (Philadelphia: Temple University Press, 1984), 61–62; Edwin George West, "The Political Economy of Alienation: Karl Marx and Adam Smith," *Oxford Economic Papers* 21, no. 1 (1969): 1–23.

75. Vincent Mosco, *The Political Economy of Communication: Rethinking and Renewal*, 2nd ed. (London: SAGE, 2009), 2.

76. Kwong-leung Tang, "Rape Law Reform in Canada: The Success and Limits of Legislation," *International Journal of Offender Therapy and Comparative Criminology* 42, no. 3 (1998): 258–70.

77. Kirk Makin, "How Canada's Sex-Assault Laws Violate Rape Victims," *The Globe and Mail*, October 5, 2013, https://www.theglobeandmail.com/news/national/how-canadas-sex-assault-laws-violate-rape-victims/article14705289/.

78. Canadian Heritage, "Rights of LGBTI Persons," October 23, 2017, https://www.canada.ca/en/canadian-heritage/services/rights-lgbti-persons.html.

79. Ibid.

80. John Ibbitson, "Canada Shows Leadership in Advancing Human Rights," *The Globe and Mail*, June 15, 2017, https://www.theglobeandmail.com/news/politics/with-

gender-identity-bill-canada-shows-leadership-in-advancing-humanrights/article35323583/.

81. Paula Chakravartty and Katharine Sarikakis, *Media Policy and Globalization* (Edinburgh: Edinburgh University Press, 2006), 11–12. For a discussion of the word *queer*, see Francisco Valdes, "Afterword & Prologue: Queer Legal Theory," *California Law Review* 83 (1995): 344–77. The reclaimed use of the word *queer* now also appears in lower-case form.

82. Canadian Heritage; Ibbitson.

83. Nancy Fraser and Axel Honneth, *Redistribution or Recognition? A Political-Philosophical Exchange* (London: Verso, 2003).

84. Ferguson, 61–62.

85. Ibid. See also Catherine Rottenberg, "The Rise of Neoliberal Feminism," *Cultural Studies* 28, no. 3 (2014): 418–37.

86. Ferguson, 61–66.

87. Valdes.

88. Bernie D. Jones, "Critical Race Theory: New Strategies for Civil Rights in the New Millennium," *Harvard Black Letter Law Journal* 18 (2002): 34–40; Derrick A. Bell, Jr., "Brown v. Board of Education and the Interest-Convergence Dilemma," *Harvard Law Review* 93 (1980): 518–33.

89. Jones, 50; Barbara Flagg, *Was Blind, but Now I See: White Race Consciousness & the Law* (New York: NYU Press, 1998), 1–9.

90. Jones, 34–40.

91. Ibid., 4.

92. Ibid., 59–60.

93. Ange-Marie Hancock, *Intersectionality: An Intellectual History* (Oxford: Oxford University Press, 2016).

94. For example, see Treasury Board of Canada Secretariat, *Canada's 2018–2020 National Action Plan on Open Government* (Ottawa: Treasury Board Secretariat, 2018).

95. Kimberlé Crenshaw, "Mapping the Margins: Identity Politics, Intersectionality, and Violence against Women," *Stanford Law Review* 43, no. 6 (1991): 1241–99.

96. Ibid.

97. Kerri A. Froc, "Multidimensionality and the Matrix: Identifying Charter Violations in Cases of Complex Subordination," *Canadian Journal of Law & Society* 25, no. 1 (2010): 21–49.

98. Nitya Duclos, "Disappearing Women: Racial Minority Women in Human Rights Cases," *Canadian Journal of Women and the Law* 6, no. 1 (1993): 25–51.

99. Treasury Board of Canada Secretariat and Open Government Partnership, *Guide to Gender-based Analysis Plus (GBA+) and Inclusive Open Government* (Washington, DC: Open Government Partnership, 2019), 5, 8.

100. Richard F. Devlin and Dianne Pothier, "Introduction: Toward a Critical Theory of Dis-Citizenship," in *Critical Disability Theory: Essays in Philosophy, Politics, Policy, and Law*, eds. Richard F. Devlin and Dianne Pothier (Vancouver: UBC Press, 2006). See also Kim Sawchuk, "Impaired," in *The Routledge Handbook of Mobilities*, eds. Peter Adey, David Bissell, Kevin Hannam, Peter Merriman, and Mimi Sheller (New York: Routledge, 2014), 409–20.

101. Lennard J. Davis, "Introduction: Normality, Power, and Culture," in *The Disability Studies Reader*, 4th ed. (New York: Routledge, 2016), 1–14.

102. The term *postcolonial* is usually used in a sense that recognizes that processes of colonialism continue, in new forms, in the present. However, some reject the term as implying that colonialism occurred in the past, preferring other terms such as *settler colonialism* to indicate processes situated in the present. Syed Mustafa Ali, "A Brief Introduction to Decolonial Computing," *XRDS: Crossroads, The ACM Magazine for Students* 22, no. 4 (2016): 16–21.

103. Anghie.

104. Ibid.

105. Ibid.

106. Truth and Reconciliation Commission of Canada, 46.

107. Ibid., 199.

108. John Borrows, *Recovering Canada: The Resurgence of Indigenous Law* (Toronto: University of Toronto Press, 2002); Borrows, *Canada's Indigenous Constitution*.

109. Hadley Friedland, "Reflective Frameworks: Methods for Accessing, Understanding and Applying Indigenous Laws," *Indigenous Law Journal* 11, no. 1 (2012): 6; Borrows, *Recovering Canada*; Borrows, *Canada's Indigenous Constitution*.

110. Alan Hunt, "Foucault's Expulsion of Law. Toward a Retrieval," *Law & Social Inquiry* 17, no. 1 (1992): 1–38.

111. Hunt, "Foucault's Expulsion of Law," 8; Foucault, *Power/Knowledge: Selected Interviews and Other Writings, 1972–1977*, ed. Colin Gordon (New York: Pantheon Books, 1980), 102.

112. Mitchell M. Dean, *Governmentality: Power and Rule in Modern Society* (London: SAGE, 1999).

113. Thomas Streeter, "Policy, Politics, and Discourse," *Communication, Culture & Critique* 6, no. 4 (2013): 489.

114. Ibid.

115. Bruno Latour argues that power results from "the actions of chains of agents each of whom 'translates' it in accordance with his/her own projects." Latour, "The Powers of Association," *The Sociological Review* 32, no. 1 (May 1984): 264. Also see John Braithwaite and Peter Drahos, *Global Business Regulation* (Cambridge: Cambridge University Press, 2000); Latour, *Science in Action: How to Follow Scientists and Engineers through Society* (Cambridge, MA: Harvard University Press, 1987).

116. Natasha Tusikov, *Chokepoints: Global Private Regulation on the Internet* (Berkeley: University of California Press, 2016).

117. Sara Bannerman, "Crowdfunding Music and the Democratization of Economic and Social Capital," *Canadian Journal of Communication*, forthcoming.

118. Ibid.

119. Lawrence Lessig, *Code*, Version 2.0 (New York: Basic Books, 2006).

120. Ibid., 4.

121. Ibid.

122. Robert E. Babe, *Telecommunications in Canada: Technology, Industry, and Government* (Toronto: University of Toronto Press, 1990), 8.

123. Harold Innis, *The Bias of Communication*, 2nd ed. (Toronto: University of Toronto Press, 2008).

124. Babe, 8.

125. Darin Barney, "One Nation Under Google," Hart House Lecture (Toronto: Hart House Lecture Committee, 2007), 24, https://darinbarneyresearch.mcgill.ca/Work/One_Nation_Under_Google.pdf.

126. Ibid., 35.

127. Ibid.

# 2 Introduction to the Canadian Legal System

## INTRODUCTION

In the last chapter, we noted that law is "the body of rules, whether proceeding from formal enactment or from custom, which a particular state or community recognizes as binding on its members or subjects."[1] Most laws, we noted, are contained in legislative statutes, court decisions, and administrative rules.[2] In this chapter, we discuss the common law and civil law legal systems. We will define public law and private law. We will also introduce the sources of law that are recognized within the Canadian legal system, including the legislative, judicial, and executive branches of government.

The Canadian legal system is rooted in Western legal tradition. While Indigenous law is often subordinated to or unrecognized by Western law in general and the Canadian legal system in particular, there are a few instances where Indigenous law is recognized. The last part of this chapter addresses the place of Indigenous law within the Canadian legal system.

## COMMON LAW AND CIVIL LAW SYSTEMS

There are two main types of Western legal systems in the world. One is known as a **common law** legal system, and the other as a **civil law** system. The common law system originates in England and can be found in England and the former British colonies, including Canada. Under a common law system, laws made by legislatures are written down and compiled in statutes. However, there are also additional laws made by judges. Judges' decisions are also considered to be laws and are contained in the judgments made by judges themselves. These are followed as what is known as **precedent**. The practice of following precedent is called *stare decisis*.

The civil law system is much older and more common, with roots in the sixth-century Roman Empire. Under Roman tradition, judges were not appointed for very long—and sometimes were only appointed for specific cases—so a written legal tradition was needed to create consistency in the law. Under a civil law system, all laws are written down and compiled in statutes. Judicial decisions are not considered to be laws; they are merely interpretations of the law. Although judges in a civil law system may refer to the decisions of other judges, those decisions do not constitute law and are not binding on other courts' decisions as they are in a common law system. At the same time, when similar cases have led repeatedly to the same decision, this constant stream of homogenous rulings may be persuasive and is referred to as *jurisprudence constante*.

The provincial, territorial, and federal legal systems in Canada are common law systems with one exception: Private law in Quebec operates under a civil law legal system. Quebec's laws are written down in the *Civil Code of Quebec*, and provincial judges in Quebec do not make or follow precedent, though they may follow *jurisprudence constante*. Canada is a **bijural** country, one in which both common law and civil law systems coexist.

## PUBLIC LAW AND PRIVATE LAW

In both civil law and common law legal systems, there are two main categories of law: **public law** and **private law**. Public law deals with the relationship between individuals and the public, represented by the state. It includes criminal law, administrative law, and constitutional law.

Criminal law, as part of public law, regulates public safety, order, or morality. The federal government makes criminal law, and most criminal offences are outlined in the *Criminal Code of Canada*. This includes some crimes we will cover in this book, such as obscenity crimes or hate speech. Since crimes are considered to be offences against the public in general and—since Canada is a constitutional monarchy—ultimately crimes against the monarch, criminal case names (e.g., *R v Smith*) include "*R*" to signify *Rex* (the king) or *Regina* (the queen) and the name of the defendant.

Private law deals not with offences against the public at large but with relationships between people or organizations. Civil cases are cases not between the state and an individual, but between two individuals or organizations. In civil cases, the names of the two parties are included in the case name (e.g., *Smith v Jones*). Private law includes the law of **tort**, which allows an individual who has suffered loss or harm to obtain a legal remedy, such as a financial award of damages. **Defamation** cases and intellectual property cases are usually civil cases, in which one person is accused of defaming or infringing the intellectual property of another person or organization. Civil cases do not result in imprisonment, but may result in the court requiring someone to do something (e.g., paying damages to the person they have defamed), prohibiting someone from doing something (e.g., from republishing a defamatory statement), or paying a fine.[3]

## BRANCHES OF GOVERNMENT

There are three main branches of government: the legislative branch, the judicial branch, and the executive branch. The legislative branch of the Canadian federal government includes the House of Commons and the Senate, together forming the Parliament of Canada. The judicial branch is comprised of the various courts of Canada. The executive branch is comprised of the Cabinet—those appointed to Cabinet by the prime minister or premier of a province or territory—and all the government departments reporting to Cabinet ministers.

### Legislature

**Legislatures** pass statutes that serve as the written law of the country, province, or territory. In Canada and other Westminster-style systems (those modelled after the system of parliament developed in the United Kingdom), legislatures are called *parliaments*. Laws passed by legislatures are called "legislation." The word *legislation* refers to the laws made by a legislature such as the Parliament of Canada or the Ontario Legislative Assembly. Many areas of communication policy and law are built upon federal legislation such as the *Privacy Act*, the *Personal Information Protection and Electronic Documents Act*, the *Broadcasting Act*, the *Telecommunications Act*, the *Copyright Act*, the *Access to Information Act*, and the *Criminal Code*.

### Judiciary

The judicial branch (the **judiciary**), or the courts, interprets the written laws of the legislature and creates law through establishing precedents. Case law, or precedent, is also referred to as *common law*. In the common law system, laws are found in courts' decisions. For example, much of defamation law was originally developed by judges and passed down as legal precedents. In copyright law, while the basic categories of activities that constitute **"fair dealing"** rather than copyright infringement are set out in legislation, the more detailed, step-by-step process for determining whether an act is "fair dealing" has been laid out by judges as precedent. It is often necessary to understand both the legislation and the precedents that interpret that legislation in order to truly understand an area of law.

### Types of Precedent

There are different types of precedents. *Binding precedent* must be followed by lower courts in the same jurisdiction. *Persuasive precedent* is precedent that is not binding on a court; it is adopted because it is persuasive.

A precedent from a higher court in a particular jurisdiction would be binding on any lower court in the same jurisdiction. For example, a decision made by the Ontario Court of Appeal, the highest court in the province, would be binding on all trial courts in Ontario. A court decision of the Manitoba Court of Appeal would not be binding on trial courts in Ontario but would be binding on lower courts in Manitoba. A decision from an appeal court in one province could be considered persuasive in another province, particularly if the decision relates to similar laws in both provinces. A decision by the Supreme Court of Canada is binding on all courts in Canada.

There are some cases were a precedent does not have to be followed. A precedent can be modified or overruled by a court with sufficient authority, such as the Supreme Court of Canada. A precedent can be overruled where a new legal issue is raised and where a change in circumstances or evidence arises.[4] As we shall see later in this book, courts have modified the laws of obscenity as attitudes toward things like pornography have changed over time.

A precedent can also be *overruled*. In 1993, the Supreme Court of Canada decided not to strike down the *Criminal Code*'s prohibitions on assisted suicide.[5] It overruled itself in 2015, when it decided that such prohibitions were unconstitutional; they violated Canadians' constitutional rights to life, liberty, and security of person.[6]

A case can also be *distinguished*. Precedent can be declared not to apply in the situation at hand if the situation is distinct from the one the precedent was meant to apply to. In the 1970s, American broadcasters were upset that Canadian cable companies were rebroadcasting their signals and (as permitted by the CRTC, the regulatory body that oversees broadcasting and telecommunications in Canada) substituting Canadian commercials in place of the original commercials. American broadcasters attempted to stop this practice, and the authorization of it by the CRTC, by arguing that a prior case affirming the jurisdiction of the Parliament of Canada (and thus the CRTC, a federal tribunal) over **broadcasting** did not apply in the case of cable, which they argued should fall under provincial jurisdiction. In other words, they attempted to **distinguish** the case of cable transmission from a precedent that had applied to over-the-air signals, arguing that the precedent did not apply to broadcast signals transmitted by cable. They were unsuccessful, and the federal power of the CRTC over cable transmission of broadcasting was upheld.[7]

### Judicial Review

Courts have the power not only to make laws through precedent but also to strike laws down. In Canada, courts have the power to review laws, in what is known as *judicial review*. Judicial review gives courts the power to strike down laws as unconstitutional.

Not all countries grant courts the power of judicial review. Civil law countries do not see judges as having the power to make—or strike down—law, and some common-law countries like the UK still see legislatures as being supreme, so courts don't have the power of judicial review over legislation.[8]

In Canada, as in the US, courts do have the power of judicial review. The extent of this power is relatively new; prior to 1982, courts could review whether legislation was within the power of legislature as granted by the Constitution. A piece of legislation that is *intra vires* is within the power of the legislature to enact, whereas a piece of legislation that falls outside the power of the legislature is *ultra vires*. However, the *Charter of Rights and Freedoms*, put in place in 1982, granted Canadian courts the additional power to overturn legislation and declare it unconstitutional if it infringed on the rights set out in the *Charter*.

### Structure of the Court System

In Canada, there are provincial or territorial and federal courts. Provincial courts deal with most criminal law, most family law, young offenders, and traffic offences. Each province has both lower courts and superior courts. Lower courts usually hear cases and call witnesses, whereas superior courts review cases on appeal from the lower courts. Superior courts also try the more serious criminal and civil cases. These may go by different names; they may be called the Supreme Court of the province (e.g., the Supreme Court of British Columbia), or the Court of Queen's Bench (e.g., in Alberta). There are also Courts of Appeal, such as the Ontario Court of Appeal and the Manitoba Court of Appeal, which serve as the top courts in the province.

The federal court system also has a trial-level court, which is based in Ottawa but holds hearings across the country. It deals with intellectual property matters, citizenship appeals, competition law, and cases involving the departments of the Government of Canada or Crown Corporations. It hears appeals from federal boards, commissions, and tribunals who can also **refer** (or ask) any question to the Federal Court. The Federal Court commonly deals with judicial review of administrative decisions of federal actors.

Appeals in the federal court system are heard by the Federal Court of Appeal. These deal with federal laws only.

The Supreme Court of Canada can take appeals from either court system and must grant "leave" to appeal. Three of the Supreme Court's nine judges review the case and grant leave if the case involves a question of public importance; "raises an important issue of law or mixed law and fact"; or is, for any other reason, significant enough to be considered.[9] Leave is granted automatically in criminal cases where a judge on a panel of a court of appeal has dissented from the **majority decision,** or where someone was found guilty who was acquitted at the original trial.[10]

The Supreme Court of Canada also acts as an advisor to the federal government; the government can refer a question to the court, asking the court to consider any important legal question, especially regarding constitutional interpretation. In 1996, the Supreme Court of Canada was asked to provide its opinion on what would be constitutionally required for the Province of Quebec to secede from Canada. The court rendered its opinion in 1998.[11] Provincial courts can also hear references from the provincial governments.

## Executive

The main role of the **executive** branch is to enforce and implement the laws and policies made by the other two branches of government. The executive branch involved with federal law enforcement includes the Royal Canadian Mounted Police (RCMP) and the Correctional Service of Canada, which administers Canada's federal prisons. The executive branch also includes departments such as Canadian Heritage and Innovation, Science and Economic Development Canada, charged with implementing the government's programs and services.

The executive branch contributes to making law through orders, administrative rules, or regulations. In Canada, **Orders in Council** are made by the **Governor in Council** (the Governor General acting on the advice of Cabinet) and are ultimately signed by the Governor General. For example, the CRTC normally operates as an independent agency. However, from time to time, the Governor in Council issues orders to the CRTC, directing it to take a particular action. These orders are binding on the CRTC.[12] Individual ministers can also make ministerial orders where legislation enables them to do so. For example, the *Aeronautics Act* allows ministerial orders to be made.[13]

Departments or administrative tribunals also make regulations where called for by legislation. For example, the copyright law sets out all the basic principles of copyright, but some details are set by regulation—by a department or agency rather than by the legislature. The Department of Agriculture, which was responsible for copyright until 1918, had the power to say exactly what forms had to be filled out to obtain a copyright and what those forms should look like.[14] These forms were an important part of the law, but creating them was a level of detail that legislature did not need to deal with, so it was set by regulation. The CRTC is also empowered by legislation to make regulations relating to the broadcasting system.[15]

## INDIGENOUS LAW

The Government of Canada asserts sovereignty, and the sovereign authority to make laws, over lands claimed as Canadian. *Sovereignty* is a Western notion, based in Western legal traditions that have been used to justify claims over Indigenous lands.[16] In most cases, the laws of Indigenous peoples have been left unrecognized in the Canadian legal system and have been displaced or subordinated to Canadian law. Under the *Indian Act*, for example, authority over on-reserve law and order, land allotment, and residence (among other things) are delegated to band councils, on the condition that laws made are consistent with the *Indian Act* or other Canadian regulations.[17] In this way, space for Indigenous lawmaking is created, but such law is subordinated to Canadian law. In many cases, the influence of Western and Canadian law and legal training is so strong that laws made on reserve virtually conform to or replicate Western law.[18] Under other laws, such as the *First Nations Land Management Act*, bands can opt out of the *Indian Act*'s provisions on land management to develop their own Land Codes that can incorporate Indigenous legal traditions to a greater degree.[19]

While the previous section of this chapter focused on centralized state sources of law, including the legislative, judicial, and executive branches of government, it is possible to recognize that other sources of law also exist, particularly in

Indigenous legal traditions. These can include sacred sources such as creation stories; nature and environmental observations; deliberative circles and feasts; proclamations, codes, rules, regulations, and teachings; customary practices; oral traditions; memory aids such as wampum belts, ceremonial repetition, and songs; and the personal authority of Elders and Knowledge Keepers.[20]

In areas of communication policy and law, there is little recognition of Indigenous legal traditions in Canada. While, for example, there are Indigenous approaches or alternatives to concepts of intellectual property or the governance of traditional knowledge, these are little recognized in the Canadian intellectual property system.[21] Similarly, rather than recognizing Indigenous laws pertaining to the stewardship of Indigenous cultural heritage,[22] the *Indian Act* and Canadian law more broadly has often played a role in denigrating and erasing Indigenous culture.[23] Indigenous legal scholars are working to encourage the preservation, revitalization, and further recognition of Indigenous law in Canada.[24]

## FURTHER READING

Baglay, Sasha. *Introduction to the Canadian Legal System*. Toronto: Pearson, 2016.

Borrows, John. *Canada's Indigenous Constitution*. Toronto: University of Toronto Press, 2010.

Coughlan, Stephen Gerard, Catherine Cotter, and John A. Yogis. *Canadian Law Dictionary*. 7th ed. Hauppauge, NY: Barrons Educational Series, 2013.

Gall, Gerald L. *The Canadian Legal System*. 5th ed. Toronto: Thomson Carswell, 2004.

Greene, Ian. *The Charter of Rights and Freedoms: 30+ Years of Decisions That Shape Canadian Life*. Toronto: James Lorimer & Company, 2014.

Hanna, Alan. "Spaces for Sharing: Searching for Indigenous Law on the Canadian Legal Landscape." *UBC Law Review* 51, no. 1 (2018): 105–59.

Napoleon, Val. "Thinking about Indigenous Legal Orders." In *Dialogues on Human Rights and Legal Pluralism*, 229–45. New York: Springer, 2013.

## NOTES

1.   *OED Online*, s.v. "law, n. 1," accessed February 15, 2019.

2.   Ashley Packard, *Digital Media Law*, 2nd ed. (Malden, MA: Wiley-Blackwell, 2013), 13.

3.   Department of Justice, "Civil and Criminal Cases," October 16, 2017, https://www.justice.gc.ca/eng/csj-sjc/just/08.html.

4.   *Carter v Canada (Attorney General)*, 2015 SCC 5 at 44.

5. *Rodriguez v British Columbia (Attorney General)*, [1993] 3 SCR 519, 107 DLR (4th) 342.

6. *Carter v Canada (Attorney General)*, 2015 SCC 5.

7. *Capital Cities Comm v CRTC*, [1978] 2 SCR 141; *The Attorney General of Quebec v The Attorney General of Canada and others*, [1932] UKPC 7, [1932] AC 304.

8. "Parliament's Authority," UK Parliament, accessed October 17, 2018, https://www. parliament.uk/about/how/sovereignty/.

9. Supreme Court of Canada, "The Canadian Judicial System," February 15, 2018, https://www.scc-csc.ca/court-cour/sys-eng.aspx.

10. Ibid.

11. *Reference re Secession of Quebec*, [1998] 2 SCR 217.

12. For example, see Canadian Heritage, "The Government of Canada Wants to Ensure the Right Balance of Investment in Content and in the Ability to Compete," December 12, 2018, https://www.newswire.ca/news-releases/the-government-of-canada-wants-to-ensure-the-right-balance-of-investment-in-content-and-in-the-ability-to-compete-640390183.html; "Order Issuing a Direction to the CRTC on Implementing the Canadian Telecommunications Policy Objectives," December 14, 2006, https://laws-lois.justice.gc.ca/eng/regulations/SOR-2006-355/FullText.html; Innovation, Science and Economic Development Canada, "Government Orders the CRTC to Investigate High-Pressure Telecom Sales Practices," June 14, 2018, https://www.newswire.ca/news-releases/government-orders-the-crtc-to-investigate-high-pressure-telecom-sales-practices-685582231.html.

13. *Aeronautics Act*, RSC 1985, c A-2, s 4.32.

14. Sara Bannerman, *The Struggle for Canadian Copyright: Imperialism to Internationalism, 1842–1971* (Vancouver: UBC Press, 2013), 85.

15. *Broadcasting Act*, SC 1991, c 11, ss 10 & 11.

16. Regarding Indigenous sovereignty, see Leanne Simpson, *Dancing on Our Turtle's Back: Stories of Nishnaabeg Re-creation, Resurgence and a New Emergence* (Winnipeg: Arbeiter Ring, 2011), 355; Dara Culhane, *The Pleasure of the Crown: Anthropology, Law, and First Nations* (Vancouver, BC: Talonbooks, 2014).

17. *Indian Act*, RSC 1985, c I-5.

18. Alan Hanna, "Spaces for Sharing: Searching for Indigenous Law on the Canadian Legal Landscape," *UBC Law Review* 51, no. 1 (2018): 129–32.

19. Ibid., 133.

20. John Borrows, *Canada's Indigenous Constitution* (Toronto: University of Toronto Press, 2010), chap. 2.

21. Jeremy de Beer and Daniel Dylan, "Traditional Knowledge Governance Challenges in Canada," in *Indigenous Intellectual Property*, ed. Matthew Rimmer (Cheltenham, UK: Edward Elgar, 2015).

22. Catherine E. Bell and Val Napoleon, eds., *First Nations Cultural Heritage and Law: Case Studies, Voices, and Perspectives* (Vancouver: UBC Press, 2008).

23. John Milloy, *Indian Act Colonialism: A Century of Dishonour, 1869–1969* (National Centre for First Nations Governance, 2008).

24. Hanna; Hadley Friedland, "Reflective Frameworks: Methods for Accessing, Understanding and Applying Indigenous Laws," *Indigenous Law Journal* 11, no. 1 (2012): 1–40; Oonagh Fitzgerald and Risa Schwartz, *UNDRIP Implementation: Braiding International, Domestic and Indigenous Laws* (Waterloo, ON: Centre for International Governance Innovation, 2017).

# 3

# Freedom of Expression and Censorship

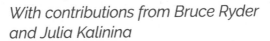

*With contributions from Bruce Ryder and Julia Kalinina*

## INTRODUCTION

The internet enables many diverse forms of expression. It facilitates forms of expression and community that were previously difficult or impossible, from live streaming to citizen reporting and activist communities. It facilitates communication among a wide range of communities from people with rare diseases, people who are sexual and gender minorities, people with disabilities, and activists, to criminals, white supremacists, and online predators.

Government may welcome many of the forms of expression the internet enables, while at the same time working to prevent its use to facilitate crimes such as sexual offences against children. Private corporations, too, increasingly regulate expression through user agreements and algorithms that determine how information is presented and what can be seen—sometimes acting at the behest of governments or in anticipation of possible government regulation.

The internet presents many dilemmas that play out in the tension between the constitutional right to freedom of expression and the limits placed on this right under the *Canadian Charter of Rights and Freedoms*. Rising concerns about online harassment, child pornography, hate speech, false information, and terrorist recruitment have all prompted debates about how online and offline speech should be regulated. Is the availability of violent and sexually degrading content on the internet a problem that should be addressed by greater regulation? Should negative, incorrect, or outdated search results about people be removed? How should rights of free expression be applied by online platforms and social media companies?

First, this chapter introduces the rights of freedom of expression and the press, as well as some of the limits on those rights. It discusses the applicability of freedom of the press to new media. Second, the chapter examines some of the limits placed on freedom of expression and the press, including those placed by laws prohibiting child pornography; obscenity; hate speech; and violent, bullying, or harassing speech. It also addresses the role of private companies in regulating speech, focusing on the role of search engines in delisting search results. The second half of the chapter asks, "Whom do laws relating to speech serve?", drawing on the liberal and critical theories introduced in Chapter 1.

## FREEDOM OF EXPRESSION

### Scope of Freedom of Expression and the Press

The *Canadian Charter of Rights and Freedoms*, in Section 2(b), protects "freedom of thought, belief, opinion and *expression*, including *freedom of the press and other media of communication*" (emphasis added).[1] All policies, laws, and services of Canadian governments (federal, territorial, provincial, and municipal) must conform to the *Charter*.

The *Charter* only applies to the actions of the state; the *Charter* does not directly regulate the actions of private individuals or businesses. For example, if a government outlawed profanity it would clearly be a limit on freedom of expression because it would place a limit on what people can say and the words they can use. Laws prohibiting profanity would be subject to challenge under the *Charter* as potentially unconstitutional restrictions on freedom of expression, although such restrictions might withstand a *Charter* challenge if they were deemed justifiable under Section 1 of the *Charter*.[2] However, if a private business put in place a similar rule for its employees, employees would not have a right to challenge the rule directly under the *Charter*, because the *Charter* applies only to *government* actions, not the actions of private businesses. Similarly, whether the *Charter* applies to an airport that prohibits protestors from demonstrating on airport property depends on whether the airport is operating as a private or governmental entity.[3] If the airport is private, the *Charter* does not apply, but if it is a government-owned and operated airport, the airport's prohibition could be subject to a *Charter* challenge.

### Limits on Freedom of Expression and the Press

The *Charter*'s guarantee of freedom of expression is limited by Section 1 of the *Charter*, which states, "The Canadian Charter of Rights and Freedoms guarantees the rights and freedoms set out in it *subject only to such reasonable limits prescribed by law as can be demonstrably justified in a free and democratic society*" (emphasis added). This limit applies not only to freedom of expression but also all the rights and freedoms set out in the *Charter*, such as freedom of conscience and religion; the right to life, liberty, and security of the person; and the right to vote.

If the court determines freedom of expression has been restricted, it proceeds to ask whether this restriction is justified under Section 1 of the *Charter*.[4] At this stage, the court applies the **Oakes test**, in which it asks:

1. Whether the restriction serves a pressing and substantial objective;
2. Whether the measure is "reasonable and demonstrably justified." This hinges on the question of whether the measure that restricts expression meets the requirements of a three-stage proportionality test:
   a. Rational connection: whether the purpose is advanced rationally;
   b. Minimal impairment: whether the measure impairs the right in question as little as reasonably possible; and,
   c. Proportionate effects: whether the negative effects of the limitation on *Charter* rights and freedoms are proportional to the objective being served (the more severe the measure, "the more important the objective must be") and to the salutary (or beneficial) effects of the measure.[5]

For example, a law prohibiting the use of abusive or insulting language could be saved if the government could show that the law serves a sufficiently important purpose, was advanced rationally, restricted freedom of expression as little as reasonably possible, and was proportional to the objective being served and the beneficial effects of the law.[6] Similarly, a ban on tobacco lifestyle advertising, along with the requirement to include warnings on tobacco products, was reasonably and demonstrably justified by the need to reduce smoking and disease and death caused by smoking.[7] On the other hand, a public transit authority's ban on all political or controversial ads was not rationally connected to the important objective of ensuring a safe and welcoming transit system because political speech did not necessarily create an unsafe or unwelcoming environment. The ban did not minimally impair freedom of expression and was struck down by the Supreme Court of Canada.[8]

## Breadth of Freedom of Expression

In Canada, we use the term **freedom of expression** rather than *freedom of speech* (the language used in the First Amendment of the US Constitution). The courts have defined *expression* to include any act that is intended to convey a message to others. With the exception of violent acts or threats of violence,[9] all expressive activity, regardless of the content of the message conveyed, is protected as expression under the *Charter*.[10] This could include, for example, parking a car in protest, making a gesture, or other expressive acts.[11]

### What Is a Press?

The right of freedom of the press applies to those institutions traditionally referred to as *the press*, such as newspapers or news broadcasters. The Supreme Court of Canada has also demonstrated willingness to protect the freedoms of "new disseminators of news and information" such as bloggers or "anyone who publishes material of public interest in any medium."[12]

## TYPES OF LIMITS ON FREEDOM OF EXPRESSION AND THE PRESS

### What Is Censorship?

**Censorship** is "the suppression or prohibition of any parts of books, films, news, etc. that are considered obscene, politically unacceptable, or a threat to security."[13] Usually, *censorship* refers to suppression of materials by the state, though it can also refer to restrictions put in place by other bodies in power. The word *censorship* is often used to refer to the criminalization of certain forms of speech but is also sometimes used to refer to routine editorial decisions made by newspapers or other publishers to publish certain things and not others, with such decisions being influenced by organizational priorities about what stories are worth telling, journalistic routines, the types of sources journalists turn to, or journalists' own interests and backgrounds.[14] This chapter focuses on the narrower sense of the word: the restriction of speech by legal or policy measures.

The word *censorship* can be used in a neutral sense to refer to any restriction on speech, whether broadly considered to be legitimate (such as in preventing the dissemination of child pornography) or illegitimate (such as in prohibiting views supportive of political opponents from being published). More often, *censorship* is used in a negative sense to refer to what are considered to be *illegitimate* uses of power over knowledge.[15]

In the following sections, we will review several types of restrictions on expression. In some cases, such as child pornography, censorship is widely accepted and viewed as legitimate. In other cases, opinions differ on the legitimacy of censorship, as in the cases of obscenity and hate speech.

## Restrictions on Freedom of Expression in Canada

### *Child Pornography*

The *Criminal Code* contains prohibitions on accessing, making, printing, publishing, transmitting, making available, distributing, selling, advertising, importing, or exporting child pornography, or possessing child pornography for many of these purposes.[16] The child pornography offence goes further than other criminal prohibitions on expression by prohibiting the possession of child pornography and accessing (knowingly viewing) child pornography. The rationale for these novel offences is to deter not just the supply but also the demand for child pornography. Police regularly lay child pornography charges against those who make and distribute child pornography on the internet. The most frequently laid charges are for possession of images downloaded from the internet.

There is a broad consensus that these core applications of the child pornography offence to the creation, distribution, or use of images of the sexual abuse of children are reasonable and demonstrably justified restrictions on expression pursuant to Section 1 of the *Charter*. For this reason, the Supreme Court has upheld the child pornography offence, although the Court found it necessary to curtail the overbreadth of the offence by adding two exceptions. The Court created an exception for (i) possession of expressive material created by oneself alone, such as private journals, drawings, and works of the imagination. It also created an exception for (ii) possession of recordings of lawful sexual activity for one's private use, which would include photos taken by a teenager of themselves or a teenage couple's private photos of themselves.[17]

Some peripheral applications of the child pornography offence have been more contentious. One is its application to creative expression that did not involve the use of children in its production.[18] The unsuccessful attempt by the Crown to destroy Canadian artist Eli Langer's drawings and paintings on the grounds that they amounted to child pornography is one example.[19] Controversy also ensued when Robin Sharpe was charged with possession of his own short stories, charges that were ultimately dismissed on the grounds that the stories had artistic merit and did not advocate or counsel the commission of sexual offences against children.[20] In 2005, parliament responded to Sharpe's acquittal on these charges by removing the artistic merit defence and expanding the definition of written material included in the definition of child pornography.[21] In 2019, Québécois author Yvon

Godbout and his publisher were charged with child pornography offences based on the description of the sexual assault of a child in Godbout's novel *Hansel et Gretel*.[22] Another contentious application of the child pornography offence is to "sexting" or other sharing of sexual images between teenagers.[23]

Child pornography is restricted not only by the state but also by private companies. As will be discussed further in Chapter 10 on internet regulation, major Canadian internet service providers (ISPs) are part of a coalition that blocks foreign websites containing child pornography.[24]

### *Obscenity*

Some forms of sexual expression are prohibited under the *Criminal Code*'s provisions on obscenity.[25] The definition of *obscenity* has evolved over time. In the nineteenth and early twentieth centuries, the test to determine if material was "obscene" was whether it tended to "deprave and corrupt those whose minds are open to such immoral influences."[26] Since then, the objective of obscenity law has shifted from protecting against moral corruption to preventing the commission of sexual violence. Consideration of community standards and artistic merit have been incorporated into the determination of whether material is obscene.[27]

In 1992, the Supreme Court of Canada set down the current interpretation of obscenity. In *R v Butler*, the court gave new emphasis to the question of whether explicit sexual representations are harmful. It categorized obscenity into three types (see Table 3.1): portrayals of explicit sex in combination with violence or threats of violence would, according to the 1992 decision, "almost always" meet the definition of obscenity, but could be saved if it passed a community standards test of having artistic merit. Portrayals of explicit sex that were not violent—but were degrading or dehumanizing—might meet the definition of obscenity and could likewise be saved by virtue of their artistic merit. Explicit sex that was not violent, degrading, or dehumanizing would not normally be considered obscene, unless it employed children in its production.[28]

*Butler* amounted to a liberalization of obscenity law in Canada, which had previously criminalized materials in the third category simply because they presented explicit representations of consensual sexual activity among adults.[29] However, some critics were concerned the law would permit the entry of feminist or religious morals into the law through the door of the community standards test: Would feminist or religious arguments be cited as community standards? However, some argue these concerns have not been borne out; obscenity prosecutions unconnected to child pornography have become uncommon since 1992, with a few exceptions (see below).[30] Material involving explicit sex

## Table 3.1: Obscenity

| TYPE | IS THE MATERIAL OBSCENE? This test focuses on whether the material causes harm, judged by community standards. | DEFENCE |
|---|---|---|
| Explicit sex + violence (including threats of violence) | The Supreme Court in *Butler* thought this material would "almost always" be considered obscene, but since 1992 the community standards test has been permissive of much of this material.* | Artistic merit |
| Explicit sex + degrading/ dehumanizing (not violent) | The Supreme Court in *Butler* thought such material might be obscene in some cases, if the risk of harm is substantial.† | Artistic merit |
| Explicit sex (not violent, degrading, or dehumanizing) | According to the Supreme Court in *Butler*, such material would not normally be considered obscene.‡ | Artistic merit |

*R v Butler*, [1992] 1 SCR 452 at 484–85; Benedet, "The Paper Tigress."
†*R v Butler*, [1992] 1 SCR 452 at 484–85.
‡*Ibid.*

in combination with violence, or in combination with degrading or dehumanizing content, has in several cases been judged to be acceptable according to the community standards test, with defendants successfully citing the widespread availability and acceptability of bondage/domination/submission/masochism (BDSM) material.[31] This is contrary to what was predicted in *Butler*, which had suggested that explicit sex in combination with violence or threats of violence would "almost always" be deemed obscene.[32] The low rate of obscenity prosecutions may also be attributable to internalization of the *Butler* norms in the mainstream pornography industry.

Some critics of the *Butler* decision were concerned that the "community standards" test might be used to persecute sexual minorities, including LGBTQ2+ materials. While obscenity convictions have become uncommon, there have been several significant cases involving sexual and gender minorities.[33]

GLAD DAY BOOKSTORE

Glad Day Bookstore in Toronto fought numerous battles against Canadian censorship laws. An **LGBTQ** bookstore, Glad Day fought against censorship of its materials by Canada Customs (now Canada Border Services Agency) and the Ontario Film Review Board. It also fought criminal charges of obscenity. The fears of those who thought that post-*Butler* obscenity law might be used against sexual minorities were proven founded when in 1992, shortly following *Butler*, the Ontario Court of Justice upheld the seizure of gay pornography by Canada Customs at the border, finding each and every item to be obscene, as the representation of gay sex was considered to be degrading and dehumanizing.[34] In 1993, Toronto police seized the magazine *Bad Attitude* from the bookstore, successfully charging Glad Day with obscenity.[35]

In 2004, Glad Day successfully challenged the Ontario Film Review Board's classification regime after selling a gay porn video that had not been approved by the Board. The court found the power of the Ontario Film Review Board to approve films as a condition of their exhibition and distribution in Ontario was defined too broadly to be upheld under Section 1 of the *Charter*; it failed the "minimal impairment" branch of the *Oakes* test.[36] Legislation passed the following year brought an end to the Board's approval powers, with the exception of "adult sex films."[37] For all other films, the role of the Ontario Film Review Board is now limited to classifying films. However, achieving this change was costly for the bookstore, which had paid more than $100,000 to fight the legal battle.[38]

### LITTLE SISTER'S BOOK AND ART EMPORIUM

Little Sister's Book and Art Emporium, a queer bookstore in Vancouver, also challenged Canada's obscenity laws, the power of Canada Customs to seize obscene materials, and Canada Customs' practice of targeting the bookstore's materials when they crossed the border. Prior to and following the *Butler* decision in 1992, the practice of Canada Customs was to classify all material depicting "anal penetration" as obscene.

Canada Customs changed this practice just prior to trial in 1994. Ultimately, the Supreme Court of Canada upheld Canada Customs' power to seize obscene materials but agreed with Little Sister's that Canada Customs had unjustly targeted gay and lesbian material, violating the protection of freedom of expression in Section 2(b) of the *Charter* and the protection of equality rights in Section 15 of the *Charter*.[39] The Court, however, gave Little Sister's no remedy other than a declaration that its rights had been violated. As Cossman notes, "After 15 years, and a court record that Canada Customs had engaged in overzealous, targeted discrimination against gay and lesbian materials, Little Sister's was told to just trust Canada Customs."[40]

Little Sister's attempted to launch another battle against further seizures of its materials by Customs in 2002, but in 2007 the Supreme Court of Canada rejected its request for advance costs, and the bookstore abandoned its efforts to fight Customs.[41] The Court's decision was not unanimous: "Given that 70 percent of Canada Customs detentions" were of gay and lesbian material, the dissenting judges noted that "there is unfinished business of high public importance left over."[42]

### Hate Speech

*Hate speech* is speech that incites or promotes hatred toward an identifiable group.[43] Public incitement of hatred, and the willful promotion of hatred other than in private conversation, are crimes under the *Criminal Code*.[44] Advocating genocide is also a crime.[45] A judge may order the removal of hate propaganda from the internet and may order an ISP to provide the court with information to identify the poster.[46]

In addition to these criminal offences, human rights legislation in three provinces and the Northwest Territories contains civil prohibitions on hate speech.[47] Until recently, the *Canadian Human Rights Act* also prohibited the communication of hate messages by telecommunications or the internet.[48] The Supreme Court of Canada has upheld federal and Saskatchewan provisions as reasonable limits on freedom of expression.[49] The Court has interpreted prohibitions on hate speech as extending only to the suppression of "extreme and egregious examples" of "detestation and vilification," and has concluded that, so understood, the prohibitions strike a reasonable balance between freedom of expression and protection against discrimination. Nevertheless, the Conservative Harper government removed the hate speech provisions from the *Canadian Human Rights Act* in 2013.[50]

The hate propaganda provision of the *Criminal Code* was used in 1990 to charge a high school teacher and former mayor of Eckville, Alberta, James Keegstra. Keegstra, between the early 1970s and his dismissal from teaching in 1982, taught his students that Jews were "child killers" who were inherently deceptive, sadistic, and evil; that they made up the Holocaust in order to garner sympathy; that they were trying to control the world; and that they were responsible for anarchy, wars, and revolution.[51] His students were required to reproduce his views in order to obtain good marks.[52] He was ultimately given a one-year suspended sentence, a year of probation, and 200 hours of community service.[53]

Criminal hate speech law was used to charge participants of a neo-Nazi protest who chanted neo-Nazi slogans outside a motel where Roma refugees were staying.[54] It was also used to charge former National Chief of the Assembly of First Nations David Ahenakew for hate speech following remarks about Jews in a speech and to a reporter. Those charges were overturned because, according to the court, Ahenakew did not set out to promote hatred or intend to convince the public of his views.[55] The hate speech provisions of the *Criminal Code* remain in place.

Some provinces also have in place laws prohibiting hate speech.[56] The civil prohibition on hate speech in Saskatchewan's *Human Rights Code* was upheld by the Supreme Court of Canada in 2013. In that case, William Whatcott had distributed flyers that portrayed gay and lesbian people as "a menace that threatens the safety and well-being of others," vilifying them as predators and child-abusers.[57] Whatcott was fined and ordered to refrain from any further distribution of the hateful flyers.[58]

Charges against David Popescu, a mayoral candidate in Sudbury, of advocating or promoting genocide and of willful promotion of hatred were eventually dropped in 2015.[59] Popescu had previously been sentenced to 18 months' probation for willful promotion of hatred after stating that "all homosexuals should be executed" during an election debate.[60] In 2019, James Sears, the editor of *Your Ward News*, a Toronto publication, and publisher LeRoy St. Germaine were found guilty of promoting hatred against women and Jews.[61]

Online environments have proven particularly ripe for hate speech to flourish, including neo-Nazi websites and Facebook groups, as well as YouTube videos and postings promoting violence against people who are racialized, women, and sexual and gender minorities. While the provisions of the *Canadian Human Rights Act* regarding online hate speech were repealed, criminal provisions remain. Under these provisions, a white supremacist webmaster, Jean-Sébastien Presseault, was sentenced to six months in prison for posting anti-Semitic content including music, cartoons, literature, and a song with the title "Skin Is Black, You Make Me Sick."[62] At the same time, criminal provisions dealing with online content can be difficult to enforce. Internet intermediaries and users may have more power than law enforcement and courts in preventing online hate from flourishing. Many ISPs have acceptable use policies that allow them to remove hate.[63] Intermediaries can also facilitate counter-speech, can educate users about false ideas and empower users to identify and complain about hateful content, and can provide tools to counter such content.[64]

### Cyberbullying, Harassment, and Promoting Terrorism

Online harassment, posting intimate images of someone online without their consent (sometimes called "revenge porn"), and terrorist recruitment are prohibited under the *Criminal Code*. In an attempt to address the problem of revenge porn, the *Protecting Canadians from Online Crime Act* modified the *Criminal Code* to make the non-consensual distribution of intimate images a crime. Other offences can also apply to in-person bullying and cyberbullying. These include the provisions of the *Criminal Code* on criminal harassment, uttering threats, intimidation, identity fraud, counselling suicide, incitement of hatred, and defamatory libel.[65]

*Criminal Code* provisions also prohibit advocating and promoting terrorism.[66] These provisions are or have been controversial because of the degree to which they restrict or chill expression. A recent study by Craig Forcese and Kent Roach conducts a detailed examination of Bill C-51, the *Security of Canada Information Sharing Act*,[67] which they call "the most radical national security law" enacted in the post-*Charter* period. They question whether the law achieves a proportionate balance between security and the protection of civil liberties.[68] Melissa Ku, similarly, argues that after the enactment of Bill C-51 the provisions of the *Criminal Code* prohibiting advocating and promoting terrorism are too broad and may not withstand a constitutional challenge.[69]

### Search Engine Regulation

While government and law enforcement play significant roles in regulating expression, private companies also regulate speech in various ways. Private companies set many of the rules governing online speech through the terms of use and the design of their services. Search engines play significant roles in regulating expression; the Google search algorithm decides what content is findable to users of Google.

Government and courts can regulate search engines, but the extent to which government intervention in search or other online services is desirable or acceptable is hotly debated. In 2017, the Supreme Court of Canada ordered Google to remove a set of websites from its global search results because the sites allegedly contained pages violating the trade secret and intellectual property rights of Equustek, a company that manufactures networking devices that allow the interconnection of industrial systems.[70] Google and other critics of the court's decision argued that the delisting order was too broad, possibly encompassing pages with innocent content.[71] The majority decision of the Court, however, decided the global delisting order was necessary to prevent irreparable harm to Equustek, noting that a court could modify the order if innocent sites were wrongly encompassed in the order.[72] The Court noted that freedom of expression does not encompass "the facilitation of the unlawful sale of goods," and that such speech does not engage freedom of expression values.[73] A US court later ruled this judgment unenforceable on the grounds that it undermined freedom of speech.[74]

In a highly controversial move, the European Union, along with Iceland, Norway, Switzerland and Liechtenstein, has implemented a **right to be forgotten**. This right allows individuals to request removal of search results from search engines if the content is "inadequate, irrelevant or no longer relevant, or excessive in relation to the purposes for which they were processed."[75] Google has received millions of requests for delisting and has complied with 43 percent of requests.[76] In October 2018, the Privacy Commissioner of Canada sought guidance from the Federal Court of Canada about whether Canadian privacy law includes a similar right to be forgotten. A response is still pending as of this writing.[77]

### Defamation

The law of defamation, discussed further in Chapter 4, aims to protect individuals from expression that tends to harm their reputations. Defamatory expression is proscribed by the *Criminal Code* as well as by the common law and Quebec civil law. In 1998, the Supreme Court of Canada upheld the *Criminal Code* prohibition on defamatory libel as a reasonable limit on freedom of expression.[78] In 1990, the Court also found that the common law of defamation achieves an appropriate balance between freedom of expression and the protection of reputation.[79] We will return to the topic of defamation in the next chapter.

### Election Spending Limits

All Canadian jurisdictions regulate certain forms of expression during political campaigns. Limits on campaign spending and campaign advertising have frequently been challenged in the courts. The goal of these provisions is to promote fair elections by limiting the ability of wealthy or powerful interests to dominate debates. The Supreme Court of Canada has upheld strict spending limits as reasonable limits on freedom of expression.[80] In the United States, in contrast, the Supreme Court has found that electoral spending limits violate the First Amendment.[81] As a result, money dominates the US electoral process to a much greater extent than it does in Canada.

## WHOM DO LAWS RELATING TO SPEECH SERVE?

### The Public Interest?

#### Pluralism

If pluralist democracy is defined by the coexistence of various economic, cultural, professional, and social groups whose competing voices challenge each other and those in power, little could be more fundamental than the freedom to express diverse views and perspectives.[82] In much of Canadian jurisprudence, the constitutional protection of freedom of expression is seen as fundamental to a pluralistic society in which a diversity of ideas and opinions are valued. The Supreme Court of Canada noted in *Irwin Toy* that "such protection is, in the words of both the Canadian and Quebec Charters, 'fundamental,' because in a free, pluralistic and democratic society we prize a diversity of ideas and opinions for their inherent value both to the community and to the individual."[83] In *R v Butler*, Justices L'Heureux-Dubé and Gonthier noted, "In a pluralistic society like ours, many different conceptions of the good are held by various segments of the population. The guarantees of s. 2 of the *Charter* protect this pluralistic diversity."[84]

Pluralism recognizes that different groups have different resources and power. Some may have more power to speak than others; for example, owners of media and entertainment conglomerates, celebrities, and business owners have far more resources than do ordinary workers. Pluralists, to a large extent, accept this, arguing that no group dominates completely or has a monopoly on the power of speech or access to government.

This acceptance of inequality in resources of speech has been criticized by many other theorists—some of whom have questioned the pluralist perspective and its tolerance of extreme inequality of resources of expression, as a basis for democratic theory.[85]

While on the one hand based on the ideal of a pluralistic vetting of views, Canadian jurisprudence has also challenged the pluralistic ideal that free competition of ideas will produce truth. The majority decision in *R v Keegstra* on hate speech stated that "individuals can be persuaded to believe 'almost anything' ... if information or ideas are communicated using the right technique and in the proper circumstances."[86] The Court also noted it was important to not "overplay the view that rationality will overcome all falsehoods in the unregulated marketplace of ideas."[87] Scholars have asked: How far should tolerance of intolerance extend? How far should the views of those who seek to undermine equality and the rights of those they target be tolerated?[88]

## Bureaucracy and Bureaucrats?

### Neoliberalism and Libertarianism

Neoliberal economic theories also place strong importance on freedom of expression, but for slightly different reasons. Speech is often equated to a "marketplace of ideas" in which government interventions, such as censorship or corporate expenditure limits on election communications, are viewed as forms of repression or distortion of the free flow of ideas. The 2010 decision of the Supreme Court of the United States to strike down a federal law limiting corporate election communication expenditures has been called "neoliberal jurisprudence," because the Court had prohibited government restrictions on corporate speech.[89] Like the pluralists mentioned above, the Court's neoliberal jurisprudence tolerates financial inequalities between speakers, viewing the legal limits on election communication expenditure intended to mitigate these inequalities as censorship of the voices of business and economic leaders.[90] Election spending limits have, on the other hand, been upheld by the Supreme Court of Canada.[91]

Libertarians, like neoliberals, generally emphasize strong free expression rights, going further than neoliberals to oppose censorship of almost any kind. Media scholar and civil libertarian C. Edwin Baker, who served as attorney for the American Civil Liberties Union, argues that the repression of hate speech is unlikely to prevent racism or genocide. Instead, he argues that prohibitions on hate speech—efforts to make hate speech "go away" or to remove racism from public discourse—might also lessen people's experience with opposing such views, thus dampening efforts to respond aggressively to critique racist views.[92] Libertarians generally agree that the remedy for bad speech is more speech, opposing most forms of speech regulation and viewing such regulation as an expansion of the powers of the state that fundamentally inhibits freedom.[93]

## The Privileged?

### *Critical Legal Studies and Critical Political Economy*
Many critical theorists view Western law as a system that supports and extends the power of a privileged few. Critical theorists view the liberal approaches to free speech presented above as supporting and extending the power of owners of capital and those whose social positions are already privileged.

Theorists in the field of critical legal studies view law as socially constructed. Notions of individual rights such as "freedom of speech" are abstract, and when applied to particular cases, such abstractions can be used in multiple ways. Whose "freedom" will be paramount? What limits on these freedoms are viewed as acceptable? While "freedom of speech" may favour the rights of individual citizens to produce films containing queer content in one instance, it may favour corporate media's freedom to decide whose voices to include—and exclude—in another.[94] These indeterminacies, critical legal theorists note, can never be resolved objectively; language, law, and legal reasoning are not neutral. Social power is always at play, and thus the judicial system is always susceptible to privileging some groups over others—often cloaking such privilege under a veneer of words like "freedom of speech."[95]

Critical political economists often focus on the role of economic resources in undermining freedom of expression. While the pluralist and liberal approaches outlined above view freedom of expression as the simple absence of government censorship, critical political economists and other thinkers argue that the absence of censorship does not sufficiently guarantee freedom of speech for all. After all, the ability to speak is dependent on sufficient access to education, cultural capital, and media resources to be heard.[96] These, in addition to inequities in access to resources of expression, may present a more significant threat to press freedom than does censorship itself.[97] "More speech," under conditions of economic and social inequality, monopoly control of the media, spin, and propaganda, could lead to further domination of the underprivileged by the privileged.[98]

Economic inequalities often see the moral codes of dominant classes prevail over those without class privilege. In *Undressing the Canadian State*, Kirsten Johnson argues that Canadian obscenity law's emphasis on community standards "perpetuates the moral hegemony of the ruling class by rearticulating and obscuring a class-based definition of 'obscenity' in democratized terms" because community standards tend to be "rooted in class privilege."[99]

### Feminist Analysis

Feminist analyses challenge many of the fundamental premises of liberal freedom of expression theory. Liberal freedom of expression theory views freedom of speech and the free competition of ideas as being important to establishing truth. Some feminists argue that what we accept as truth is socially constructed—that we select certain shared aspects of our experience as "truth," and that this selection process is fundamentally guided by our values and by who is doing the selecting. In a patriarchal system, men's experiences are often considered as "universal" and determining what constitutes "truth." For example, until the 1980s, heart attack symptoms were defined by scientific studies of male subjects; the heart attack symptoms of women were, and still are, often overlooked.[100] If we wish to live in a world where truth is constructed by all affected, feminists suggest that it is not enough to prohibit censorship; we also need to ensure equitable access to the resources of expression and truth construction.[101]

Chris Demaske draws on feminist theories of relationality to argue that American law regarding freedom of speech and hate speech should, to a greater extent, consider inequalities of power between speakers when considering whether prohibitions on speech are constitutionally valid. Like many critical race theorists (see below), feminist theories of relational autonomy note that individuals and groups are socially constructed in ways that empower some groups, while disempowering others, including women. The liberal approach to freedom of speech analysis, which views individuals as theoretically equal "atoms" with equal rights does not sufficiently take this context into account.[102]

Some feminists have also engaged in a longstanding critique of obscenity law. Many feminists have argued that current obscenity law does little to combat stereotypical and degrading images of women and women's sexuality. Kirsten Johnson argues that current Canadian obscenity law does not serve women in that it does not ask, first and foremost, whether violent pornographic material harms women.[103] Rather, the law, in incorporating a community standards test, serves contemporary Canadian community standards as defined mostly by men. These standards, Janine Benedet argues, are now such that almost any kind of violence against women is deemed acceptable under the test, including degrading or dehumanizing content and sexualized portrayals of the murder of women.[104]

Other feminists take a "pro-sex" position about pornography, arguing that women's choices to make, participate in, or consume pornography should be respected. Pornography, they argue, provides sexual information and allows women to experience sexual alternatives in a safe environment. Pornography, they argue, is a part of women's sexual and expressive freedom.[105]

### Queer Studies

For lesbian, gay, bisexual, pansexual, transgender, gender nonbinary, Two-Spirited, gender diverse, and other queer people, freedom of expression is particularly important because members of these groups often experience silencing and invisibility, and many of our experiences of liberation have come through the ability to name and express our experiences and identities—sometimes in ways that dominant majorities find objectionable.[106] These groups are significantly affected by censorship and hate speech.

Perhaps because of the importance of freedom of expression to the affirmation of queer identity, many activists and academics have favoured a liberal approach to free speech and obscenity law in relation to queer publications and pornography.[107] Doubtful that censors would use their power to upset the patriarchal system (by censoring misogynistic pornography, for example), some commentators have suggested that the powers of censorship afforded under Canadian law are more likely to be used against women and queer communities than in support.[108] Queer bookstores and queer written and visual materials, including pornography, have been significant sites for the affirmation of queer identities and, some argue, for the destabilization of oppressive gender norms.[109] As we have seen, many of the battles over free expression in Canada have been fought on these sites. Such battles continue in Canada and elsewhere.[110]

While many queer activists and academics may oppose censorship, many also support restrictions on hate speech.[111] At the same time, some commentators recognize the power of freedom of expression for queer communities and have thus been reluctant to see it curtailed in any way, even in the case of hate speech.[112]

Gender expression has sparked significant controversy in debates about freedom of expression.[113] In 2017, the passage of Bill C-16, *An Act to amend the Canadian Human Rights Act and the Criminal Code*, led to heated debates about freedom of expression in Canada. The bill added gender identity to the list of prohibited grounds of discrimination under the *Canadian Human Rights Act*; to Sections 318 and 319 of the *Criminal Code* prohibiting advocating genocide, publicly inciting hatred, and the willful promotion of hatred; and to Section 718(2)(a)(i) of the *Criminal Code*, which permits hatred to be taken account in sentencing (permitting a crime to be considered a *hate crime* where there is "evidence that the offence was motivated by bias, prejudice or hate based on race, national or ethnic origin, language, colour, religion, sex, age, mental or physical disability, sexual orientation, or gender identity or expression, or on any other similar factor").[114] Critics of the bill argued that the new provisions would infringe freedom of expression by forcing the use of gender-neutral or alternative pronouns such as "they"—a form of compelled speech. Law professor Brenda Cossman argues, however, that such claims have no legal basis; the incorrect use of gender pronouns would only contravene the revised *Criminal Code* provisions on hate speech, hate crime, and advocating genocide if used in the context of murdering, assaulting, sexually assaulting, advocating the genocide of, threatening violence against, or advocating the extreme vilification and detestation of, for example, trans or nonbinary individuals.[115] The modified provisions of the *Canadian Human Rights Act* preventing discrimination against individuals on the grounds of their gender expression could require the use of the pronoun "they" in the context of federal government and businesses that fall within federal jurisdiction (such as banks and airlines).[116] In such contexts, the right to be referred to by one's chosen gender pronoun would be balanced against the freedom of expression of the speaker.[117] Similar requirements exist in provincial contexts; for example, the *Ontario Human Rights Code* also protects Ontarians against discrimination on the basis of gender identity and gender expression.[118]

### Critical Race Theory and Intersectionality

Critical race theorists have presented some significant challenges to free speech ideals. Richard Delgado and Jean Stefancic, two leading critical race theorists, question whether freedom of speech principles actually do what they are supposed to do: Do they really permit free democratic dialogue and facilitate community? American protection of freedom of speech did little, they argue, for protestors calling for racial equality who were arrested and convicted for marching, holding sit-ins, and distributing leaflets.[119] Free speech theory, they argue, may do more to protect racism than to protect minority speakers.

Critical race theorists note that harmful and hateful speech can be silencing to those who are the subject of it, making the ideals of open debate impossible to achieve. Such ideals are even more impossible to achieve on the internet, where like-minded people communicate in relatively closed communities where ideas are reinforced rather than challenged.[120] The racism that pervades our societies may mean that "persons of color can easily become demoralized, blame themselves, and not speak up vigorously"; they may not be able to afford to participate in exchanges of ideas; and when they speak, they may be accorded less credibility than other speakers.[121]

Freedom of speech, critical race theorists emphasize, does not benefit everyone equally; it protects the (predominantly white) powerful, while failing to protect racialized minorities. Exceptions to free speech doctrines, Delgado and Stefancic note, are skewed to favour the rich and powerful:

> If one says something disparaging of a wealthy and well-regarded individual, one discovers that one's words were not free after all; the wealthy individual [can sue for defamation]. Similarly, if one infringes the copyright or trademark of a well-known writer or industrialist, again it turns out that one's action is punishable. Further, if one disseminates an official secret valuable to a powerful branch of the military or defense contractor, that speech is punishable. If one speaks disrespectfully to a judge, police officer, teacher, military official, or other powerful authority figure, again one discovers that one's words were not free.... Yet the suggestion that we create new exception to protect lowly and vulnerable members of our society ... is often met with consternation: the First Amendment must be a seamless web; minorities, if they knew their own self-interest, should appreciate this even more than others. This one-sidedness of free-speech doctrine makes the First Amendment much more valuable to the majority than to the minority.[122]

The idea that there is a "marketplace of ideas" not only fails to protect all, it functions to legitimate racist speech. Racism is subtle and based in hidden assumptions that may be viewed as acceptable by white majorities; racist speech is therefore often not recognized or challenged. For whites, "the existence of an ostensibly free marketplace of ideas," Delgado and Stefancic argue, "renders [the effort of justifying whites' own superior position] unnecessary. Rationalization is easy: our ideas, our culture competed with their more easygoing ones and won."[123] The false idea that there is a "marketplace of ideas" lends false legitimacy to racial and cultural hierarchies.

Critical race theorists argue that free speech doctrines must be changed to permit the prevention of harmful speech and keep hate speech from silencing those who experience it and from reproducing racial hierarchies. Critical race theorists have often argued for more robust provisions prohibiting hate speech.[124] Richard Delgado has proposed that courts should recognize a right to sue for the injuries suffered from "language intended to demean through reference to race."[125] He argues that, as the First Amendment does not protect threats, neither should racial insults be protected given the severe harm they cause to minorities.[126] He argues that regulation of disparaging remarks and slurs is necessary to ensure equality under the law.[127]

At the same time, some critical race theorists believe that the law is a tool for maintenance of the status quo and white supremacy and not an effective tool for change. Some are pessimistic that the law will ever be an effective force for combating racism and hate speech. Nevertheless, critical race theorists see fighting for change as a moral obligation, even if they are uncertain of success.[128]

Theorists who use an intersectional approach point to the relevance of multiple categories of identity or oppression in analyzing the regulation of speech. In the case of hate speech, victims of hate speech may be targeted due to multiple identity categories that may be relevant to the administration of justice. Victims may be targeted because of their race, gender, religion, indigeneity, national or ethnic origin, disability, or class.[129] The form and effects of hate speech may differ based on the intersecting identity categories of its victim(s). For example, Tutsi women were targeted by hate propaganda during the 1994 Rwandan genocide based both on their gender and ethnicity. They were portrayed as evil seductresses seeking to oppress Hutu men in propaganda that promoted sexual violence against, and the genocide of, Tutsi women.[130] Cisgender racialized men may be targeted by different forms of hate speech than racialized trans women and may experience the effects of hate speech differently. Intersectionality theorists argue that multiple intersecting identity categories and systems of oppression should be considered when analyzing and administering the regulation of speech.[131]

### Critical Disability Theory

People with disabilities often experience verbal and physical harassment.[132] They are often subject to medical and mental health systems that restrict their freedom of expression and other fundamental freedoms.[133] For reasons similar to critical race theorists, some critical disability theorists also support state restriction of hate speech. Ian Cram, for example, points to the severe and all-too-common harms caused by hate speech to people who are differently abled, and to the potential for eugenic thinking to take hold if states do not take a stand against hate speech and eugenic theories that have too often been applied to people with disabilities.[134]

Some scholars advocate for greater protection of the expressive freedom of people who are differently abled.[135] Fleur Beaupert argues that mental health service users, survivors of psychiatry, and people with psychosocial disabilities experience extreme infringements on their freedom of expression when they interact with the mental health and psychiatric systems. Many legal systems provide for the restraint, detention, and non-consensual medical treatment of people with a mental disorder in certain circumstances, such as if a person presents a risk of harm to themselves or others.[136] These threats of involuntary detention and treatment, along with the power of psychiatric systems to define, classify, interpret, and enact rules and regimes of behaviour affecting the experiences of its users can so undermine people's own sense of self and point of view that it enacts "epistemic disqualification of an individual as a legitimate 'knower' who can speak on their own behalf."[137] People with disabilities are thus frequently excluded from the protections that the right of freedom of expression is supposed to provide.

### Indigenous and Postcolonial Analysis

Postcolonial theorists argue that the right of freedom of expression and the regulation of speech does not equally benefit all.[138] Postcolonial theorist Gayatri Spivak argues that the power of speech, including language and the ability to express, is sometimes unavailable to groups, such as Indigenous peoples, who are not represented in dominant ways of thinking. Judy Iseke-Barnes and Deborah Danard suggest that Indigenous peoples are often represented online by outsiders, according to an outsider world view that draws on racist stereotypes and distances representations of Indigenous peoples from local contexts and from Indigenous control.[139] Wendy Brown notes that while freedom of expression is available to all, including disempowered groups, freedom of expression can also reinforce the subordination of some groups by expanding the power of those who already possess strong capacities and resources of speech.[140] This tension plays out in questions over whether the right to freedom of the press, guaranteed under the Canadian *Charter*, applies in contexts where the right to press freedom might conflict with Indigenous rights to self-governance.[141]

Colonial tensions over freedom of expression and the press have a long history. During the 1970s, alliances of former colonies attaining independence argued that the international media ecosystem required reordering. Freedom of expression and the free flow of information internationally, they argued, did not guarantee that everyone could express themselves or access media equally. Rather, free media markets tended to reproduce unequal flows of information and Western media and cultural dominance—a "continuation of imperialism by other means."[142] Building a supportive environment that could ensure all countries and groups would have equal voices in the international media ecosystem would require something even broader than freedom of expression: a right to communicate, including a right to a diverse media ecosystem, and a right of access for minority voices to contribute to media programming.[143] However, in other senses, a right to communicate and associated policies designed to ensure that all groups and countries had access to media to communicate could conflict with freedom of the press; such a right would likely require policy measures to ensure that media outlets represented diverse voices in their employment and content.[144] Debates about whether such measures were necessary and whether they represented an unacceptable level of interference with freedom of the press caused strong divisions within the United Nations Educational, Scientific and Cultural Organization (UNESCO) in the 1970s and 1980s.[145] The United States, the United Kingdom, and Singapore saw such measures as unacceptable and withdrew from membership in UNESCO in 1984 as a result of the organization's support of such measures.[146] Similar debates have been echoed more recently with regard to the international digital divide, asking whether a right to communicate, broader than simple freedom of expression, is required to bridge the gap.[147] However, due to the tensions over this issue and concerns that such a right might interfere with freedom of expression, a right to communicate has not, to date, been recognized in international law.[148]

### Governmentality, Networked Governance, Technology, and Geography

Scholars who examine freedom of expression through the lenses of governmentality, networked governance, the history of technology, and geography note that freedom of expression and the press exists within specific historical, geographical, political, and technological contexts.[149] Those of us lucky enough to hold rights of freedom of expression and the press have been historically and discursively constructed as free, democratic subjects possessing civic responsibility.[150] Freedom of expression and the press are discourses that help to construct us as holders of those rights. They are discourses of power that enable some persons to exercise these rights, but at the same time, some people are excluded from their ambit. Historically, freedom of expression and the press were constructed by imperial powers as belonging only to "civilized" white citizens; rights and freedoms thus were not considered to be appropriate modalities of governance in nations considered to be "uncivilized" by their imperial governors.[151] Thus, freedom of expression is a discourse constructed along lines of an imperial racializing cartography.

Freedom of expression and the press, like all liberal rights, are tied to the rise of the nation state and nationalism, which were enabled by the propagation of technologies of mass printing and publishing.[152] The role of government is, as Michel Foucault argues, to construct subjects who are capable of exercising those rights and to regulate knowledge.[153] States secure power through the mastery of information and through control of, and monopolies on, knowledge.[154] Freedoms of expression and speech arose historically and geographically, as communications scholar Harold Innis argues, as a part of efforts by states and publishers to control knowledge and communication.[155] Freedom of the press, according to Innis, entrenched the printed word as primary over oral traditions. It served "vested interests" such as publishing powerhouses and encouraged mass production/reproduction as the dominant form of social production.[156] Freedom of the press became "the bulwark of monopolies of the press," which was, in turn, enrolled in the project of empire.[157]

Rights of freedom of expression and the press are not static; they change according to their historical, technological, and discursive context. As we see dramatic changes in communication technologies, on one hand expanding communicative freedoms and on the other enabling state surveillance on a scale never before known, some scholars argue that theories of freedom of expression must equally change. Perhaps to an extent greater than law alone, communication technologies play a role in enabling or restricting freedom of expression and in regulating speech. Still, we cannot fall prey to technological determinism or to the idea that greater communicative freedom will naturally flow from the advent of new technologies. Rights of freedom of expression prohibit state interference with expression, but do not guarantee a right to express oneself on a particular platform.[158] The private owners of platforms set the rules that prohibit certain types of speech or speakers on their platforms in ways that may inhibit or encourage communicative freedoms. Surveillance and other technologies are a threat to communicative freedoms even as they are enablers of communication.[159] Governments, in protecting freedom of expression, must therefore not stop at preventing censorship; they should also promote participation in communication technologies and facilitate technological designs that incorporate free speech values such as access, openness, participation, interactivity, and democratic control.[160] These concepts are encompassed under the idea of a "right to communicate" or "communication rights."[161]

## FURTHER READING

Benedet, Janine. "The Paper Tigress: Canadian Obscenity Law 20 Years after *R v Butler*." *Canadian Bar Review* 93, no. 1 (2015): 1–37.

Cossman, Brenda, Shannon Bell, Lise Gotell, and Becki Ross. *Bad Attitude/s on Trial: Pornography, Feminism, and the Butler Decision.* Toronto: University of Toronto Press, 1997.

Demaske, Chris. "Modern Power and the First Amendment: Reassessing Hate Speech." *Communication Law and Policy* 9, no. 3 (2004): 273–316.

Johnson, Kirsten. *Undressing the Canadian State: The Politics of Pornography from Hicklin to Butler.* Halifax: Fernwood, 1995.

Matsuda, Mari J. *Words That Wound: Critical Race Theory, Assaultive Speech, and the First Amendment.* New York: Routledge, 2018.

Moon, Richard. *The Constitutional Protection of Freedom of Expression.* Toronto: University of Toronto Press, 2000.

Sumner, Leonard Wayne. *The Hateful and the Obscene: Studies in the Limits of Free Expression.* Toronto: University of Toronto Press, 2004.

Williams, Susan H. "Feminist Theory and Freedom of Speech." *Indiana Law Journal* 84, no. 2009 (2009): 999–1013.

## NOTES

1.  *Canadian Charter of Rights and Freedoms*, s 2(b), Part I of the *Constitution Act, 1982*, being Schedule B to the *Canada Act 1982* (UK), 1982, c 11.

2.  *Bracken v Niagara Parks Police*, 2018 ONCA 261.

3. *Calgary Airport Authority v Canadian Centre for Bio-Ethical Reform*, 2019 ABQB 29 (*Charter* does not apply to an airport operating autonomously from government); *Committee for the Commonwealth of Canada v Canada*, [1991] 1 SCR 139 (*Charter* does apply to an airport owned and operated by government).

4. See also Marc Raboy, William J. McIver, and Jeremy Shtern (eds.), *Media Divides: Communication Rights and the Right to Communicate in Canada* (Vancouver: UBC Press, 2010), 64.

5. *R v Oakes*, [1986] 1 SCR 103; *R v Edwards Books Ltd.*, [1986] 2 SCR 713; *Dagenais v Canadian Broadcasting Corporation*, [1994] 3 SCR 835; *Alberta v Hutterian Brethren of Wilson Colony*, [2009] 2 SCR 567; Richard Moon, *The Constitutional Protection of Freedom of Expression* (Toronto: University of Toronto Press, 2000), 35.

6. See *Bracken v Niagara Parks Police*.

7. *JTI MacDonald Corp v Canada (Procureure générale)*, 2007 SCC 30. See also *RJR-MacDonald v Canada*, 3 SCR 199, [1995] SCJ No. 68.

8. *Canadian Federation of Students v Greater Vancouver Transportation Authority*, 2009 SCC 31.

9. *R v Khawaja*, [2012] 3 SCR 555.

10. Moon, 33–35; *Irwin Toy Ltd v Quebec (Attorney General)*, [1989] 1 SCR 927 at 968. Note that laws having the effect but not the purpose of restricting expression can be challenged only if the restricted speech can be shown to advance the values underlying freedom of expression. *Irwin Toy Ltd v Quebec (Attorney General)* at 976.

11. *Irwin Toy Ltd v Quebec (Attorney General)* at 969.

12. *Grant v Torstar Corp* at 96. See also Raboy, McIver, and Shtern, 70; Teresa Scassa, "Journalistic Purposes and Private Sector Data Protection Legislation: Blogs, Tweets, and Information Maps," *Queen's Law Journal* 35 (2010): 733–81.

13. *Lexico: Powered by Oxford*, s.v. "censorship, n.," accessed August 19, 2019, https://www.lexico.com/en/definition/censorship.

14. Bob Hackett and Richard Gruneau, "Is Canada's Press Censored?", in *The Missing News: Filters and Blind Spots in Canada's Media* (Ottawa: Canadian Centre for Policy Alternatives, 2000), 22–51.

15. Bruce Ryder, "Undercover Censorship: Exploring the History of the Regulation of Publications in Canada," in *Interpreting Censorship in Canada*, eds. K. Petersen and A.C. Hutchinson (Toronto: University of Toronto Press, 1999), 129.

16. *Criminal Code*, RSC 1985, c C-46, s 163.1(1)–(4.3).

17. *R v Sharpe*, 2001 SCC 2 at para 75–76. The scope of the private use exception is discussed in *R v Barabash*, 2015 SCC 29.

18. Brenda Cossman, *Censorship and the Arts: Law, Controversy, Debate, Facts* (Toronto: Ontario Association of Art Galleries, 1995); Bruce Ryder, "The Harms of

Child Pornography Law," *University of British Columbia Law Review* 36, no. 1 (2003): 101–35.

19. *Ontario (Attorney General) v Langer*, (1995) 123 DLR (4th) 289, 1995 CanLII 7422 (ONSC).

20. *R v Sharpe*, 2002 BCSC 423.

21. *An Act to amend the Criminal Code (protection of children and other vulnerable persons) and the Canada Evidence Act*, SC 2005, c 32.

22. Pierre Trudel, "Inhibition Collatérale [Chilling Effect]," *Le Devoir*, March 26, 2019.

23. Lara Karaian and Dillon Brady, "Revisiting the 'Private Use Exception' to Canada's Child Pornography Laws: Teenage Sexting, Sex Positivity, Pleasure, and Control in the Digital Age," *Osgoode Hall Law Journal* 56 (forthcoming).

24. "Cleanfeed Canada," accessed October 30, 2018, https://cybertip.ca/app/en/projects-cleanfeed.

25. *Criminal Code*, RSC 1985, c C-46, s 163.

26. *Regina v Hicklin*, 1868 LR 3 QB 360; Kirsten Johnson, *Undressing the Canadian State: The Politics of Pornography from Hicklin to Butler* (Halifax: Fernwood, 1995), 42.

27. Brenda Cossman, Shannon Bell, Lise Gotell, and Becki Ross, *Bad Attitude/s on Trial: Pornography, Feminism, and the Butler Decision*; Johnson, *Undressing the Canadian State* (Toronto: University of Toronto Press, 1997), 43–45.

28. *R v Butler*, 1992 1 SCR 452 at 484–85.

29. Janine Benedet, "The Paper Tigress: Canadian Obscenity Law 20 Years after *R v Butler*," *The Canadian Bar Review* 93, no. 1 (2015): 10–11.

30. Ibid., 7, 11.

31. Ibid., 25–33.

32. See Figure 4.1; *R v Butler* at 484–85.

33. Benedet downplays the significance of these cases. See Benedet, 11, 20.

34. *Glad Day Bookshop v Deputy Minister of National Revenue for Customs & Excise*, [1992] OJ No. 1466; Brenda Cossman, "Censor, Resist, Repeat: A History of Censorship of Gay and Lesbian Sexual Representation in Canada," *Duke Journal of Gender Law & Policy* 21 (Fall 2014): 45–66.

35. *R v Scythes*, [1993] OJ No 537 (Prov Div)(QL) (1993); Brenda Cossman, "Censor, Resist, Repeat," 55. See also Moon, 123.

36. *Glad Day Bookshop v Deputy Minister of National Revenue for Customs & Excise*.

37. *Film Classification Act, 2005*, SO 2005, c 17, and O Reg 452/05.

38. *R v Glad Day Bookshops Inc*, 70 OR (3d) 691; [2004] OJ No. 1766; Sheryl Hamilton, *Law's Expression: Communication, Law and Media in Canada* (Toronto: LexisNexis, 2009), 27.

39. *Canadian Charter of Rights and Freedoms*, c 11, s 15.

40. Cossman, "Censor, Resist, Repeat," 57; *Little Sisters Book and Art Emporium v Canada*, 2000 SCC 69.

41. Ibid.

42. *Little Sisters Book and Art Emporium v Canada*, 2007 SCC 2, [2007] 1 SCR 38 at 110.

43. *Criminal Code*, RSC 1985, c C-46, ss 319 (1) and 319 (2); see also *OED Online* (2018), s.v. "hate, n.," accessed February 15, 2019.

44. *Criminal Code*, RSC 1985, c C-46, s 319.

45. *Criminal Code*, RSC 1985, c C-46, s 318.

46. *Criminal Code*, RSC 1985, c C-46, s 320.1.

47. *Human Rights Code*, RSBC 1996, c 210, s 7(1)(b); *Alberta Human Rights Act*, RSA 2000, c A-25.5, s 3(1)(b); *Saskatchewan Human Rights Code*, 2018, SS 2018, c S-24.2, s 14(1)(b); *Human Rights Act*, SNWT 2002, c 18, s 13(1)(c).

48. *Canadian Human Rights Act*, RSC 1985, c H-6, s 13 (repealed). For a review of the enforcement of this provision, see Moon, "Report to the Canadian Human Rights Commission."

49. *Canada (Human Rights Commission) v Taylor* [1990] 3 SCR 892; *Saskatchewan (Human Rights Commission) v Whatcott*, 2013 SCC 11; see also *Lemire v Canada (Human Rights Commission)*, 2014 FCA 18 (affirming that s 13 of the *Canadian Human Rights Act* remained a reasonable limit on freedom of expression prior to its repeal).

50. "'Hate Speech' No Longer Part of Canada's Human Rights Act," *National Post*, June 27, 2013, https://nationalpost.com/news/politics/hate-speech-no-longer-part-of-canadas-human-rights-act.

51. Tu Thanh Ha, "Holocaust Denier and Former Alberta Teacher Jim Keegstra Dead at 80," *The Globe and Mail*, June 13, 2014, https://www.theglobeandmail.com/news/national/holocaust-denier-and-former-alberta-teacher-jim-keegstra-dead-at-the-age-of-80/article19155171/.

52. *R v Keegstra*, [1990] 3 SCR 697 at 714.

53. "This Day in 1985—Former Teacher Jim Keegstra Fined for Promoting Hatred against Jews," *Calgary Herald* (blog), July 20, 2012, https://calgaryherald.com/news/local-news/this-day-in-1985.

54. *R v Krymowski*, 2005 SCC 7.

55. *R v Ahenakew*, 2009 SKPC 10.

56. Luke McNamara, "Negotiating the Contours of Unlawful Hate Speech: Regulation under Provincial Human Rights Laws in Canada," *UBC Law Review* 38, no. 1 (2005): 1–82.

57. *Saskatchewan (Human Rights Commission) v Whatcott*, 2013 SCC 11 at 187 and 189.

58. Ibid.

59. Harold Carmichael, "Out-of-Town Crown Dropped Charges vs Sudbury Man," *Sudbury Star*, December 30, 2015, https://www.thesudburystar.com/2015/12/31/out-of-town-crown-dropped-charges-vs-sudbury-man/wcm/9b90e126-4220-e0da-9e3e-afb5e4a414db.

60. Ibid.

61. Colin Perkel, "James Sears Fires Lawyer; Sentencing for Your Ward News Delayed," *680 News* (blog), May 30, 2019, https://www.680news.com/2019/05/30/james-sears-fires-lawyer-sentencing-for-your-ward-news-delayed/; Colin Perkel, "Editor Found Guilty of Peddling Hate, Says Your Ward News Gave 'Angry Men' a Voice," April 26, 2019, https://nationalpost.com/news/canada/crown-seeks-one-year-jail-term-against-editor-convicted-of-promoting-hate; *R v Sears*, 2019 ONCJ 104.

62. "Racist Webmaster Gets 6 Months for Hate Propaganda," *CBC News*. January 23, 2007, https://www.cbc.ca/news/canada/montreal/racist-webmaster-gets-6-months-for-hate-propaganda-1.662779; *R v Presseault*, 2007 QCCQ 384.

63. Jane Bailey, "Private Regulation and Public Policy: Toward Effective Restriction of Internet Hate Propaganda," *McGill Law Journal* 49 (2004): 59.

64. Danielle Keats Citron and Helen Norton, "Intermediaries and Hate Speech: Fostering Digital Citizenship for Our Information Age," *Boston University Law Review* 91 (2011): 1435–84.

65. *Criminal Code*, RSC 1985, c C-46, ss 264 (criminal harassment), 264.1 (uttering threats), 243(1) (intimidation), 403 (identity fraud), 241 (counselling suicide), 319 (incitement of hatred), and 298–301 (defamatory libel).

66. *Criminal Code*, RSC 1985, c C-46, s 83.221

67. *Anti-Terrorism Act*, SC 2015, c 20.

68. Craig Forcese and Kent Roach, *False Security: The Radicalization of Canadian Anti-Terrorism* (Toronto: Irwin Law, 2015); see especially "Delete: Criminalizing and Censoring Extremist Speech."

69. Melissa Ku, "Walking the Tightrope between National Security and Freedom of Expression: A Constitutional Analysis of the New Advocating and Promoting Terrorism Offence," *Appeal: Review of Current Law and Law Reform* 21 (2016): 83–98.

70. *Google Inc v Equustek Solutions Inc*, 2017 SCC 34.

71. "Google v Equustek," Electronic Frontier Foundation, October 24, 2016, https://www.eff.org/cases/google-v-equustek.

72. *Google Inc v Equustek Solutions Inc* at 45–49.

73. Ibid. at 48.

74. "Canada's Top Court Overstepped, Can't Enforce Google to Delist Search Results in U.S., Judge Rules," *Toronto Star*, November 3, 2017, https://www.thestar.com/business/2017/11/03/canadas-top-court-overstepped-cant-enforce-google-to-delist-search-results-in-us-judge-rules.html

75. *Google Spain SL and Google Inc. v Agencia Española de Protección de Datos (AEPD) and Mario Costeja González*, case C-131/12.

76. Theo Bertram, Elie Bursztein, Stephanie Caro, Hubert Chao, Rutledge Chin Feman, Peter Fleischer, Albin Gustafsson, Jess Hemerly, Chris Hibbert, and Luca Invernizzi, "Three Years of the Right to Be Forgotten" (Mountain View, CA: Google, 2018), https://drive.google.com/file/d/1H4MKNwf5MgeztG7OnJRnl3ym3glT3HUK/view.

77. *Reference re subsection 18.3(1) of the Federal Courts Act, RSC 1985, c F-7*, 2019 FC 261; Teresa Scassa, "Right to Be Forgotten Reference to Federal Court Attracts Media Concern," April 17, 2019, https://www.teresascassa.ca/index.php?option=com_k2&view=item&id=305:right-to-be-forgotten-reference-to-federal-court-attracts-media-concern&Itemid=80; Office of the Privacy Commissioner of Canada, "Privacy Commissioner Seeks Federal Court Determination on Key Issue for Canadians' Online Reputation," October 10, 2018, https://www.priv.gc.ca/en/opc-news/news-and-announcements/2018/an_181010/.

78. *R v Lucas*, [1998] 1 SCR 439, [1998] SCJ No 28.

79. *Hill v Church of Scientology of Toronto*, [1995] 2 SCR 1130, [1995] SCJ No 64.

80. *Harper v Canada*, 2004 SCC 33.

81. *Citizens United v Federal Electoral Commission*, (2010) 558 US 310.

82. Seymour Martin Lipset, "The Social Requisites of Democracy Revisited: 1993 Presidential Address," *American Sociological Review* 59, no. 1 (1994): 4, 12.

83. *Irwin Toy Ltd v Quebec (Attorney General)*.

84. *R v Butler*.

85. David Schultz, "The Case for a Democratic Theory of American Election Law," *University of Pennsylvania Law Review Online* 164, no. 2 (2016): 259–68.

86. *R v Keegstra* at 747. As quoted in Richard Moon, "Hate Speech Regulations in Canada," *Florida State University Law Review* 36, no. 1 (2008): 88.

87. *R v Keegstra* at 763. As quoted in Moon, "Hate Speech Regulations," 88.

88. Wayne Sumner, "Hate Speech and the Law: A Canadian Perspective," in *Pluralism and Law*, ed. Arend Soeteman (Dordrecht: Springer Netherlands, 2001), 37, https://doi.org/10.1007/978-94-017-2702-0_3.

89. *Citizens United v Federal Election Commission*; Timothy K. Kuhner, "Citizens United as Neoliberal Jurisprudence: The Resurgence of Economic Theory," *Virginia Journal of Social Policy and the Law* 18, no. 3 (2011): 395–468.

90. *Citizens United v Federal Election Commission*; Kuhner, 404–5.

91. *Harper v Canada (AG)*, 2004 SCC 33.

92. C. Edwin Baker, "Hate Speech," in *The Content and Context of Hate Speech*, eds. Michael Herz and Peter Molnar (Cambridge: Cambridge University Press, 2012), 57–80, https://doi.org/10.1017/CBO9781139042871.007.

93. *Whitney v California*, 274 US 357 (1927) at 377.

94. Thomas Streeter, "Beyond Freedom of Speech and the Public Interest: The Relevance of Critical Legal Studies to Communications Policy," *Journal of Communication* 40, no. 2 (1990): 43–63.

95. Ibid.

96. Smeltzer and Hearn discuss the long tradition of free speech activism at universities and the role of neoliberalism in putting pressure on free speech on campus. Sandra Smeltzer and Alison Hearn, "Student Rights in an Age of Austerity? 'Security,' Freedom of Expression and the Neoliberal University," *Social Movement Studies* 14, no. 3 (May 4, 2015): 352–58, https://doi.org/10.1080/1474 2837.2014.945077.

97. Tony Burman, "The Real Danger to Press Freedom," in *The Unfulfilled Promise of Press Freedom in Canada*, eds. Lisa Taylor and Cara-Marie O'Hagan (Toronto: University of Toronto Press, 2017), 15–30; Leigh Felesky, "Exploring How Emerging Digital Business Models and Journalistic Innovation May Influence Freedom of the Press," in *The Unfulfilled Promise of Press Freedom in Canada*, eds. Lisa Taylor and Cara-Marie O'Hagan (Toronto: University of Toronto Press, 2017), 31–46; Ben H. Bagdikian, *The New Media Monopoly* (Boston: Beacon Press, 2014).

98. C. Edwin Baker, "Scope of the First Amendment Freedom of Speech," *University of California Law Review* 25 (1978): 965.

99. Johnson, 45.

100. Caroline Criado Perez, *Invisible Women: Data Bias in a World Designed for Men* (New York: Abrams, 2019).

101. Susan H. Williams, "Feminist Theory and Freedom of Speech," *Indiana Law Journal* 84 (2009): 999–1013.

102. Chris Demaske, "Modern Power and the First Amendment: Reassessing Hate Speech," *Communication Law and Policy* 9, no. 3 (2004): 273–316. See also Moon, *Constitutional Protection* for a relational (but not necessarily a feminist) view of freedom of expression.

103. Moon, *Constitutional Protection*, 106. See also Johnson, 45.

104. Benedet.

105. Wendy McElroy, "A Feminist Defense of Pornography," *Free Inquiry* 17, no. 4 (1997): 14–17; Wendy McElroy, *XXX: A Woman's Right to Pornography* (New York: St. Martin's Press, 1995); Robert Scott Stewart, "Is Feminist Porn Possible?" *Sexuality & Culture* (2018): 1–17; see also, generally, Rebecca Sullivan and Alan McKee, *Pornography: Structures, Agency and Performance* (Hoboken, NJ: John Wiley & Sons, 2015).

106. William B. Rubenstein, "Since When Is the Fourteenth Amendment Our Route to Equality: Some Reflections on the Construction of the Hate Speech Debate

from a Lesbian/Gay Perspective," *Law & Sexuality: A Review of Lesbian & Gay Legal Issues* 2, no. 19 (1992): 22.

107. Carl F. Stychin, "Exploring the Limits: Feminism and the Legal Regulation of Gay Male Pornography," *Vermont Law Review* 16 (1991): 857–900; Susan R. Taylor, "Gay and Lesbian Pornography and the Obscenity Laws in Canada," *Dalhousie Journal of Legal Studies* 8 (1999): 94–129.

108. Paul Wollaston, "When Will They Ever Get It Right—A Gay Analysis of *R. v. Butler*," *Dalhouise Journal of Legal Studies* 2 (1993): 261.

109. Stychin. But see Ann Scales, "Avoiding Constitutional Depression: Bad Attitudes and the Fate of *Butler*," *Canadian Journal of Women and the Law* 7 (1994): 349–92.

110. Monika Zalnieriute, "The Anatomy of Neoliberal Internet Governance: A Queer Critical Political Economy Perspective," in *Queering International Law: Possibilities, Alliances, Complicities, Risks*, ed. Dianne Otto (Abingdon, UK: Routledge, 2018), 53–74. In this volume, see Chapter 10, "Internet Regulation."

111. Christopher N. Kendall, *Gay Male Pornography: An Issue of Sex Discrimination* (Vancouver: UBC Press, 2005).

112. Rubenstein; Martha T. Zingo, *Sex/Gender Outsiders, Hate Speech, and Freedom of Expression: Can They Say That about Me?* (Westport, CT: Greenwood Publishing Group, 1998).

113. Gender expression is a form of speech deserving of protection: Danielle Weatherby, "From Jack to Jill: Gender Expression as Protected Speech in the Modern Schoolhouse," *NYU Review of Law & Social Change* 39 (2015): 89; Jeffrey Kosbie, "(No) State Interests in Regulating Gender: How Suppression of Gender Nonconformity Violates Freedom of Speech," *William and Mary Journal of Women and the Law* 19 (2012): 187–254.

114. *Criminal Code*, RSC, 1985, c C-46, s 718.2(a)(i); Bill C-16, *An Act to amend the Canadian Human Rights Act and the Criminal Code*, SC 2017, c 13.

115. Brenda Cossman, "Gender Identity, Gender Pronouns, and Freedom of Expression: Bill C-16 and the Traction of Specious Legal Claims," *University of Toronto Law Journal* 68, no. 1 (2018): 37–79.

116. Provincial and territorial governments virtually all provide similar protections. See Cossman, "Gender Identity."

117. Cossman, "Gender Identity," 54–57.

118. *Human Rights Code*, RSO 1990, c H.19, s 1.

119. Delgado and Stefancic, "Images of the Outsider in American Law and Culture: Can Free Expression Remedy Systemic Social Ills?" 1285.

120. Richard Delgado and Jean Stefancic, "Hate Speech in Cyberspace," *Wake Forest Law Review* 49 (2014): 319; Philip M. Napoli, "What If More Speech Is no

Longer the Solution: First Amendment Theory Meets Fake News and the Filter Bubble," *Federal Communications Law Journal* 70, no. 1 (2018): 55–104.

121. Delgado and Stefancic, 1287.

122. Ibid., 1285–86.

123. Ibid., 1286.

124. Mari J. Matsuda, *Words That Wound: Critical Race Theory, Assaultive Speech, and the First Amendment* (New York: Routledge, 2018).

125. Richard Delgado, "Words That Wound: A Tort Action for Racial Insults, Epithets, and Name-Calling," *Harvard Civil Liberties Law Review* 17 (1982): 179.

126. Ibid., 173.

127. Richard Delgado, "Campus Antiracism Rules: Constitutional Narratives in Collision," *Northwestern University Law Review* 85 (1990): 343–87.

128. Delgado and Stefancic, 1289.

129. Nazila Ghanea, "Intersectionality and the Spectrum of Racist Hate Speech: Proposals to the UN Committee on the Elimination of Racial Discrimination," *Human Rights Quarterly* 35, no. 4 (2013): 935–54. See also Pete Burnap and Matthew L. Williams, "Us and Them: Identifying Cyber Hate on Twitter across Multiple Protected Characteristics," *EPJ Data Science* 5, no. 1 (December 2016), 11, https://doi.org/10.1140/epjds/s13688-016-0072-6.

130. Lezlie L. Green, "Gender Hate Propaganda and Sexual Violence in the Rwandan Genocide: An Argument for Intersectionality in International Law," *Columbia Human Rights Law Review* 33 (2001): 733–76.

131. Kerri A. Froc, "Multidimensionality and the Matrix: Identifying Charter Violations in Cases of Complex Subordination," *Canadian Journal of Law & Society* 25, no. 1 (2010): 21–49.

132. Ian Cram, "Hate Speech and Disabled People: Some Comparative Constitutional Thoughts," *Disability Rights in Europe: From Theory to Practice* (2005): 69.

133. Fleur Beaupert, "Freedom of Opinion and Expression: From the Perspective of Psychosocial Disability and Madness," *Laws* 7, no. 1 (2018): 3.

134. Cram, 76.

135. Beaupert.

136. Ibid., 12.

137. Ibid., 9.

138. Gayatri Chakravorty Spivak, "Can the Subaltern Speak?" in *Can the Subaltern Speak? Reflections on the History of an Idea*, ed. Rosalind C. Morris (New York: Columbia University Press, 2010), 21–78.

139. Judy M. Iseke-Barnes and Deborah Danard, "Indigenous Knowledges and Worldview: Representations and the Internet," in *Information Technology and Indigenous People* (Hershey, PA: IGI Global, 2007), 27–29.

140. Wendy Brown, "Suffering the Paradoxes of Rights," in *Left Legalism/Left Critique*, eds. Wendy Brown and J. Halley (Durham, NC: Duke University Press, 2001), 423.

141. Wawmeesh Hamilton, "Treaties Are No Guarantee of Freedom of the Press, but There's Little Media Coverage of First Nations Anyway," *Policy Options*, December 1, 2016, https://policyoptions.irpp.org/magazines/december-2016/in-first-nations-freedom-of-the-press-is-unclear/.

142. Cees Hamelink and Julia Hoffmann, "The State of the Right to Communicate," *Global Media Journal* 7, no. 13 (2008): 1–16.

143. Raboy, McIver, and Shtern.

144. Hamelink and Hoffmann.

145. Alia Dakroury and Julia Hoffmann, "Communication as a Human Right: A Blind Spot in Communication Research?", *International Communication Gazette* 72, no. 4–5 (2010): 315–22.

146. Hamelink and Hoffmann.

147. Ibid.; Dakroury and Hoffmann.

148. Hamelink and Hoffmann.

149. Paul Passavant, *No Escape: Freedom of Speech and the Paradox of Rights* (New York: NYU Press, 2002).

150. Ibid.

151. Ibid.

152. Benedict Anderson, *Imagined Communities: Reflections on the Origin and Spread of Nationalism* (New York: Verso Books, 2006).

153. Passavant.

154. Monroe E. Price, *Free Expression, Globalism, and the New Strategic Communication* (New York: Cambridge University Press, 2015), 4.

155. Ibid.

156. Harold A. Innis, *The Bias of Communication*, 2nd ed. (Toronto: University of Toronto Press, 2008).

157. Ibid.

158. *Baier v Alberta*, 2007 SCC 31; *Native Women's Assn of Canada v Canada*, [1994] 3 SCR 627; [1994] SCJ No. 93.

159. Hamelink and Hoffmann.

160. Jack M. Balkin, "Digital Speech and Democratic Culture: A Theory of Freedom of Expression for the Information Society," *NYU Law Review* 79 (2004): 1–55.

161. Hamelink and Hoffmann.

# 4 Defamation

## INTRODUCTION

Defamation is the act of damaging a person's reputation—of bringing dishonour or disrepute to a person.[1] In Canada, a person who has been defamed can **sue** the person who defamed them.

Defamation can take many forms. It can take the form of a verbal statement, an article in a newspaper, a blog post, a social media posting, or an email to friends. In the online environment, defamation frequently occurs on a worldwide scale, crossing international borders, and it often occurs anonymously. This presents difficult problems for those seeking to sue for defamation. It also presents potentially severe consequences for casual users of email and social media, who may not realize that their emails and social media postings are subject to defamation law, especially when they make posts in what they consider to be a personal or semi-private context.

This chapter introduces defamation law in Canada by first introducing basic concepts and principles in defamation law, including the elements of defamation and defences to defamation suits. It discusses strategic lawsuits against public participation (SLAPP)—suits used by individuals or companies seeking to chill criticism. The second half of the chapter asks, "Whom does defamation law serve?", drawing on the theories introduced in Chapter 1.

## LIBEL AND SLANDER

Defamation can be divided into two categories: libel and slander. **Libel** is defamation in print or broadcast form, such as newspaper articles, YouTube videos, blog posts, emails, and other communications that leave a record. **Slander** encompasses *verbal* statements, such as defamatory comments made around a water cooler.

## INTENT

In Canada, statements can be defamatory even where there is no intent to defame someone.[2] The defamer's intent is only relevant in assessing the damages to be paid to a successful plaintiff in a case.[3] For example, the defamer may think their comments are true and may make their statements without malice. They may still be successfully sued for defamation if the statements are not, in fact, true and if they are defamatory.

## WHO CAN BE DEFAMED?

Individuals can be defamed. So can corporations and non-profit organizations. This is different from some other areas of law. For example, only people are protected by privacy law—not corporations. Some countries, like Australia, have changed the law so that corporations cannot sue for libel.[4]

Case law in some provinces suggests that government cannot be defamed. According to the Ontario Superior Court of Justice, "In a free and democratic system, every citizen must be guaranteed the right to freedom of expression about issues relating to government as an absolute privilege, without threat of civil action for defamation being initiated against them by that government."[5] However, individual government officials, or groups of officials, can sue for defamation.[6] In most provinces and territories, the dead cannot be defamed.[7]

## DEFAMATION AND THE *CHARTER*

As a tort, defamation law is not subject to *Charter* scrutiny in the same way that government legislation is. Torts are private actions taken by individuals, not governments, and the *Charter* applies to government conduct. At the same time, the Supreme Court of Canada has said that *Charter* values should guide the development of common law, including defamation law.[8] The Supreme Court of Canada has held up defamation law as compatible with *Charter* values while, from time to time, adjusting the law and the defences available under it to conform with *Charter* values.[9]

# ELEMENTS OF DEFAMATION

To successfully sue for defamation, a plaintiff must show:

1. **Defamation:** that the words are defamatory;
2. **Publication:** that the words were published; and
3. **Identification:** that the plaintiff is identified in the words as the person being defamed.

## Defamation

The plaintiff must argue that the defamatory words, according to their ordinary meaning, are damaging to their reputation, lowering them in the estimation of "right-thinking" people.[10] Defamatory libel is assumed to be damaging; it is not necessary to demonstrate damage to reputation.

The defamatory words are presumed to be false. If the defendant can prove the words are not false but can be shown to be true, then this could act as a defence to the libel suit.[11] For example, most right-thinking people would find the statement "Esther is a thief" to be defamatory; assuming that Esther is not already well-known as a criminal, such words would tend to lower many people's opinion of Esther. It is presumed, at the initial stage of determining whether a statement is libelous, that Esther is not a thief. Later, a defendant might raise a defence of truth if they can show that Esther is, in fact, a thief.

Canada differs from most comparable jurisdictions in that it leaves the defendant to prove that the speech was not defamatory. This is burdensome to the defendant, costly, and places a greater restriction on freedom of speech.

## Publication

The plaintiff must show that the defamatory material has been conveyed to a third party other than the plaintiff and the defendant. While this is called "publication," it can include any act, from oral remarks, to putting a poster that contains defamatory content on a hydro pole, to traditional publication in a book or newspaper, to posting something on social media, to emailing the material to a third party.[12]

Republishing defamatory material can constitute defamation. However, hyperlinking to defamatory material does not constitute publication unless the hyperlink repeats the defamatory content to which it links.[13] For example, if Rex were to email the statement "Esther is a thief" to 56 people, this could constitute the second element (publication) in Esther's libel suit against Rex.

## Identification

Finally, the plaintiff must show they are the subject of the defamatory material. They must show that the defamatory words did, in fact, refer to the plaintiff.[14] For example, if Esther can show that Rex referred to Esther by name in his email to 56 of their mutual friends and that the friends would recognize Esther as the person he was referring to, this could constitute the third prong (identification) in Esther's libel suit against Rex.

# DEFENCES AND MITIGATING FACTORS

## Truth

If the plaintiff can demonstrate that the three elements of libel are present, the respondent can raise the defence that the statements were, in fact, substantially true. For example, if Rex can prove that his statement is true and Esther is, in fact, a thief, this could act as Rex's defence in Esther's libel suit against him.

It can sometimes be difficult to prove that a statement is true. A journalist, for example, might have a great deal of supporting evidence for a statement made about a person, and the statement could still turn out to be untrue.

In one case, a golf course owner applying for government approval for expansion of their golf course was also a friend of the then-premier of Ontario. Some onlookers felt that the owner's political connections might help the owner get approval for the expansion. When the *Toronto Star* published an article raising this issue, quoting a cottager opposing government approval of a golf course development as saying "everyone thinks it's a done deal," the *Toronto Star* was sued for libel by the golf course owner. The defence of truth failed, apparently because it was not proven that political influence was involved in the golf course's approval.[15]

In Quebec, truth is only a defence to a defamation claim if the statement is true *and* its disclosure is in the public interest.[16] In cases where unfavourable but true statements are made "without any valid reason for doing so," truth may not be a defence.[17]

## Privilege

Defendants to a libel case can, as a defence, claim that their speech was privileged. **Privilege** is a right of immunity from being sued. Speech in parliament or in legal proceedings receives *absolute privilege*. Other forms of speech, such as in reference letters or credit reports, have been protected from defamation claims by *qualified privilege* due to a special relationship between the sender and receiver of the information: The speaker has a duty to communicate the information, and the recipient has a legitimate interest in receiving it.[18] A qualified privilege defence can be defeated if the defendant acted with malice.[19] Qualified privilege has occasionally been successfully argued by some media defendants, but the Supreme Court of Canada noted that it is "uncertain when, if ever, a media outlet can avail itself of the defence of qualified privilege."[20] The Supreme Court of Canada therefore created a new defence of "responsible communication," intended for use by media defendants as well as others.[21] The responsible communication defence is described below.

## Fair Comment

A defendant can claim the defence of fair comment by arguing that the statement in question was a statement of opinion rather than fact. A statement of opinion cannot be proven.[22] For example, the statement "Esther is a thief" is a statement of fact, not opinion. It is possible to prove that Esther stole something. However, it would not be possible to prove the statement "Esther is a bad person" because such a statement is a matter of opinion and judgment. A person who was sued for defamation because they published the statement "Esther is a bad person" might claim the defence of fair comment.

Hyperbolic speech can be considered fair comment.[23] For example, the statement "Esther is a traitor" could be taken not as a statement of fact—not as a claim that Esther had actually committed an act of treason—but as a hyperbolic or exaggerated expression of a disapproving opinion of Esther's decision to change sides in an issue under debate. The speaker, if sued by Esther for libel, might claim the defence of fair comment.

The defence of fair comment can be defeated if the speaker acted with malice.[24] For example, if the person who published the claim "Esther is a traitor" wished to harm or get revenge against Esther, the defence of fair comment could be defeated.

## Responsible Communication on Matters of Public Interest

In 2009, the Supreme Court of Canada elaborated an additional defence of *responsible communication on matters of public interest.*[25] Prior to the establishment of the responsible communication defence, statements of fact that could not be proven true in a court of law and were not privileged left their publishers open to libel suits. This was a problem for media outlets that published statements of fact, where the facts were well-supported by journalistic research and reporting but could not necessarily be proven true in a court of law. Here, journalists and media outlets might not be able to rely on the defences of truth, privilege, or fair comment, as with the case with the *Toronto Star* reporting about the golf course approval. It was this case that established the new defence of responsible communication. While the defence was intended to address the dilemma that media faced, it is available to anyone publishing in any medium.[26]

A defendant making use of the responsible communication defence must show, first, that the publication is on a matter of public interest. Second, they must show that they acted responsibly: researching diligently, especially in cases of serious allegations and matters of grave public importance; balancing urgency of reporting with fact-checking appropriately; treating untrustworthy and anonymous sources with diligence and caution; seeking out the plaintiff's side of the story and making an effort to be fair; reporting damaging information only where relevant and justifiable; taking specific precautions in re-reporting other news reports; and the like.[27] If a defendant can show that they have acted responsibly in all of these ways, the responsible communication defence gives them, in a sense, the right to be (responsibly) wrong.

## Consent

If a plaintiff consented to a publication, this can also act as a defence to a libel suit. If the plaintiff sowed false information about themselves or started false rumours about themselves, this can be considered consent to the publication.[28]

## Innocent Dissemination

In Canada, actors who play a secondary role in distributing libelous material, such as libraries, booksellers, and internet service providers can claim "innocent dissemination" as a defence.[29] Internet service providers, in some cases, are deemed not to engage in publication in the first place and are, therefore, not subject to claims of libel.[30] In other cases, such as internet message board operators who play a more active role, moderating forums, banning users, or refusing to remove defamatory postings, claims of innocent dissemination may not succeed.[31]

## Mitigation of Damages

An apology to the plaintiff and/or a retraction of the publication can play a significant role in reducing the award of damages in a libel case.[32]

## SLAPP

Sometimes defamation lawsuits are used to attempt to intimidate and silence critics. These are called **strategic lawsuits against public participation** or "SLAPP." Some jurisdictions, including Quebec and Ontario, have put in place legislation that allows courts to dismiss SLAPP and award lawyers' fees to a person unfairly pursued by a defamation claim.[33]

## CRIMINAL DEFAMATION

This chapter, so far, has addressed the private law of defamation. In Canada, there is also a law of criminal defamation, punishable by imprisonment.[34] Many other countries, and most American states, have abolished criminal laws of defamation.[35] Criminal defamation law was held up as constitutional by the Supreme Court of Canada in 1998.[36]

In Canada, cases of criminal defamation can be grouped into two main categories: First, there are "slut-shaming" cases where women are defamed, often online, and often by former male romantic partners whom they are no longer interested in.[37] Second, criminal libel is used by police and prosecutors to pursue those who have criticized government officials.[38] Concerns have therefore been raised that criminal defamation law in Canada is being used by police and prosecutors to punish those who criticize police and other government officials.[39] Even where no charges are laid or if charges are withdrawn, the process of being investigated for criminal libel—which can include search and seizure of computers and cellphones and the threat of jail time—is itself a significant punishment that threatens to chill speech.[40]

# WHOM DOES DEFAMATION LAW SERVE?

## The Public Interest?

### *Pluralism*

Defamation law can, at best, be said to foster the ideal of pluralism where it helps to foster democratic debate by encouraging truth and discouraging damaging falsity in speech. Defamation law has been held by the Supreme Court of Canada to be compatible with a pluralist society and the principle of freedom of expression. The Supreme Court of Canada, while prizing a pluralistic society and a diversity of ideas, has simultaneously held up defamation law as compatible with *Charter* values, suggesting that defamation law places limits on speech that are appropriate and not "unduly restrictive or inhibiting."[41] However, many around the world have argued that defamation law, and in particular criminal defamation legislation, is anti-democratic and anti-pluralist because of the restrictions it places on speech and its potential to create a libel chill that inhibits potential speech.[42]

## Bureaucracy and Bureaucrats?

### *Libertarianism and Neoliberalism*

Libertarians, as has been noted in earlier chapters, tend to strongly favour free speech and to critique speech regulation, including its regulation via defamation law. Libertarians argue that even gross examples of libel must be defended. After all, they argue, a person's reputation is not their own; ideas about a person exist in *other people*'s heads and are therefore property of *other people*. A person cannot reasonably own or control their reputation if it exists in other people's heads.[43] Defamation law, according to libertarians, requires too great a restriction on individual liberty of thought and speech to be defendable.[44]

Neoliberal theorists, as we have noted in earlier chapters, also tend to favour a liberal "marketplace of ideas" approach to speech, resisting encroachments on freedom of expression. Neoliberal theory associates the history of press freedom with the liberalization of the press from government regulation, including from laws of seditious libel and defamation.[45]

The loss of long-term employment and labour protections and the rise of the "gig economy," both associated with a neoliberal economy, have placed an increased burden on individuals' reputations. Workers in the "gig economy" often rely on user reviews of their work and services. Professionals as well as many other individuals have become increasingly concerned about their online reputations. Many have been encouraged to develop a "personal brand."[46] Workers with few labour protections available to them must go to great lengths to protect their online reputations.

While such workers may turn to defamation law to address what they feel are false or malicious negative reviews or other online content, defamation lawsuits may be unaffordable or too slow to address the problems they face.[47] Many workers turn not to the law but to private actors to manage negative reviews. Often, these reputation management services solve the problem of negative speech with more speech, using the tools available to request removal of negative online content and burying negative content with additional promotional content.[48]

## The Privileged?

### Critical Political Economy and Critical Legal Studies

Recognizing that the marketplace of ideas metaphor does not account for the enormous power discrepancies between large media companies, politicians, and individual citizens and workers, some political scientists, political economists, and legal scholars have criticized the liberal approach to libel law.[49] Critical scholars argue that defamation law, particularly when used to attempt to silence activists and political debate, is a symptom of a justice system that integrates and reproduces inequalities.[50] Those influenced by critical legal studies and its predecessor, legal realism, have argued that the doctrine of libel is not a neutral, coherent legal doctrine, but rather is (like all legal doctrine) largely incoherent and open to judicial interpretation.[51] This leads to widely disparate outcomes in different cases, leaving defamation law open to bias and manipulation—largely by those holding power, but also by political movements.[52] These critics have suggested the creation of various legal rights, intended to give greater power to those without the means to use defamation law to defend their reputations. These have included, most prominently, a right of reply, which would give a person or government criticized in media a right to reply to such criticism; and laws requiring the retraction of defamatory material.[53] Such proposals have been rejected by dominant liberal theorists as infringements on freedom of the press.

### Feminist and Queer Studies

Feminist analysis of defamation law has shown that, in some ways, defamation law treats women and men differently. American studies have shown that most plaintiffs in defamation cases are elite men.[54] This suggests that defamation law may be less accessible to women and to the less wealthy. Men tend to receive higher damage awards than women. While women have been more likely to win defamation cases where their chastity and morality are defamed, they have tended to lose in cases where their occupational status is injured.[55] Historically, women's reputations tended to be defamed through in-person speech, a form of slander with lower penalties than libel, while men tended to be defamed through written speech, permitting men to claim higher damages.[56] This discrepancy reflected, in part, media's exclusion of women from the public sphere and from their coverage.[57]

Defamation law has reflected and reinforced sexist attitudes about gender roles, instituting a special category of defamation for imputation of immorality of a woman.[58] In American law, it was assumed, and needed not be proven, that an allegation of sexual impropriety was injurious to a woman's reputation. Sex workers, under some versions of this law, were not eligible to take action under this category of libel, presumably either because they did not have a reputation of chastity to protect or because they were deemed unworthy of such protection.[59] Until the mid-nineteenth century, married women were considered the property of their husbands. They could neither initiate legal action on their own behalf nor own any damages rewarded independently of their husbands.[60]

Sexual orientation and gender norms have also influenced the law of defamation as it pertains to queer people. It was once the case that falsely calling someone gay or lesbian was clearly defamatory and akin, in many jurisdictions where homosexuality was illegal, to calling them a criminal. Calling a woman a lesbian was likened to alleging lack of chastity. As acceptance of same-sex relationships has increased, and as same-sex relations have been decriminalized, courts have reached various conclusions in cases involving falsely calling someone queer.[61]

Defamation cases, unlike obscenity cases, ask whether a person's reputation would be diminished in the minds of "right-thinking people" (whereas obscenity law asks about the standards of *average* people).[62] Whom do courts consider to be "right-thinking people?" Are members of a relatively homophobic community "right-thinking," and thus might a person whose reputation within a homophobic community is diminished due to a false allegation of homosexuality be eligible to sue for defamation, while a person living in a relatively queer-positive community who was falsely called gay would not?

Defamation law has done little to serve minority groups in general, including queer communities and racialized groups. In the United States and Canada, efforts to claim group defamation have led to mixed results.[63] Since defamation actions focus on the harm to individuals, it can be hard to show that specific individuals have been identified in defamatory statements or that they have suffered injury to their reputation.[64] In Canada, it has proven difficult to pursue such claims as a class action.[65] However, individual members of a group may attempt to pursue a defamation claim in a case of defamation against a group. For example, a claim of defamation was brought by two gay men on behalf of the LGTBTQ2SI (lesbian, gay, transgender, bisexual, transsexual, queer, Two-Spirit, and intersex) community against William Whatcott and a group known as "Gay Zombies," who distributed pamphlets allegedly containing hate speech at Toronto's Pride parade in 2016. As a class action, the claim was unsuccessful, but the judge ruled that the claim could be pursued by other means.[66]

Women who have been "slut shamed" online have successfully turned to police in Canada.[67] Criminal defamation law in Canada permits charges to be laid, leading to possible jail time. Because such charges are laid by police, this approach can be less costly to victims and can proceed relatively quickly.[68]

### Critical Race Theory

Defamation law is marked by racialization. Cultural and racialized communities sometimes differ in what they view as respectable and which statements might harm a person's reputation. For example, in 2011 the Supreme Court of Canada, which has never had an Arab or Haitian judge and on which there are, as of this writing, no visible minorities, determined that what its judges imagined as "an ordinary person" would "not have formed a less favourable opinion of each Arab or Haitian taxi driver" based on a Montreal shock jock's negative and racist comments.[69] It is possible that white judges, who have never personally experienced anti-Black or anti-Arab racism, do not have a full awareness of, or overlook, how *ordinary* racism is.

Similar examples in Canada and other countries abound. For example, calling a person a Communist might have little significance in many communities today, but in the American case *Pham v Le*, a Vietnamese American who had been imprisoned by the North Vietnamese Communists following the Vietnam War, and who had incorporated the Vietnamese Community of Minnesota after moving to the United States, was called a "Communist lackey" by a rival Vietnamese group. Pham successfully sued for defamation, since the judge considered Pham's reputation through the eyes of the Vietnamese community in his area, where the "Communist lackey" statement may have lowered people's opinions of Pham. Here, the Vietnamese community constituted an important minority, "'respectable' enough to garner the law's attention and respect."[70] However, in many cases, judges' decisions are made through the lens of their own—often white male—eyes and perspectives.

## Indigenous and Postcolonial Analysis

Indigenous and other marginalized groups are subject to more negative and racist media portrayals than dominant groups. Indigenous peoples are often known by majority populations through (often negative) mainstream media representations, because majority white/settler populations often have little personal experience with Indigenous peoples.[71] Despite the higher rate of negative or racist portrayals, and despite Indigenous peoples' vulnerability to mainstream media portrayals, Indigenous peoples may be less able than more privileged groups to utilize defamation law to protect their reputations. While there has been no equivalent study in Canada, an Australian study found that "those who lacked money and influence," such as Indigenous peoples, were "more likely to be the subject of potentially defamatory" newspaper articles. It was theorized this was due to journalists believing these groups would be unlikely to mount a defamation lawsuit.[72]

Indigenous peoples may, like other racialized or minority ethnic and cultural groups, have different views from those of what courts consider to be "ordinary" or "reasonable" people in considering defamation cases. When Taiwanese Indigenous groups unsuccessfully sued the Japanese public broadcaster for defamation in its portrayal of these groups in a documentary series, they lost, in part because their own view of the portrayals as negative and defamatory was not reflected in the judges' views of what a "general audience" would think when viewing the documentary series.[73]

More broadly, defamation law has played a role in supporting colonialism. British defamation law, and particularly criminal defamation law (in which a fine or jail term can be imposed), was used by colonial administrations in British colonies to silence criticism of colonialism, exploitation, and colonial governments.[74] A broad definition of slander was used in some places to punish expressions of dissent, including "foot-dragging, shuffling, foot-thumping, whistling, sighing, coughing, clearing one's throat, rolling one's eyes, spitting, laughing, [*sic*] or giggling, drumming, dancing, standing, sitting, wearing African masks and masquerades without authorization at the wrong time, in the wrong place, in the right location, at the wrong time, or in the wrong manner."[75] While the African Commission on Human and People's Rights began a campaign in 2010 to eradicate criminal defamation law, defamation law has nevertheless played a significant role in supporting authoritarian governments under postcolonialism.[76] At the same time, American free speech protections have begun to be incorporated, translated, and transposed into the legal systems of former colonies, in many cases contributing to greater freedom of the press.[77] In Canada, as already noted, criminal defamation law remains.

# FURTHER READING

Borden, Diane L. "Reputational Assault: A Critical and Historical Analysis of Gender and the Law of Defamation." *Journalism & Mass Communication Quarterly* 75, no. 1 (Spring 1998): 98–111.

Brown, Raymond E. *Defamation Law: A Primer.* Toronto: Carswell, 2013.

———. *The Law of Defamation in Canada.* 2nd edition, 2 volumes. Scarborough, ON: Carswell, 1999.

*Grant v Torstar,* 2009 SCC 61 [2009] 3 SCR 640.

Kary, Joseph. "The Constitutionalization of Quebec Libel Law, 1848–2004." *Osgoode Hall Law Journal* 42, no. 2 (2004): 229–70.

Landry, Normand. "Strategic Lawsuits against Public Participation and Freedom of the Press in Canada." In *The Unfulfilled Promise of Press Freedom in Canada*, edited by Lisa Taylor and Cara-Marie O'Hagan, 47–65. Toronto: University of Toronto Press, 2017.

———. *Threatening Democracy: SLAPPs and the Judicial Repression of Political Discourse.* Black Point, NS: Fernwood Publishing, 2014.

Rosenberg, Norman. "Taking a Look at the Distorted Shape of an Ugly Tree: Efforts at Policy-Surgery on the Law of Libel during the Decade of the 1940s." *Northern Kentucky Law Review* 15 (1988): 11–56.

Rosenberg, Norman L. *Protecting the Best Men: An Interpretive History of the Law of Libel.* Chapel Hill: University of North Carolina Press, 1986.

Taylor, Lisa, and David Pritchard. "The Process Is the Punishment: Criminal Libel and Political Speech in Canada." *Communication Law and Policy* 23, no. 3 (2018): 243–66.

# NOTES

1.  *OED Online* (2018), s.v. "defamation, n.," accessed February 15, 2019.

2.  *Grant v Torstar,* 2009 SCC 61 at 28.

3.  Antonin I. Pribetic and Marc Randazza, "'War of the Words': Differing Canadian and American Approaches to Internet Defamation," in *Annual Review of Civil Litigation*, ed. Todd L. Archibald (Toronto: Carswell Thomson Reuters, 2015), 403.

4.  Hilary Young, "Why Canada Shouldn't Let Businesses Sue for Defamation," *The Toronto Star*, September 16, 2012, https://www.thestar.com/opinion/editorialopinion/2012/09/16/why_canada_shouldnt_let_businesses_sue_for_defamation.html.

5.  *Montague (Township) v Page*, 79 OR (3d) 515; [2006] OJ No 331. See also *Dixon v Powell River (City)*, 2009 BCSC 406.

6. *Halton Hills (Town) v Kerouac*, 80 OR (3d) 577; 270 DLR (4th) 479; [2006] OTC 384; 142 CRR (2d) 285; *Montague (Township) v Page*; James Rusk, "Municipalities Can't Sue for Libel, Judges Say," *The Globe and Mail*, April 18, 2006, https://www.theglobe-andmail.com/news/national/municipalities-cant-sue-for-libel-judges-say/article18160475/.

7. Zvulony, "What Is Defamation in Ontario Law," accessed October 31, 2018, https://zvulony.ca/2010/articles/defamation-articles/definition-defamation/. Regarding a possible exception in Quebec, see "Decisions," *Columbia Law Review* XL, no. 7 (1940): 1267.

8. *Hill v Church of Scientology of Toronto*, [1995] 2 SCR 1130 at 97; see also *Grant v Torstar* at 44.

9. *Hill v Church of Scientology of Toronto*; *Grant v Torstar* at 44; Johnathon Feasby, "Who Was That Masked Man? Online Defamation, Freedom of Expression, and the Right to Speak Anonymously," *Canadian Journal of Law and Technology* 1, no. 1 (2002).

10. *WIC Radio Ltd v Simpson*, 2008 SCC 40 at 67–69; *Grant v Torstar* at 28.

11. *Grant v Torstar* at 28.

12. *Crookes v Newton*, 2011 SCC 47 at 16.

13. Ibid.

14. *Grant v Torstar* at 28.

15. Ibid., at 137–39.

16. Joseph Kary, "The Constitutionalization of Quebec Libel Law, 1848–2004," *Osgoode Hall Law Journal* 42, no. 2 (2004): 268.

17. *Prud'homme v Prud'homme*, 2002 SCC 85 at 36.

18. *Grant v Torstar* at 34; see also Joseph Brean, "Can Your Old Boss Badmouth You to a Potential Employer?" *National Post*, April 20, 2017, https://nationalpost.com/news/canada/can-your-old-boss-badmouth-you-to-a-potential-employer-absolutely-says-an-ontario-court.

19. *Grant v Torstar* at 30.

20. Ibid. at 37.

21. Ibid.

22. Ibid. at 31.

23. *WIC Radio Ltd. v Simpson*; Andrew Duff, "Defamation of Blogger Was 'Fair Comment,' Judge Rules," Canadian Justice Review Board, March 4, 2015, https://www.canadianjusticereviewboard.ca/articles-caselaw/articles/defamation-of-blogger-was-%e2%80%98fair-comment,%e2%80%99-judge-rules.

24. *Grant v Torstar* at 31.

25. Ibid.

26. *Grant v Torstar*.

27. For a full account of how courts would examine a defence of responsible communication, see *Grant v Torstar* at 98–126. For a summary, see Dean Jobb, "The Responsible Communication Defence," J-Source, December 23, 2009. http://j-source.ca/article/the-responsible-communication-defence-whats-in-it-for-journalists/. See also Tim Currie, "Process Journalism and Responsible Communication," in *The Unfulfilled Promise of Press Freedom in Canada*, eds. Lisa Taylor and Cara-Marie O'Hagan (Toronto: University of Toronto Press, 2017), 66–83.

28. Carolin Ann Bayer, "Re-Thinking the Common Law of Defamation: Striking a New Balance between Freedom of Expression and the Protection of the Individual's Reputation," LLM Thesis (University of British Columbia, 2001) 61–62, https://doi.library.ubc.ca/10.14288/1.0077572.

29. *Crookes v Newton* at 20.

30. Ibid. at 21.

31. *Baglow v Smith*, 2015 ONSC 1175 at 186; *Carter v BC Federation of Foster Parents Assn*, 2005 BCCA 398 at 21.

32. Bayer, 62.

33. Normand Landry, "Strategic Lawsuits against Public Participation and Freedom of the Press in Canada," in *The Unfulfilled Promise of Press Freedom in Canada*, eds. Lisa Taylor and Cara-Marie O'Hagan (Toronto: University of Toronto Press, 2017), 55; Ministry of the Attorney General, "Protection of Public Participation Act," October 28, 2015, https://news.ontario.ca/mag/en/2015/10/protection-of-public-participation-act.html.

34. *Criminal Code*, RSC 1985, c C-46, ss 297–317.

35. Committee to Protect Journalists, "Critics Are Not Criminals: Comparative Study of Criminal Defamation Laws in the Americas," 2016, https://cpj.org/reports/2016/03/critics-are-not-criminals.php.

36. *R v Lucas*, [1998] 1 SCR 439.

37. Lisa Taylor and David Pritchard, "The Process Is the Punishment: Criminal Libel and Political Speech in Canada," *Communication Law and Policy* 23, no. 3 (2018): 243–66, https://doi.org/10.1080/10811680.2018.1467155.

38. Ibid.

39. Taylor and Pritchard; David Pritchard and Lisa Taylor, "In Canada, We Criminalize Public-Interest Speech," *The Globe and Mail*, April 3, 2018, https://www.theglobeandmail.com/opinion/article-in-canada-we-criminalize-public-interest-speech/?utm_medium=Referrer:+Social+Network+/+Media&utm_campaign=Shared+Web+Article+Links.

40. Ibid.

41. *Hill v Church of Scientology of Toronto* at 137; Feasby.

42. Elena Yanchukova, "Criminal Defamation and Insult Laws: An Infringement on the Freedom of Expression in European and Post-Communist Jurisdictions," *Columbia Journal of Transnational Law* 41 (2002): 861–94.

43. Walter Block, *Defending the Undefendable* (Auburn, AL: Ludwig von Mises Institute, 2003), 47–50; but see Walter Block, "A Libertarian Analysis of Suing for Libel," September 5, 2014, https://www.lewrockwell.com/2014/09/walter-e-block/may-i-sue-the-ny-times/; Murray Newton Rothbard, *The Ethics of Liberty* (New York: New York University Press, 2002), 126–28.

44. Block, *Defending the Undefendable*, 49.

45. Johnathan Hardy, *Critical Political Economy of the Media: An Introduction* (London: Taylor & Francis Group, 2014), xiii.

46. Ben Medeiros, "Right to Be Forgotten or Right to Not Be Talked About? Public and Private Speech Regulation and the Panic about Critical Speech on the Interactive Web" (University of California San Diego, 2016), 98.

47. David S. Ardia, "Reputation in a Networked World: Revisiting the Social Foundations of Defamation Law," *Harvard Civil Rights-Civil Liberties Law Review* 45 (2010): 261.

48. Medeiros, 95.

49. Norman Rosenberg, *Protecting the Best Men: An Interpretive History of the Law of Libel* (Chapel Hill: University of North Carolina Press, 1986), 11; Norman Rosenberg, "Taking a Look at the Distorted Shape of an Ugly Tree: Efforts at Policy-Surgery on the Law of Libel during the Decade of the 1940s," *Northern Kentucky Law Review* 15 (1988): 31.

50. Norman Landry, *Threatening Democracy: SLAPPs and the Judicial Repression of Political Discourse*, trans. Howard Scott (Black Point, NS: Fernwood, 2014).

51. Rosenberg, "The Distorted Shape of an Ugly Tree."

52. Ibid., 37–38.

53. Ibid., 44.

54. Diane L. Borden, "Reputational Assault: A Critical and Historical Analysis of Gender and the Law of Defamation," *Journalism & Mass Communication Quarterly* 75, no. 1 (1998): 101; Diane L. Borden, "Patterns of Harm: An Analysis of Gender and Defamation," *Communication Law and Policy* 2, no. 1 (1997): 105–41.

55. Ibid.

56. Ibid.

57. Ibid.

58. Borden, "Reputational Assault"; *Libel and Slander Act*, RSO 1970, c 243, s 17.

59. Borden, "Reputational Assault," 103.

60. Ibid., 102.

61. Abigail A. Rury, "He's So Gay—Not That There's Anything Wrong with That: Using a Community Standard to Homogenize the Measure of Reputational Damage in Homosexual Defamation Cases," *Cardozo Journal of Law & Gender* 17 (2011): 655–82.

62. Ibid., 663.

63. *Bou Malhab v Diffusion Métromédia CMR Inc*, 2011 SCC 9; see also Bennett Jones, "Group Defamation Clarified," accessed December 13, 2018, https://www.bennettjones.com/Publications-Section/Updates/Group-Defamation-Clarified.

64. *Hudspeth v Whatcott*, 2017 ONSC 1708 at 262–63 and 225.

65. *Bou Malhab v Diffusion Métromédia*; *Hudspeth v Whatcott*, at 11–13.

66. *Hudspeth v Whatcott*; Osler, Hoskin & Harcourt LLP, "Court Approves US-Style Group Claim for Hate Speech," accessed December 13, 2018, http://www.osler.com/en/blogs/classactions/april-2017/court-approves-us-style-group-claim-for-hate-speec.

67. Taylor and Pritchard; see also Kaitlynn Mendes, *SlutWalk: Feminism, Activism and Media* (New York: Springer, 2015).

68. *R v Lucas*, at 74.

69. *Bou Malhab v Diffusion Métromédia*; Michael Tutton, "Advocates for Minority Supreme Court Judge Disappointed by Trudeau's Pick," *The Toronto Star*, October 18, 2016, https://www.thestar.com/news/canada/2016/10/18/advocates-for-minority-supreme-court-judge-disappointed-by-trudeaus-pick.html.

70. Rury, 665.

71. Rong-Xuan Chu and Chih-Tung Huang, "Indigenous Peoples in Public Media: A Critical Discourse Analysis of the Human Zoo Case," *Discourse & Society* 30, no. 4 (2019): 403.

72. Jacqui Ewart, "The Scabsuckers: Regional Journalists' Representation of Indigenous Australians," *Asia Pacific Media Educator* 1, no. 3 (1997): 113.

73. Chu and Huang.

74. Lyombe Eko, "Globalization and the Diffusion of Media Policy in Africa: The Case of Defamation of Public Officials," *Africa Policy Journal* 12 (2017/2016): 17–44.

75. Ibid., 23.

76. Ibid.; see also David Streckfuss, *Truth on Trial in Thailand: Defamation, Treason, and Lèse-Majesté* (New York: Routledge, 2010).

77. Eko.

# 5  Privacy

## INTRODUCTION

In an age of sharing, is privacy still important? How can privacy regulation keep up with the constant threat of hackers, leaked data, and complex privacy agreements and settings? In a world where big data allows intimate details about us, such as our sexual orientation, personality type, or political orientation, to be inferred from our "likes" on Facebook or our shopping habits, can and should privacy law provide protection to inferences made about us? When privacy is balanced against the freedom to express private or personal information about others, how far should privacy protection go? Should individuals have the right to erase information about themselves from the internet? This chapter explores some of these complex questions, asking whose interests are served by privacy law and regulation.

Canadian privacy law is set out in provincial and federal legislation, as well as in judge-made common law. It is regulated by the Canadian Privacy Commissioner alongside provincial and territorial information and privacy commissioners. But privacy in Canada is also increasingly regulated by private contracts or terms of service that we "consent" to when we sign up to use online services, and by the technologies, security measures, and computer code that structure our online and offline activities.

This chapter reviews privacy law in Canada, defining the right to privacy, discussing the history of privacy regulation, and reviewing both privacy legislation and the common law torts of privacy. It discusses privacy in the context of new technologies and the internet, including the emerging European "right to be forgotten" and its applicability in Canada. The second half of the chapter asks, "Whom does privacy law serve?", drawing on the theories introduced in Chapter 1.

## PRIVACY: A *CHARTER* RIGHT?

A right of privacy is not mentioned in the *Canadian Charter of Rights and Freedoms* but is taken as implied in the right granted in Section 7 of the *Charter*'s right to liberty and security of the person, and in Section 8 of the *Charter*'s prohibition of unreasonable search and seizure.[1] The right of privacy in Canada has been recognized as having a quasi-constitutional status, because privacy is seen as fundamental to individual autonomy and freedom, which is, in turn, a foundation of democracy itself.[2]

## WHOSE PRIVACY?

Privacy rights are granted, in Canadian legislation, to individuals. Most privacy rights are applicable to "any individual" whose personal information is collected.[3] A right of access to personal information held by government is granted to Canadian citizens and permanent residents.[4] Privacy rights do not generally extend directly to groups or corporations.

## THE IMPORTANCE OF PRIVACY

Alan Westin, author of the foundational book *Privacy and Freedom* (1967), described why privacy is important in modern democratic society. He gave four main reasons:

1. **Personal autonomy.** Privacy makes individual autonomy possible. It is a zone in which a person is not manipulated or dominated by anyone else. It is the place where one's "core self" and ultimate secrets are held. In privacy, one can grow, develop, and explore. One can form thoughts and opinions without fear of judgment. One can decide whether, and when, to express an opinion or make it public. Without privacy, the unexpected exposure of secrets or thoughts one does not want to share can be very painful. Freedom involves choosing what to show as one's public self.

2. **Emotional release.** Privacy provides a kind of emotional release from the constraints of everyday social life. Erving Goffman notes that we play a series of roles, called on by the situations we are in; we play the

roles of student, parent, friend, or employee. For each role we play, we have different social "masks." Goffman notes that it is important to be able to remove one's mask, as roles or masks can only be sustained for limited periods. Such ability is especially important during times of stress or sorrow. Privacy also allows the occasional breaking of rules and norms—such as to vent anger or deviate from sexual norms. Westin notes, "the firm expectation of having privacy for permissible deviations is a distinguishing characteristic of life in a free society."[5]

3. **Self-evaluation and creativity.** Privacy permits time to reflect, process, plan, and organize in solitude. Such reflection is crucial to creativity, as it is in times of solitude that most creative thought takes place. Solitude also allows one to reflect on one's own ideals, to consider whether one is living up to morals and ideals, as in religious contemplation or self-contemplation.

4. **Limited and protected communication.** The ability to be limited in one's communications is crucial to social life. A society of constant and utter candor would be full of unnecessary confrontation and exhausting intimacy. We set boundaries and create mental distance in communications across work hierarchies, on the subway, in crowded spaces, and even in intimate relationships where we try to preserve respect and mystery. We have private gestures and words, and we learn to ignore each other as a way of achieving privacy in crowded situations. Communication with strangers can be liberating, as confidences will not be shared back to the home sphere, and certain communications with lawyers, doctors, or psychiatrists may be protected legally against disclosure.[6]

The journalist Glenn Greenwald has become an activist for privacy and against government surveillance. A former journalist for *The Guardian* and *Salon. com*, he was responsible for breaking much of the news about the American National Security Agency (NSA) mass surveillance programs, drawing on documents leaked by Edward Snowden (discussed in Chapter 6). In a talk, Greenwald pointed out that:

We all need places where we can go to explore without the judgmental eyes of other people being cast upon us.... Only in a realm where we're not being watched can we really test the limits of who we want to be. It's really in the private realm where dissent, creativity and personal exploration lie.[7]

Responding to Google chairman Eric Schmidt, who had commented, "if you have something that you don't want anyone to know, maybe you shouldn't be doing it in the first place," Greenwald noted that all people do things that they don't want others to know. The ability to do something privately is sometimes crucial to encouraging personally and socially desirable actions, such as having an HIV test or calling a suicide hotline.[8] To be a person who never does anything that one does not want made public, according to Greenwald, is to say, "I have agreed to make myself such a harmless and unthreatening and uninteresting person that I actually don't fear having the government know what it is that I'm doing."[9]

## WHAT IS PERSONAL INFORMATION?

The Organisation for Economic Co-operation and Development (OECD) defines *personal data* as "any information relating to an identified or identifiable individual (data subject)."[10] The Canadian *Privacy Act* defines **personal information** as "information about an identifiable individual that is recorded in any form."[11]

### De-Identified Information

Because privacy law deals with "personal information" that is about an "identifiable individual," aggregate data that has been anonymized or dissociated from particular users may be treated differently. Many companies, including social media companies and data brokers, sell or share such aggregate or **de-identified information** with their clients or other business partners.

The sharing and sale of de-identified information remains a concern, given that data can sometimes be re-identified or easily re-associated with specific individuals. For example, a team of researchers studying student friendships gathered all Facebook posts made over a four-year period by a large set of university students and released the data online. The names of students, their school, and their location had been erased from the data in an effort at anonymization. However, it was possible, without difficulty, to identify the school that was part of the study by examining the list of students' majors; only Harvard College offered the specific subject majors in the data set. It was then possible to re-associate the Facebook data with particular students, especially in cases where there was only one individual of a particular nationality and gender studying a particular major.[12] In this manner, students' Facebook posts, along with their names, were revealed to outsiders without students' consent. Data from one seemingly anonymous data set can sometimes be de-anonymized when combined with data from other data sets (such as by combining the Facebook data set with the list of majors at Harvard College). This is known as the **mosaic effect**.

While aggregated or anonymized data may appear to fall outside the scope of privacy legislation, the Office of the Privacy Commissioner has taken "a contextual approach" to assessing whether information is identifiable, and thus whether it is "personal information" that is regulated by privacy law. If there is a "serious possibility that an individual could be identified through the information," whether the information is taken alone or combined with other information, then even anonymized or aggregate data could be considered personal information.[13]

## PRIVACY LEGISLATION

### The *Privacy Act*

The federal *Privacy Act* regulates federal government institutions' collection, use, and disclosure of personal information. It grants individuals the rights to access and to correct personal information held by the federal Government of Canada.

### The *Personal Information Protection and Electronic Documents Act* (PIPEDA)

The *Personal Information Protection and Electronic Documents Act* (PIPEDA) regulates companies' collection, use, and disclosure of personal information. The OECD principles mentioned above helped to inspire a set of Canadian principles, developed through public consultation and established in 1996 by the Canadian Standards Association, that have been incorporated into PIPEDA. These, referred to as Canada's "Fair Information Principles," are:

#### Principle 1—Accountability
An organization is responsible for personal information under its control and shall designate an individual or individuals who are accountable for the organization's compliance with the following principles.

#### Principle 2—Identifying Purposes
The purposes for which personal information is collected shall be identified by the organization at or before the time the information is collected.

### Principle 3—Consent

The knowledge and consent of the individual are required for the collection, use, or disclosure of personal information, except where inappropriate.

### Principle 4—Limiting Collection

The collection of personal information shall be limited to that which is necessary for the purposes identified by the organization. Information shall be collected by fair and lawful means.

### Principle 5—Limiting Use, Disclosure, and Retention

Personal information shall not be used or disclosed for purposes other than those for which it was collected, except with the consent of the individual or as required by law. Personal information shall be retained only as long as necessary for the fulfillment of those purposes.

### Principle 6—Accuracy

Personal information shall be as accurate, complete, and up-to-date as is necessary for the purposes for which it is to be used.

### Principle 7—Safeguards

Personal information shall be protected by security safeguards appropriate to the sensitivity of the information.

### Principle 8—Openness

An organization shall make readily available to individuals specific information about its policies and practices relating to the management of personal information.

### Principle 9—Individual Access

Upon request, an individual shall be informed of the existence, use, and disclosure of his or her personal information and shall be given access to that information. An individual shall be able to challenge the accuracy and completeness of the information and have it amended as appropriate.

### Principle 10—Challenging Compliance

An individual shall be able to address a challenge concerning compliance with the above principles to the designated individual or individuals accountable for the organization's compliance.[14]

PIPEDA permits individuals whose privacy rights have been infringed to complain to the Office of the privacy commissioner of Canada. The Office may conduct an investigation and issue a report, issuing findings and recommendations. If unsatisfied, the individual may then take their complaint to the Federal Court in certain circumstances.[15]

## Provincial Legislation

Each province has its own legislation governing privacy in public sector organizations, and several have legislation governing the private sector as well. In cases where provincial legislation governing the private sector is deemed to be substantially similar to PIPEDA, provincial legislation supersedes PIPEDA.[16]

# PRIVACY COMMISSIONERS

The Privacy Commissioner of Canada reports directly to parliament. The Commissioner is empowered to investigate privacy complaints, conduct privacy audits, pursue court action under the *Privacy Act* or under PIPEDA, publicly report on the privacy practices of organizations (whether in the public sector or in the private sector), research privacy issues, and promote public awareness of privacy issues.[17] All Canadian provinces and territories also have information and privacy commissioners or a similar office to regulate privacy in their respective provinces and territories.[18]

# PRIVACY TORTS

While American privacy law is well-developed in the realm of torts, privacy torts are relatively less developed in Canada. Canadian law relies more heavily on privacy legislation and complaint processes through the privacy commissioners. The following are the main privacy torts available in Canadian law.[19]

## Intrusion upon Seclusion

Perhaps the most significant of the privacy torts is the common law right to sue for **intrusion upon seclusion**, or invasion of a person's space or affairs. As of this writing, the common law tort of intrusion upon seclusion has been recognized in

Ontario and has been considered, but not recognized, in British Columbia and Alberta. Four provinces have created a tort of invasion of privacy through statute: British Columbia, Manitoba, Saskatchewan, and Newfoundland and Labrador.[20]

Ontario courts definitively recognized the tort of intrusion upon seclusion in 2012 when Sandra Jones won a case against Winnie Tsige, her ex-husband's common-law partner. Tsige had surreptitiously examined Jones's banking records at least 174 times over the course of four years, accessing them through her computer at the bank where she worked.

In this case, the privacy legislation in place afforded little recourse to Jones. PIPEDA has jurisdiction over the Bank of Montreal (BMO), the bank where both Tsige and Jones worked. However, PIPEDA affords no measure for individuals to take actions against other individuals; it governs organizations. This would have left Jones with the option of lodging a complaint against BMO, her own employer, but not against Tsige, the wrongdoer. Neither does PIPEDA afford the option of suing for damages. Thus, Jones would have gained little from launching a PIPEDA complaint. Instead, the Ontario Court of Appeal, recognizing the tort of intrusion upon seclusion, awarded Jones $10,000 in damages.

To successfully sue for intrusion upon seclusion, a plaintiff must demonstrate four things:

1. that there was an unauthorized intrusion;
2. that the intrusion was highly offensive to the reasonable person;
3. that the matter intruded upon was private (and that the plaintiff had a reasonable expectation of privacy); and
4. that the intrusion caused anguish and suffering.[21]

All four elements were in place in *Jones v Tsige*, as the intrusion on Jones's banking records was unauthorized and highly offensive; her banking records were private; and Jones experienced anguish and suffering as a result.

The Quebec *Civil Code* also recognizes entry into a dwelling, intercepting or using private communications, keeping a person's private life under observation, and using a person's "correspondence, manuscripts, or other personal documents" as invasions of privacy.[22]

## Appropriation of Personality

While there is no exclusive right to use a particular name (there are many people with the name "John Smith," "Zhang Wei," or "Muhammed Ahmed"), using someone else's name without permission to one's own benefit, such as to promote one's own business, can be the basis of a lawsuit under the tort of **appropriation of personality**. This privacy tort has been recognized in Canada since 1973.[23] To be successful in their suit, the plaintiff must show at least two things:

1. that the exploitation of the plaintiff's identity was for a commercial purpose (it was used to sell a piece of merchandise, as opposed to being used as the basis of a biography about the plaintiff, where the purpose is to tell a story about the plaintiff); and
2. that the exploitation clearly and primarily captured the plaintiff (that the plaintiff was, for example, the primary subject of a photograph used in the defendant's advertising, as opposed to a bystander in the photo, and that the plaintiff was recognizable in the photo).[24]

The Quebec *Civil Code* also grants a right of privacy in the use of one's "name, image, likeness or voice for a purpose other than the legitimate information of the public."[25] Quebec's *Charter of Human Rights and Freedoms* grants a privacy right in the use of one's image without consent.[26] In 1998, the Supreme Court of Canada ruled that a woman's right to privacy under the Quebec *Charter* was infringed when a photograph of her sitting on the steps of a building was published in an arts magazine without her consent.[27]

## THE RIGHT TO BE FORGOTTEN

There are many occasions where personal information (such as reports of crimes, including the names of the accused and the victims; accounts of alleged wrongdoing; unflattering photos; or personal stories) is legitimately published, often by media outlets or in court documents. Here, there is a legitimate reason for the information to be publicly accessible, and individuals' privacy interests must be balanced against the rights to freedom of the press and expression, as well as against the transparency and accessibility of the justice system. There are also cases where false, defamatory, unfair, or outdated personal information is posted online. If the information is defamatory, it may be possible to use the legal system to have the information taken down. However, removal of some data may prove difficult if it is not defamatory and if the organization that posted it does not want to take it down.[28]

The European Union has adopted, in response to such concerns, a *right to be forgotten*, which permits individuals to request that results be deleted for search terms that include their own name. Individuals making such requests must explain how the information is "irrelevant, outdated, or otherwise inappropriate," and their request is balanced against "the public's interest to know and the right to distribute information."[29]

The right to be forgotten has been controversial in Canada. The Privacy Commissioner of Canada has consulted the public and the courts on whether such a right should be instituted in Canada.[30] In response, some have argued that such a right would unconstitutionally infringe on freedom of expression.[31] Critics have also warned against entrusting private organizations like Google with arbitrating such a right.[32]

At the same time, Canadian courts have the power to issue injunctions to have material taken down from websites. For example, as discussed in Chapter 3, in 2017 the Supreme Court of Canada controversially granted a worldwide injunction prohibiting Google from displaying search results for websites of a distributor of counterfeit goods.[33] It remains to be seen whether a right to be forgotten will be adopted in Canada.

## PRIVACY BY DESIGN

In the 1990s, Ontario Privacy Commissioner Ann Cavoukian developed an approach called **privacy by design**. Recognizing that government regulation cannot alone ensure privacy, Cavoukian commented, "the future of privacy cannot be assured solely by compliance with regulatory frameworks; rather, privacy assurance must ideally become an organization's default mode of operation." The principles of privacy by design require that organization processes and technologies be designed from the start to prevent privacy risks, and that privacy be the default setting of information systems and business practices.[34] These principles have been adopted by privacy commissioners internationally as a gold standard.[35]

Massive data leaks occur with regularity. Sometimes data is hacked, as in the case of the leak in 2015 of Ashley Madison user data from the website dedicated to enabling extramarital affairs;[36] sometimes it is accidentally published; sometimes computers or digital media containing data are lost or stolen; and sometimes data is accessible due to poor security measures, as was the case when criminals were able to obtain tax information from the American Internal Revenue Service in 2015.[37] These leaks continue to demonstrate the need for organizations to adopt privacy by design.

There are a number of good examples of privacy by design. It has been used in targeted advertising screen systems that, using video analytics, identify the gender and age of customers looking at an advertising screen in order to display customized advertising. However, the data generated is deleted as soon as the ad is displayed, eliminating any risk of personal data breaches. In another example, Bering Media has designed a system that allows online ads to be targeted at particular user locations without either the ad-serving companies' or internet service providers' information on user location being exchanged, isolating and protecting personal information from disclosure.[38] The Ontario Lottery and Gaming Corporation (OLG) designed a system of facial recognition to allow customers who may have gambling problems to self-exclude themselves from casinos. The facial recognition system does not store images of customers entering casinos unless they match the biometric data of a person who has signed up for self-exclusion. To further protect personal information, the records in the self-exclusion database are locked by biometric encryption; each record can only be unlocked by the biometric data and thus the physical presence of the self-excluded person, ensuring that the self-exclusion database is secure.[39]

## PRIVACY REFORM

In the wake of March 2018 revelations that personal information had been harvested and obtained by political consulting firm Cambridge Analytica, and in light of massive data breaches that exposed the personal information of millions of people, there have been calls around the world for privacy law reform. Some groups, including the Canadian House of Commons Standing Committee on Privacy, Access to Information and Ethics (the Ethics Committee), have called for Canada to adopt laws similar to the European General Data Protection Regulation, imposing greater fines and penalties on companies and social media platforms for privacy breaches, ensuring that Canadians have opt-in consent to use of personal information, implementing a right of data portability that would allow Canadians to access their personal information in standardized formats and port that information to other platforms, and potentially implementing a right to be forgotten that would apply, as a minimum, to minors.[40] The Ethics Committee has recommended that Canadian federal privacy law be brought to apply to political parties, who as of this writing are able to collect personal information about Canadians in large databases, virtually unregulated except in British Columbia.[41] The Ethics Committee has recommended the expansion of the powers of the Privacy Commissioner of Canada to ensure that the Commissioner can audit companies' privacy practices and impose penalties large enough to deter global companies from breaking privacy laws.[42]

# WHOM DOES PRIVACY LAW SERVE?

## The Public Interest?

### Pluralism

Privacy rights are important, in part because, as Alan Westin argued, they protect a private zone where individuals can maintain their own private preferences, relatively free from outside influence. Privacy safeguards "individuality from social processes which inevitably tend towards homogeneity and conformity."[43] By preserving a space outside of public intervention, privacy permits people to "control their own destiny" within a private sphere, thus supporting a diversity of destinies, visions of the good life, and tolerance for such diversity.[44] It is a way of "respecting the pluralism of citizens' values, opinions, and life projects."[45] Privacy rights protect the pluralism of private beliefs and preferences. As such, they act as a pillar of democracy.[46]

## Bureaucracy and Bureaucrats?

### Bureaucratic Theory

There is little doubt that privacy governance has changed over time. Privacy has recently become a matter increasingly subject to government intervention. Although eavesdropping or opening and reading personal letters could land one in court between the fourteenth and eighteenth centuries, government enforcement of privacy norms has since ballooned.[47] Beginning in the 1970s, the use of new technologies, such as small recording devices, computer databases, and networked data transmission, disrupted accepted privacy norms. Many governments began to consider putting in place legal protections of privacy. Some have criticized the layers of bureaucracy, both in government and in private organizations, that such privacy protections can involve.[48] We might ask whether the current approach to privacy regulation in Canada, which relies on the bureaucracies of information and privacy commissioners, is effective. Has this approach to privacy governance been effective in protecting Canadians' privacy? Has it been more or less effective than the private laws of torts?

### Liberalism and Neoliberalism

The rise of modern democracy, public institutions, and the press has been accompanied by a greater recognition of the importance of privacy, coinciding with a liberal individualist view of privacy. Here, privacy, and the recognition of the right to privacy, is associated with increasing levels of liberty, freedom, and democracy.

The emphasis on privacy arose, arguably, alongside Western liberal capitalism; attitudes about privacy have changed significantly over time and across social conditions, though the extent of these changes is a matter of dispute. According to the philosopher Jürgen Habermas, what we consider to be the *public sphere*—the sphere of life where individuals come together to discuss the problems they hold in common and to influence political action—arose in the eighteenth century as a result of the establishment of cafés and other venues, as well as the rise of critical journalism, where such public discussions could be held.[49] The public sphere gave rise to its opposite: the *private sphere*, or the realm of life like the home or family, where individuals are free of intrusions from outside institutions. These two realms, some historians argue, became increasingly separated during the eighteenth century and the onset of "modernity," affecting everything from architecture of our homes and living spaces to sexual and relationship norms.[50] A rising valuation of privacy is also associated with wealth, home ownership, and land ownership, which afford a sense of privacy in everyday life. This stands in contrast to conditions in which shared dwellings with few physical separations afford little sense of privacy.[51]

Western liberal governments and, since the 1980s, neoliberal governments have put in place privacy laws that protect privacy to some extent. However, they also provide a large measure of freedom to businesses, enabling businesses to limit privacy rights of their customers and users or to require individuals to waive their privacy rights through private contracts and terms of use. This is permitted based on the liberal idea that individuals and private businesses know best their own preferences and concerns as well as that the market will provide appropriate protections for people's privacy. Negotiations over privacy are therefore best left to the involved parties.[52]

### Libertarian Theory

Many cyber-libertarians place a strong emphasis on privacy and freedom from surveillance. However, they often turn to technological rather than government regulatory approaches. Libertarians tend to support strong self-regulatory approaches such as privacy by design, the use of encryption and other technological measures, and the use of blockchain technologies to protect privacy.[53] Cypherpunk Eric Hughes argued:

> We cannot expect governments, corporations, or other large, faceless organizations to grant us privacy out of their beneficence.... We must defend our own privacy if we expect to have any. We must come together and create systems which allow anonymous transactions to take place. People have been defending their own privacy for centuries with whispers, darkness, envelopes, closed doors, secret handshakes, and couriers. The technologies of the past did not allow for strong privacy, but electronic technologies do.[54]

The cyber-libertarian stance toward privacy may be reflected by some Silicon Valley companies, which often emphasize privacy in terms of individual control over data.[55] For example, Mark Zuckerberg emphasizes users' control over their data, rather than their right of privacy. This emphasis on individual control shifts attention to users' control over how their posts and data are shared socially, but away from potential privacy controls and regulations that could protect individuals from corporations' power to collect user data and to use that data in ways that are not transparent, which may be harmful to individuals.[56]

## The Privileged?

### Critical Political Economy

The establishment of privacy rights has been driven, on the one hand, by public concern, beginning in the 1960s, with invasions of privacy: Governments saw a need to regulate in light of the storage of (sometimes inaccurate) personal data, the abuse of personal data, and the unauthorized disclosure of personal data that was enabled by computers and digitization.[57] On the other hand, governments were also driven by concern that a growing patchwork of national laws, all responding in different ways to changing privacy norms and threats, might make it difficult for transnational corporations, including insurance and banking companies, to transmit personal data across borders.[58] Critical political economists note that privacy law is rooted not only in governments' efforts to protect individuals' privacy as a human right; it is just as much rooted in government efforts to serve the interests of transnational corporations and to ensure the free flow of personal data in the interests of business. Thus, privacy law and regulation are the products of government, but also of private businesses' efforts to regulate and protect the flow of data, using governments to do so.

One example of how privacy law serves the interests of businesses and corporate owners is the law surrounding consent. Privacy law permits businesses to collect, retain, and use personal information, in many cases, as long as they obtain consent. So-called consent is obtained by asking people to click on "I agree" when they sign up for user accounts. Many have noted, however, that users rarely read privacy policies and terms of use.[59] Nevertheless, the law legitimates privacy practices such as asking users to "consent" to terms that everyone knows few will ever read or actually agree to. The law does this, in part, because it facilitates business transactions. It also massively favours the businesses who write the terms of use over the users who click on "I agree."

Marxian and other critical legal scholars argue that the law and government always, ultimately, serve transnational corporations and the capitalist class. Privacy laws are no different, as accepted privacy principles permit pervasive corporate and even government surveillance (see Chapter 6), with few effective safeguards for citizens. Many people realize this. Low-income and marginalized people, Virginia Eubanks suggests, may see privacy as a pipedream.[60] After all, privacy laws do little to protect those forms of legal and legitimized surveillance to which low-income and marginalized people are subject, such as monitoring by social services authorities, carding, or CCTV. However, as Eubanks argues, those same forms of surveillance to which marginalized people are subject spawn "repressive political environments" wherever used, and will "eventually be used on everyone."[61]

### Feminist and Queer Studies

Habermas's account of the rise of the public sphere and its accompanying private sphere has been criticized as overly simplistic and as overly laudatory of the private sphere as a space of freedom.[62] Feminist critics note that privacy can be used to hide abuse and exploitation.[63] They also note that consigning certain issues to the private sphere—such as issues of concern to women—can serve to halt women's empowerment and divert public attention from issues women consider important.[64]

Feminist, socialist, and other critical scholars have critiqued the dominant liberal view of privacy as privileging masculine individualist ideals, noting that the oppressed rarely have a space of privacy and safety to which they can retreat to reflect and find their "true selves," and that private spaces such as the home or institutions can be places that obscure privilege, oppression, and exploitation, hiding these from public view.[65]

Privacy is also experienced differently by queer people. Queer theorist Eve Sedgwick has noted this difference, observing that heterosexual couples may be able to navigate between public and private spaces without problem, being granted a right of privacy in their intimate relations. Same-sex couples have been exposed to public scrutiny in their private lives (particularly when sodomy was a crime) while often being compelled to keep aspects of their lives private in public:

> Think of how a culturally central concept like public/private is organized so as to preserve for heterosexuality the unproblematicalness, the apparent naturalness, of its *discretionary* choice between display and concealment: "public" names the space where cross-sex couples *may*, whenever they feel like it, display affection freely, while same-sex couples must always conceal it; while "privacy," to the degree that it is codified in US law, has historically been centred on the protection-from-scrutiny of the married, cross-sex couple, a scrutiny to which (since the 1986 decision in *Bowers v Hardwick*) same-sex relations on the other hand are unbendingly subject.[66]

Such differences are also reflected in the differing ways that queer people navigate their privacy settings and presentation of identity online and in social media.[67]

Privacy is also experienced differently by those who are gender non-conforming. Trans and gender non-conforming people often face a variety of dilemmas and decisions about whether and how to present themselves as gender-conforming—to conform either to the gender they were assigned at birth, or to their real self-identified gender identity—and whether to take hormones or undergo surgery that, in part, may serve to "evade any surveillance (whether visual, auditory, social, or legal) that would reveal one's trans status."[68] To the extent that the "medico-legal system itself works to track and document gender-nonconforming bodies and transgender identities," Toby Beauchamp notes, "at some level, trans people's medical and legal information was never private or privileged."[69]

### Critical Race Theory and Intersectional Analysis

Privacy laws and norms are experienced and granted unevenly, permitting the privileged their "minor infractions" while subjecting the working class, the racialized, and the criminalized to constant surveillance and scrutiny.[70] As Virginia Eubanks has shown, poor, working-class, racialized, and marginalized people are subject to higher levels of privacy invasions and surveillance:[71]

> Marginalized people are subject to some of the most technologically sophisticated and comprehensive forms of scrutiny and observation in law enforcement,

the welfare system, and the low-wage workplace. They also endure higher levels of direct forms of surveillance, such as stop-and-frisk in New York City.[72]

Privacy can hide racism and shield racism and discrimination from being addressed. Liberalism, as David Eng notes, consigns most forms of racial discrimination that occur within family and private relationships to the private realm, making "the state regulation of race and racial discrimination within the private realm of family and kinship relations" into a "preposterous idea, a fundamental affront to our sense of individual liberty and freedom."[73] The hierarchies and relationships of dominance (including capitalist, gendered, racialized, or heteronormative relationships) in the private sphere, left unaddressed, are reproduced in the public sphere, which "presupposes the hierarchies of the private sphere, guided and regulated by norms that are not neutral but conditioned by the particular interests of the dominant group."[74]

### *Indigenous and Postcolonial Analysis*
Indigenous peoples in Canada have historically been denied the range of privacy protections that many non-Indigenous people enjoy. For Indigenous peoples in Canada, Mary Caldbick notes, "virtually every aspect of privacy has been under assault since at least the colonial period."[75] Indigenous peoples' lives have been "unduly susceptible to government interference."[76] Government and religious institutions historically collected and used "information about virtually all aspects of Aboriginal peoples' lives."[77] Information gathered has included reports of Indian agents about Indigenous people, church records, and census data.[78]

A huge archive of personal information about Indigenous peoples is held by the Canadian government. This information has played a significant role in colonial rule, facilitating the management and governance of Indigenous populations.

The uneven distribution of privacy goes hand-in-hand with colonial and postcolonial distributions of labour, in which, on an international scale, a privileged core is granted privacy and rights that are unavailable to labourers in the world periphery, from which wealth is extracted. Internationally, regions with low privacy standards are left out of privacy protection, leaving "the techno-oligarchs such as Facebook, Twitter, Amazon, and Google [to compute the] data of much of [the world outside the West] given the weak or nonexistent privacy and data protection laws. This expansionist outreach of pervasive datafication of the 'peripheries' by the 'core'" contributes to reproduce the power inequities of colonialization.[79]

Privacy law can be seen as an element of the liberal legal order that has been used to justify and legitimize settler colonialism.[80] Privacy can also act as a "technology of erasure and forgetting," where privacy rights are mobilized to justify the erasure of the records and testimonials of Indigenous peoples about their experiences under the Indian residential schools regime—and thus the record of state violence perpetuated against Indigenous peoples—or to restrict access to information about Indigenous peoples, preserving or presenting a sanitized version of history and settler colonialism.[81]

Personal information is not always readily available and accessible to Indigenous peoples themselves for their own use and benefit. Although privacy legislation provides a right of access to personal information, First Nations in Western Quebec and Eastern Ontario were initially denied access to personal information in a case involving the First Nations' request for access to personal information contained in census data.[82] They sought the census data from Statistics Canada to help evidence a land claim. Access to the census data was initially denied by the chief statistician due to concerns about releasing personally identifiable information. However, the census data was ultimately ordered released after the Information Commissioner intervened on the First Nations' behalf.[83] This case demonstrated the difficulties that First Nations can have in accessing and controlling the personal information of Indigenous peoples for their own benefit.

Privacy law also fails to serve Indigenous peoples because ethnocentric and racist concepts are employed at the core of privacy law. Studies of privacy are ethnocentric, often drawing disproportionately from, as Payal Arora notes, "empirical evidence on privacy attitudes and behaviors of Western-based, white, and middle-class demographics."[84]

For example, ideas about what is "reasonable" and "ordinary" are often part of key legal tests in privacy, as well as in areas of law. Several American court cases, known as the *portrait cases*, have seen Indigenous peoples attempt, and often fail, to sue organizations for the unauthorized use of their portraits.[85] According to the traditional beliefs of the plaintiffs in these cases, unauthorized uses of their image could bring misfortune to the subject of the portrait. Courts in several of the cases found that the privacy claims of the plaintiff were not justifiable because a defendant could only be liable if they should have realized that their action would offend a person of "ordinary sensibilities."[86] The Indigenous plaintiffs were deemed by the court not to be people of "ordinary sensibilities";

instead, they were people who subscribed to traditional beliefs (to which the "ordinary" white population did not subscribe), and thus the defendant was not liable. "We cannot," ruled the court, "equate an offense to persons holding a traditional belief with an offense to persons of ordinary sensibilities."[87]

Legal concepts about what is "ordinary" or "reasonable"—or a "reasonable expectation of privacy"—change over time and differ somewhat among court systems. "The concept of the reasonable expectation of privacy is clearly entrenched in Canadian common law," Caldbick noted in 2007, "but it remains to be seen whether the reasonableness can be extended to cover perspectives other than that of the dominant society."[88] This indeterminacy leaves room for uneven and discriminatory applications of privacy law. At the same time, Canadian courts may have begun to consider the specific experiences of racialized and Indigenous peoples who have been disproportionately subject to privacy invasions by law enforcement and government as a part of a "reasonable person" standard. In a 2019 decision, the Supreme Court considered what a "reasonable person" "*with a similar experiential history*" of being Indigenous or racialized would expect.[89]

### Governmentality, Networked Governance, Technology, and Geography

As we have seen, some are excluded from the exercise of privacy rights, falling outside the racialized, gendered, geographical, capitalist, or technological boundaries and affordances of privacy law. The role of technologies in constructing and distributing privacy is growing. In some senses, technology and the corporations that design it, rather than governments, govern the collection, use, and disclosure of personal information. The design and coding of social network sites, the options available to users, and the transparency of the design as to when and what personal information is being collected have a huge role to play in privacy. Government regulators may be unaware of what, when, or how personal information is being collected by individuals and organizations, and may have relatively little power to regulate this.

Privacy, and the persons who exercise the rights and privileges of privacy, exist within specific historical, geographical, political, and technological contexts. Governmentality theorists note that privacy, and the subjects who claim a right of privacy, have been historically and discursively constructed as free liberal subjects.[90] Such a construction takes privacy as a "defining characteristic of liberal democratic citizenship,"[91] but it is also, as Foucault noted, a "dividing practice" that individualizes legal rights and responsibilities.[92]

## FURTHER READING

Eng, David L. *The Feeling of Kinship: Queer Liberalism and the Racialization of Intimacy.* Durham, NC: Duke University Press, 2010.

Eubanks, Virginia. *Automating Inequality: How High-Tech Tools Profile, Police, and Punish the Poor.* New York: St. Martin's Press, 2018.

Fullenwieder, Lara, and Adam Molnar. "Settler Governance and Privacy: Canada's Indian Residential School Settlement Agreement and the Mediation of State-Based Violence." *International Journal of Communication* 12 (2018): 1332–49.

Greenwald, Glenn. *Transcript of "Why Privacy Matters."* 2014. https://www.ted.com/talks/glenn_greenwald_why_privacy_matters/transcript.

Prosser, William L. "Privacy." *California Law Review* 48, no. 3 (1960): 383–422.

Warren, Samuel D., and Louis D. Brandeis. "The Right to Privacy." *Harvard Law Review* (1890): 193–220.

Weinberg, Lindsay. "Rethinking Privacy: A Feminist Approach to Privacy Rights after Snowden." *Westminster Papers in Communication and Culture* 12, no. 3 (2017).

Westin, Alan. *Privacy and Freedom.* New York: Atheneum, 1967.

## NOTES

1. *Jones v Tsige*, 2012 ONCA 32 at paras 39–40.
2. See also *Alberta (Information and Privacy Commissioner) v United Food and Commercial Workers Local 401*, 2013 SCC 62 at para 22.
3. E.g., *Privacy Act*, RSC 1985, c P-21, ss 5(1), 5(2), 7, 8(1), and 8(5).
4. *Privacy Act*, s 12(1).
5. Alan F. Westin, "Science, Privacy, and Freedom: Issues and Proposals for the 1970s. Part I—The Current Impact of Surveillance on Privacy," *Columbia Law Review* 66, no. 6 (1966): 1925.
6. Ibid., 1024–29. For an alternative view, see Sara Bannerman, "Relational Privacy and the Networked Governance of the Self," *Information, Communication & Society* 2018: 1–16.
7. Kathleen Miles, "Glenn Greenwald on Why Privacy Is Vital, Even if You 'Have Nothing to Hide,'" June 20, 2014, https://www.huffingtonpost.ca/entry/glenn-greenwald-privacy_n_5509704.
8. Ibid.
9. Glenn Greenwald, *Transcript of "Why Privacy Matters,"* 2014, https://www.ted.com/talks/glenn_greenwald_why_privacy_matters/transcript.

10. OECD, *The OECD Privacy Framework* (Paris: OECD, 2013), 13.

11. *Privacy Act*, s 3.

12. Michael Zimmer, "'But the Data Is Already Public': On the Ethics of Research in Facebook," *Ethics and Information Technology* 12, no. 4 (2010): 313–25.

13. Office of the Privacy Commissioner of Canada, "Data Brokers: A Look at the Canadian and American Landscape—September 2014," October 10, 2014, 9, https://www.priv.gc.ca/en/opc-actions-and-decisions/research/explore-privacy-research/2014/db_201409/.

14. Quoted from Office of the Privacy Commissioner of Canada Canada, "PIPEDA Fair Information Principles," September 16, 2011, https://www.priv.gc.ca/en/privacy-topics/privacy-laws-in-canada/the-personal-information-protection-and-electronic-documents-act-pipeda/p_principle/.

15. *Personal Information Protection and Electronic Documents Act*, SC 2000, c 5, s 11–17. See also Office of the Privacy Commissioner of Canada, "How to Apply for a Federal Court Hearing under PIPEDA," September 2016, https://www.priv.gc.ca/en/privacy-topics/privacy-laws-in-canada/the-personal-information-protection-and-electronic-documents-act-pipeda/pipeda-complaints-and-enforcement-process/federal-court-applications-under-pipeda/; and Office of the Privacy Commissioner of Canada, "Federal Court Applications under the *Privacy Act*," September 2016, https://www.priv.gc.ca/en/privacy-topics/privacy-laws-in-canada/the-privacy-act/federal-court-applications-under-the-privacy-act/.

16. Office of the Privacy Commissioner of Canada, "Summary of Privacy Laws in Canada," May 15, 2014, https://www.priv.gc.ca/en/privacy-topics/privacy-laws-in-canada/02_05_d_15/.

17. Office of the Privacy Commissioner of Canada, "About the OPC," September 14, 2016, https://www.priv.gc.ca/en/about-the-opc/.

18. Office of the Privacy Commissioner of Canada, "Provincial and Territorial Privacy Laws and Oversight," accessed February 16, 2019, https://www.priv.gc.ca/en/about-the-opc/what-we-do/provincial-and-territorial-collaboration/provincial-and-territorial-privacy-laws-and-oversight/.

19. See William L. Prosser, "Privacy," *California Law Review* 48, no. 3 (1960): 383–422, https://doi.org/10.15779/z383j3c; see also Ashley Packard, *Digital Media Law*, 2nd ed. (Malden, MA: Wiley-Blackwell, 2013), 257–301; and Chris D.L. Hunt, "The Common Law's Hodgepodge Protection of Privacy," *University of New Brunswick Law Journal* 66 (2015): 161–84.

20. *Jones v Tsige* at para 52.

21. Ibid. at para 56; drawing on William L. Prosser, *Law of Torts* (St. Paul: West Publishing Company, 1971), 808–12.

22. *Civil Code of Québec*, SQ 1991, c 64, ss 35 and 36.

23. *Krouse v Chrysler Canada Ltd*, (1973), 1 OR (2d) 225 (Ont. CA).

24. Anna Shahid, *A Short Overview on the Tort of Appropriation of Personality*, http://www.iposgoode.ca/2009/04/a-short-overview-on-the-tort-of-appropriation-of-personality/

25. *Civil Code of Québec*, c 64, s 36.

26. *Charter of Human Rights and Freedoms*, RSQ, c C-12, s 5; *Aubry v Éditions Vice-Versa*, [1998] 1 SCR 591.

27. *Aubry v Éditions Vice-Versa*.

28. "How Do You Fight Back against Online Defamation?" *CBC News*, May 7, 2013, https://www.cbc.ca/news/technology/how-do-you-fight-back-against-online-defamation-1.1314609.

29. Google, "EU Privacy Removal," accessed October 31, 2018, https://www.google.com/webmasters/tools/legal-removal-request?complaint_type=rtbf&visit_id=636765972026970240-3559955740&rd=1.

30. *Reference re subsection 18.3(1) of the Federal Courts Act, RSC 1985, c F-7*, 2019 FC 261; Teresa Scassa, "Right to Be Forgotten Reference to Federal Court Attracts Media Concern," April 17, 2019, https://www.teresascassa.ca/index.php?option=com_k2&view=item&id=305:right-to-be-forgotten-reference-to-federal-court-attracts-media-concern&Itemid=80; Office of the Privacy Commissioner of Canada, "Privacy Commissioner Seeks Federal Court Determination on Key Issue for Canadians' Online Reputation," October 10, 2018, https://www.priv.gc.ca/en/opc-news/news-and-announcements/2018/an_181010/.

31. Eloïse Gratton and Jules Polonetsky, "Submission: Privacy above All Other Fundamental Rights? Challenges with the Implementation of a Right to Be Forgotten in Canada—August 2016," https://fpf.org/wp-content/uploads/2016/04/PolonetskyGratton_RTBFpaper_FINAL.pdf.

32. Ibid.

33. *Google Inc v Equustek Solutions Inc*, 2017 SCC 34; David Murakami Wood, "What Is Global Surveillance?: Towards a Relational Political Economy of the Global Surveillant Assemblage," *Geoforum* 49 (October 2013): 318, https://doi.org/10.1016/j.geoforum.2013.07.001.

34. Ann Cavoukian, "The 7 Foundational Principles" (Toronto: Information and Privacy Commissioner of Ontario, 2011), https://www.ipc.on.ca/wp-content/uploads/Resources/7foundationalprinciples.pdf.

35. "Resolution on Privacy by Design," Israel: 32nd International Conference of Data Protection and Privacy Commissioners, 2010, https://edps.europa.eu/sites/edp/files/publication/10-10-27_jerusalem_resolutionon_privacybydesign_en.pdf.

36. Kim Zetter, "Hackers Finally Post Stolen Ashley Madison Data," *Wired*, August 18, 2015, https://www.wired.com/2015/08/happened-hackers-posted-stolen-ashley-madison-data/.

37. Jose Pagliery, "Criminals Use IRS Website to Steal Data on 104,000 People," *CNN Money*, May 26, 2015, https://money.cnn.com/2015/05/26/pf/taxes/irs-website-data-hack/index.html.

38. "Privacy by Design: Strong Privacy Protection—Now, and Well into the Future," 33rd International Conference of Data Protection and Privacy Commissioners, 2011, 15, https://www.ipc.on.ca/wp-content/uploads/Resources/PbDReport.pdf.

39. OLG, "OLG PlaySmart—Gambling Facts, Tools and Advice," accessed October 31, 2018, https://www.playsmart.ca/#FacialRecognition.

40. House of Commons Standing Committee on Access to Information, Privacy, and Ethics, "Towards Privacy by Design: Review of the Personal Information Protection and Electronic Documents Act" (Ottawa: House of Commons, February 2018); House of Commons Standing Committee on Access to Information, Privacy, and Ethics, "Addressing Digital Privacy Vulnerabilities and Potential Threats to Canada's Democratic Electoral Process" (Ottawa: House of Commons, June 2018); House of Commons Standing Committee on Access to Information, Privacy, and Ethics, "Democracy under Threat: Risks and Solutions in the Era of Disinformation and Data Monopoly" (Ottawa: House of Commons, December 2018).

41. House of Commons Standing Committee, "Democracy under Threat," 25–26; Colin J. Bennett and Robin M. Bayley, *Canadian Federal Political Parties and Personal Privacy Protection: A Comparative Analysis* (Ottawa: Office of the Privacy Commissioner of Canada, 2012); Office of the Information and Privacy Commissioner of British Columbia, "Full Disclosure: Political Parties, Campaign Data, and Voter Consent" (Vancouver: Office of the Information and Privacy Commissioner of British Columbia, February 6, 2019), https://www.oipc.bc.ca/investigation-reports/2278.

42. House of Commons Standing Committee, "Addressing Digital Privacy," Recommendations 4–7.

43. Judith Squires, "Private Lives, Secluded Places: Privacy as Political Possibility," *Environment and Planning D: Society and Space* 12, no. 4 (1994): 390.

44. Ibid., 391.

45. Clive Barnett, "Convening Publics: The Parasitical Spaces of Public Action," in *The SAGE Handbook of Political Geography*, eds. Kevin Cox, Murray Low, and Jennifer Robinson (London: SAGE, 2008), 406.

46. Ibid., 405–6; Squires.

47. Jan Holvast, "History of Privacy," in *The Future of Identity in the Information Society*, eds. Vashek Matyáš, Simone Fischer-Hübner, Daniel Cvrček, and Petr Švenda (Berlin: Springer, 2009), 15.

48. Michi Iljazi, "TPA Submits Comments to FCC on Broadband Privacy Rule," Taxpayers Protection Alliance, March 8, 2017, https://www.protectingtaxpayers. org/blog/a/view/tpa-submits-comments-to-fcc-on-broadband-privacy-rule; Ross Marchand, "Pai and Ohlhausen Lead FCC and FTC's Fight Against Misguided Rules," Taxpayers Protection Alliance, April 21, 2017, https://www. protectingtaxpayers.org/blog/a/view/pai-and-ohlhausen-lead-fcc-and-ftcs-fight-against-misguided-rules.

49. Jürgen Habermas, *The Structural Transformation of the Public Sphere: An Inquiry into a Category of Bourgeois Society* (Cambridge, MA: MIT Press, 1989), 27.

50. Tim Meldrum, "Domestic Service, Privacy and the Eighteenth-Century Metropolitan Household," *Urban History* 26, no. 1 (1999): 27–39.

51. Holvast, 15.

52. Richard A. Posner, "The Right of Privacy," *Georgia Law Review.* 12 (1977): 393; Richard A. Posner, "The Economics of Privacy," *The American Economic Review* 71, no. 2 (1981): 405–9; George J. Stigler, "An Introduction to Privacy in Economics and Politics," *The Journal of Legal Studies* 9, no. 4 (1980): 623–44. For a critique of this position, see Anita L. Allen, "Coercing Privacy," *William and Mary Law Review* 40, no. 3 (1999): 723–24.

53. Gabor Soos, "Smart Decentralization? The Radical Anti-Establishment Worldview of Blockchain Initiatives," *Smart Cities and Regional Development (SCRD) Journal* 2, no. 2 (2018): 35–49; Robert Kutis, "Bitcoin: Light at the End of the Tunnel for Cyberlibertarians?" *Masaryk University Journal of Law and Technology* 8, no. 2, accessed February 15, 2019, https://journals.muni.cz/mujlt/article/viewFile/2656/2220.

54. Eric Hughes, "A Cypherpunk's Manifesto," accessed February 15, 2019, https://www.activism.net/cypherpunk/manifesto.html.

55. Andrew McStay, *Privacy and the Media* (New York: SAGE, 2017), 64–65; Alyson Leigh Young and Anabel Quan-Haase, "Privacy Protection Strategies on Facebook: The Internet Privacy Paradox Revisited," *Information, Communication & Society* 16, no. 4 (2013): 479–500.

56. McStay, 78.

57. "OECD Guidelines on the Protection of Privacy and Transborder Flows of Personal Data—OECD," accessed October 31, 2018, http://www.oecd.org/sti/ieconomy/oecdguidelinesontheprotectionofprivacyandtransborderflowsofpersonaldata. htm. For a broader history of privacy, see Holvast.

58. "OECD Guidelines."

59. Jonathan A. Obar and Anne Oeldorf-Hirsch, "The Biggest Lie on the Internet: Ignoring the Privacy Policies and Terms of Service Policies of Social Networking Services," *Information, Communication & Society* (2018): 1–20.

60. Virginia Eubanks, "Want to Predict the Future of Surveillance? Ask Poor Communities," *The American Prospect*, January 15, 2014, https://prospect.org/article/want-predict-future-surveillance-ask-poor-communities.

61. Ibid.

62. Nancy Fraser, "Rethinking the Public Sphere: A Contribution to the Critique of Actually Existing Democracy," *Social Text*, no. 25/26 (1990): 56–80.

63. Elizabeth M. Schneider, "The Violence of Privacy," *Connecticut Law Review* 23 (1990): 973–99; Sally F. Goldfarb, "Violence against Women and the Persistence of Privacy," *Ohio State Law Journal* 61, no. 1 (2000): 1–87.

64. Ibid.

65. Lindsay Weinberg, "Rethinking Privacy: A Feminist Approach to Privacy Rights after Snowden," *Westminster Papers in Communication and Culture* 12, no. 3 (2017); Bannerman; Anita L. Allen, *Uneasy Access: Privacy for Women in a Free Society* (Lanham, MD: Rowman & Littlefield, 1988).

66. Eve Kosofsky Sedgwick, *Tendencies* (London: Taylor & Francis, 2004), 9.

67. Danah Boyd, "Facebook's Privacy Trainwreck: Exposure, Invasion, and Social Convergence," *Convergence* 14, no. 1 (2008): 16.

68. Toby Beauchamp, "Artful Concealment and Strategic Visibility: Transgender Bodies and US State Surveillance after 9/11," *Surveillance & Society* 6, no. 4 (2009): 357.

69. Beauchamp, 362; Shoshana Magnet, *When Biometrics Fail: Gender, Race, and the Technology of Identity* (Durham, NC: Duke University Press, 2011); Rachel E. Dubrofsky and Shoshana Magnet, eds., *Feminist Surveillance Studies* (Durham, NC: Duke University Press, 2015), 5.

70. Virginia Eubanks, *Digital Dead End: Fighting for Social Justice in the Information Age* (Cambridge, MA: MIT Press, 2011).

71. Virginia Eubanks, *Automating Inequality: How High-Tech Tools Profile, Police, and Punish the Poor* (New York, NY: St. Martin's Press, 2018); Seeta Peña Gangadharan, "The Downside of Digital Inclusion: Expectations and Experiences of Privacy and Surveillance among Marginal Internet Users," *New Media & Society* 19, no. 4 (2017): 597–615; Payal Arora and Laura Scheiber, "Slumdog Romance: Facebook Love and Digital Privacy at the Margins," *Media, Culture & Society* 39, no. 3 (2017): 408–22; Payal Arora, "Decolonizing Privacy Studies," *Television & New Media* 20, no. 4 (2019): 366–78; Nathalie Maréchal, "First They Came for the Poor: Surveillance of

Welfare Recipients as an Uncontested Practice," *Media and Communication* 3, no. 3 (2015): 56–67.

72. Eubanks, "Want to Predict the Future of Surveillance?"

73. David L. Eng, *The Feeling of Kinship: Queer Liberalism and the Racialization of Intimacy* (Durham, NC: Duke University Press, 2010), 8.

74. Ibid.

75. Mary Caldbick, "Privacy and Access to Information of Aboriginal Peoples in Canada," LLM Major Research Paper (University of Ottawa, 2007), 4.

76. Ibid., 10.

77. Ibid., 12.

78. Ibid.

79. Arora, 268.

80. Lara Fullenwieder and Adam Molnar, "Settler Governance and Privacy: Canada's Indian Residential School Settlement Agreement and the Mediation of State-Based Violence," *International Journal of Communication* 12 (2018): 1332–49.

81. Ibid.

82. *Canada (Information Commissioner) v Canada (Minister of Industry)*, 2007 FCA 212; Caldbick, 37–40.

83. Ibid.

84. Arora, 368.

85. Caldbick, 26–29.

86. *Bitsie v Walston*, 515 P.2d 659 (N.M. Ct. App. 1973) at 661.

87. Ibid. at 662.

88. Caldbick, 29.

89. *R v Le*, 2019 SCC 34 at 107. Emphasis added.

90. Paul Passavant, *No Escape: Freedom of Speech and the Paradox of Rights* (New York: NYU Press, 2002).

91. Fullenwieder and Molnar.

92. Ibid.

# 6 Government Surveillance

## INTRODUCTION

In 2013, the world was rocked by revelations of mass surveillance programs being operated by the American government, as well as the Canadian government and others around the world. The scale and invasiveness of such programs raised many questions: Are such programs legal and constitutional? When is surveillance appropriate? What type of oversight should be in place over surveillance programs? When, if ever, can we reasonably expect not to be surveilled or have our communications intercepted by government? Do we have a reasonable expectation of privacy when using computers, the internet, mobile phones, or in our living rooms while using smart home devices?

This chapter defines surveillance and lawful access, and introduces the history of government surveillance in Canada, the *Criminal Code* provisions that apply to the interception of private communications, and mass surveillance programs that operate in Canada and internationally. The second half of the chapter asks, "Whom does government surveillance serve?", drawing on the theories introduced in Chapter 1.

## WHAT IS SURVEILLANCE?

**Surveillance** is the act of keeping a close watch on someone. Surveillance by government occurs in many contexts, including criminal investigations and monitoring for national security threats such as terrorist plots.

There are two main types of surveillance: surveillance conducted in person and surveillance conducted through electronic devices. In-person surveillance typically has a specific target, such as a criminal or criminal organization. Electronic surveillance can be conducted against specific targets but has more recently been deployed on a mass scale, such that everyone is potentially a target;

potentially all networked communications may be monitored through big data processing. This type of surveillance, conducted on such a large scale, is called **mass surveillance**.

## OVERSIGHT

There is little court oversight or constitutional restriction on human intelligence gathering. A warrant is not required for police or security to deploy undercover agents to conduct surveillance operations.[1] However, interception of electronic communications, except under specific circumstances, can be illegal. Certain exceptions are therefore made in the *Criminal Code of Canada* to permit law enforcement and security services to intercept communications. This is called "lawful access." National security and intelligence activities in Canada are overseen by the National Security and Intelligence Review Agency, established in 2019.

## WHAT IS LAWFUL ACCESS?

The term **lawful access** refers to the lawful or legal interception of communications and the lawful search and seizure of information. Lawful access permits the interception of communications such as phone calls, text messaging, communication via apps, or other internet communications. It also permits the search or seizure of records or devices containing such communications. This interception or seizure is lawful because it is done by government agencies such as police or security agencies with legal authority such as a court order.

## HISTORY

**Wiretapping**, or the interception of telecommunications, has a long history.[2] Telegraphs were wiretapped during the American Civil War of 1861 to 1865. Police in Canada began using wiretaps to investigate crimes in the late 1950s and early 1960s.[3] However, the use of wiretaps was not consistently regulated, and concerns about wiretapping began to arise to prominence in Canada around the 1970s.[4] Laws about wiretapping and warrant requirements for conducting wiretap investigations were put in place in the *Criminal Code* under what is now Part VI, titled "Invasion of Privacy."[5]

# CRIMINAL CODE PROVISIONS: PRIVATE COMMUNICATIONS

Under Part VI of the *Criminal Code*, the willful interception of a private communication without authorization is a crime.[6] Authorization to intercept private communications can be obtained under specific circumstances. This authorization takes two major forms. First, *Part VI authorization* can be obtained. Part VI of the *Criminal Code* provides for the lawful interception of *live* communications—interception of the message in transit—under specific circumstances, especially for law enforcement investigations. Second, *pre-existing stored communications*, such as emails stored on a server or text messages stored on an individual's telephone, can be accessed by law enforcement under a regular search warrant or production order.[7]

*Private communication* is defined, in part, as a communication in which there is a reasonable expectation of privacy.[8] When do individuals have a reasonable expectation of privacy in their private communications? Courts' answers to this question have varied over time. When cordless and mobile phones first came into use, courts held that there was no reasonable expectation of privacy, since it was seen to be widely known that such transmissions could be easily intercepted.[9] However, today it is recognized that individuals do have a reasonable expectation of privacy in their mobile phone conversations and text messages.[10] This means that Part VI authorization is required for the lawful interception of phone conversations and text messages.

Since 2001, Canadian governments have undertaken a number of efforts to expand the lawful access provisions of the *Criminal Code* to permit broader surveillance powers.[11] Such efforts have sparked heated debate and have been opposed by civil liberties organizations, some academics, privacy commissioners, and, in some cases, telecommunications companies.[12]

# MASS SURVEILLANCE PROGRAMS

In 2013, Edward Snowden, a former contractor with the American National Security Agency (NSA), leaked classified documents to media outlets that revealed mass surveillance programs conducted by the NSA, as well as by other governments, including the Canadian Communications Security Establishment (CSE).[13]

The CSE and four other intelligence agencies—the NSA, the United Kingdom's Government Communications Headquarters (GCHQ), New Zealand's

Government Communications Security Bureau (GCSB), and the Australian Signals Directorate (ASD)—are collectively known as the "Five Eyes." The Five Eyes has installed equipment around the world in telecommunication networks to collect the contents of telephone, email, social media, and internet communications, web activity, and file downloads.[14] They also collect **metadata** about those communications, such as the "time and duration of a communication, the particular devices, addresses, or numbers contacted, which kinds of communications services we use, and at what geolocations."[15] Such metadata can be used to infer life patterns, political leanings, and intimate relationships. It may be easier to infer more intimate details from metadata than from the actual contents of communications, because the processes of drawing inferences from data can be automated through data mining.[16]

All of this data could potentially be accessed by law enforcement and security agencies by lawful requests.[17] Lisa Austin has called the mass surveillance done by Canada and its Five Eyes partners "lawful illegality," because the legal infrastructure that makes mass surveillance legal also creates a space in which the structures of legal accountability are so vague, and in which the level of discretion and secrecy are so high, that the *rule of law*—the idea that the state itself should be subject to the law—is called into question.[18]

## WHOM DOES GOVERNMENT SURVEILLANCE SERVE?

### The Public Interest?

*Pluralism*

Pluralists generally view law and policy as arising from healthy competition between a diversity of groups who seek to influence public policy, providing checks and balances to each other. On the matter of government surveillance, however, pluralists raise concerns. Mass surveillance programs have been constructed in secret, meaning that a diversity of voices was likely not heard in the formulation of such programs. In fact, pluralists see government surveillance as a threat to pluralist democracy. Security and surveillance measures, according to William E. Connolly, a major theorist of pluralism, foster "more closed surveillance states."[19] He argues that installing surveillance and security without addressing the grievances that lead to crime or terrorism is ineffective; instead, they produce a "national security machine that pushes numerous issues outside the range of legitimate dissent."[20] Political pluralism is suspended, limited, or sacrificed to secure order and security.[21] Surveillance systems should not be thought of as the result of balancing competing interests but as technologies that change the infrastructures within which these contests take place.[22]

## Bureaucracy and Bureaucrats?

### *Bureaucratic Theory*

Surveillance and the use of surveillance data to track and categorize individuals represents an extension of the iron cage of bureaucracy that Max Weber described in 1978.[23] They permit the digital scoring and ranking of individuals into categories according to risk (does the person represent a risk to individual persons or to national security?), eligibility for benefits, and targeting for more intensive surveillance. Such measures and practices can create an "iron cage" of bureaucracy from which it can be difficult to escape.[24] For example, individuals wrongly placed on no-fly lists have had a very difficult challenge in correcting that problem. The systems and procedures that surround surveillance and the big-data classification of people can certainly resemble an iron cage of bureaucracy to those caught up in them.[25]

### *Neoliberalism*

Neoliberal theorists have pointed to surveillance as a method of encouraging self-regulation, thus permitting the downsizing of government bureaucracy. Public servants who are subject to internal workplace surveillance can, like other workers, be held accountable to management and citizens through internal systems that track their performance and activities. They can then be subject to cutbacks where surveillance leads to finding "efficiencies." Citizens who are subjected to surveillance, for their part, might better self-regulate and might be deterred from crime and misdemeanours. This, according to neoliberal logic, could lead to savings, reducing the costs of law enforcement. Surveillance has also been used as a cost-saving measure in the provision of government services. Recipients of welfare have been subjected to forms of surveillance by neoliberal governments, on the grounds that such surveillance would reduce welfare fraud.[26]

Surveillance and security standards and technologies are also employed on an international scale. Viewing differing national standards relating to security and privacy as a problem that stands in the way of transnational business transactions, international standards are developed to clear the way for international markets.[27] Here, the tracking and surveillance of financial and regulatory data about, and credit-scoring of, nation states affords risk assessments and information provision that facilitates flows of neoliberal capitalism.[28]

## Libertarian Theory

Where neoliberals see possible efficiencies and savings, libertarians fear that a surveillance society could lead down the road toward totalitarianism. Libertarian socialist George Orwell warned of this in his novel *1984*, which portrayed a dystopian picture of a future society (the novel was published in 1949) in which citizens were subject to continuous omnipresent surveillance, and in which independent thought was undermined by government propaganda and disinformation.[29]

Some libertarians have been at the forefront of efforts to halt government surveillance. The Electronic Frontier Foundation and the Electronic Privacy Information Centre (EPIC) are just two cyber-libertarian organizations that have campaigned against government surveillance.[30] Cyber-libertarians have opposed government surveillance of the internet in many forms, from FBI access to encryption keys to government wiretapping.[31]

## The Privileged?

### Critical Political Economy

A critical political economy of big data surveillance takes note of the use and ownership of surveillance data and capabilities as a source of political power. Governments, and particularly security and law enforcement, were once the most significant users of surveillance technologies. However, the use, ownership, and control of surveillance technologies, political economists note, is shifting to a greater extent into the hands of private companies.[32] Private companies use market surveillance, consumer monitoring, and security surveillance to understand and mitigate market risks, and to create, understand, and acquire new markets domestically and globally.[33] Governments, for their part, continue to play an important role, helping to foster the legal norms, technical standards, markets, and international institutions that enable the forms of surveillance that corporations make use of.[34]

### Feminist, Queer, and Intersectional Analysis

Gender non-conforming and trans-identified people are subject to increased and disproportionate levels of national security surveillance as a result of measures taken after September 11, 2001, to increase security measures in immigration, border, and air travel. The American Department of Homeland Security raised concerns about male terrorists disguising themselves as women, painting gender non-conforming people as potential security threats. Increased scrutiny of identity documents, which may conflict with each other and with the gender presentation of individuals, has had a disproportionate impact on gender non-conforming and trans-identified individuals. Such individuals may face increased scrutiny, may be identified as national security threats, and must decide whether to be open and out about their gender identity with security officials, in some cases bringing name- and gender-change paperwork with them for travel so as to prove that they are "good citizens who have nothing to hide."[35] Technologies of surveillance, including airport X-ray and body scanners, can out trans people in airport screening.[36]

Feminists note that surveillance structures are often gendered; in many cases, men are the "watchers" and women are either invisible in employment and public institutions, or hyper-visible and subject to the male gaze.[37] Girls and women—particularly racialized women—feminists note, are often over-surveilled. Feminists, drawing on intersectionality theory, note that race, sexuality, class, and ability all play in to people's experiences of surveillance.[38] Racialized women are rarely situated as the spectator or "watcher."[39] Prisoners, recipients of welfare and social services, people in institutions, people with disabilities, immigrants, and refugees are all subject to greater levels of surveillance through the government institutions with which they interact.[40] Women who are subject to aggression and assault are often just as much under surveillance as are aggressors and perpetrators of violence.[41]

### Critical Race Theory

Government surveillance plays a role in reproducing racializing categories and hierarchies. Racialized people are subject to greater levels of government surveillance than many others. Surveillance plays a role in categorizing and sorting people—whether for the purposes of marketing or management and control.[42] In some cases, especially in national security and law enforcement, these categories are highly racialized, targeting racialized populations with increased surveillance and categories of difference.[43] Carding, or the stopping and documenting by police of civilians who are not investigated for any particular offence, is experienced disproportionately by racialized people, as are other forms of government surveillance.[44] Critical race theorists have argued that police surveillance of racialized people has historical roots in slave patrols of Black slaves in the southern United States.[45] Surveillance, Tina Patel argues, "is a powerful means by which negative labels are created and strengthened." It marks certain people or types of bodies as "suspicious" and "carries out more often than not, visible displays of enhanced attention."[46]

Surveillance systems can be construed to indicate that there is "permission to hate," or to indicate that racialized people deserve to be subject to extra scrutiny or treated with extra suspicion. Such systems can even be construed to indicate that subjecting racialized people to extra suspicion and scrutiny is a civic duty and "an acceptable response" to a risk of terrorism.[47] In this way, surveillance systems act as a normalized part of everyday racism.

Government surveillance has significant psychological effects, as well as damaging effects on relationships between racialized communities and the state. Those who are subject to carding, household raids, or detention experience significant psychological and emotional effects.[48]

Counter-surveillance of police and surveillance systems, particularly during interactions between racialized individuals and police or at protests against police brutality, has often been adopted as a strategy by anti-racism protesters.[49] While some are optimistic that counter-surveillance might bring a level of accountability for police wrongdoing, some scholars, drawing on critical race theory, are not so optimistic; Lindsey Beutin argues that counter-surveillance efforts have resulted in few police convictions, partly because racism so colours the interpretation of police brutality that even clear video does not often result in strong convictions against police.[50]

Surveillance has been used as a tool of repression against Black activists and the civil rights movement. The American Federal Bureau of Investigation (FBI) conducted surveillance against the civil rights movement, including Martin Luther King, Jr., and decolonization activists like Frantz Fanon.[51]

### Indigenous and Postcolonial Analysis

Surveillance of Indigenous peoples has long been a strategy of colonialism. Surveillance practices of monitoring and managing Indigenous peoples were an integral part of racialization and oppression by settler governments.[52] These practices direct the gaze of the state onto Indigenous and racialized peoples "to monitor, measure, and account for their 'dysfunctional' behaviours," while making invisible the colonial logics, the expropriation of Indigenous lands, Indigenous laws, and rights that created the conditions that led to the oppression of Indigenous peoples.[53]

Canada's Truth and Reconciliation Commission recognized the perception among Indigenous peoples that government documents and archives have often acted as mechanisms "of colonization, cultural appropriation by Western society and hyper-surveillance and objectification of Aboriginal peoples."[54] The National Centre for Truth and Reconciliation, the TRC noted, would therefore need to work to ensure that its own archives would not be perceived the same way, so that those archives could act as a force for reconciliation.[55]

Surveillance is conducted on entire countries, as well as on individual people and populations. Governments, international institutions, and private credit rating companies "collect, collate and perform algorithmic operations on data relating to nation-states to assess their credit-worthiness, rank their relative place in global markets, and create profiles to build into simulations of future trajectories and likely behavior." Such national credit-scoring systems can reproduce the economic and political inequalities of colonialism, condemning "large sections of national populations to economic marginality," limiting "individual and collective life chances," and undermining national government policies as indebted countries must consider credit ratings above domestic priorities.[56]

### Governmentality and Networked Governance

Surveillance is a technique and a way of ordering the world employed by governments to facilitate neoliberalization.[57] In his lectures on *Security, Territory, Population* (2007), Michel Foucault argued that the most fundamental role of government was in providing

> "security," accomplished through biopolitics: the management of entire populations in particular territorial configurations. The development of surveillance from the early modern period can be linked to the identification of these populations through rationalism and science, and in particular through new forms of counting and statistics.[58]

According to Ian Hacking, counting and statistics as governance practices

> started to emerge prior to the creation of the modern territorial nation-state system, indeed helped to construct the very idea of an apparently necessary coincidence between a national population and a territorial state. Biopolitical surveillance thereafter comes to function as what Foucault would later call "an art of government" or "governmentality," which seeks to maximize the capacity of the national population in a variety of ways "to participate productively in the market" by differentiating good and bad circulations and maximizing the former whilst preventing the latter.[59]

In *Discipline & Punish* (1975), Foucault argued that we increasingly live in a society where permanent visibility is instituted as a form of discipline and control—a means of power that does not entail physical bars or violence, but that instills a form of consciousness of visibility such that discipline is maintained through the mere threat of constant observation. He called this a "panoptic society," drawing on the image of a panopticon—a prison built to allow all prisoners to be observed by a single prison guard, without their being able to observe the guard or know whether they were being observed—to illustrate this form of control.[60]

### Technology and Geography

Whereas many Canadian communication policies mentioned in this text have taken nation-building as their impetus, surveillance and mass surveillance draw on narratives of national security—securing what is already built—and on narratives of networked society that portray mass surveillance as a natural technological response to events driven by technology: globally networked threats such as terrorist networks operating on social media and through encrypted communications.

Surveillance, like other communication technologies and the politics and policies by which they are employed, changes our geographical relationships. Surveillance expands the scale at which governments and corporations can act, affording global seeing and global action that would otherwise be impossible.[61] The massive scale of the surveillance programs Snowden revealed have the potential to "reconfigure power politics at a world scale."[62]

## FURTHER READING

Dubrofsky, Rachel E., and Shoshana Magnet, eds. *Feminist Surveillance Studies*. Durham, NC: Duke University Press, 2015.

Geist, Michael. *Law, Privacy and Surveillance in Canada in the Post-Snowden Era*. Ottawa: University of Ottawa Press, 2015.

Kealey, Gregory S. *Spying on Canadians: The Royal Canadian Mounted Police Security Service and the Origins of the Long Cold War*. Toronto: University of Toronto Press, 2017.

Lyon, David. *Surveillance after Snowden*. Hoboken, NJ: John Wiley & Sons, 2015.

Smith, Andrea. "Not-Seeing: State Surveillance, Settler Colonialism, and Gender Violence." In *Feminist Surveillance Studies*, edited by Rachel E. Dubrofsky and Shoshana Magnet, 21–38. Durham, NC: Duke University Press, 2015.

Turner, Anne. "Wiretapping Smart Phones with Rotary-Dial Phones' Law: How Canada's Wiretap Law Is in Desperate Need of Updating." *Manitoba Law Journal* 40 no. 2 (2017): 249–98.

Van der Meulen, Emily, and Robert Heynen, eds. *Expanding the Gaze: Gender and the Politics of Surveillance*. Toronto: University of Toronto Press, 2016.

# NOTES

1.  Steve Hewitt, "Chapter II. Forgotten Surveillance: Covert Human Intelligence Sources in Canada in a Post-9/11 World," in *Law, Privacy and Surveillance in Canada in the Post-Snowden Era*, ed. Michael Geist (Ottawa: University of Ottawa Press, 2017), 45–67.

2.  Anne Turner, "Wiretapping Smart Phones with Rotary-Dial Phones' Law: How Canada's Wiretap Law Is in Desperate Need of Updating," *Manitoba Law Journal* 40 no. 2 (2017): 252–56.

3.  Ibid., 253.

4.  Ibid.

5.  *Criminal Code*, RSC 1985, c C-46, s 184(1).

6.  Ibid.

7.  Part VI authorization has been used to apply to stored text messages. However, there is legal uncertainty around when Part VI provisions, as opposed to a regular search warrant, should be used by law enforcement in accessing stored communications. Turner, 266–72.

8.  *Criminal Code*, s 183.

9.  Turner, 281.

10. Ibid.

11. Christopher Parsons, "Stuck on the Agenda: Drawing Lessons from the Stagnation of 'Lawful Access' Legislation in Canada," in *Law, Privacy and Surveillance in Canada in the Post-Snowden Era*, ed. Michael Geist (Ottawa: University of Ottawa Press, 2017), 257–83; Turner.

12. Parsons.

13. Andrew Clement, "Limits to Secrecy: What Are the Communications Security Establishment's (CSE) Capabilities for Intercepting Canadians' Internet Communications?" in *National Security Intelligence and Surveillance in a Big Data Age*, eds. David Lyon and David Murakami Wood (Vancouver: UBC Press, forthcoming).

14. Christopher Parsons, "Law Enforcement and Security Agency Surveillance in Canada: The Growth of Digitally-Enabled Surveillance and Atrophy of Accountability," 2018, 6, https://papers.ssrn.com/sol3/papers.cfm?abstract_id=3130240; Christopher Parsons, "Beyond Privacy: Articulating the Broader Harms of Pervasive Mass Surveillance," *Media and Communication* 3, no. 3 (2015): 1–11.

15. Ann Cavoukian, "A Primer on Metadata: Separating Fact from Fiction" (Toronto: Information and Privacy Commissioner of Ontario, 2013), 3, https://www.ipc.on.ca/wp-content/uploads/Resources/metadata.pdf; Parsons, "Beyond Privacy."

16. Cavoukian, "Primer on Metadata"; Ron Deibert, "The Geopolitics of Cyberspace after Snowden," *Current History* 114, no. 768 (2015): 9.

17. Parsons, "Law Enforcement and Security Agency Surveillance," 6.

18. Lisa Austin, "Lawful Illegality: What Snowden Has Taught Us about the Legal Infrastructure of the Surveillance State," in *Law, Privacy and Surveillance in Canada in the Post-Snowden Era*, ed. Michael Geist (Ottawa: University of Ottawa Press, 2017), 103–25.

19. William E. Connolly, *Pluralism* (Durham, NC: Duke University Press, 2005), 53.

20. Ibid., 54.

21. Zygmunt Bauman, Didier Bigo, Paulo Esteves, Elspeth Guild, Vivienne Jabri, David Lyon, and Rob BJ Walker, "After Snowden: Rethinking the Impact of Surveillance," *International Political Sociology* 8, no. 2 (2014): 121–44.

22. Kate O'Riordan and David J. Phillips, eds., *Queer Online: Media Technology & Sexuality* (New York: Peter Lang, 2007), 13–30.

23. Max Weber, *Economy and Society: An Outline of Interpretive Sociology* (Los Angeles: University of California Press, 1978).

24. Sarah Brayne, "Big Data Surveillance: The Case of Policing," *American Sociological Review* 82, no. 5 (2017): 977–1008.

25. Patricia Williams, "In-Laws and Outlaws," *Arizona Law Review* 46 (2004): 199.

26. Virginia Eubanks, *Digital Dead End: Fighting for Social Justice in the Information Age* (Cambridge, MA: MIT Press, 2011); Krystle Maki, "Neoliberal Deviants and Surveillance," *Surveillance & Society* 9, no. 1/2 (November 30, 2011): 47, https://doi.org/10.24908/ss.v9i1/2.4098.

27. David Murakami Wood, "What Is Global Surveillance? Towards a Relational Political Economy of the Global Surveillant Assemblage," *Geoforum* 49 (October 2013): 322, https://doi.org/10.1016/j.geoforum.2013.07.001.

28. Ibid.

29. David Lyon, *The Electronic Eye: The Rise of Surveillance Society* (Minneapolis: University of Minnesota Press, 1994), 61–62.

30. Jason Krause, "Cyber-Libertarians: A Legal Group Formed to Defend Civil Liberties on the Web Gears up to Fight the USA Patriot Act," *ABA Journal* 89, no. 11 (2003): 50–56.

31. Ibid.

32. Mark Andrejevic and Kelly Gates, "Big Data Surveillance," *Surveillance & Society* 12, no. 2 (May 9, 2014): 187–88, https://doi.org/10.24908/ss.v12i2.5242.

33. Murakami Wood.

34. Ibid.

35. Toby Beauchamp, "Artful Concealment and Strategic Visibility: Transgender Bodies and US State Surveillance after 9/11," *Surveillance & Society* 6, no. 4 (2009): 356–66.

36. Dubrofsky and Magnet, 5.

37. Emily Van der Meulen and Robert Heynen, *Expanding the Gaze: Gender and the Politics of Surveillance* (Toronto: University of Toronto Press, 2016), 7–14.

38. Dubrofsky and Magnet, 3–4.

39. Van der Meulen and Heynen, 7–14.

40. Dubrofsky and Magnet, 4.

41. Ibid., 5.

42. Van der Meulen and Heynen, 4.

43. Ibid.

44. Jim Rankin and Patty Winsa, "Carding Drops but Proportion of Blacks Stopped by Toronto Police Rises," *Toronto Star*, July 26, 2014, https://www.thestar.com/news/insight/2014/07/26/carding_drops_but_proportion_of_blacks_stopped_by_toronto_police_rises.html.

45. Lyndsey P. Beutin, "Racialization as a Way of Seeing: The Limits of Counter-Surveillance and Police Reform," *Surveillance & Society* 15, no. 1 (2017): 6, 11.

46. Tina Girishbhai Patel, "Surveillance, Suspicion and Stigma: Brown Bodies in a Terror-Panic Climate," *Surveillance & Society* 10, no. 3/4 (2012): 217.

47. Ibid., 220.

48. Ibid., 217.

49. Beutin.

50. Ibid.

51. Jules Boykoff, *The Suppression of Dissent: How the State and Mass Media Squelch USAmerican Social Movements* (New York: Routledge, 2013), chap. 6; Simone Browne, *Dark Matters: On the Surveillance of Blackness* (Durham, NC: Duke University Press, 2015).

52. Andrea Smith, "Not-Seeing: State Surveillance, Settler Colonialism, and Gender Violence," in *Feminist Surveillance Studies*, eds. Rachel E. Dubrofsky and Shoshana Magnet (Durham, NC: Duke University Press, 2015), 21–38.

53. Ibid.

54. TRC, NRA, Government of Northwest Territories—Education, Culture and Employment, Miscellaneous Hostel Reports RIMS ID# 1209, box 9, "Student Residences (Hostels)," undated. [RCN-007183], as cited in Truth and Reconciliation Commission of Canada, "Honouring the Truth, Reconciling for the Future: Summary of the Final Report of the Truth and Reconciliation Commission of Canada" (Winnipeg: Truth and Reconciliation Commission of Canada, 2015), 266, http://www.trc.ca/.

55. Ibid.

56. Murakami Wood, 323.

57. Ibid., 317.

58. Ian Hacking, *The Taming of Chance* (Cambridge: Cambridge University Press, 1990).

59. Murakami Wood, 318, quoting Ceyhan, "Surveillance as Biopower," and citing Hacking.

60. Michel Foucault, *Discipline & Punish* (New York: Vintage Books, 1995).

61. Murakami Wood, 318.

62. Bauman et al.

# 7

## Intellectual Property

## INTRODUCTION

When is it appropriate to make a copy of a photo without getting permission? Doesn't "owning" a word or phrase infringe on freedom of expression? Who benefits from the intellectual property system? Does the intellectual property system adequately serve the purpose of fostering creativity and innovation?

This chapter introduces the main categories of intellectual property and the key concepts used in each. It then proceeds to ask, "Whom does the intellectual property system serve? Does intellectual property provide equal benefits to all?"

## WHAT IS INTELLECTUAL PROPERTY?

**Intellectual property law** grants ownership rights of intangible things—in works of the mind, works of creativity, and works of expression. While, at times, analogies are drawn between intellectual property rights and the law of property in land or objects, the legal regimes governing intellectual property and other forms of property are distinct. Owning a copy of a book does not usually include ownership of the intellectual property in the book or the right to print and sell copies of the book.

There are many different types of intellectual property law, applying to everything from creative works, inventions, product branding, plant breeding, and integrated circuit topographies to rights in Indigenous knowledge. This chapter will discuss the three main types of intellectual property: copyright, patent, and trademark law.

## Copyright, Patent, and Trademark Law

**Copyright** law grants a set of rights in original literary, dramatic, musical, and artistic works, including the exclusive right to reproduce the work and to authorize its reproduction.[1] It grants rights to the authors of original books, articles, songs, musical compositions, paintings and drawings, television shows, movies, and computer software. (The term *authors* is used broadly in copyright law, to include artists, painters, sculptors, composers, software writers, and the full range of creators of literary, dramatic, musical, and artistic works.)

**Patent** law grants rights in new and useful inventions. For example, it grants rights to inventors of machines, computer parts, and drugs, and to inventors of processes for making products, such as yeast or robots.[2]

**Trademark** law grants rights in words, symbols, drawings, shapes, packaging, sound, or colours used to distinguish the goods or services of one person or organization from the goods and services of others.[3] For example, the exclusive rights to use the word *NIKE*, the Nike swoosh, the triangular packaging of a Toblerone chocolate bar, the start-up chime of a Macintosh computer, and the colour of a pill (of a specific shape and size) in the sale of goods and services are granted under trademark law.[4]

The process of obtaining rights under the copyright, patent, and trademark regimes differ. Authors of copyright works receive most of their rights automatically when the work is created, though registration of copyright can be helpful in proving copyright ownership in the context of a legal action. Inventors of patented inventions, however, must apply to register their patent (in Canada, with the Canadian Intellectual Property Office) to receive rights in their invention. Some trademark rights are granted automatically once a mark becomes recognized as associated with a particular product or service, but registration of a mark can be advantageous because it confers greater rights.

Intellectual property rights expire. This ensures that the monopolies granted in creative works, inventions, and trademarks are limited; those rights are theoretically calibrated to be strong enough to provide an incentive for creation and innovation, while also being limited so that when such rights expire, innovations, creative works, and words and phrases become available to all to use, serving to benefit the public. However, the questions of whether this theory works in practice, whether intellectual property law does actually serve to foster creativity and innovation, and how long the term of intellectual property rights should last in order to best serve these goals are matters of significant debate.[5]

**Table 7.1:** Intellectual Property

|  | **Copyright** | **Patent** | **Trademark** |
|---|---|---|---|
| **Subject matter** | Original literary, dramatic, musical, and artistic works | Inventions that are new and useful | Words, symbols, draw-ings, shapes, packag-ing, sounds, or colours used to distinguish wares or services |
| **Process for obtaining rights** | Automatic<br><br>Optional additional rights through registration | Apply for through Canadian Intel-lectual Property Office (CIPO) | Automatic once distinc-tiveness is established<br><br>Optional additional rights through registration |
| **Term of rights** | Life of the author + 50 years* | 20 years | 15 years (renewable) |

*The copyright term is expected to be extended to life of the author + 70 years when the *US-Mexico-Canada Agreement* comes into effect, expected in 2020.

Copyright, in most cases in Canada, expires 50 years after the death of the author, though this is expected to be extended to 70 years after the death of the author when the *US-Mexico-Canada Agreement* comes into effect. Patents expire 20 years after the patent application is filed. Trademark rights can last the longest, as they can be in effect as long as the mark is used and recognized as distinguishing a product or service. A trademark registration is valid for 15 years and renewable as long as the mark is in use. Some trademarks registered in the nineteenth century are still in use; the Coca-Cola trademark was first registered in 1893.

## COPYRIGHT

### Ideas vs. Expressions

Copyright law grants authors rights in *expressions* of ideas, but does not grant rights in ideas themselves. For example, an author of an original short story about a character going out on a dark and stormy night could have copyright in their story. However, they would not have copyright over the *idea* of a character going out on a dark and stormy night; other authors are free to write stories about characters going out on dark and stormy nights using different events, different language, and so on. Stock characters, situations, and settings are not protected; only original expressions are.

## Originality

Copyright grants rights in works that are original. Under Canadian law, this does not mean that the work must be ground-breaking, high quality, or new. However, the work must originate from the author (it must not be copied from elsewhere), and it must involve a "non-mechanical and non-trivial exercise of skill and judgment."[6]

## Rights

Copyright law grants to authors the right:

- "to *produce or reproduce* the work, or any substantial part thereof;"[7]
- "to *perform* the work or any substantial part thereof in public;"[8]
- "to *publish* the work or any substantial part thereof;"[9]
- "to produce, reproduce, perform or publish any *translation* of the work;"[10]
- to *convert or adapt* works (for example, to adapt a novel into a film);[11]
- "to communicate the work to the public by *telecommunication*;"[12]
- to *publicly exhibit* an artistic work;[13]
- to *rent out* a work that is a computer program or sound recording;[14]
- to make the *first sale* of a work that is a tangible object, such as a painting;[15] and
- to *authorize* someone else to do any of these things.[16]

Copyright law also grants to authors rights known as **"moral rights,"** or the right:

- to the integrity of the work (to prevent it from being altered), and
- the right, "where reasonable in the circumstances, to be associated with the work as its author by name or under a pseudonym and the right to remain anonymous."[17]

Anyone who infringes these rights, such as by reproducing a work without the authorization of the copyright owner, can be subject to civil and criminal penalties under the *Copyright Act*.[18]

## Fair Dealing and Other Exceptions

Canadian copyright law contains many exceptions, including an important exception called fair dealing, which allows people to make uses of works without the authorization of the copyright owner. These are sometimes referred to as *user rights*.[19] There are exceptions permitting the use of an existing work to create non-commercial, user-generated content (the source of the original work should be mentioned); for private purposes (for example, to make a copy of an MP3 file you already own for private purposes, provided no digital locks are broken to do so; the original copy was not borrowed, rented, or illegally obtained; and the copy is not given away); for time-shifting (for example, recording a broadcast to watch later); and for making backup copies.[20] There are also exceptions that apply to libraries, archives, museums, and educational institutions.[21]

Fair dealing permits the use of a work, for the specific purpose of:

- research,
- private study,
- education,
- parody or satire,
- news reporting (with attribution), or
- criticism or review (with attribution).[22]

Such use is permitted only if the use is fair. The Supreme Court of Canada has outlined a six-part test to determine whether a use is fair. This test considers:

1. the purpose of the dealing (whether it was used for one of the permitted purposes of news reporting, criticism or review, research or private study, education, parody, or satire);
2. the character of the dealing (whether a single copy was made, or multiple; whether the copies were widely distributed; what the customary practices are in the trade or industry);
3. the amount of the dealing (was a trivial amount of the work taken, or was the work copied in its entirety?);
4. the alternatives to the dealing (was there a non-copyrighted equivalent work available? Could a criticism have been equally valid without reproducing a work?);
5. the nature of the work (was the work published or unpublished? Was the work confidential?); and
6. the effect of the dealing on the work (is the reproduction likely to compete, in the market, with the original work?)[23]

# PATENTS

In Canada, an invention must meet specific standards before it qualifies to be patented. The invention must be new, useful, and non-obvious. To qualify for a patent, an invention must be novel or new; it must not already exist, be known to the public, or have been previously patented.[24] It must also be useful; it must have a commercial or industrial use, and it must do what it is supposed to do. A patent for a can opener that does not open a can would be invalid.[25] Finally, to be patentable, an invention must be non-obvious; a patent on an invention that is obvious—that involved no inventive step or ingenuity—would be invalid.[26] For example, using a pressure washer to clean the inside of a distillery is an obvious (rather than an inventive) step.[27]

## Disclosure

The "bargain" of patent law is that, in exchange for patent rights, the inventor must disclose their invention to the public by registering the invention in a public database. The patent registration describes the invention in a way that could be used by someone skilled in the trade to produce the invention. In exchange for disclosing their invention, the inventor receives a monopoly on the invention for 20 years. Registration of a patent can be done through a patent agent or lawyer. A public database of all patents registered in Canada is publicly available online on the website of the Canadian Intellectual Property Office.

## Rights

A patent gives an inventor or their assignee a set of exclusive rights to make, construct, use, or sell their invention, or to authorize or license others to make, construct, use, or sell their invention.[28] Anyone who makes, constructs, uses, or sells a patented invention in Canada without such a licence or authorization can be sued for damages, subject to an injunction, or charged with an indictable offence.[29] At the same time, the sale of a patented invention exhausts the patent holder's rights to use or resell the invention, or grants an implied licence to the purchaser, such that the person who bought the invention is free to use it or resell it.[30]

## Things That Can't Be Patented

Scientific principles, abstract theorems, and the laws of nature cannot be patented.[31] Discoveries, such as the discovery of ultraviolet rays, are not patentable—though the invention of a process of using ultraviolet rays to purify water could be patentable.[32] Professional skills and methods are not patentable, such as surgical methods, or methods of medical treatment, though diagnostic methods and cosmetic surgery may be patentable.[33] Computer calculations are not patentable in Canada, though computer software can be.[34] Games are not patentable.[35] Higher life forms are also not patentable.[36]

# TRADEMARK

Trademark law grants rights over words, symbols, drawings, shapes, packaging, sounds, or colours that are used in the branding of goods and services.[37] Trademark law helps consumers know what the source of a product or service is, prevents confusion over the source of a product or service, and prevents the goodwill associated with particular brands from being misappropriated by others.[38]

## Registration

Some trademarks are registered, while others are not. The symbol ™ indicates a mark that is not registered, while the symbol ® indicates a registered mark.[39] Trademark law grants rights in both unregistered and registered marks; even if a mark is not registered, it can still be a valid trademark, recognized and protected by trademark law. Registered marks receive national protection, while unregistered marks are protected only in the region where they are used. Registration can also be helpful to an owner who seeks to claim and enforce their trademark rights.[40] Trademarks can be registered through a trademark agent or lawyer. A public database of all registered Canadian trademarks is available online on the website of the Canadian Intellectual Property Office.

## Unregistrable Marks

Some things cannot be registered as trademarks. These include, for example, the names of people; a word that is "primarily merely the names or surname of an individual" who is alive, or who died in the past 30 years, cannot be registered as a trademark unless it has become distinctive.[41] Since it is important that words typically used to describe a particular good or service must be open to use by all competitors who sell a good or service, descriptive (or mis-descriptive) words cannot be registered as a mark for selling those same products or services. For example, one cannot register the mark *BANANORANGE* to sell juice containing bananas and oranges.[42] This is because the words *banana* and *orange* must be available for other people who sell juice containing bananas and oranges; otherwise, they would not be able to describe their product. For the same reason, the actual name of a good or service, in any language, is not registrable. For example, the words *SHREDDED WHEAT* cannot be registered alone as a trademark for use in selling cereal made of shredded wheat (though a design or a longer phrase containing those words could potentially be registered).[43]

## Rights and Infringement

Registering a trademark gives the owner of the mark the exclusive right to use the mark in commerce, to be free of confusingly similar marks (to take legal action against others who are making use of marks that consumers might confuse with their own), and to take action against uses of the mark that might depreciate the goodwill associated with the mark.[44] Owners of unregistered marks (who have established ownership of the mark by using it in commerce to distinguish their goods or services from those of others) also have some rights, including the exclusive right to use the mark in association with the products or services it has become associated with, to be free of confusingly similar marks, and to take action against those who may be passing off their goods and services as those of the mark owners.[45]

# WHOM DOES INTELLECTUAL PROPERTY SERVE?

## The Public Interest?

According to the most mainstream theories, intellectual property rights are granted as a means to serve the public interest. In the case of copyright and patent law, intellectual property law serves public interests by rewarding creators and innovators for their work, encouraging creative work to be published and exhibited, and ensuring that innovations are disclosed to the public in the furtherance of science and innovation. Trademark law, for its part, serves as a form of consumer protection, ensuring that the source of products and services can be correctly identified using names, logos, and other marks. It also protects the goodwill that business owners have acquired from being appropriated by counterfeiters.

### *Pluralism*
Pluralist theories of intellectual property pose intellectual property law as a matter of "balancing" between various competing interest groups. Various

intellectual property owners' interests in protecting their intellectual property must be balanced against the interest of a wide variety of intellectual property users. This includes the interests of individual authors, artists, translators, and performers, as well as the competing interests of numerous large corporations, ranging from those who own trademarks, movie rights, rights in sound recordings, or broadcasting stations. It also includes students; educators; music, film, and television consumers; and internet users. Pluralist theories of intellectual property see no one of these interests as being completely dominant, although they do acknowledge that some groups have more resources than others.

The pluralist view of intellectual property has been, to a large extent, adopted by Canadian courts and policymakers. The Supreme Court of Canada has, in various decisions, emphasized the necessity of balancing competing interests under copyright law.[46] However, numerous scholars have questioned this portrayal of intellectual property law as being "balanced" or potentially balanceable. Alan Story argues that "balanced copyright is an oxymoron, a contradiction in terms.... Every one of the central principles or elements of copyright is one-sided and unbalanced, that is, they favour the owners of copyrighted goods."[47]

### Neoliberalism

Intellectual property law, like many areas of communication policy, is tightly tied to liberal individualism—to a legal paradigm that takes the world as made up of individuals who possess (or potentially possess) individual autonomy or free will, and that believes this free will is best supported by limiting government constraints and granting rights to individuals. Canadian legal scholar Carys Craig explains:

> The theoretical framework of intellectual property law, and copyright law in particular, is premised upon liberal and neo-liberal assumptions. At the core of copyright's functionality are the concepts of private rights, property, ownership, exclusion, and individualism. At the core of copyright's justifications are the concepts of individual entitlement or desert, on one hand, and economic rationality and self-interest on the other. Within this model, authors are individuated, proprietary personalities with a claim to ownership of their intellectual works; these works are the original, stable, and propertizable results of the authors' independent efforts.[48]

This vision of intellectual property law as a form of property justified by authors' individual creative efforts, while challenged by some feminist scholars—as we shall read below—has deepened and expanded globally over the past 125 years.

Global intellectual property law has been dramatically expanded since the 1990s. This expansion is tied to the rise of neoliberal economics—to the liberalization of trade, foreign direct investment, and international markets; the liberalization of telecommunications; and, in turn, the globalization of markets. The neoliberal economic approach emphasizes a reliance on markets and property mechanisms to drive economic development, as opposed to social planning. In the case of intellectual property, the neoliberal approach is associated with the grant of strong global intellectual property rights and enforcement. Transnational corporations' and governments' efforts to expand intellectual property regimes over geographical and digital space has supported the construction of global markets, especially in computers, communications, and data, under neoliberalism since the 1980s. According to neoliberal theory, this global expansion of intellectual property rights should drive global development, research, and innovation, thus ultimately serving the public interest, even if it may cause pain to those who cannot afford to access patented drugs or educational materials.[49]

## Bureaucracy and Bureaucrats?

### *Libertarian Theory and Bureaucratic Theory*
Libertarians are divided in their views on intellectual property rights. Most libertarians agree on, and support, property rights in things like land and possessions, and—perhaps most importantly of all—in one's own body. Some libertarians have similarly expressed support for intellectual property rights. For example, Ayn Rand viewed intellectual property rights as an extension of the property right in one's body—as property in the product of one's mind and in the fruits of one's labour.[50]

Other libertarians reject intellectual property rights, arguing that intellectual property law should be abolished. They argue that property rights should be granted only in scarce resources, and ideas are not scarce. As well, following the libertarian argument against defamation law (see Chapter 4), they argue that a person should not be able to control the ideas and speech of other people.[51] **Cyberlibertarians** have advocated the abolition of intellectual property rights. In his famous "Declaration of the Independence of Cyberspace," cyberlibertarian John Perry Barlow declared, "Your legal concepts of *property*, expression, identity, movement, and context do not apply to us. They are all based on matter, and there is no matter here."[52] Cyberlibertarians often support a vision of the free flow of information and ideas on the internet, unimpeded by intellectual property rights.

Those libertarians who oppose intellectual property argue that it promotes inefficient bureaucracy (patent offices being a prime example).[53] They argue that intellectual property law produces and requires large bureaucracies and companies that rest on their intellectual property monopolies, rather than producing competitive products.[54] Intellectual property, in this view, benefits bureaucrats at the cost of much freedom.

## The Privileged?

### Critical Political Economy

Critical political economists are often, like libertarians, critical of intellectual property law and, in some but not all cases, advocate its abolishment. Communication scholar Ronald Bettig, in *Copyrighting Culture: The Political Economy of Intellectual Property*, critiqued copyright as primarily serving to line the pockets of global entertainment multinationals, while Joost Smiers (with van Schijndel) argues that copyright, because it serves primarily multinational entertainment corporations who use it to lock up cultural monopolies, should be largely abolished.[55]

Many people once thought that the rise of downloading and the internet, beginning in the 1990s, would lead to the end of the recording industry along with copyright. Instead, copyright law adapted, making it illegal to make works under copyright available on the internet without authorization, or to break digital locks; mandating real-time surveillance of platforms, monitoring for copyright infringement; and facilitating the continued centralization of ownership of intellectual property in the hands of a few companies.[56] Rather than collapsing, the copyright system adapted to meet the needs of industry.

Numerous scholars have focused on the ways that copyright laws facilitate the exploitation of cultural labourers or employees more generally.[57] Here, copyright law is seen as part of a broader system of exploitation of labour by capital.

Copyright has also been criticized as an element of unjust international economic structures. Alan Story argues that the international intellectual property system benefits mainly intellectual property owners who are situated in rich countries while offering little to countries of the South (developing countries).[58] Economist Ha-Joon Chang, in *Kicking Away the Ladder*, argues that "developed" countries like the United States, the United Kingdom, Germany, and France have followed a path of development that was facilitated by low levels of intellectual property protection, allowing the import and emulation of foreign works and technology. However, having achieved "development," they have moved to "kick away the ladder" by insisting that developing countries today adopt high levels of intellectual property protection, thus preventing those countries from taking the same path they themselves followed.[59]

### Feminist Analysis and Queer Theory

Property relationships in general are interwoven with, and have often reinforced, gender hierarchies. Both women and property are objects of desire, sought out for possession by men.[60] In some cases, historically, a woman's property and/or wages were owned by her husband. Property ownership was required to be eligible to vote and was thus was associated with full civic personhood. Intellectual property law, similarly, has reinforced gender hierarchies and has therefore been the subject of feminist critique.

Ann Bartow and Debora Halbert have argued that copyright, while appearing gender-neutral, actually has significant gendered effects, in part because it embodies a male-centred vision of authorship, creativity, and commerce.[61] Second-wave feminists argued that culture is a masculine construction, in which women are more often situated as the inspiration for male creativity than they are as creators themselves.[62] Scientific discovery is also, most often, conducted by men in ways that focus on men's needs.[63] Bartow argues that copyright tends to recognize, and tends to be used to enforce rights in, highly successful commercial works, a field in which men, she notes, are dominant. The same thing could be said for trademark and patent law, which are used in commercial ventures and in businesses often dominated by men. Copyright, feminists note, offers less to producers of non-commercial works and to the sorts of crafts and domestic creativity that may have been traditionally produced by women.[64] In fact, much of the work that women have traditionally done in the home is not protected by any form of intellectual property law. Like other areas of communication law, intellectual property law, while appearing neutral, has a gendered history and gendered effects.

Some feminists challenge the liberal individualist assumptions that underlie intellectual property law. They challenge the assumption that creation or innovation can be attributed to a single author or inventor; after all, the skills, capacities, supportive systems—and even language itself—come from our families, friends, and the institutions around us. All creativity and innovation, they argue, is part of an ongoing dialogue and relationship between creators, innovators, and users. Intellectual property law must therefore make room for such dialogic processes, attributing value and authority to the full range of voices who participate in creative processes.[65]

Queer theory seeks to challenge the gender hierarchies and categories at play in property and intellectual property discourse. It does so in part by attempting to disrupt some of the fundamental concepts upon which property and intellectual property are built. Margaret Davies suggests disrupting the concept of the autonomous legal subject whose personhood is realized through property ownership and replacing it with a concept of property that recognizes people as constituted by relationships, rather than by independence propped up by property ownership. Davies suggests recognizing property as a relationship between people that affords responsibilities as well as rights.[66]

### Critical Race Theory and Postcolonial Analysis

Some of the most potent critiques of intellectual property law have pointed to its roots in Western conceptualizations of creativity and innovation and to its historical ties to colonialization. Copyright, as many scholars have noted, is based on Enlightenment ideals of originality and in historically and culturally constructed Western conceptualizations of the Romantic author,[67] ownership, protection of property,[68] piracy, and the public domain.[69] Each of these has roots not only in the West and Enlightenment traditions but also in cultural imperialism; the concepts in which copyright is based fail to register Indigenous forms of authorship and ownership, relegating much of the traditional knowledge and cultural expressions of Indigenous peoples to the public domain, a realm free for plunder by the West.[70]

The copyright system, paired with inequitable contracts granted to racialized people, has failed to protect racialized people from—and in fact, has facilitated—cultural appropriation; Black artists have often not received the credit or compensation for their work, which is then appropriated by white artists who have used or built on their work.[71] Such patterns play out across the field of intellectual property where, as Vats and Keller note:

> Whites have historically constructed information regimes in ways which devalue the knowledge and practices of non-whites; whites have historically held the power and authority to determine the legal structures which govern intellectual property rights; whites have historically crafted legal doctrines which favor the protection of Western understandings of creativity; and whites largely continue to manage domestic and international intellectual property rights regimes.[72]

Trademark law has done little to prevent the registration and use of racist and offensive trademarks, such as the marks of the Washington Redskins, the Cleveland Indians, or the Edmonton Eskimos. In the United States, the provisions of trademark law used to cancel the trademark registrations of the Washington Redskins were struck down as a violation of First Amendment rights.[73] In Canada, provisions prohibiting the registration of offensive trademarks remain.

It is no surprise that intellectual property has generally reinforced the hierarchies of racialization; property law in general has also reinforced these hierarchies. The law of property has historically facilitated the commodification and ownership of racial minorities as slaves, has failed to recognize Indigenous custodianship of land, and has generally situated white men as property owners.[74]

### Indigenous Theory

Copyright and patent law, like Eurocentric knowledge systems more generally, have historically taken minimal account of Indigenous and traditional knowledge and cultural expressions. In some cases, Eurocentric and colonial knowledge systems have worked to erase Indigenous knowledge and culture; in others, these systems have trivialized Indigenous science and technologies as "art." They fail to value or systematically store Indigenous knowledge, including cultural, scientific, technical, and environmental knowledge that has been passed down and improved over generations.[75] Indigenous peoples have successfully challenged many assumptions about the superiority of Western thought and systems of knowledge governance. In doing so, they have created space for the demonstration and elaboration of valuable and extensive bodies of Indigenous knowledge that have gained greater recognition in Canada and internationally.[76]

Like Eurocentric thought generally, Western intellectual property law has failed to value or protect Indigenous knowledge, often considering it to be part of the public domain. Intellectual property law has facilitated the appropriation of traditional knowledge as the "raw material" of Western creativity.[77] Profits often flow to the Western intellectual property holders, who appropriate traditional knowledge and cultural expressions as a part of their works, while the originating nations, communities, Elders, and Knowledge Keepers are left unrecognized and uncompensated.

Indigenous peoples have approaches to governing knowledge that differ, in many cases, from those embedded in the Western intellectual property system.[78] In some countries, laws have been put in place to recognize traditional communities and Indigenous peoples' rights in, and approaches to governing, Indigenous knowledge.[79] In contrast to the speed with which copyright, patent, and trademark law has been internationalized, efforts to internationalize the recognition of rights in traditional knowledge have been slow-paced, with few concrete results.[80] For this reason, the international intellectual property system has been subject to extensive postcolonial critique.[81]

### Critical Disability Theory

Critical disability theorists have noted that intellectual property law is premised on **ableist** assumptions about perception, cognition, and expression.[82] As with many areas of law, intellectual property law often rests on assumptions about an abstract person who does not have any disabilities. Thus, judicial decisions about, in the realm of trademark, what words or images might be confusing; in the realm of patent law, what "ordinary" skill or knowledge is; and, in the realm of copyright, whether a use is commercial or non-commercial (for example, in the context of a fair dealing test) all rest on assumptions about people's abilities and normative uses of things.[83] A person who does not read or perceive colour, or who perceives differently, may be confused by trademarks or may not be able to benefit from a patent disclosure in the same way as others. A person who is visually or cognitively impaired might use three-dimensional objects, such as busts or figurines, for information or education, even if such objects are usually considered as having only commercial or entertainment value.

While copyright law has in place certain exceptions that permit the making of accessible works, these provisions are limited, in part to preserve for book publishers and other copyright owners the requirement of purchase of accessible-format works, where such works are available.[84] Canadian copyright law has restricted the making of accessible versions of copyright works. Until 2016, there was no exception permitting the circumvention of digital locks in order to make a work accessible.[85] Critical disability studies scholars note that the legal system often works to serve corporate copyright owners, rather than people with disabilities.[86]

### Governmentality and Networked Governance

A broad range of actors are involved in the regulation of intellectual property; courts and legislators certainly play a role, but so do technologies. In some cases, regulation is carried out by internet service providers, who take down content that infringes copyright or inform their users of possible copyright infractions. Digital locks that stop CDs or files from being copied or keep content behind paywalls play a role in copyright enforcement. Words also matter. Words like *property* or *pirate* play a role in shaping people's ideas of themselves and their actions and in guiding the norms of behaviour.[87] Intellectual property is an excellent example of *networked governance*, or regulation by a plurality of actors.[88]

Michel Foucault's theory of governmentality points to the importance of discourse—the internalized moral, ethical, and practical norms and practices that guide behaviour, as conveyed by language such as *pirate*, *property*, or *theft*. These words, when applied to unauthorized downloading of books or songs, shape our thinking about what is possible and what is or should be permitted, as well as our thinking about what problems intellectual property law should or should not address.[89]

Foucault's theory of governmentality points to the specific *mentalities*, discursive constructions, problematizations, and concrete practices that underpin intellectual property law as a form of governance that extends beyond state power. It examines, in historical perspective, how the problems that intellectual property law is intended to address have been discursively produced and how the state came to be constructed as the solution to those problems.[90] The state has been constructed as having a role to play in the regulation of cultural and commercial production. However, the governance of creativity and innovation extends beyond the law itself to involve a multiplicity of interpersonal relationships, institutions, and tactics that enable the kind of creative work valued under a specific governance regime. Families, schools, friends, workplaces, and previous creative works all contribute to and help to produce the norms, tools, and resources of creative production of a particular governance regime.[91]

Foucault observed that the sort of author recognized and enabled through a particular governmentality may be different from that recognized under another. The status granted to authors (as the "creative genius"), and the texts that are seen as having authors (whereas most books today have authors, medieval books were not signed by specific authors) changes depending on the historical governmentality regime in place.[92]

### Technology and Geography

New technologies and globalization are often seen as the drivers of change in intellectual property law. The rise of digital and internet communications, the difficulty of preventing digital copying, the ease of transmitting copyright works over the internet, the ease of creating parodies and knock-offs of trademarked products, and the ease of reproduction using 3D printing are all pointed to as driving the need for intellectual property revision. Intellectual property owners in particular see technological change as requiring stronger intellectual property laws. Others see technological change as requiring either the abolishment of intellectual property laws or greater emphasis on sharing and exceptions to enable greater freedom to reuse and interact with intellectual property. To avoid the trap of technological determinism, it is essential to look at the political, economic, and social interests that lie behind these two points of view. It is not technology itself but rather people, institutions, and economic and social forces that shape technology and the regulatory regimes that govern technology. It is the people who have economic, social, and cultural interests in shaping technology and regulation who drive technological change.

## FURTHER READING

Boldrin, Michele, and David Levine. *Against Intellectual Monopoly.* Cambridge: Cambridge University Press, 2008.

Gervais, Daniel J., and Elizabeth F. Judge. *Intellectual Property: The Law in Canada.* 2nd ed. Toronto: Carswell, 2011.

Kratz, Martin. *Canada's Intellectual Property Law in a Nutshell.* 2nd ed. Toronto: Carswell, 2010.

Lessig, Lawrence. *Free Culture: How Big Media Uses Technology and the Law to Lock Down Culture and Control Creativity.* New York: Penguin, 2004.

Murray, Laura J., and Samuel E. Trosow. *Canadian Copyright: A Citizen's Guide.* Toronto: Between the Lines, 2013.

## NOTES

1. *Copyright Act,* RSC 1985, c C-42, s 5(1).
2. Mike Murphy, "Google Patented Building Robots with Personalities," *Quartz,* March 31, 2015, https://qz.com/373658/google-patented-building-robots-with-personalities/.
3. Elizabeth Frances Judge and Daniel J. Gervais, *Intellectual Property: The Law in Canada,* 2nd ed. (Toronto: Carswell, 2011), 317.
4. "'1586637—MAC START UP CHIME,' Canadian Trademarks Database," report, accessed October 31, 2018, https://ic.gc.ca/app/opic-cipo/trdmrks/srch/viewTrademark?id=1586637&lang=eng&tab=reg; "'0832993—TOBLERONE & DESIGN (COLOR),' Canadian Trademarks Database," report, accessed October 31, 2018, https://ic.gc.ca/app/opic-cipo/trdmrks/srch/viewTrademark?id=0832993&lang=eng&tab=reg; *Smith Kline & French Canada Ltd v Canada Registrar of Trademarks,* [1987] 2 FC 633 (FCTD); Judge and Gervais, 331–36.
5. Michele Boldrin and David K. Levine, *Against Intellectual Monopoly* (Cambridge: Cambridge University Press, 2008); Peter Drahos and John Braithwaite,

*Information Feudalism: Who Owns the Knowledge Economy* (New York: Routledge, 2017); Brian Martin, "Against Intellectual Property," *Philosophy and Social Action* 21 (1995): 7–22; Edwin C. Hettinger, "Justifying Intellectual Property," *Philosophy & Public Affairs* (1989): 31–52; Lawrence Lessig, *Free Culture: How Big Media Uses Technology and the Law to Lock Down Culture and Control Creativity* (New York: Penguin, 2004).

6.  Judge and Gervais, 55; *CCH Canadian Ltd. v Law Society of Upper Canada*, 2004 SCC 13.

7.  *Copyright Act*, s 3(1).

8.  Ibid.

9.  Ibid.

10. *Copyright Act*, s 3(1)(a).

11. *Copyright Act*, s 3(1)(b, c, and e).

12. *Copyright Act*, s 3(1)(f).

13. *Copyright Act*, s 3(1)(g).

14. *Copyright Act*, s 3(1)(h–i).

15. *Copyright Act*, s 3(1)(j).

16. *Copyright Act*, s 3(1).

17. Ibid., s 14.1 (1).

18. Ibid., Part IV.

19. Myra J. Tawfik, "The Supreme Court of Canada and the Fair Dealing Trilogy: Elaborating a Doctrine of User Rights under Canadian Copyright Law," *Alberta Law Review* 51 (2013): 191.

20. *Copyright Act*, ss 29–29.24.

21. Ibid., ss 29.3–29.30.5.

22. Ibid., ss 29–29.2.

23. *CCH Canadian Ltd v Law Society of Upper Canada* at 54–60.

24. Judge and Gervais, 652, 708–24. A grace period applies.

25. Ibid., 724.

26. *Patent Act*, RSC 1985, c P-4, s 28.3; Judge and Gervais, 735–48.

27. Canadian Intellectual Property Office (CIPO) Government of Canada, "Manual of Patent Office Practice (MOPOP)—Canadian Intellectual Property Office," s 15.02.02e, accessed October 31, 2018, https://www.ic.gc.ca/eic/site/cipointernet-internetopic.nsf/eng/h_wr00720.html.

28. *Patent Act*, s 42.

29. *Patent Act*, ss 55, 57, and 75.

30. Jeremy de Beer and Robert Tomkowicz, "Exhaustion of Intellectual Property Rights in Canada," *Canadian Intellectual Property Review* 25 (2009): 3–31.

31. *Patent Act*, s 27(8); Judge and Gervais, 654, 657.

32. Judge and Gervais, 658–59.

33. Ibid.

34. Stacy Rush, Giselle Chin, and Andrew Kaikai, "Software Patent Eligibility in Canada: IP Year in Review," *Canadian Lawyer Mag*, December 29, 2016, https://www.canadianlawyermag.com/article/software-patent-eligibility-in-canada-ip-year-in-review-3474/; CIPO, "MOPOP."

35. CIPO, "MOPOP," s 12.03.09.

36. Judge and Gervais, 671–703.

37. Ibid., 317.

38. Ibid., 318.

39. These symbols have no legal significance in Canada, but American law requires their use. Dave Macdonell, "How to Use the TM and R Symbols—Trademark Registration," *The Trademark Group—Trademark Registration* (blog), September 18, 2012, https://trademarkshop.ca/trademark-symbols/.

40. Judge and Gervais, 321–22.

41. *Trade-Marks Act*, RSC 1985, c T-13, s 12(1)(a); Judge and Gervais, 344.

42. *Trade-Marks Act*, s 12(1)(b); *Lassonde Inc v Canada (Registrar of Trade-marks)* (2000), 5 CPR (4th) 517, 180 FTR 177 (Fed TD), affirmed (2001), 281 NR 365 (Fed CA); Judge and Gervais, 355.

43. *Trade-Marks Act*, c T-13, s 12(1)(c); Judge and Gervais, 371.

44. *Trade-marks Act*, ss 19, 20, and 22; Martin P.J. Kratz, *Canada's Intellectual Property Law in a Nutshell*, 2nd ed. (Toronto: Carswell, 2010), 137.

45. *Trade-marks Act*, s 7; Kratz, 158.

46. *Théberge v Galerie d'Art du Petit Champlain Inc*, 2002 SCC 34; *CCH Canadian Ltd. v Law Society of Upper Canada*.

47. Alan Story, "'Balanced' Copyright: Not a Magic Solving Word," *Intellectual Property Watch* (blog), February 27, 2012, www.ip-watch.org/2012/02/27/%e2%80%98balanced%e2%80%99-copyright-not-a-magic-solving-word/. See also Drahos, "Six Minutes to Midnight: Can Intellectual Property Save the World?"

48. Carys J. Craig, "Reconstructing the Author-Self: Some Feminist Lessons for Copyright Law," *Journal of Gender, Social Policy and the Law* 15, no. 2 (2007): 208.

49. Margaret Chon, "Intellectual Property and the Development Divide," *Cardozo Law Review* 27, no. 6 (2005): 2853.

50. Ayn Rand, *Capitalism: The Unknown Ideal* (New York: Signet Books, 2007).

51. N. Stephan Kinsella, "Against Intellectual Property," *Journal of Libertarian Studies* 15, no. 2; SEAS SPR (2001): 1–54; N. Stephan Kinsella, "Intellectual Property and Libertarianism," *Liberty* 23, no. 11 (2009): 27–46.

52. John Perry Barlow, "A Declaration of the Independence of Cyberspace," Electronic Frontier Foundation, January 20, 2016, https://www.eff.org/cyberspace-independence. Emphasis added.

53. Kinsella, "Against Intellectual Property."

54. Butler Shaffer, *A Libertarian Critique of Intellectual Property* (Auburn, AL: Mises Institute, 2013), 42–49, https://mises.org/library/libertarian-critique-intellectual-property.

55. Ronald V. Bettig, *Copyrighting Culture: The Political Economy of Intellectual Property* (New York: Routledge, 2018); Joost Smiers and Marieke van Schijndel, *Imagine There Is No Copyright and No Cultural Conglomerates Too: An Essay*, vol. 4 (Morrisville, NC: Lulu.com, 2009).

56. Derek Hrynyshyn, *The Limits of the Digital Revolution: How Mass Media Culture Endures in a Social Media World* (Santa Barbara, CA: Praeger, 2017), chap. 6; Nick Srnicek, *Platform Capitalism* (Cambridge: Polity, 2017).

57. Matt Stahl, "From Seven Years to 360 Degrees: Primitive Accumulation, Recording Contracts, and the Means of Making a (Musical) Living," *TripleC: Cognition, Communication, Co-Operation* 9, no. 2 (2011): 668–88; Christian Fuchs, "A Contribution to the Critique of the Political Economy of Google," *Fast Capitalism* 8, no. 1 (2011): 1–24.

58. Christopher May, *The Global Political Economy of Intellectual Property Rights: The New Enclosures* (New York: Routledge, 2015); Story.

59. Ha-Joon Chang, *Kicking Away the Ladder: Development Strategy in Historical Perspective* (London: Anthem Press, 2002).

60. Margaret Davies, "Queer Property, Queer Persons: Self-Ownership and Beyond," *Social & Legal Studies* 8, no. 3 (September 1999): 338, https://doi.org/10.1177/096466399900800303.

61. Ann Bartow, "Fair Use and the Fairer Sex: Gender, Feminism, and Copyright Law," *American University Journal of Gender, Social Policy & the Law* 14, no. 3 (2006): 551–84; Debora Halbert, "Feminist Interpretations of Intellectual Property," *Journal of Gender, Social Policy and the Law* 14, no. 3 (2006): 431–60.

62. Halbert, 435–36.

63. Ibid., 437.

64. Bartow.

65. Craig.

66. Davies, 345.

67. Martha Woodmansee and Peter Jaszi, *The Construction of Authorship: Textual Appropriation in Law and Literature* (Durham, NC: Duke University Press, 1994); Brad Sherman, "From the Non-Original to the Ab-Original: A History," in *Of Authors*

*and Origins*, eds. Brad Sherman and Alain Strowel (New York: Oxford University Press, 1994); Roland Barthes, "The Death of the Author," *Contributions in Philosophy* 83 (2001): 3–8; Michel Foucault, "What Is an Author?" *Screen* 20, no. 1 (March 1, 1979): 13–34, https://doi.org/10.1093/screen/20.1.13.

68. Rosemary J. Coombe and Andrew Herman, "Rhetorical Virtues: Property, Speech, and the Commons on the World-Wide Web," *Anthropological Quarterly* 77, no. 3 (2004): 559–74; Jessica Silbey, *The Eureka Myth: Creators, Innovators, and Everyday Intellectual Property* (Stanford: Stanford University Press, 2014); Laura Murray, "Protecting Ourselves to Death: Canada, Copyright, and the Internet," *First Monday* 9, no. 10 (2004).

69. Eva Hemmungs Wirtén, *Terms of Use: Negotiating the Jungle of the Intellectual Commons* (Toronto: University of Toronto Press, 2008); Sherman; Adrian Johns, *Piracy: The Intellectual Property Wars from Gutenberg to Gates* (Chicago: University of Chicago Press, 2010).

70. Wirtén; Madhavi Sunder, "The Invention of Traditional Knowledge," *Law and Contemporary Problems* 70, no. 2 (2007): 97–124.

71. Toni Lester, "Blurred Lines—Where Copyright Ends and Cultural Appropriation Begins—The Case of Robin Thicke versus Bridgeport Music, and the Estate of Marvin Gaye," *Hastings Communications and Entertainment Law Journal* 36, no. 2 (2014): 217–42. But see Toni Lester, "Oprah, Beyonce, and the Girls Who Run the World—Are Black Female Cultural Producers Gaining Ground in Intellectual Property Law?" *Wake Forest Journal of Business & Intellectual Property Law* 15 (2014): 537.

72. Anjali Vats and Deidre A. Keller, "Critical Race IP," *Cardozo Arts & Entertainment Law Journal* 36, no. 3 (2018): 759.

73. Roxanne Goodon, "An Update on Disparaging Marks," Intellectual Property Institute of Canada, February 8, 2018, https://ipic.ca/english/blog/an-update-on-disparaging-marks-2018-02-08.htm; Lauren Blaiwais and Scott Miller, "Offensive Trademarks: The Canadian and American Perspectives," *Intellectual Property Journal* 30, no. 2 (2018): 205–15; Tamara Céline Winegust, Noelle Engle-Hardy, and Susan J. Keri, "Redskins, Eskimos, and Indians: The Canadian Approach to Disparaging Trademarks," *Trademark Rep.* 105 (2015): 938.

74. Davies, 329.

75. Marie Battiste, "Indigenous Knowledge: Foundations for First Nations," *World Indigenous Nations Higher Education Consortium-WINHEC Journal* (2005): 2.

76. Ibid., 4–5.

77. Sunder.

78. Rob McMahon, Amanda Almond, Greg Whistance-Smith, Diana Steinhauer, Stewart Steinhauer, and Diane P. Janes, "Sweetgrass AR: Exploring Augmented Reality as a Resource for Indigenous–Settler Relations," *International Journal of Communication* 13 (2019): 4540–41.

79. Chidi Oguamanam, *International Law and Indigenous Knowledge: Intellectual Property, Plant Biodiversity, and Traditional Medicine* (Toronto: University of Toronto Press, 2006); Peter Drahos, *Intellectual Property, Indigenous People and Their Knowledge* (Cambridge: Cambridge University Press, 2014).

80. Sara Bannerman, *International Copyright and Access to Knowledge* (Cambridge: Cambridge University Press, 2016).

81. Andreas Rahmatian, "Neo-Colonial Aspects of Global Intellectual Property Protection," *The Journal of World Intellectual Property* 12, no. 1 (2009): 40–74; Sunder; Sherman; Pradip Thomas and F. Nyamnjoh, "Intellectual Property Challenges in Africa: Indigenous Knowledge Systems and the Fate of Connected Worlds," *Indigenous Knowledge Systems and Intellectual Property in the Twenty-First Century: Perspectives from Southern Africa,* (Oxford: African Books Collective, 2007), 12; Ruth L. Okediji, "The International Relations of Intellectual Property: Narratives of Developing Country Participation in the Global Intellectual Property System," *Singapore Journal of International & Comparative Law* 7 (2003): 315.

82. Eric E. Johnson, "Intellectual Property's Need for a Disability Perspective," *George Mason University Civil Rights Law Journal* 20 (2009): 189–90.

83. Ibid.

84. *Copyright Act*, s 32.

85. OpenCanada, "How the Marrakesh Treaty Makes the Intellectual Property System More Inclusive," accessed February 17, 2019, https://www.opencanada.org/features/how-marrakesh-treaty-makes-intellectual-property-system-more-inclusive/. See also Katie Ellis and Mike Kent, *Disability and New Media* (New York: Routledge, 2011), 133–37.

86. Ibid.

87. James Meese, *Authors, Users, and Pirates: Copyright Law and Subjectivity* (Cambridge, MA: MIT Press, 2018).

88. Drahos.

89. Chris Dent, "Copyright, Governmentality and Problematisation," *Griffith Law Review* 18, no. 1 (January 2009): 129–50, https://doi.org/10.1080/10383441.2009.10854633.

90. Ibid.

91. Ibid.

92. Foucault.

# 8 Telecommunications Regulation

## INTRODUCTION

Telecommunications, whether telegraph, telephone, or the internet, are the networks that link people together. They provide the means for families, communities, publics, and politics to bridge great distances. They are also the foundation upon which the global operations of electronic capitalism are built; they provide the networks that allow transnational businesses, internet communication, and global media to operate.[1] Sometimes, as we shall see, visions about the future of how telecommunications networks could operate conflict. This makes telecommunications regulation a hotly contested arena. To what extent should telecommunications be provided as a public service? Should telecom operators be allowed to interfere in network communications? If so, under what circumstances should this be permitted?

The telecommunications industry, and telecom regulation, has undergone massive change. Once a highly regulated industry built on public monopoly service provision, it was deregulated in the 1980s and 1990s. This sparked new technological innovations, including the development of the internet. Liberalization challenged the principles of universal service, national flagship enterprise, and the stable labour conditions that had come with monopoly service provision. Deregulation was tied to the rise of the neoliberal economic regime and a free trade agenda that saw the liberalization of the cross-border provision of telecommunications products and, to some extent, telecommunications services.

Telecommunications regulation serves as the basis on which some elements of internet regulation have been built. Chapter 10 will examine internet regulation. In this chapter, we explore the regulation of landline telephones, mobile phone services, and the provision of data network services.

This chapter starts by defining telecommunications and discussing the history of telecommunications regulation in Canada. It then reviews the major forms of telecommunications regulation, from basic service and price regulation to the regulation of spectrum and foreign ownership of telecommunications services. In the second half, it asks, "Whom does Canadian telecommunications policy serve?", drawing on the theories introduced in Chapter 1.

## WHAT ARE TELECOMMUNICATIONS?

To "telecommunicate" is to communicate over distance. **Telecommunications services** are services that permit the transmission of communication—whether voice, images, or data—over a distance by radio or wire.[2] These include mobile phone, landline, data, and internet services.

## WHO REGULATES?

The CRTC regulates telecommunication companies by granting, renewing, and reviewing telecom licences, and by creating the rules that govern them. For example, the CRTC enforces the *Unsolicited Telecommunications Rules* and the *National Do Not Call List*.

The CRTC regularly revokes telecommunication licences from companies that fail to follow the rules, especially annual reporting requirements. Corporations that are caught operating telecommunications services without a licence can be fined up to $500,000 for a first offence or $1 million for a subsequent offence.[3]

## WHAT JUSTIFIES TELECOMMUNICATIONS REGULATION?

The objectives of telecommunications law and policy in Canada are outlined in the *Telecommunications Act*. They are:

a.  to facilitate the orderly development throughout Canada of a telecommunications system that serves to safeguard, enrich and strengthen the social and economic fabric of Canada and its regions;

b.  to render reliable and affordable telecommunications services of high quality accessible to Canadians in both urban and rural areas in all regions of Canada;

c.   to enhance the efficiency and competitiveness, at the national and international levels, of Canadian telecommunications;

d.   to promote the ownership and control of Canadian carriers by Canadians;

e.   to promote the use of Canadian transmission facilities for telecommunications within Canada and between Canada and points outside Canada;

f.   to foster increased reliance on market forces for the provision of telecommunications services and to ensure that regulation, where required, is efficient and effective;

g.   to stimulate research and development in Canada in the field of telecommunications and to encourage innovation in the provision of telecommunications services;

h.   to respond to the economic and social requirements of users of telecommunications services; and

i.   to contribute to the protection of the privacy of persons.[4]

Three main reasons are typically given to justify the regulation of Canadian telecommunications. They are:

1.   **Competition:** to encourage competition and address market failure,
2.   **Technological determinism:** to address technological requirements such as spectrum scarcity, and
3.   **Technological nationalism:** to foster Canadian ownership and control of telecommunications services.

## Competition

Since 2006, Canadian telecommunications policy has focused on encouraging competition in the provision of services. Economic regulation (regulation of prices or competition) is being pared back and is now justified only in limited circumstances.

A Telecommunications Policy Review Panel was commissioned in 2005 by the federal government. The panel recommended that the *Telecommunications Act* should be revised to hasten **deregulation** of Canadian telecommunications and that market forces should be relied upon. Although the objectives of the *Telecommunications Act* have not been revised, following the report of the panel in 2006, the federal government directed the CRTC to "rely on market forces to the maximum extent feasible."[5] As a result of the federal government's order, telecommunications regulation, such as pricing regulations for telephone services, has been cut back. The existence of competitive market forces as a means to address the needs of Canadians is used to justify deregulation. Where regulation exists, it must clearly address one of the objectives of the *Telecommunications Act*.[6] Under this policy, economic regulation should be used only to address market failure. In 2019, this policy direction was updated, placing less emphasis on market forces.

**Market failure** is an occasion where the market does not "provide the optimum level of production or quality of product or service."[7] For example, market failure exists when insufficient competition exists in a region for the provision of competitive telecommunications services. This market failure justifies the regulation of consumer prices for telephone services, preventing monopoly telecommunication companies from making unreasonable rate increases.[8]

## Technological Determinism

Technological requirements and developments have often been used to justify both the regulation and deregulation of telecommunications. The licensing of the wireless spectrum used to transmit wireless telephone and data signals has been justified as necessary for ensuring that multiple players do not try to transmit signals on the same frequency, thus causing interference. The need to maintain the integrity of telecommunications equipment and networks was also used as a justification for the maintenance of a regulated monopoly system in Canada and many other countries. Today, the pace of technological change is used as a justification for deregulation of telecommunications, to permit markets to move quickly, allow new entrants, and respond to technological innovation.[9]

## Technological Nationalism

Communications technologies have often been seen as crucial to the construction of Canada and a sense of Canadian nationhood. Just as broadcasting technologies have been seen as playing a role in binding together, creating space for, and/or producing "Canadian" people, so have telecommunications technologies been considered important to the construction of Canada. Nationalism is one reason for the Canadian ownership and control requirements built into the *Telecommunications Act*.

However, given the extent that economic and communication networks are networked between Canada and the United States, Canadian communications scholar Robert E. Babe has argued that "Canada as a nation persists despite, not because of, communication media."[10] Historically, telegraph and telephone lines were constructed to link Canadian centres with big American cities. Satellite technologies facilitated the globalization of culture, permitting access to communications around the world.[11] Canadian internet traffic travels through the United States and beyond, even between Canadian users and sites.[12]

Nationalist telecommunications policies, such as restrictions on foreign ownership, are often justified by reference to national security. Hacking or cyber-attacks, it is argued, are better addressed by Canadian companies than by foreign countries. The security and privacy of Canadians' personal information and messages are sometimes linked to Canadian ownership and control of telecommunications.[13] Cybersecurity is also a potential reason to bar foreign telecommunications providers from offering services in Canada. The Chinese telecommunications company Huawei has been barred from supplying 5G telecommunications equipment in several countries due to concerns about its close ties to the Chinese government and the Chinese Communist Party. Some argue that the company should also be barred in Canada; as of this writing, no ban has been put in place.[14]

## WHAT IS A COMMON CARRIER?

For much of history, telecommunication companies provided the means of communications, but did not supply, censor, edit, prioritize, or otherwise involve themselves with the content of those communications. The content and the carriage of that content were provided separately, and telecommunication companies offered carriage to all communications without discrimination. This is known as the *common carrier principle*: Carriage was open to "the common," or all people and communications on a non-discriminatory basis.[15] That is, telecommunications services would be offered to all without discrimination as to the sender, recipient, or the contents of the communications.

The term **common carrier** is drawn from the realm of transportation. A *common carrier* is a person or company that transports goods or passengers on regular routes at set rates, such as on a bus or in an airplane.

The *Telecommunications Act* states, "except where the [CRTC] approves otherwise, a Canadian carrier shall not control the content or influence the meaning or purpose of telecommunications carried by it for the public."[16] Moreover it states, "No Canadian carrier shall, in relation to the provision of a telecommunications service or the charging of a rate for it, unjustly discriminate or give an undue or unreasonable preference toward any person, including itself, or subject any person to an undue or unreasonable disadvantage."[17]

The principle of common carriage forms the basis for a related principle, to be explored in Chapter 10; network neutrality is the principle that computer networks and internet providers should not prioritize, slow, or block messages based on their origin or content.

## WHAT IS CONVERGENCE?

Prior to the 1990s, telecommunications services provided common carriage for voice/telephone and data (such as company internal networks or internet services). They did not provide content or media. The opposite was also true; broadcast companies did not provide telecommunication services. However, beginning around the 1990s, the distinction between telecommunications companies and broadcast companies began to blur. For example, Rogers, up to that point a broadcast distribution and media company, entered the telecommunications market, providing mobile phone and internet services. Telus, up to then a telecommunications company providing retail phone services, entered the broadcasting market. Both telecommunications companies (such as Bell) and media companies (such as Rogers) began to offer internet access services. This blurring of lines between telecommunications and broadcast or media companies is known as convergence. Convergence also happens on devices; smartphones now offer access to both broadcast media and telecommunications services.

### Challenges to the Common Carrier Concept

Convergence challenges the principle of common carriage, because companies that offer telecommunications services might decide to prefer their own broadcasting content for delivery to their smartphone services. Convergence raises all kinds of questions: Should phone companies be able to provide special content to their customers on smartphones? Is it fine for a phone company to provide exclusive access to certain sports content that it owns, such that only the company's customers can access it? Should internet companies (considered telecom companies) be able to give faster access to certain content or block content? These are all cases where telecommunications or internet companies cross over and take an editorial role, breaking the common carrier principle. When companies try to do these things, the principle of common carriage is eroded.

Common carriage is important because it permits anyone to access the means of communication without censorship. It prevents communications companies from taking an unfair advantage in the market by giving preference to their own media content. Even more important, as Canadian communications scholar Dwayne Winseck argues, the principle of common carriage protects freedom of expression. Many critics argue that "media freedoms belong to those who own the media because citizens' access to the media is entirely dependent on [media companies'] discretion."[18] In contrast, "the common-carrier principle prevents private arrogation of freedom of expression by erecting barriers to censorship by the state and private interests."[19]

## HISTORY OF TELECOMMUNICATIONS REGULATION IN CANADA

Canada has been at the centre of many of the most significant developments in the history of telecommunications. Canadian Alexander Graham Bell patented the telephone and transmitted voice by wire in 1877. The first transatlantic radio link was established by Guglielmo Marconi between what would become the Canadian province of Newfoundland and the British coast in 1901.[20]

### The Telephone

In 1878, the telephone was introduced in Canada, two years after it was invented by Alexander Graham Bell. Initially, two companies competed to provide telephone services in major Canadian cities.[21] In 1880, Bell took over telephone services and held an unregulated monopoly.[22] Bell was given the right to manufacture telephone/telegraph equipment to operate telephone systems and to construct telephone lines along public rights of way.[23] Bell also made agreements with the Canadian Pacific Railroad Company to construct lines along the railway in exchange for free phone services.[24] However, in 1885, Bell's patent on the telephone was declared void by the Canadian government, and other companies began offering competing services.[25]

### The Beginning of Telecommunication Regulation

While telecommunications in Canada was regulated beginning in 1852 with the *Electric Telegraph Act*, such regulation was minimal.[26] In 1898, the Supreme

Court of Canada determined that telecommunications was a federal matter.[27] In 1906, the Board of Railway Commissioners (BRC) was mandated to regulate Canadian telephone systems under the *Railway Act*.[28] The *Railway Act* regulated the interconnection of phone companies, the technical standards, the tolls companies paid each other, and prices—sometimes demanding lower prices for rural users.[29]

## Monopolization

By 1916, nearly 1,700 telecommunications companies existed, alongside provincial monopoly services in Manitoba, Saskatchewan, and Alberta.[30] However, a decision of the BRC that year would virtually impose a monopoly system nationwide. The BRC refused to order Bell to permit independent phone companies to interconnect to the Bell long-distance system after Bell had refused to grant such a connection.[31] This decision, backed up by the Supreme Court of Canada, meant that independent telephone operators were cut off from the long-distance network and could not provide long-distance service. As a result, competition in the Canadian telecommunications market disappeared in favour of a set of geographical monopolies.[32] The last competing phone company had disappeared by 1925, though non-competing companies continued to thrive.[33]

## National Integration

In 1932, the TransCanada Telephone System (TCTS; later known as Stentor) formed with the purpose of integrating national telephone services into a cross-Canada long-distance network.[34] Its members were the major provincial telephone companies. TCTS worked as the national lobby organization for its membership, set technical standards and performance indicators, coordinated rates, and discouraged competition.[35]

## Natural Monopoly

Between 1916 and the 1980s, the idea that the telecommunications industry naturally tended toward monopoly, or that there was a "natural monopoly," was dominant. This idea justified the policy decisions that structured Canadian telecommunications around monopoly provision for decades.

Several arguments were made in support of "natural monopoly" in telecommunications.

### Network Effects

First, when telephone networks competed, they sometimes refused to interconnect with each other. Subscribers to one network could not call subscribers of another network. This meant people always wanted to join the biggest phone network, which tended to lead to a monopoly, as the biggest network bought the smaller players.

It is desirable to have a telephone system in which everyone can connect to each other. There are two possible ways of bringing this about. First, it can be done by permitting monopolies to form. This was the solution that dominated in Canada between 1916 and the 1980s. Second, it is also possible to permit people on different competing networks to connect to each other by putting in place interconnection requirements, forcing any network operator to grant access to its networks to users of other systems. This second option, currently in place, permits the existence of multiple networks, while also allowing everyone to connect to each other.[36]

### Economies of Scale

There are tremendous costs associated with building a network. Even if a new entrant to the market is able to interconnect with an existing player, the costs of starting up its own network could include, in the case of landlines, the costs of digging trenches for cable, stringing up wires on poles, or, in the case of wireless or cellular technologies, buying licences to use wireless transmission frequencies. These costs must be met before acquiring customers. Thus, it is easier for an existing company to expand to new regions, scaling up, by drawing on the fees paid by its current customers, than it is for a new entrant with no customers to start up a service.[37] These economies of scale further justified the idea of a natural monopoly in telecommunications.

Eventually, this logic broke down. **Wholesale access** (the ability of competitors to obtain access to existing networks) and leased capacity to networks (the ability of competitors to lease network capacity) allowed competition to thrive, circumventing economies of scale by reducing competitors' need to build new networks. Universal service funds were established in Canada and the United States, to which all telecommunications companies contributed. This ensured the subsidized provision of telecommunications services in rural areas would continue, even in a competitive context.

### Economies of Density

In dense urban areas, it is less expensive to construct networks because cables and phone lines can be much shorter and fewer cell towers are needed. It is much more expensive to provide network services in rural areas, where distances from a central exchange and between residences are much longer. The urban market would thus attract competitors, while the rural market would not. The dominant providers argued that the monopoly system allowed the money earned in cities to subsidize rural or poorer areas. Permitting other providers to compete in urban areas would siphon off profits, reducing the amount available to subsidize the rest of the network. This, too, was used to justify monopoly provision of telecommunications services.[38]

### Systems Integrity

Telecommunications companies also argued that they required end-to-end control over the telecommunication system in order to protect the equipment and to ensure the integrity and uninterrupted operation of telecommunications. In the 1980s and 1990s, this logic broke down. Interconnection requirements solved the problem of network effects, ensuring that no matter which telephone system a subscriber joined, they could connect with subscribers on other networks. Despite the loss of end-to-end technical control of the networks by monopoly providers, the operation of the telecommunications system was uninterrupted. In fact, the freedom to connect outside companies' technologies to the network would lead to significant technological developments such as the modem and, ultimately, the internet. Monopoly providers had arguably had the capability to develop internet services and other innovations, but had been content to collect monopoly rents, with no real incentive to innovate.[39]

## Deregulation

As the dominance of the natural monopoly concept faded, the CRTC would oversee the deregulation of Canadian telecommunications, beginning in 1976.[40] That year, responsibility for telecommunications regulation had been transferred to the CRTC from the Canadian Transport Commission, which had taken responsibility for telecommunications in 1936.[41]

The rising international free trade agenda was partly responsible for the shift in policy from monopoly to competition. Former monopoly providers saw competition in their markets as an acceptable trade-off for the ability to raise rates and compete in foreign markets.[42]

## Breakup of Monopoly System

By the 1980s, the monopoly system of telecommunications service provision began to break up in favour of a model of relatively free market competition. The breakup of the monopoly system occurred in several steps.

The Canadian National Canadian Pacific (CNCP, a telegraph company that was transforming itself into a telecommunications company) was granted the right to interconnect with phone company lines for the purposes of private-line voice and data services and dial-up data service, permitting competition to occur. However, monopoly providers still controlled the market in other telecommunications services and devices. Prior to 1982, attaching unauthorized equipment to the monopoly network was not permitted. In 1982, the CRTC changed the rule to allowed other equipment to attach to the monopoly network.[43] This opened the door to the possibility of competition in telecommunications devices, and markets in numerous devices flourished, including fax machines, answering machines, and modems.

In 1992, the CRTC also allowed competition in long-distance markets. They had opened the door to the idea in a previous 1985 decision but had not approved any competitor. In 1992, they approved Unitel (now AT&T) as a competitor in long-distance services.

In 1993, the federal government passed a new *Telecommunications Act*, which included "increased reliance on market forces for the provision of telecommunications services" as one of its objectives.[44]

## Free Trade in Telecommunications

In 1986, negotiations began between the governments of Canada and the United States, culminating in the 1987 *Canada–US Free Trade Agreement* (CUSFTA). In 1994 the *North American Free Trade Agreement* (NAFTA) came into effect, and in 1995, the *General Agreement on Trade in Services* (GATS) came into effect under the World Trade Organization (WTO). The GATS, as NAFTA and CUSFTA before it, distinguishes between basic telecommunications services (such as phone service) and enhanced telecommunications services (such as email, voicemail, or online databases), requiring countries to permit foreign competition in the provision of the latter.[45] These agreements opened telecom markets to international competition. They would prevent monopoly providers from squeezing out competition in competitive areas like long distance.[46] These measures led to the introduction of competition, most prominently in the provision of long-distance services; for the first time, many Canadians had a choice among long-distance providers. Rather than paying by-the-minute for long-distance service, they could now choose long-distance providers offering flat-rate plans.

It was not until 1998 that the Canadian monopoly system was more fully broken up, and not just in long distance. BCTel and Telus, which had previously operated in Western Canada, merged to put together a national network that would compete with Bell to provide telephone service in the east. Bell, having operated previously in Ontario, Quebec, and the Northwest Territories, entered the markets in Alberta and British Columbia. As a result, the Stentor alliance broke up.[47]

Since 1994, the provision of telecommunication services in Canada has been increasingly governed by competition. However, some argue there is still not enough competition to ensure the provision of low-cost telecommunication services.

## CURRENT REGULATIONS

### 2006: Cabinet Direction

In 2006, the federal Cabinet directed the CRTC to "rely on market forces to the maximum extent feasible."[48] Therefore, in telecom markets where there is competition, the CRTC has lifted regulation, including much of the price regulation that formerly applied to providers of telecommunications services.[49] However, telecommunications services continue to be regulated in several respects, discussed below. These include price regulation of basic telephone services (in limited cases) and regulations that ensure fair competition in the telecommunications market, as well as consumer protection initiatives.

### Price Regulation

In some cases, the CRTC limits the prices of basic telephone services. This is called **price-cap regulation**, which replaced the rate-of-profit regime that had existed until 1997.[50] Under it, the prices of a basket of services considered "basic" are regulated. **Basic services** include individual touchtone landline service, dial-up internet access, 9-1-1 access, operator and directory assistance, and long-distance calling.[51] In markets where there is sufficient competition, the CRTC forbears (refrains) from regulating the price of basic services.[52] The CRTC is, as of this writing, in the process of reviewing the basic service and price-cap regimes,[53] and in light of what it sees as near-ubiquitous access to basic services, has recently shifted the focus of basic service provision to broadband access.[54]

### Competition

The Canadian telecommunications regime has, since the 1990s, encouraged competition in telecommunications services primarily by reducing regulations that had prevented competition and encouraged monopoly services. It has also put in place measures intended to encourage and protect competition.

Still, at the level of infrastructure, there is less competition in Canada; many companies operate by using the same underlying network.[55] Most Canadians are served by one telephone network and one cable network; they can choose to purchase internet and telephone landline services that operate over cable or over the landline network. Although there may be no competition among cable companies in the same area, the telephone company (often offering DSL internet service) and the cable company compete in offering internet services. This is known as *facilities-based competition*, where competition takes place between different types of networks, such as cable and telephone.[56] Wireless infrastructure is also concentrated among a few players. Most Canadians can, as of this writing, choose between four wireless networks: Bell, Rogers, Telus, and a regional carrier. Bell, Rogers, and Telus's subsidiaries—Virgin, Fido, and Koodo respectively—share their parents' networks.[57]

### Undue Preference

The *Telecommunications Act* says that no Canadian carrier shall "unjustly discriminate or give an undue or unreasonable preference toward any person, including itself, or subject any person to an undue or unreasonable disadvantage."[58] The CRTC is charged with enforcing this provision.

With **vertical integration**—the ownership of both content and the means of transmitting that content by a single entity—there is a danger that distributers, whether telecommunications companies, broadcast companies, or internet companies, may give preferential treatment to their own content. A distributor may do so by providing that content only to its own customers or by charging less for its own content than it charges for competitors' content.

For example, in 2011, Bell had made a deal with the National Hockey League and the National Football League to offer their games exclusively on Bell cellphones. Telus complained. In December 2011, the CRTC ruled that Bell had given itself an unfair advantage.

The chairman of the CRTC said, "Canadians shouldn't be forced to buy a mobile device from a specific company or subscribe to its internet service simply to access their favourite television programs."[59] The CRTC tried to force Bell to sublicense the rights to the games to other carriers, but Bell did not have the rights to sublicense the content.[60]

In 2017, the CRTC directed Vidéotron, a Quebec-based telecommunications company, to cease its practice of exempting a particular music streaming program from data charges.[61] Such practices are seen as inhibiting competition by disadvantaging customers who use, or want to use, other content and the providers of other music services.[62]

### Wholesale Access

As an alternative to the formidable cost of constructing a new national wireless network, new cellphone companies must obtain access to the existing national wireless networks of Bell, Rogers, and Telus, which allow the new entrants' customers to "roam" on the national carriers' networks. This form of access to a national carrier's network is called wholesale access. In 2015, the CRTC examined whether the national carriers (Bell, Rogers, and Telus) were providing wholesale access to their competitors at competitive rates and found evidence of "rates and ... terms that would not prevail in a competitive market."[63] The CRTC therefore decided to regulate wholesale wireless prices.[64]

The CRTC also regulates wholesale prices for wireline (landline or broadband) services. While this form of regulation is in the process of being phased out for older copper telephone landline services, a regulatory regime remains in place for broadband.[65]

### Foreign Ownership

While free trade in telecommunications services has allowed foreign telecommunications companies to compete in the Canadian market, the rules of free trade agreements have not prohibited Canadian ownership requirements in telecom. As of this writing, foreign ownership of telecommunications companies is limited to 46.7 *percent*.[66] Some have suggested that one way of increasing competition in the Canadian wireless market is to reduce foreign ownership limits and thus permit a foreign-owned mobile service provider to compete in the Canadian market. Along these lines, in 2012, the Canadian government announced that it would exempt telecommunications companies that have less than a 10 percent share of the Canadian telecommunications market, in order to encourage limited foreign entrants.[67]

### Spectrum Management

In order for cellular telephone and wireless service carriers to operate, they must acquire the use of **spectrum** over which they can send their wireless signals. The process of allocating and managing the use of radio spectrum is called **spectrum management**. The federal government manages spectrum, in part, by licensing the use of spectrum to carriers.

The main way of allocating spectrum to companies in Canada has histori-cally been a comparative selection process whereby the government would issue a "Call for Licence Applications." The government would then evaluate the writ-ten submissions based on their business plan and the services and benefits the company promised to provide. More recently, the government has begun to auc-tion spectrum off, producing greater revenue. This change entails shifting from a concept of spectrum as a publicly owned resource to a market-based model of spectrum management.[68]

Many argue that the Canadian market for wireless services (such as cell-phone service) is uncompetitive, resulting in high prices for Canadian consumers. In the pursuit of more competition in cellular telephone and wireless services, the Canadian government has set caps on the amount of spectrum that can be owned by one company and has reserved wireless spectrum for new players.[69] In its 2019 auction of 5G wireless spectrum, the government permitted Bell, Rogers, and Telus to bid on only 64 of the 104 available licences, reserving the rest for smaller companies. The government made $3.5 billion in the auction.[70]

## Consumer Protection

### Wireless Code of Conduct

The CRTC has put in place consumer protection policies, including a *Wireless Code of Conduct*. This code places a cap of $50 on data overage charges and a $100 cap on data roaming, limits the length of cellular telephone contracts to two years, requires carriers to unlock phones, and eliminates fees for paper billing.[71]

# WHOM DOES TELECOMMUNICATIONS REGULATION SERVE?

## The Public Interest?

### Pluralism

A pluralist perspective sees telecommunications policy as serving the various interest groups at play in the field of telecommunications. Not all groups' voices are equal, as Winseck notes; workers, low-income Canadians, and consumers are represented by groups with limited resources and weaker networks than those held by powerful industry associations and groups.[72] However, according to plu-ralist theory, the voices of less powerful groups still matter, and policymaking processes should not be seen as driven by any one group alone.

Pluralist theory takes into account the changing power of different groups. Regulatory changes, such as telecommunications liberalization, can be seen as driven by the rise of new groups, such as competitive long-distance providers and new technology producers, as they attempt to enter the previously monopolistic market. The strengthening of such groups, along with the weakening of civil society and labour can explain the major changes we have seen in telecommunications policy history.[73]

## Bureaucracy and Bureaucrats?

### Neoliberalism

Neoliberal theory views regulation and subsidies as serving not those who cannot otherwise afford access to telecommunications services but the businesses that provide subsidized services. Neoliberal theory advocates deregulation and competition in telecommunications, as in other sectors. Legacy telecommunications like AT&T in the United States and Bell Canada long benefited from a regulated market that preserved their monopoly status. Neoliberal theorists argue (and non-neoliberals may agree) that regulatory agencies can be "captured" by businesses; in other words, they can be enrolled or brought to view things in the same way as the businesses they regulate. As a result, regulations that appear or purport to serve the public interest may actually entrench and preserve the positions of the dominant players.[74]

In the neoliberal view, regulation can also negatively affect markets. Long-distance services were priced high in order to subsidize local telephone services in rural or less affluent neighbourhoods. Neoliberal theory views such subsidies as distorting markets and benefiting the telephone companies that serve rural and less affluent areas.[75]

Many telecommunications historians have been highly critical of neoliberalism. They have argued that the neoliberal approach widens inequities in access to telecommunications services, and reduces job security, in that employment opportunities in stable monopoly providers are reduced.[76] However, neoliberals might counter that deregulation has also helped to foster the growth of the information technology sector, the establishment of internet and social media companies, internet innovation, and the globalization of telecommunications and information technology companies. It has also contributed to new forms of precarious employment and the current rise of *platform capitalism*—a form of capitalism under which private internet platform companies play a central and growing role in how we communicate and conduct our personal and working lives.[77]

## The Privileged?

### *Critical Political Economy*

Critical political economists see the state not as a "neutral arbiter among competing interests" but as serving the interests of business owners.[78] Business interests, critical political economists note, have privileged access to the state and have power to put pressure on states that other groups do not have, such as by threatening to move business out of the country. This special access is especially apparent in the negotiation of international agreements, where businesses often have access to negotiations that other groups do not; indeed, corporations and coalitions of companies often drive and set the agenda for such negotiations.[79]

The state is a neutral arbiter neither under monopoly conditions nor under conditions of competition. Under monopoly conditions, the state, in some cases captured by monopoly providers, facilitates private companies like Bell Canada in profiting from monopoly service provision.[80] Under conditions of competition, the state paves the way for private companies to earn profits from domestic and foreign telecommunication markets.

Critical political economists have historically objected to telecommunications deregulation and privatization. They did so on the grounds that privatization would erode universal service and that it would disrupt "several decades of harmonious industrial relations in the telecommunications industry."[81] They also have objected to the shift away from public interest objectives such as universal service, to a focus on growth and profit.[82]

Critical political economists have long emphasized equal access to communication resources and widespread digital literacy as facilitating equal access to information and equal participation in policy debate.[83] However, access is rarely equal. Critical political economists emphasize the ways in which business owners and increasingly large corporations have benefited from government subsidies, favourable corporate tax treatment, and government licences to use of the public spectrum—far more than those who do not have the resources to access or control information systems.[84]

### *Feminism*

Feminists, for their part, have noted that the digital divide disproportionately affects women; members of racialized, ethnic, and linguistic communities; and the elderly.[85] Feminists have emphasized the importance of women's access to telecommunications services,[86] as well as the fact "access and control of spectrum are regulated by occupations and organizations that tend to be gender-biased."[87]

Telecommunications companies have often prioritized the interests of businesses, failing to consider the ways that women may use telecommunications technologies—even as women find new and perhaps unexpected uses for technologies.[88] Regulators, too, have often failed to consider women; UNESCO, for example, has at times taken a limited view of the roles of women in telecommunications, failing to see women as potential investors in and owners of telecommunications.[89] Information and communication technologies are often masculinized, while work is feminized and job security is reduced, especially for women. Telecommunications institutions often devalue work that is done by women, privileging the disciplines and jobs dominated by men.[90] Telecommunications and the internet are male-dominated. However, women had a tremendous influence on the history and development of telephony; Michèle Martin's *"Hello Central?"* recounts the role of women in transforming what Bell Canada originally envisioned as a business technology into a social and public utility—one that would transform the labour practices and social lives of women as well as all people.[91]

### Critical Disability Studies

People with disabilities often face barriers of access to telecommunications. Telecommunications networks have "built in disability" by basing technologies around ableist norms.[92] In other words, "disability is created when telecommunications systems are designed in accordance with ableist norms."[93] The telephone itself was invented by Alexander Graham Bell, who promoted eugenics and the sterilization of deaf people. Bell's work was part of an ableist program to help people who are deaf communicate in spoken English rather than sign language.[94] When telephone systems were put in place in many countries, people with disabilities were excluded. People who are deaf or speech impaired and people who are hearing impaired have fought successfully for diversity programs that rendered many technologies more accessible.[95] However, the availability of accessible telecommunications technologies may have been slowed or limited due to privatization, which means market forces guide, to some extent, what technologies are (and are not) put in place.[96]

### Critical Race Theory

Some studies have documented disparities in the availability and quality of telecommunications services available to racialized people living in rural and urban areas, particularly in the United States.[97] Such disparities can exist in both monopoly and free-market environments as telecommunication companies move more quickly to serve more affluent white consumers.[98]

Regulatory measures, such as penalties for substandard service and reporting requirements that allow regulators to see demographic inequity, can help to reduce such disparities.[99] Critical race theory, and a race-conscious lens in policymaking, "is particularly important," note communication scholars Rachel Moran and Matthew Bui, "due to the tendency for more so-called 'objective' and race-neutral approaches to research to reify structural inequalities through their legal and policy recommendations."[100] They emphasize that:

> a failure to consider the racial contexts of inequalities in relation to digital inequities and the social construction of technologies (Pinch & Bijker, 1984) will result in lackadaisical communications policymaking, non-equitable internet access and development, increased divisiveness between privileged and marginalized communities, and the promulgation of whiteness (and relatedly, white supremacy) as the norm and starting point for policymaking.[101]

Because telecommunications policymaking is often not race-conscious, it can be difficult for those representing racialized communities to place these issues and concerns high on the telecommunications policy agenda. Not only are significant resources and technical knowledge required to participate in public proceedings about telecommunications policy but groups representing racialized communities must also battle presumptions that technology, law, and policy are neutral, despite evidence to the contrary.[102] These difficulties in achieving policy outcomes can mean it is important to find alignments and common interests with other, more powerful policy actors, or solutions must be sought outside the regulatory system.[103]

### Indigenous Theory and Postcolonial Analysis

Researchers who have studied telecommunications policy with a focus on Indigenous peoples have shown that, while hopes are often pinned to new technologies, technology alone cannot solve problems of colonialism, inequitable distribution of resources and land, poor healthcare and health services, and limited access to economic and community development opportunities. In fact, network technologies, while vital, are often promoted in ways that echo the "civilizing mission" of colonialism—as having liberating or development potential.[104]

The rising availability of telecommunication services does not solve the problems of colonialism. The federal government's close ties with telecommunications companies, and the corporate interests of telecommunications companies themselves, help to create and reproduce relationships of dependency and colonialism:

> Historically the federal government has a legal responsibility to ensure that First Nations are not exploited in their dealings with corporate entities, also known as the Crown's fiduciary relationship. However the federal government's close links with telecommunications companies, as well as its policies that flow public funding directly to this industry instead of to the First Nations or their organizations, have called the fiduciary relationship into question. Forcing First Nations to be dependent on the telecoms is yet another form of paternal colonial governance that furthers the relationships that benefit these urban centres at the expense of developing remote and rural communities. These relationships also means [sic] that many First Nations communities end up being disempowered and unable to deal with the issues themselves as all the government resources are used to take care of the telecommunication corporations.[105]

Thus, some scholars and Indigenous peoples argue for Indigenous self-determination—for "development processes grounded in a recognition of the inherent laws, institutions, and practices of sovereign Indigenous peoples and for Indigenous-controlled telecommunications services."[106] "In this context," Rob McMahon notes, "Indigenous peoples are providing alternatives to sociotechnical development paths that position state and corporate entities as the dominant nodes in a centralized network society."[107] Indigenous peoples have advocated at the CRTC and in other venues for policies and measures to support those paths.[108] Telephone services and other telecommunications infrastructure were late to arrive in remote Northern communities in Canada, but Indigenous peoples leveraged evidence from their local initiatives to demonstrate the need for and benefits of advanced telecommunications services to support telemedicine, distance learning, and videoconferencing.[109] Indigenous ownership, control, access, and possession (OCAP) of infrastructure and telecommunications is emphasized as an important part of establishing self-determination.[110]

In international context, telecommunications services have often been posed as a modernizing force. However, postcolonial theorists have questioned linear portrayals of development that see all societies traversing the same path on the up-escalator of progress. Instead, they encourage appreciating that there are multiple conflicting visions of the future, ideals of progress, and strategies for moving toward them.[111] Mahatma Gandhi was critical of technology and popularized a vision of austere development based on self-reliance in India, whereas subsequent Indian leaders pursued a strategy of technological nationalism, including the development of domestic technologies and networks.[112]

The privatization of telecommunications services around the world has raised specific difficulties for some countries. The rise of deregulation of the telecommunications industry has led to the decline of national telecommunications companies, once a source of national pride, especially in some countries of the South. Telecommunications regulators are, in many cases, weak in terms of their capacity to stand up against corruption and corporate influence.[113] At the same time, access to telecommunications services has risen dramatically. For example, there was less than 1 landline per 100 people in India in 1990 (compared with Canada, which had 55 landlines and 2 cellphones per 100 people). By 2014, there were 74 mobile phones per 100 people in India (compared to 81 in Canada).[114]

## FURTHER READING

Babe, Robert E. *Telecommunications in Canada: Technology, Industry, and Government.* Toronto: University of Toronto Press, 1990.

Intven, Hank, and Grant Buchanan. *Canadian Telecommunications Regulatory Handbook.* 3rd ed. Toronto: McCarthy Tétrault, 2016.

MacDougall, Robert. *The People's Network: The Political Economy of the Telephone in the Gilded Age.* Philadelphia: University of Pennsylvania Press, 2013.

Martin, Michèle. *"Hello, Central?": Gender, Technology, and Culture in the Formation of Telephone Systems.* Montreal: McGill-Queen's University Press, 1991.

McMahon, Rob. "From Digital Divides to the First Mile: Indigenous Peoples and the Network Society in Canada." *International Journal of Communication* 8 (January 2014): 2002–26.

Moll, Marita, and Leslie Regan Shade, eds. *For Sale to the Highest Bidder: Telecom Policy in Canada.* Ottawa: Canadian Centre for Policy Alternatives, 2008.

Mussio, Laurence. *Telecom Nation: Telecommunications, Computers, and Governments in Canada.* Montreal: McGill-Queen's University Press, 2001.

Rideout, Vanda. *Continentalizing Canadian Telecommunications: The Politics of Regulatory Reform.* Montreal: McGill-Queen's University Press, 2003.

Winseck, Dwayne Roy. *Reconvergence: A Political Economy of Telecommunications in Canada.* Cresskill, NJ: Hampton Press, 1998.

# NOTES

1. Vanda Rideout, *Continentalizing Canadian Telecommunications: The Politics of Regulatory Reform* (Montreal: McGill-Queen's University Press; Combined Academic, 2004), 1.

2. Dwayne Winseck defines "telecoms" as "wire- or radio-based communication networks that carry information—regardless of whether that information is voice, data, television, computer-enhanced services, and so on—from one point to another without editorial intervention." Winseck, *Reconvergence: A Political Economy of Telecommunications in Canada* (Cressville, NJ: Hampton Press, 1998), 1–2. See also Robert E. Babe, *Telecommunications in Canada: Technology, Industry, and Government* (Toronto: University of Toronto Press, 1990), 22. The *Telecommunications Act*, SC 1993 c 38, s 2, defines *telecommunications* as "the emission, transmission or reception of intelligence by any wire, cable, radio, optical or other electromagnetic system, or by any similar technical system." *Intelligence* is defined as "signs, signals, writing, images, sounds or intelligence of any nature." The act does not apply to "broadcasting by a broadcasting undertaking" (s 4).

3. CRTC, "Revocation of Basic International Telecommunications Services Licences," Decisions, February 3, 2017, https://crtc.gc.ca/eng/archive/2017/2017-37.htm.

4. *Telecommunications Act*, s 7.

5. "Order Issuing a Direction to the CRTC on Implementing the Canadian Telecommunications Policy Objectives," December 14, 2006, https://laws-lois.justice.gc.ca/eng/regulations/SOR-2006-355/FullText.html.

6. Ibid.

7. *OED Online* (2018), s.v. "market failure, n.," accessed February 15, 2019. Telecommunications Policy Review Panel, *Final Report*: 3–17.

8. CRTC, "Telecom Regulatory Policy CRTC 2012-211: Bell Aliant Regional Communications, Limited Partnership and Télébec, Limited Partnership—Application Regarding the Price Ceiling Applicable to Residential Primary Exchange Services in Regulated Non-High-Cost Serving Areas," Regulatory Policies, May 5, 2012, https://crtc.gc.ca/eng/archive/2012/2012-211.htm.

9. Babe, 9–18.

10. Ibid., 7–8.

11. Ibid.

12. Tribe, "Canadian Internet Traffic Is Travelling through the U.S.—Making Canadians Even More Vulnerable to NSA Surveillance." *OpenMedia*, December 16, 2015, https://openmedia.org/en/canadian-internet-traffic-travelling-through-us-making-canadians-even-more-vulnerable-nsa.

13. Marita Moll, "Trading Sovereignty for Surveillance in the Telecommunications Sector," in *The Internet Tree: The State of Telecom Policy in Canada 3.0*, eds. Marita Moll and Leslie Regan Shade (Ottawa: Canadian Centre for Policy Alternatives, 2011), 93–99.

14. Steve Proceviat, "Evening Update: U.S. Senators Urge Trudeau to Block Huawei; Belinda Stronach Offered to Settle Dispute Weeks before Father's Lawsuit," accessed November 29, 2018, https://www.theglobeandmail.com/canada/article-evening-update-us-senators-urge-trudeau-to-block-huawei-belinda/.

15. Winseck, 4–7.

16. *Telecommunications Act*, s 36.

17. Ibid., s 27(2).

18. Winseck, 6–7.

19. Ibid.

20. Monica L. Auer, "Foreign Ownership in Canadian Telecommunications," in *The Internet Tree: The State of Telecom Policy in Canada 3.0*, edited by Marita Moll and Leslie Regan Shade (Ottawa: Canadian Centre for Policy Alternatives, 2011); Marc Raboy, *Marconi: The Man Who Networked the World* (New York: Oxford University Press, 2016).

21. Winseck, 87.

22. Ibid.

23. Babe, 68.

24. Ibid.

25. Ibid., 74–90; Winseck, 131. See generally Winseck, chap. 4; Rideout, chap. 2.

26. Winseck, 87–88.

27. Sheryl Hamilton, *Law's Expression: Communication, Law and Media in Canada* (Toronto: LexisNexis, 2009), 16–17.

28. Babe, 91–101.

29. Winseck, 130–31. See generally Winseck, chap. 4; Rideout, chap. 2; Laurence B. Mussio, *Telecom Nation: Telecommunications, Computers, and Governments in Canada* (Montreal: McGill-Queen's University Press, 2001), chap. 1.

30. Winseck, 132, 137.

31. Ibid., 135, 137; Babe, 118–19.

32. *Ingersoll Telephone Co. v Bell Telephone Co. of Canada*, (1916) 53 SCR 583; Winseck, 135, 137; Babe, 118–19.

33. Babe, 121; Winseck, 156.

34. Winseck, 156, 176–78.

35. Rideout, 27.

36. Jonathan E. Nuechterlein and Philip J. Weiser, *Digital Crossroads: Telecommunications Law and Policy in the Internet Age*, 2nd ed. (Cambridge, MA: MIT Press, 2013), 3–8. See generally Winseck, chap. 2; Rideout, chap. 2.

37. Nuechterlein and Weiser, 3–8.

38. Ibid.

39. Mark A. Lemley and Lawrence Lessig, "The End of End-to-End: Preserving the Architecture of the Internet in the Broadband Era," *UCLA Law Review* 48 (2000): 925–72.

40. Winseck.

41. CRTC, "CRTC Origins: History and Chronology," December 20, 2013, http://web.archive.org/web/20131220213318/http://www.crtc.gc.ca/eng/backgrnd/brochures/b19903.htm; Mussio, chaps. 2–7.

42. Winseck, 237.

43. Rideout, 75; Winseck, 241.

44. *Telecommunications Act*, s 7(f); Winseck, 238.

45. Dwayne Winseck, "Reconstructing the Political Economy of Communication for the Digital Media Age," *The Political Economy of Communication* 4, no. 2 (2017), 225–26; Rideout, 156–60; Olga Batura, *Universal Service in WTO and EU Law: Liberalisation and Social Regulation in Telecommunications* (The Hague: Asser Press, 2015), 36.

46. CUSFTA, Annex 1404, Art 5; NAFTA, Art 1305; GATS, Art VIII.

47. Rideout, 27.

48. "Order Issuing a Direction to the CRTC on Implementing the Canadian Telecommunications Policy Objectives."

49. CRTC, "Telecom Decision CRTC 2006-15: Forbearance from the Regulation of Retail Local Exchange Services," Regulatory Policies, April 6, 2006, https://crtc.gc.ca/eng/archive/2006/dt2006-15.htm; see also the unofficial consolidated version at CRTC, "Telecom Regulatory Policy CRTC 2011-291: Obligation to Serve and Other Matters," Regulatory Policies, May 3, 2011, https://crtc.gc.ca/eng/archive/2011/2011-291.htm.

50. CRTC, "CRTC, Telecom Decision CRTC 97-9: Price Cap Regulation and Related Issues," Decisions, May 1, 1997, https://crtc.gc.ca/eng/archive/1997/DT97-9.htm.

51. For a complete list of basic services, see CRTC, "Telecom Decision CRTC 99-16: Telephone Service to High-Cost Serving Areas," Decisions, October 19, 1999, https://crtc.gc.ca/eng/archive/1999/dt99-16.htm, referenced in CRTC, "Forbearance," para 382; referenced in CRTC, "Telecom Regulatory Policy CRTC 2009-379: Framework for Forbearance from Regulation of Retail Local Exchange Services in the Serving Territories of the Small Incumbent Local

Exchange Carriers," Regulatory Policies, June 23, 2009, https://crtc.gc.ca/eng/archive/2009/2009-379.htm, referenced in CRTC, "Obligation to Serve."

52. CRTC, "Obligation to Serve," para 12.

53. CRTC, "Telecom Regulatory Policy CRTC 2016-496: Modern Telecommunications Services—The Path Forward for Canada's Digital Economy," Regulatory Policies, December 21, 2016, paras 187–89, https://crtc.gc.ca/eng/archive/2016/2016-496.htm.

54. Ibid., para 180.

55. Catherine Middleton, "Structural and Functional Separation in Broadband Networks: An Insufficient Remedy to Competitive Woes in the Canadian Broadband Market," in *The Internet Tree: The State of Telecom Policy in Canada*, eds. Marita Moll and Leslie Regan Shade (Ottawa: Canadian Centre for Policy Alternatives, 2011), 61–72; Catherine Middleton, "An Introduction to Telecommunications Policy in Canada," *Journal of Telecommunications and the Digital Economy* 5, no. 4 (2017): 97–124.

56. Ibid.

57. Middleton, "An Introduction."

58. *Telecommunications Act*, s 27(2).

59. "Press Release: CRTC Takes Action to Ensure a Wide Choice of Television Programming on All Platforms," *Canada News Wire*, September 21, 2011, https://www.newswire.ca/news-releases/crtc-takes-action-to-ensure-a-wide-choice-of-television-programming-on-all-platforms-521676221.html.

60. Tasneem Chipty, "Vertical Integration, Market Foreclosure, and Consumer Welfare in the Cable Television Industry," *American Economic Review* 91, no. 3 (2001): 428–53; Girard, "CRTC Drops NFL Content Case against Bell Canada," *Toronto Star*, March 1, 2012, https://www.thestar.com/sports/2012/03/01/crtc_drops_nfl_content_case_against_bell_canada.html.

61. CRTC, "Telecom Decision CRTC 2017-105: Complaints against Quebecor Media Inc., Videotron Ltd., and Videotron G.P. Alleging Undue and Unreasonable Preference and Disadvantage Regarding the Unlimited Music Program," Decisions, April 20, 2017, https://crtc.gc.ca/eng/archive/2017/2017-105.htm.

62. Ibid.

63. CRTC, "Telecom Regulatory Policy CRTC 2015-177: Regulatory Framework for Wholesale Mobile Wireless Services," Regulatory Policies, May 5, 2015, para 74, https://crtc.gc.ca/eng/archive/2015/2015-177.htm.

64. Ibid., paras 4–7. *Economic Action Plan 2014 Act, No. 1* SC 2014, c 20. This decision followed federal legislation passed in 2014 to regulate wholesale roaming rates and led to their repeal. *Telecommunications Act*, s 27.1. See also CRTC, "Telecom

Decision CRTC 2014-398: Wholesale Mobile Wireless Roaming in Canada— Unjust Discrimination/Undue Preference," Decisions, July 31, 2014, https://crtc. gc.ca/eng/archive/2014/2014-398.htm.

65. CRTC, "Telecom Regulatory Policy CRTC 2015-326: Review of Wholesale Wireline Services and Associated Policies," Regulatory Policies, July 22, 2015, https:// crtc.gc.ca/eng/archive/2015/2015-326.htm.

66. Sharon K. Black, *Telecommunications Law in the Internet Age* (San Francisco: Morgan Kaufmann Publishers, 2002), 453; *Telecommunications Act*, s 16.

67. *Telecommunications Act*, s 16(2)(c). For further reading on foreign ownership of Canadian telecommunications, see Monica Auer, "Foreign Ownership in Canadian Telecommunications," in *The Internet Tree: The State of Telecom Policy in Canada 3.0*, eds. Marita Moll and Leslie Regan Shade (Ottawa: Canadian Centre for Policy Alternatives, 2011), and Julie White, *Losing Canadian Culture: The Danger of Foreign Ownership of Telecom* (Ottawa: Canadian Centre for Policy Alternatives, 2005).

68. Gregory Taylor, "Oil in the Ether: A Critical History of Spectrum Auctions in Canada," *Canadian Journal of Communication* 38 (2013): 121–37.

69. Gregory Taylor, "Spectrum Policy in Canada," *IEEE Wireless Communications* 22, no. 6 (2015): 8–9; Kris Joseph, "Analysis of Canadian Wireless Spectrum Auctions: Licence Ownership and Deployment in the 700 MHz, 2500 MHz and 3500 MHz Frequency Ranges," Gatineau, QC: Canadian Radio-television and Telecommunications Commission, 2018, https://crtc.gc.ca/eng/acrtc/prx/2018joseph. htm; Industry Canada, "Government Opts for More Competition in the Wireless Sector," 2007, https://www.canada.ca/en/news/archive/2007/11/government-opts-more-competition-wireless-sector.html.

70. "5G Wireless Spectrum Auction Nets Ottawa $3.5 Billion," *MarketWatch* (blog), April 11, 2019, www.marketwatch.com/press-release/5g-wireless-spectrum-auction-nets-ottawa-35-billion-2019-04-11-91975053.

71. CRTC, "Telecom Regulatory Policy CRTC 2013-271: The Wireless Code," Regulatory Policies, June 3, 2013. https://crtc.gc.ca/eng/archive/2013/2013-271.htm; CRTC, "The Wireless Code, Simplified," Consumer Information, June 3, 2013, https://crtc.gc.ca/eng/phone/mobile/codesimpl.htm.

72. Winseck, 233–34. See also Tamara Shepherd, Gregory Taylor, and Catherine Middleton, "A Tale of Two Regulators: Telecom Policy Participation in Canada," *Journal of Information Policy* 4 (2014): 1–22.

73. Rideout, 6–7.

74. Reza Rajabiun and Catherine Middleton, "Public Interest in the Regulation of Competition: Evidence from Wholesale Internet Access Consultations in Canada," *Journal of Information Policy* 5 (2015): 32–66; William H. Melody, "On the Meaning

and Importance of 'Independence' in Telecom Reform," *Telecommunications Policy* 21, no. 3 (1997): 195–99.

75. John Wenders, "Equity and Politics in the US Telecommunications Industry," In *Telecommunications and Equity: Policy Research Issues Proceedings of the Thirteenth Annual Telecommunications Policy Research Conference, Airlie House, Airlie, Virginia, USA, April 21–24, 1985*, ed. James Miller (Amsterdam: North-Holland, 1986), 53–60.

76. Rideout, 15.

77. Ibid.; Srnicek.

78. Winseck, 235.

79. Rideout, 160; Sell, *Public Power, Private Law.*

80. Babe; Winseck.

81. Vincent Mosco, "Changing Telecommunications Policy in Canada," in *Telecommunications and Equity: Policy Research Issues Proceedings of the Thirteenth Annual Telecommunications Policy Research Conference, Airlie House, Airlie, Virginia, USA, April 21–24, 1985*, ed. James Miller (Amsterdam: North-Holland, 1986), 189–95; see also Rideout.

82. Winseck.

83. Oscar Gandy, "Inequality: You Don't Even Notice After a While," in *Telecommunications and Equity: Policy Research Issues Proceedings of the Thirteenth Annual Telecommunications Policy Research Conference, Airlie House, Airlie, Virginia, USA, April 21–24, 1985*, ed. James Miller (Amsterdam: North-Holland, 1986), 9–20.

84. Dallas Smythe, "National Policy on Public and Private Sectors," in *Telecommunications and Equity: Policy Research Issues Proceedings of the Thirteenth Annual Telecommunications Policy Research Conference, Airlie House, Airlie, Virginia, USA, April 21–24, 1985*, ed. James Miller (Amsterdam: North-Holland, 1986), 21–30. See also Marita Moll and Leslie Regan Shade, eds., *For Sale to the Highest Bidder: Telecom Policy in Canada* (Ottawa: Canadian Centre for Policy Alternatives, 2008).

85. Barbara Crow and Graham Longford, "Digital Restructuring: Gender, Class and Citizenship in the Information Society in Canada," *Citizenship Studies* 4, no. 2 (2000): 217; Kim Sawchuk and Barbara Crow, "Into the Grey Zone: Seniors, Cell Phones and Milieus that Matter," in *Observing the Mobile User Experience*, 17, 2010.

86. Kiran Prasad, "Gender-sensitive Communication Policies for Women's Development: Issues and Challenges," in *Feminist Interventions in International Communication: Minding the Gap*, eds. Katharine Sarikakis and Leslie Regan Shade. (Lanham, MD: Rowman & Littlefield, 2008), 74–89.

87. Barbara Crow and Kim Sawchuk, "The Spectral Politics of Mobile Communication Technologies: Gender, Infrastructure and International Policy," in *Feminist Interventions in International Communication: Minding the Gap*, eds. Katharine Sarikakis and Leslie Regan Shade (Lanham, MD: Rowman & Littlefield, 2008), 102.

88. Michèle Martin, *"Hello, Central?": Gender, Technology, and Culture in the Formation of Telephone Systems* (Montreal: McGill-Queen's University Press, 1991).

89. Micky Lee, "UNESCO's Conceptualization of Women and Telecommunications 1970–2000," *Gazette (Leiden, Netherlands)* 66, no. 6 (2004): 533–52.

90. Wendy Cukier, Samantha Jackson, Mohamed A. Elmi, Erin Roach, and Darren Cyr, "Representing Women? Leadership Roles and Women in Canadian Broadcast News," *Gender in Management: An International Journal* 31, no. 5/6 (2016): 374–95.

91. Martin.

92. Gerard Goggin and Christopher Newell, *Digital Disability: The Social Construction of Disability in New Media* (Lanham, MD: Rowman & Littlefield, 2003), 40.

93. Ibid., 41.

94. "Through Deaf Eyes. Deaf Life. Signing, Alexander Graham Bell and the NAD," PBS.org, accessed February 17, 2019, https://www.pbs.org/weta/through-deafeyes/deaflife/bell_nad.html; Goggin and Newell, 42; Michael Rosenwald, "Your iPhone's Secret Past: How Cadaver Ears and a Talking Dog Led to the Telephone," *Washington Post*, November 3, 2017.

95. Goggin and Newell, 39–62.

96. Ibid.

97. Philip Howard, Laura Busch, and Penelope Sheets, "Comparing Digital Divides: Internet Access and Social Inequality in Canada and the United States," *Canadian Journal of Communication* 35, no. 1 (2010); Leonard M. Baynes, "Deregulatory Injustice and Electronic Redlining: The Color of Access to Telecommunications," *Administrative Law Review* 56 (2004): 263–352.

98. Baynes.

99. Ibid., 348–49.

100. Rachel E. Moran and Matthew N. Bui, "Race, Ethnicity, and Telecommunications Policy Issues of Access and Representation: Centering Communities of Color and Their Concerns," *Telecommunications Policy* 43, no. 5 (2019): 462.

101. Ibid.

102. Ibid.

103. Ibid.

104. Cynthia J. Alexander, "Wiring the Nation! Including First Nations? Aboriginal Canadians and Federal e-Government Initiatives," *Journal of Canadian Studies* 35, no. 4 (2001): 282.

105. Duncan Philpot, Brian Beaton, and Tim Whiteduck, "First Mile Challenges to Last Mile Rhetoric: Exploring the Discourse between Remote and Rural First

Nations and the Telecom Industry," *Journal of Community Informatics* 10, no. 2 (2014): 13.

106. Rob McMahon, "From Digital Divides to the First Mile: Indigenous Peoples and the Network Society in Canada," *International Journal of Communication* 8 (2014): 25.

107. Ibid.

108. Rob McMahon, Heather E. Hudson, and Lyle Fabian, "Indigenous Regulatory Advocacy in Canada's Far North: Mobilizing the First Mile Connectivity Consortium," *Journal of Information Policy* 4 (2014): 228–49.

109. Rob McMahon, Heather E. Hudson, and Lyle Fabian, "Canada's Northern Communication Policies: The Role of Aboriginal Organizations," *The Shifting Terrain: Public Policy Advocacy in Canada* (2017): 268.

110. Brian Beaton, Terence Burnard, and Adi Linden, "Keewaytinook Mobile: An Indigenous Community-Owned Mobile Phone Service in Northern Canada," in *Indigenous People and Mobile Technologies*, eds. Laurel Evelyn Dyson, Stephen Grant, and Max Hendriks (New York: Routledge, 2015), 123–39.

111. Arturo Escobar, *Encountering Development: The Making and Unmaking of the Third World* (Princeton, NJ: Princeton University Press, 2011).

112. Paula Chakravartty, "Telecom, National Development and the Indian State: A Postcolonial Critique," *Media, Culture & Society* 26, no. 2 (2004): 227–49.

113. Amin Alhassan, "Telecom Regulation, the Post-Colonial State, and Big Business: The Ghanaian Experience," *West Africa Review* 4, no. 1 (2003).

114. International Telecommunications Union, "ICT Statistics Database," https://www.google.com/publicdata/explore?ds=emi9ik86jcuic_&ctype=l&strail=false&bcs=d&nselm=h&met_y=i91&scale_y=lin&ind_y=false&rdim=country&idim=country:IN:CA&ifdim=country&hl=en_US&dl=en&ind=false&icfg.

# 9 Broadcasting Regulation

## INTRODUCTION

Do Canadians want the programming available on television, radio, cable, satellite, and streaming services to be Canadian? Is it important that this programming include Canadian places, stories, actors, and points of view? Should policies be in place to ensure that television, film, and music production occurs in Canada? Is it important that Canadian companies own broadcast and distribution networks in Canada? If so, what policies best serve these goals?

This chapter explores many of these questions, discussing the problems that broadcasting regulation attempts to solve. It begins by defining broadcasting. The chapter then reviews the major justifications for broadcasting regulation in Canada and discusses CRTC regulation of broadcasters, broadcast distribution undertakings, and programming undertakings. Following an overview of the history of broadcasting regulation in Canada, the chapter discusses various types of broadcasting policy: media ownership regulation; and policies on content, representation, and accessibility. In the second half, it asks, "Whom does broadcasting regulation serve?", drawing on the theories introduced in Chapter 1.

## WHAT IS BROADCASTING?

Broadcasting is the transmission of audio and video signals by radio and television.[1] It is a one-to-many form of communication, with one broadcasting source (the broadcaster) and many recipients.[2] Audio and video programming received over the internet, such as through podcasts and streaming services, are technically considered to be "broadcasting" under the current Canadian regulatory regime, but these are regulated with a far lighter touch than over-the-air, satellite, and cable television and radio.[3] This book discusses internet-based audio and video programming in Chapter 10. This chapter will focus on the regulation of radio and television transmitted over the air, by satellite, and by cable television services.

## WHO REGULATES?

The CRTC regulates broadcasting and telecommunications in Canada. Broadcasters in Canada (with the exception of internet and mobile broadcasters and some Indigenous broadcasters) are required to have a broadcasting licence. The CRTC regulates broadcasters by granting, renewing, and revoking broadcasting licences. It regularly grants new broadcasting licences and renews existing licences. It also occasionally revokes broadcasting licences.[4] For example, in 2004, the CRTC decided not to renew the broadcasting licence of CHOI-FM, a Quebec radio station. CHOI-FM had failed to comply with a number of regulations, including the CRTC policy on abusive comment (see below); the requirement to submit logger tapes of its broadcasts to the CRTC; requirements on the broadcast of French-language vocal music; and requirements on sex-role portrayal.[5]

## WHAT JUSTIFIES BROADCASTING REGULATION?

Most media in Canada are not as heavily regulated as broadcasting. Why is broadcasting regulated? A number of different reasons are typically given to justify the regulation of Canadian broadcasting. These include:

1. **Technological determinism**: spectrum scarcity;
2. **Technological and cultural nationalism**: the promotion of Canadian content and a Canadian broadcasting system;
3. **Market failure**;
4. **The protection of values**; and
5. **The pervasiveness, invasiveness, and influence of broadcasting**.

### Technological Determinism: Spectrum Scarcity

Because there is a limited range of frequencies that are useable for over-the-air broadcasting, the first justification for the regulation of broadcasting is that broadcasting uses a scarce public resource: the radio spectrum. This resource must be regulated so that it can be used effectively in the public interest.

The technical definition of broadcasting used in the *Broadcasting Act* refers to the transmission of programs "by radio waves or other means of telecommunication."[6] A radio wave is "an electromagnetic wave propagated by a vibrating antenna."[7] Radio waves operate on a range of frequencies called the "radio spectrum." Television and radio programming can be transmitted on specific frequencies within this spectrum and, in order to receive a specific radio or television transmission, it is necessary to tune the receiving device to the frequency on which the program is being transmitted. For example, CBC Radio One in Toronto transmits at a frequency of 99.1FM. Each radio or television station needs its own frequency; if two radio signals are transmitted on the same frequency, they interfere with each other and impede reception. To prevent this, the CRTC grants licences to radio and television stations to operate on specific frequencies in a specific geographical region.

The idea of **spectrum scarcity** has become less meaningful with the advent of digital technologies for several reasons. First, a digital broadcast uses less bandwidth in the radio spectrum. While the radio spectrum is still limited, it can transmit a greater number of digital signals. This has permitted some bandwidth to be freed up for cellular telephone communications.[8] Second, digital technology makes it possible to "broadcast" without using the radio spectrum, for example by online audio or video streaming. Third, digital technology makes it possible to more effectively share the radio spectrum, such that a single frequency could theoretically be shared by multiple transmitters without impeding each other's signals.[9] However, broadcasters continue to obtain licences for and to use the radio spectrum for over-the-air broadcasting, and many Canadians receive radio and television signals over the air via broadcast receiving antenna.[10]

## Technological and Cultural Nationalism: The Promotion of Canadian Content and a Canadian Broadcasting System

A free or unregulated market can fail to encourage the Canadian ownership of broadcasting stations and the production of Canadian broadcasting content. The most salient reason for broadcasting regulation in Canada is technological and cultural nationalism: the promotion of a Canadian broadcasting system and Canadian content in radio and television.[11] Broadcasting regulation in Canada has therefore mandated the Canadian ownership of broadcasting stations, as well as the production and broadcast of Canadian content. Canadian broadcasting regulation is justified by the idea that there should be a Canadian broadcasting system meeting the values and standards of Canadians.

The promotion of Canadian content as part of a state project to foster a sense of Canadian nationalism was, in part, a historical strategy to reinforce the legitimacy of the Canadian state and to bolster Canadian nationalism in light of the powerful influence of continentalism, American culture, and the American economy on Canada.[12] Like the Canadian National Railway, the Canadian broadcasting system was a nation-building project—a project to build and legitimize the Canadian nation across spaces that were occupied by people with a variety of national and ethnic identities, including Indigenous peoples.[13]

## Market Failure

In some cases, a free-market system creates the incentive for private businesses to produce products and services for which there is consumer demand. However, in the case of private radio and television broadcasting, it is advertisers and not consumers who pay broadcasters. Broadcasters tailor their programming to reach the largest audience in order to command the greatest possible advertising revenue. Advertising-funded programming tends to produce programming appealing to a large audience, such as comedy, popular music, and reality television. The most inexpensive programming, often American, is used in order to produce the greatest profit. A free market can fail to produce other types of programming, such as news, educational, or documentary programming. This market failure to produce high-quality Canadian programming is corrected through Canadian content (**CanCon**) regulation that requires minimum amounts of news and Canadian content to be produced and aired.[14]

## The Protection of Values

An unregulated market can fail to meet public interest objectives. Regulation can help to protect values that are widely held but might be at risk if left to market forces alone.[15] Such values include pluralism, diversity (of media ownership, media content, voices in media content, types of media content), accessibility, fairness, and standards of decency. A number of broadcast regulations have been put in place to protect such values. Broadcast policies on equitable portrayal, Indigenous broadcasting, ethnic broadcasting, accessibility, and abusive comment are discussed later in this chapter.

## Pervasiveness, Invasiveness, and Influence

Many countries, including the United States, have justified the regulation of broadcasting more than other media of communication because of the pervasiveness, invasiveness, and potential influence of broadcasting.[16] Broadcasting is pervasive in the sense that it is everywhere—anyone with a radio or TV has immediate and direct access to over-the-air broadcasting. The accessibility of broadcasting also makes it invasive, as it is carried over the air by satellite and cable into the homes of audiences. It can be especially invasive because audiences have no say in what they are going to hear until they hear it. Unlike film or the internet, where audiences can decide what they are going to watch or look at, television and radio audiences have relatively little choice over what they are going to view, as the programming lineup is decided by broadcasters.[17]

The pervasiveness and invasiveness of broadcasting gives it great potential power over its audiences. Internet and social media may now be the main way of accessing news content, but in the past many Canadians accessed news primarily through broadcast media.[18] This gave broadcast media enormous power to influence the agenda of political discussion.[19] As well, its pervasiveness makes broadcasting a crucial medium for the dissemination of public service messages and emergency communications.

## WHAT DOES THE CRTC REGULATE?

The Canadian broadcasting system is, as of this writing, considered to be a single system containing multiple elements.[20] The following elements of that system are regulated by the CRTC.

### Broadcasters

Companies owning radio and television stations that transmit radio and television signals over the air are called **broadcasters.** Other entities transmitting television signals over other means, such as cable, are also sometimes called *broadcasters.* Often, a *network* is owned by the same broadcast company or is a set of stations that agree to broadcast content from a particular source. Examples include the CBC, BBC, and NBC.

### Broadcast Distribution Undertakings

*Broadcast distribution undertakings* (BDUs) are also regulated by the CRTC. This includes cable companies and satellite distributors who receive programming from a source, such as an over-the-air broadcaster, and retransmit it to customers.[21] Examples include Rogers cable service and Bell satellite television.

## Programming Undertakings

Some television companies do not transmit programming themselves, but rather sell television programs to broadcasters and programming undertakings. These are called *programming undertakings*. Examples include pay TV, video on demand, specialty services, and specialty channels.[22]

# HISTORY OF BROADCASTING REGULATION IN CANADA

The earliest form of wireless transmission consisted of transmissions of Morse code, starting with the experiments of Guglielmo Marconi in 1895. Experiments with the broadcast of audio signals started about ten years later, along with amateur use of radio technology. Commercial radio broadcasting began in the 1920s.[23]

## The Aird Commission (1928–1929)

As commercial radio broadcasting grew, questions arose about how it should be regulated. Amateur radio broadcasters were required to have broadcast licences beginning in 1913, and commercial broadcasters could obtain a commercial broadcasting licence beginning in 1922.[24]

In order to determine a path forward for radio regulation in Canada, the government appointed a Royal Commission on Radio Broadcasting, with John Aird, president of the Canadian Bank of Commerce, as its chair.[25] Its most well-known conclusion was that "Canadian radio listeners want Canadian broadcasting."[26]

The Commission based its conclusions on hearings held in 25 cities across the country. At these hearings, it heard concerns that radio was too commercial, that there was too much advertising in radio broadcasts, that there was insufficient radio service in rural areas, and that Canadians, and youth especially, were exposed to too much American content.[27] It heard arguments that the educational potential of broadcasting and broadcasting's potential to connect different parts of the country were important.[28]

In order to meet the demand for more Canadian radio, including educational radio service, the Commission made a set of radical recommendations that followed the European model of *public* broadcasting, rather than the American model of *private* broadcasting.[29] Taking the view that a national public broadcaster was the only viable alternative to American domination, it recommended that the private broadcasters then in existence should be taken over by a single public broadcaster, that Canadian broadcasting should be entirely public, and that Canadian broadcasts should feature no advertising.[30]

While the Aird Commission's vision of an entirely public broadcasting system would not be implemented, it produced two traditions that have stood at the core of Canadian broadcasting policy. First, it established a tradition of public consultation in Canadian broadcast regulation.[31] Second, the idea that Canadians want Canadian broadcasting has stood at the core of the Canadian broadcasting policy since 1929; Canadian broadcasting is regulated based on the idea that there should be a Canadian system, meeting the values and standards of Canadians.

## Canadian Radio Broadcasting Commission (CRBC; est. 1932)

Shortly after the Aird Commission issued its report in 1932, Canada's first *Broadcasting Act* was put into place. The Canadian Radio Broadcasting Commission (CRBC) was established and tasked with setting up a national radio broadcasting network, with the idea that private radio would eventually be taken over by the public system. The new *Broadcasting Act* prohibited national private radio networks but did allow for regional private broadcasting.[32]

However, an entirely public broadcast system was never fully implemented. By the 1930s, Canada was in the midst of the Great Depression. This made the establishment of a national broadcasting system financially difficult.[33] Opponents of public broadcasting lobbied against the establishment of an entirely public system. Groups based in Quebec were particularly loath to see the federal government take over Canadian broadcasting.[34] The radio network that was established by the CRBC did not live up to expectations; there were complaints that the quality of programming was poor.[35] Newscasts in 1935 were modest and, by 1936, national broadcasts still failed to reach more than half of the population.

## Canadian Broadcasting Corporation (CBC; est. 1936)

The CBC was created in 1936 under the *Broadcasting Act*.[36] Upon its creation, the CBC was mandated to create a national radio service. The CBC took over for the CRBC, acting both as broadcaster and broadcasting regulator. By 1941, the CBC News Service and Radio-Canada's news division were established.[37] The CBC expanded its program offerings and its radio network, affiliating with private radio stations and establishing an international service.[38]

In 1945, the Federal Communications Commission (FCC), the American broadcasting regulator, began to issue licences for television broadcasting.[39] In 1947, the CBC set out a plan for a national television service. The CBC established two television stations in Toronto and Montreal in 1952. More television stations were established in the following years.

## Massey Commission (1949–1951)

In 1949, the federal government struck a Royal Commission on National Development in the Arts, Letters and Sciences, led by Vincent Massey, Chancellor of the University of Toronto and eventual Governor General. Its mandate was broad: It was tasked with studying the overall state of culture in Canada, and part of its investigation dealt with Canadian broadcasting. The Commission viewed broadcasting as a public service that should operate in the public interest, with a significant or primary role for public broadcasting. It recommended that the CBC should continue in its roles both as broadcaster and broadcast regulator, and that it should regulate in order to avoid excessive commercialism.[40] However, the Massey Commission also recognized the role of private broadcasters in Canadian broadcasting—and their viability; since the 1920s, private broadcasters had flourished.[41]

Private broadcasters would continue to lobby for a separate regulator and for a reduced role for the CBC. The regulation of broadcasting and the establishment of national public broadcasting by the federal government were viewed as a problem in Quebec. Many Quebec-based groups saw federal involvement in broadcasting as a threat to Quebec's sovereignty.[42]

## The Fowler Commission (1955–1957)

In 1955, another Royal Commission on Broadcasting was established, this time led by Robert Fowler.[43] The Fowler Commission affirmed, again, the role of private broadcasting in Canada alongside public broadcasting, both as part of a single Canadian broadcasting system. Unlike its predecessors, it called for more advertising, including on the CBC.[44] It also recommended greater budgetary independence of the CBC from Parliament through longer-term financial commitments.[45] Opting not for separate regulatory bodies for private and public broadcasting, the Commission recommended the creation of a single regulator, to be called the Board of Broadcast Governors.[46]

## Board of Broadcast Governors (BBG; est. 1959)

The BBG was created in 1959 under a new *Broadcasting Act*, taking the role of regulator from the CBC.[47] The Board had the authority to make recommendations on new broadcasting licences to the Minister of Transport and to regulate broadcasters, including the CBC.[48]

The BBG created Canada's first set of broadcasting content regulations. In November 1959, it put in place a policy that 55 percent of television broadcast time should be dedicated to Canadian content.[49] It would later add that 40 percent of broadcast prime time (between 6 PM and midnight) be filled with Canadian content.[50]

The CBC had previously acted in the dual role of broadcaster and regulator. The establishment of the BBG meant that the CBC would no longer regulate both itself and its competitors; it also meant the public broadcaster would no longer have pre-eminence in the Canadian broadcasting system. Both public and private broadcasters would be viewed as equals in the sense that they would both be subject to the same regulatory body. Some were concerned this would lead to the withering away of public broadcasting and the dominance of private broadcasting.[51]

Several concerns dominated debates about public broadcasting in the decade to follow. First, concerns about the status of the public broadcaster and its pre-eminence or place in Canadian broadcasting would continue to be hotly debated. Second, support for sovereignty was growing in Quebec, and the role of the CBC in debates about Quebec sovereignty was at issue: Should the CBC and Radio-Canada allow sovereigntist views to be aired or sovereigntists to be employed? Views within CBC, Radio-Canada, and the government were polarized on these questions. Third, new cable television technology was not yet regulated, and government and broadcasters feared that cable could harm or even replace over-the-air broadcasting. Could the BBG regulate cable? A new *Broadcasting Act* in 1968 was established to partly answer these questions.[52]

## Canadian Radio-television and Telecommunications Commission (CRTC; est. 1968)

The 1968 *Broadcasting Act* replaced the BBG with the CRTC. The new act could be interpreted as placing the CBC in a paramount position in relation to private broadcasters, as it stated that where the interests of the two conflicted, the objectives of the CBC should be considered paramount.[53] The objectives of the CBC and of the broadcasting system as a whole were set out in the act.[54] In addition, the CRTC was given power to grant broadcast licences.

Two Supreme Court of Canada decisions affirmed the CRTC had jurisdiction over cable.[55] In the years to follow, the CRTC would establish a regulatory framework for cable television. In the 1980s, it would also establish a regulatory framework for specialty television services for which consumers paid extra, such as pay-per-view television and video on demand.[56]

## CBC *Northern Broadcasting Plan* (1974)

Prior to 1958, broadcasting in the Yukon and Northwest Territories was not focused on serving the local populations; rather, services were established to serve military and commercial (including mining) operations.[57] Up to the late 1960s, temporary workers from the south were the envisioned audience of radio broadcasting, not local northern populations.[58]

In 1958, the CBC decided to supply broadcast services to these northern territories, envisioning that programming from southern stations, primarily in English and French, would be broadcast in the north. The CBC's 1974 *Northern Broadcasting Plan* extended the CBC's service in the north.[59]

Tensions surrounded the CBC's northern expansion, which was seen by some as a form of cultural imperialism.[60] Radio was seen as a significant tool for preserving Inuit and Indigenous languages and culture. However, rather than broadcasting local programming in local Inuit and Indigenous languages, for many years, the CBC broadcast programming from the south, primarily in English and French.[61] While the CBC has historically been envisioned as a bulwark against American cultural imperialism, it was also seen as facilitating cultural imperialism by southern anglophone and francophone elites.[62]

## *Broadcasting Act* (1991)

Between 1985 and 1991, public consultations were held that led to the creation of the current *Broadcasting Act* in 1991. Under this act, the goal of the Canadian broadcasting system was set out as follows:

The Canadian broadcasting system should

    i.   serve to safeguard, enrich and strengthen the cultural, political, social and economic fabric of Canada,

ii.   encourage the development of Canadian expression by providing a wide range of programming that reflects Canadian attitudes, opinions, ideas, values and artistic creativity, by displaying Canadian talent in entertainment programming and by offering information and analysis concerning Canada and other countries from a Canadian point of view,

iii.   through its programming and the employment opportunities arising out of its operations, serve the needs and interests, and reflect the circumstances and aspirations, of Canadian men, women and children, including equal rights, the linguistic duality and multicultural and multiracial nature of Canadian society and the special place of aboriginal peoples within that society, and

iv.   be readily adaptable to scientific and technological change.[63]

Groups who took part in the consultations called for the inclusion of various goals and objectives under the new *Broadcasting Act*. Some wanted to make sure that both broadcasting content and employment were reflective of Canadian interests. Some fought successfully for the act to reflect Canada's bilingualism, its multiculturalism, the interests of women as well as men, and the interests of children. Some fought for the special place of Indigenous peoples in Canadian society to be reflected in the act. While the interests of women, children, cultural minorities, people with disabilities, and Indigenous peoples were, in one way or another, reflected in the new *Broadcasting Act*—often over the objections of private broadcasters—there were also some losses. The act recognized Canada's "linguistic duality" but not the multiple languages spoken by Canadians. It recognized the special place of Aboriginal peoples and the need for programming that was accessible to people with disabilities, but it stated that programming reflecting Aboriginal cultures should be offered "as resources become available for the purpose."[64]

## MEDIA OWNERSHIP REGULATION

The *Broadcasting Act* says, "the Canadian broadcasting system shall be effectively owned and controlled by Canadians."[65] This requires that, in order to be eligible to hold a broadcast licence, the majority of voting shares in a company must be owned by Canadian citizens.[66] Media ownership is regulated by the CRTC, through its ability to grant broadcasting licences, and the Competition Bureau.

While Canadian regulators have long required that broadcasting licences be owned by Canadians, Canada did not have legislation, regulations, or a policy on cross-media ownership (limiting the ownership of several types of media outlets in the same area) or audience share prior to 1998.[67] Such regulations have been used in other countries, such as the United States, to ensure that media ownership does not become too concentrated in the hands of one person or business. In 2008, the CRTC set new limits on the concentration of media ownership. It restricted media ownership such that one person or business could own no more than two types of media in a given market.[68] It limited the ownership of broadcasting licences "to ensure that one party does not control more than 45 percent of the total television audience share as a result of a transaction."[69] It also decided it would not permit transactions between broadcast distributors "(such as cable or satellite companies) that would result in one person effectively controlling the delivery of programming in a market."[70]

The 2008 decision of the CRTC was criticized because the limits set were so high that they would not have an effect on what critics saw as an already concentrated media market. Although broadcast ownership currently falls well below the 45-percent threshold, the "big four" control more than half of the market share in Canada.[71] The Canadian Media Concentration project has found a great deal of concentration in Canadian broadcasting, with big, vertically integrated companies holding a huge segment of Canadian media.[72]

## POLICIES ON CONTENT, REPRESENTATION, AND ACCESSIBILITY

The goal of Canadian broadcasting policy is to ensure content serves the needs and interests of Canadians and reflects Canada's multicultural, multiracial, and bilingual environment, and the special space for Aboriginal peoples in Canadian society. The CRTC implements this mandate via several policies, including Canadian Content (CanCon) regulation, policies on equitable portrayal, Indigenous broadcasting, ethnic broadcasting, campus and community radio,[73] accessibility policies, and its policy on abusive comment.

### Canadian Content Regulation

One of the most important objectives of Canadian broadcasting regulation is the promotion of the production and broadcast of Canadian content, including Canadian music, Canadian film and television productions, and Canadian news. These objectives are met through several regulatory measures.

First, the CRTC establishes *exhibition requirements*: Canadian broadcasters are required to broadcast minimum amounts of Canadian content. Second, the CRTC sets spending and *financial contribution requirements* for broadcasters and broadcast distribution undertakings—these require spending on and financial contributions toward the creation of Canadian content. For example, radio broadcasters are required to contribute toward funding programs for the development of Canadian talent, including the Foundation Assisting Canadian Talent on Recordings (FACTOR), which provides grants to musical artists. Third, broadcast distribution services are required to provide Canadian programming services.[74]

In 2010, the CRTC began to shift its focus away from exhibition requirements and toward spending requirements. It raised financial contribution requirements and reduced exhibition requirements, shifting focus toward the funding of big-budget productions.[75] Nevertheless, exhibition requirements continue to be important.

For private television stations, 50 percent of prime-time television programming (from 6 PM through until midnight) aired by broadcasters must be Canadian content. The former requirement that broadcasters air 55 percent Canadian content throughout the broadcast day (6 AM to midnight) has been removed.[76] For the CBC, Canadian content requirements are much higher. For specialty and pay television channels, the requirements are lower.[77]

Recently, these regulations were revised following the *Let's Talk* hearings held by the CRTC. *Let's Talk TV* was a massive overhaul of Canadian broadcasting regulations, which included replacing exhibition quotas with expenditure quotas, as well as changes to CanCon regulations that meant that 55 percent of all content overall must be Canadian, and content aired during prime time must include 50 percent Canadian programming.[78]

### *What Is Canadian Content?*

CANADIAN CONTENT ON TELEVISION

Programs produced in-house by broadcasters themselves, by Canadian federal or provincial governments, or by the National Film Board are considered Canadian.[79] For independently produced programs, a points system is used to determine whether a television production qualifies as Canadian.[80] Under this system, a production receives two points if the director is Canadian, two points if the screenwriter is Canadian, one point if the first lead (highest-paid) performer is Canadian, one point if the second lead performer (second highest-paid) is Canadian, one point if the production designer is Canadian, one point if the director of photography

**Figure 9.1**: Points System for Canadian Content in Film and Television

| | | |
|---|---|---|
| Producer | N/A | Must be Canadian |
| Director | 2 points | } Either the director or the screenwriter |
| Screenwriter | 2 points | must be Canadian |
| Lead performer 1 | 1 point | } One lead performer must be |
| Lead performer 2 | 1 point | Canadian |
| Director of photography | 1 point | |
| Music composer | 1 point | |
| Picture editor | 1 point | |
| | 6 points = Canadian | |
| Service costs used to produce the work | 75% must be paid to Canadians | |

is Canadian, one point if the music composer is Canadian, and one point if the picture editor is Canadian. To qualify as Canadian content, the producer must be Canadian, the work must obtain six points, and either the director or screenwriter and one of the two lead performers must be Canadian.[81]

In addition, to qualify as Canadian content, 75 percent of the service costs used to produce the work must be paid to Canadians.[82] Examples of service costs include:

- Remuneration for producer(s) and co-producer(s) (except for producer-related positions);
- Remuneration for key creative personnel eligible for points;
- Post-production/lab costs;
- Accounting and legal fees;
- Insurance brokerage and financing costs;
- Indirect expenses;
- Contingency costs;
- Goods purchased, such as film/video tape supplies; or
- Other costs not directly related to production.[83]

Some programs, in addition to those mentioned above, are generally recognized as being Canadian without being subject to the points system. These programs include:

- News and public affairs programs;
- Music video clips five minutes in length or less, which satisfy the music, artist, production, and lyrics (**MAPL**) points system (see below in this chapter);

- Public service announcements less than five minutes in length; and
- Some official co-ventures and co-productions between Canadian and non-Canadian partners.[84]

In 2015, the CRTC decided it would create a pilot-project exemption for productions based on Canadian-authored novels.[85] In addition, exemptions were made for high-cost productions. As long as the script and one lead performer was Canadian, and as long as 75 percent of production costs are paid to Canadians, the production would qualify as Canadian.

There are instances where productions are not eligible to qualify for CanCon certification. These productions include infomercials and television ads, as well as promotional and corporate videos or films.[86]

In addition to exhibition requirements, many broadcasters are also required to spend a percentage of their gross revenues on Canadian programming—often between 10 and 37 percent—though some broadcasters are not subject to a spending requirement.[87] In recent years, the CRTC has shifted to this method of promoting Canadian content. In 2015, the CRTC indicated that it would, in some cases, lift expenditure requirements in favour of relying on market forces for the production of some types of Canadian content.[88]

CANADIAN CONTENT ON RADIO

Canadian content requirements for radio primarily focus on popular music, rather than on spoken word and other types of music (such as classical music, jazz, or world music). CRTC regulations require that 35 percent of popular music broadcast on Canadian radio stations must be Canadian.[89] Commercial radio stations must also ensure that 35 percent of music played Monday through Friday between 6 AM and 6 PM is Canadian, and French-language radio stations must play at least 65 percent French-language popular music, including 55 percent of popular music played between 6 AM and 6 PM.[90] On satellite radio services like Sirius, 10 percent of channels offered must be Canadian-produced.[91]

For music, the MAPL system is used to determine whether music is Canadian. Two of the four MAPL elements (music, artist, production, and lyrics) must be Canadian in order for a song to qualify as Canadian.

## Simultaneous Substitution Policy

Most Canadian broadcasters make money by selling advertising or commercials on their programs. Many purchase American programming to fill part of their

**Figure 9.2:** MAPL System for Canadian Content in Music

| | |
|---|---|
| **M** (music): | The music is composed entirely by a Canadian. |
| **A** (artist): | The music is, or the lyrics are, performed principally by a Canadian. |
| **P** (production): | The musical selection consists of a live performance that is recorded wholly in Canada or performed wholly in Canada and broadcast live in Canada. |
| **L** (lyrics): | The lyrics are written entirely by a Canadian. |
| Two of the four MAPL elements (music, artist, production, and lyrics) must be Canadian in order for a song to qualify as Canadian. | |

schedule. However, American programs are also carried on American networks, received by cable or satellite subscribers in Canada. To give Canadian broadcasters the ability to have the full benefit of advertising sales in the programs for which they have purchased the rights to the Canadian market, CRTC regulations on **simultaneous substitution** allow Canadian broadcasters to request that their own advertising be substituted in place of the American advertising on American channels. That way, advertisers who wish to reach the Canadian market by placing a commercial in an American program must purchase that spot from a Canadian broadcaster. Further, Canadian broadcasters can sell their advertisements at a higher rate because they reach a larger audience, encompassing both the audience of the Canadian broadcaster and also recipients of American network broadcasting transmitted by cable or satellite.[92]

Due to complaints received from consumers who wish to see the specialized American advertising broadcast during the Super Bowl, the CRTC changed its policy in 2016 to stop simultaneous substitution during that event. (This decision has been appealed to the Supreme Court of Canada; a decision is awaited as of this writing.[93]) Without simultaneous substitution, the original American commercials—rather than the simultaneous substituted Canadian commercials—appear.[94] However, in 2018, Canada signed the *United States-Mexico-Canada Free Trade Agreement*, which restored simultaneous substitution to the Super Bowl.

## Equitable Portrayal Code

Gender is often portrayed in stereotypical ways on television, and women are generally underrepresented.[95] The CRTC has attempted to address these problems through the development of the ***Equitable Portrayal Code***, which was created in partnership with broadcasters and members of the public. The *Equitable Portrayal Code* is administered by the Canadian Broadcast Standards Council (CBSC).

The CBSC is an industry self-regulatory group put together by the Canadian Association of Broadcasters (CAB). At the behest of the CRTC, the CBSC began setting up codes of conduct for the broadcasting industry in the 1980s. These received CRTC sanction in 1991.

Today's *Equitable Portrayal Code* replaced an earlier code of conduct, the *Sex-Role Portrayal Code*, in 2008.[96] It requires that "television and radio programming shall respect the principle of equitable portrayal of all individuals" and prohibits "abusive or unduly discriminatory material or comment which is based on matters of race, national or ethnic origin, color, religion, age, gender, sexual orientation, marital status or physical or mental disability," along with negative, stereotypical, degrading, and exploitative programming. However, it provides that "individuals who are themselves bigoted or intolerant may be part of a fictional or non-fictional program, provided that the program is not itself abusive or unduly discriminatory" and permits some "comedic, humorous or satirical content" even if discriminatory or stereotypical, that may be "light and relatively inoffensive" along with other programming in the public interest.[97]

Complaints under the *Equitable Portrayal Code* are adjudicated not by the CRTC but by the CBSC. The CBSC has the power to publish decisions about its cases and to require that a station make on-air announcements and apologies when the code is broken.

### The Native Broadcasting Policy and Aboriginal Peoples Television Network

The *Broadcasting Act* states that the Canadian broadcasting system should "through its programming and employment opportunities arising out of its operations" recognize "the special place of aboriginal peoples within [Canadian] society."[98] As well, "programming that reflects the aboriginal cultures of Canada should be provided within the Canadian broadcasting system as resources become available for the purpose."[99]

Canada's Truth and Reconciliation Commission noted that the *Broadcasting Act* does not prioritize broadcasting in Indigenous languages in the same way that English- and French-language broadcasting is prioritized.[100] The words "as resources become available for the purpose" has allowed public and private broadcasters to deprioritize Indigenous broadcasting if they did not feel they had the resources. For example, the TRC noted that the CBC faced limitations in its ability to provide Indigenous content and to increase the number of Indigenous people among its ranks and leadership (where Indigenous representation was far below demographic levels), especially due to budgetary cutbacks.[101] The TRC therefore called on the federal government to increase the CBC's resources.[102]

Indigenous broadcasters have played an important, though marginalized, role in the Canadian broadcasting system. There is a rich history of Indigenous radio broadcasting in Canada.[103] When a Native Broadcasting Policy was established in 1983, greater priority began to be placed on programming produced by Indigenous peoples, in contrast to the CBC's previous focus. A Northern Native Broadcast Access Program was established to help fund the protection of Indigenous content.[104] In 1990, the CRTC announced a revised Native Broadcasting Policy to encourage Indigenous broadcasting in all regions of Canada.[105] Under the policy, a *native undertaking* is a broadcast undertaking that is:

> owned and controlled by a non-profit organization whose structure provides for board membership by the native population of the region served. Its programming can be in any native Canadian language or in either or both of the two official languages, but should be specifically oriented to the native population and reflect the interests and needs specific to the native audience it is licensed to serve. It has a distinct role in fostering the development of aboriginal cultures and, where possible, the preservation of ancestral languages.[106]

In 1998, some "native undertakings"—those serving remote areas with no other commercial stations—were exempted from broadcast licensing requirements.[107] In issuing this exemption, the CRTC based its decision "on the fact that, although culturally important, these stations have limited resources, provide radio services in unique circumstances and, by definition, operate in areas where no commercial stations are operating."[108]

The exemption recognizes the lack of resources faced by Indigenous broadcasters. Funding cutbacks and the precarious financial resources available to Indigenous broadcasters has made it difficult for licensed Indigenous broadcasters, in many cases, to meet their conditions of licence (such as to submit required annual reports).[109] Although Indigenous ("native") broadcasters play much the same public service broadcasting role as does the CBC, they do not receive the same supports, legislative recognition,[110] and funding. As Szwarc notes, the contributions of unlicensed Indigenous broadcasters to meeting the goals of the *Broadcasting Act* cannot be tracked, due to the exemption from reporting requirements.[111] This means, by extension, that the CRTC cannot measure the success of the broadcasting system in serving Indigenous peoples and, by extension, its own success (or lack thereof) in this regard.[112]

Even before this exemption, unlicensed Indigenous radio stations played an important role in Indigenous broadcasting in Canada. Some Indigenous groups founded radio broadcasting stations without acquiring a licence from the CRTC because the licensing process is long and expensive.[113] Others chose not to pursue a CRTC licence because they do not recognize the CRTC's authority over the airwaves. For example, Secwepemc Radio, established on the Neskonlith Reserve in British Columbia, took the position that "As aboriginal people we did not give up our right to make use of the electromagnetic spectrum to carry on our traditions, language and culture."[114] Neskie Manuel, who worked at Secwepemc Radio, noted, "our expression of sovereignty was our ability to choose what was going onto the airwaves and exposing what is going on in other Indigenous communities around the world."[115]

Indigenous groups' claims of sovereignty over the broadcasting spectrum are based in section 35 of the *Constitution Act, 1982*, which recognizes Aboriginal and treaty rights. Spectrum rights of Indigenous peoples have been recognized, to some extent, in the United States and New Zealand, but have not been formally affirmed in Canada.[116]

Indigenous broadcasters play an important role. Many Indigenous languages are endangered, in a large part due to assimilationist policies and the residential school system, where children were taken away from their families and communities and forbidden from speaking their own languages.[117] Indigenous owned and controlled broadcasters can play a role in the preservation of Indigenous languages, cultures, and identities. Some argue that radio broadcasting is particularly suited to Indigenous cultures because "radio is an oral and aural medium."[118]

In 1999, the Aboriginal Peoples Television Network (APTN) was licensed by the CRTC.[119] It expands on the "native undertakings" mentioned above. It is mandatory that basic cable and satellite carriers include APTN in all their packages.[120] The TRC noted that APTN could provide media leadership in supporting reconciliation.[121]

Following the TRC, questions have been asked about how Canadian broadcasting policy should be revised to further reconciliation. A revised Indigenous broadcasting policy, recommended by a group of Indigenous people and broadcasting experts in 2019, could focus on improved consultation and representation. It could see Indigenous governance structures, rather than the CRTC, grant broadcasting licences and control broadcasting spectrum as related to Indigenous broadcasting.[122] Content regulation could allocate greater space to Indigenous languages and prioritize funding for Indigenous content production, possibly including quotas for Indigenous language programming and Indigenous music.[123]

In June 2019, the CRTC announced that it would "co-develop a new Indigenous broadcasting policy with First Nations, Métis, and Inuit broadcasters, content creators, and audiences."[124] The co-development process would begin with engagement sessions, public consultations with Indigenous and non-Indigenous people, and a presentation of preliminary views to Indigenous peoples for further feedback.[125]

Support of Indigenous broadcasting has been emphasized as crucial to Indigenous rights and culture. The *United Nations Declaration on the Rights of Indigenous Peoples* (UNDRIP) declares:

1. Indigenous peoples have the right to establish their own media in their own languages and to have access to all forms of non-indigenous media without discrimination.
2. States shall take effective measures to ensure that State-owned media duly reflect indigenous cultural diversity. States, without prejudice to ensuring full freedom of expression, should encourage privately owned media to adequately reflect indigenous cultural diversity.[126]

## Ethnic Broadcasting Policy

Under the CRTC's Ethnic Broadcasting Policy, the CRTC licenses ethnic broadcasting stations. The policy defines ethnic broadcasting as "programming directed to any culturally or racially distinct group other than one that is Aboriginal Canadian, or from France or the British Isles. Such programming may be in any language or combination of languages."[127] Ethnic broadcasting stations are required to meet Canadian content requirements, and must also dedicate 60 percent of broadcast time each month to ethnic programming, and 50 percent of broadcast time to third-language programming (programming in languages "other than English, French, or an Aboriginal language").[128] Ethnic broadcasting stations must each serve a variety of ethnic groups.[129]

## CRTC Accessibility Policies

The CRTC is required under the *Broadcasting Act* to provide programming accessible to people who are disabled. However, the act notes that this is required "as resources become available."[130]

To ensure broadcast programming is accessible, the CRTC has created policies on closed captioning, described video, and targeted accessibility services.[131]

Closed captioning must be included on all broadcast programming.[132] A minimum number of hours of described video, a service where a narrator describes what is happening in the video for people who are blind or visually impaired, is required per week.[133] This is put on a separate audio track. Broadcasters are required to provide a minimum amount of described video per work. The CRTC also encourages programs specifically designed for people with disabilities. In 2007, the CRTC approved a new specialty channel titled The Accessibility Channel. This channel provides services in accessible format without the need for special equipment. The channel is now called Accessible Media, Inc., or AMI-TV.[134]

### CRTC Policy on Abusive Comment

While broadcaster content is mainly regulated through the CBSC, the CRTC has power to prohibit abusive comment in some cases. Regulations under the *Broadcasting Act* prohibit:

> any abusive comment or abusive pictorial representation that, when taken in context, tends to or is likely to expose an individual or a group or class of individuals to hatred or contempt on the basis of race, national or ethnic origin, colour, religion, sex, sexual orientation, age or mental or physical disability.[135]

In some cases, complaints have been raised under the CRTC's abusive comment policy. In one 2007 complaint about an episode of the television show *Little Mosque on the Prairie*, in which various characters voiced opposition to a same-sex marriage and the gay couple ultimately left town, the CRTC concluded that there was stereotyping. However, this in and of itself did not constitute "abusive comment." The CRTC argued that the show did not promote or encourage hateful behaviour.[136] The CRTC found no evidence that the CBC was promoting hate or hateful messages; it called the program "well intentioned."[137] However, in other cases, the CRTC has found content to be "abusive comment."

## WHOM DOES CANADIAN BROADCASTING REGULATION SERVE?

### The Public Interest?

#### *Pluralism*
Some Canadian communication scholars, including broadcast historian Marc Raboy, argue that Canadian broadcast policy serves the public interest to some

extent, in part because Canadian broadcasting draws on a strong and deep tradition of public consultation.[138] Consultation with a cross-section of Canadians
on the role and purposes that should be reflected in Canadian broadcasting regulation allows, according to pluralism theory, a diversity of Canadians to see
their interests reflected in the Canadian broadcasting system and the regulation
thereof. Not all groups have an equal say, as some are more well-funded and/or
more motivated to present their views during the consultation process, but no
single group dominates the process. Canadian broadcasting policy serves the
public interest in a general sense, especially where a variety of groups participate
in policymaking processes.

However, Raboy also critiques Canadian broadcast policy, and he demon-
strates that, despite the diversity of voices in the processes of broadcast policymaking, Canadian broadcasting has become increasingly commercialized.
Public broadcasting has been deprioritized over the long term and has been
forced to compete with commercial broadcasters in ways that prevent it from
focusing on fostering dialogue among Canadians, greater community-building,
more grassroots production, and greater educational content. Many of the poten-
tials of broadcasting were lost as a result.[139]

Such losses are a significant blow to media pluralism. As Canadian communications scholar Robert Hackett notes, mainstream for-profit media are
constrained by their ideological and economic ties to global capitalism. Many
major media companies are transnational and have corporate links throughout
the economy. "Any challenge to the structures and ideology of contemporary
capitalism is also a challenge to dominant media," notes Hackett.[140]

> Can ecologically sustainable economies be achieved without challenging a media/
> advertising complex that cultivates the desire for limitless consumption? Can a
> level playing field for diverse political parties be achieved in the US without bitter
> opposition from the television networks with a vested interest in hyper-expensive
> political advertising? Can ethnic and gender equality be achieved while media
> representations and employment practices continue to stereotype, marginalize
> or under-represent women and minorities? Do progressive policies on social pro-
> grams and workers' rights have much chance when the agenda-setting media are
> closely tied to the corporate elite and its interests?

For this reason, it is crucial that a variety of media models, including
non-profit, alternative, and publicly funded media and information sources exist,
in order to support a true diversity of voices.

Even if there is a mix of media models, some are disadvantaged in policy processes. Szwarc notes that "There are currently no advocacy groups or organizations dedicated to Indigenous broadcasting in Canada, making it difficult for individuals to intervene with the CRTC or lobby parliamentarians on behalf of Indigenous listeners in Canada."[141] The ideal of pluralism is strained and compromised under conditions where groups are unable to participate in policy processes.

## Bureaucracy and Bureaucrats?

### *Bureaucratic, Neoliberal, and Libertarian Theory*

Others have drawn on bureaucratic, neoliberal, and libertarian theories to suggest that broadcast regulation in Canada has tended to serve the state itself by expanding the power of bureaucrats, such that it impedes freedom of thought and expression. During the Massey Commission's tenure, Raboy notes that "a kind of libertarian right grouped around the private broadcasters."[142] Private broadcasters tended to see public broadcasting as being tied to a "nanny state" or an expanding welfare state.[143] Popular commentators, including Fox News' Tammy Bruce, have argued that broadcasting regulation has gone too far, and standards such as the *Sex Role Portrayal Code* and the current *Equitable Portrayal Code* represent an invasion on freedom of thought and expression, likening such standards to thought police.[144]

Arguments that state regulation and ownership of broadcasting services stand in the way of growth and consumer choice have been central to the rise of neoliberalism in broadcasting. Neoliberal theorists have advocated for the deregulation and privatization of broadcasting and for reduced state intervention in broadcasting.[145] Such policies are advocated by transnational corporations, who have invested in domestic communication industries around the world and by the owners of domestic broadcasting companies, who benefit financially from growth powered by international investment. This has led to the rise of "mega-global" communication companies; the privatization of public broadcasters; an increasingly international advertising market; the development of new technologies of broadcasting, including new media broadcasting by transnationals; and vertical and horizontal integration in broadcasting.

Vertical integration, or the integration of the ownership of broadcasters or broadcast distributors with the ownership of the broadcasted programming, as well as the **horizontal integration** of broadcast companies through mergers and acquisitions, can drive broadcasters' profits.[146] Vertical integration allows companies to reduce the costs of content while raising costs for rivals, thus driving profits and, possibly, reducing consumer prices.[147] Horizontal integration, also known as consolidation, allows broadcast owners to increase profits by accessing new markets previously served by acquired or merged companies and by sharing the same content over a larger audience.

## The Privileged?

### *Critical Political Economy*

Much of the writing and analysis about Canadian broadcasting history and regulation has been based in the field of critical political economy. This literature has pointed to broadcasting content's dual and contradictory role both as a commodity and as a public good—an important medium of culture, empowerment (and oppression), and community—and the role that regulation has played in shaping the Canadian broadcasting system.[148]

Many communication theorists argue that neoliberal broadcast policies serve the private owners and stockholders of broadcast companies, rather than the public interest in a broader sense. Raboy has pointed to the ways that technological nationalism in Canadian broadcast policy gave way to policies that ultimately served private broadcasters' interests, by whittling away support for nation-building and public broadcasting.[149] Horizontal and vertical integration may drive company profits, but they also reduce competition and choice for consumers. For example, a broadcast distributor may seek to either exclude or increase the prices of competitor-owned content, making that content either more expensive or inaccessible altogether.[150] Neoliberal broadcast policies tend to reduce the production of local content. Partly through the privatization of, and thus reduction of, public broadcasting, neoliberal policies support the production of content serving advertisers' interests rather than the public interest. For example, Toby Miller notes that food channels are vehicles of product advertising, rather than educating citizens about the global fast-food industry and the treatment of animals, labourers, and the environment within the food industry. Similarly, private weather reporting is apolitical, rather than providing education and public engagement on climate change, ecological risk, and water politics.[151]

### *Feminist and Queer Studies*

Although the *Broadcasting Act* states that Canadian broadcasting should "serve the needs and interests, and reflect the circumstances and aspirations, of Canadian men, women and children," policymakers and broadcasters have failed to meet the goal of gender equality in broadcasting.[152] Many feminists have critiqued Canadian broadcast policy for its failures to address the underrepresentation of women in broadcasting, the character of the portrayal of women in broadcasting, and the underrepresentation of women in roles of leadership in the broadcasting industry.

Women are underrepresented in broadcasting content, making up just 40 percent of speaking characters on television.[153] In broadcast news, women are underrepresented in news stories about politics, government, and economics, while they are overrepresented in stories about celebrity, arts, and media.[154] This underrepresentation draws on a history of broadcasting that was originally uncomfortable with women's voices on the air. As Copeland notes, historically, women confronted attitudes that were "very patriarchal and heteronormative toward the role of women and the amount of physical (sonic, visual, and embodied) space a woman could inhabit."[155]

Feminists have also challenged the character of women's portrayal in broadcasting, and the inadequacy of policy efforts to change stereotypical or sexist portrayals of women. Linda Trimble's history and analysis of the CBSC's *Sex-Role Portrayal Code*, predecessor to the *Equitable Portrayal Code*, suggests the code placed considerable demands on broadcasters to portray women and men equitably, but was ineffective. Broadcasters were resistant to implementing such a code when women's groups called for a policy that would address sex-role stereotyping on television, and the CRTC, though it did encourage the establishment of the code, did little to ensure that it was enforced.[156]

Women's representation in broadcasting remains, in many cases, gendered; women are less likely to be represented in broadcast news as leaders, experts, or news anchors and are more likely to be represented as victims.[157] Women's issues, furthermore, are more likely to be portrayed as particular special-interest topics rather than issues of general importance. When women's issues are portrayed as of universal concern, the critical component of relevance to women is often lost, as when reporting on assaults, murders, and mass shootings of women does not address the problem of male violence against women.[158]

Feminists have also focused on women's status as workers in the broadcasting industry. Women are severely underrepresented in key positions in television, making up just 26 percent of overall employees in television, and just 17 percent of directors, 38 percent of writers, and 0 percent of cinematographers in Canadian English television drama series in 2012–13.[159] Women are also underrepresented in work in film.[160] Working roles in broadcasting and television remain very much gendered, and women's experiences are mediated by intersecting identities, including age, racialization, and parental status.[161] The #MeToo movement has highlighted women's experiences of sexual violence and harassment in the film and broadcasting industries, but "an entirely 'new day' of gendered and sexual relations still seems," according to some researchers, "a long way off."[162]

**LGBTQ2**+ communities have also had significant interests in broadcasting policy in Canada. Community and campus radio, supported by community radio policies, have been sites of queer broadcasting in Canada since the 1970s. Such broadcasts were, on the one hand, extremely important to queer people, especially before relatively positive representations of queer identities began to appear in mainstream media in the late 1990s.[163] At the same time, mainstream representations often present queer people in commodified and stereotypical roles, with representations of queer women often produced for the heterosexual male gaze.[164]

### Indigenous Theory, Postcolonial Analysis, and Critical Race Theory

Race and ethnicity are, as critical race theorists note, social constructs; they are also categories that have played a significant role in the Canadian broadcasting system.[165] The system was put in place to foster a sense of Canadian identity and nationalism that privileged white voices and legitimized a Canadian colonial state that treated non-European immigrants as resources and worked to erase Indigenous peoples and culture.[166] Canadian broadcasting policy reinforces categories of "Native" and "ethnic" in its broadcasting licensing systems. It marginalizes Indigenous, ethnic, and racialized people's voices. Rather than ensuring that Indigenous, ethnic, and racialized people have voice and space within mainstream broadcast programming that are free of stereotypical and abusive portrayals, Canada's ethnic and "Native" broadcasting policies have structured a system that segregates Indigenous and ethnic programming in alternative "Native broadcasting" and "ethnic broadcasting" stations.[167] The CBC historically prioritized expansion of its network in the north to serve people from the south working, usually temporarily, in the north, with southern broadcast programming.[168]

Lorna Roth's work on Canadian broadcasting policy has pointed to the ways that policies on Indigenous and ethnic broadcasting have often served to marginalize Indigenous and ethnic communities, preserving white dominance in broadcasting.[169] She argues that the Ethnic Broadcasting Policy obscures the fact that "anglophones and francophones have ethnicity too,"[170] and thus masks and perpetuates, rather than addressing, cultural and racial inequality:

I suggest that Canadian policymakers (though not necessarily in a self-reflexive manner) have taken existing evidence of "inequality" and renamed it "diversity," a more neutral category. Re-labelling inequality as "diversity" makes it easier to mask cultural and racial hierarchy and marginalization within mainstream and specialized organizations of Canadian society. There is an unequal distribution of power between those who talk about ethnicity and those who are talked about. The shift in terminology from "inequality" to "diversity" may be viewed as a discursive strategy of those ethnic peoples in power, that is, mostly anglophones and francophones, to disguise institutional and cognitive inequities embedded in their very manner of thinking about, building, and controlling institutional structures.[171]

Roth argues that CRTC policy, including its Ethnic Broadcasting Policy and its decision to require carriage of APTN on basic cable, has made, to some extent, a positive contribution to the visibility and culture of Indigenous peoples; these have affirmed the (marginal) place of Indigenous peoples and ethnic minorities in the Canadian broadcasting system.[172] In order to reduce this level of marginalization, some have called for affirmative action programs. Critical race theorists have called for minority broadcast ownership provisions to facilitate the ownership of broadcast facilities by people of colour and other minority groups.[173] Other affirmative action programs would require private and public broadcasters to guarantee representation at all levels of hiring and decision-making off-screen, as well as in on-screen representations.[174] Critical race theorists call not for "colourblind" broadcast policies but for policies that confront the racial inequities and substantive injuries to which media and governments have contributed.[175]

## FURTHER READING

Armstrong, Robert. *Broadcasting Policy in Canada*. 2nd ed. Toronto: University of Toronto Press, 2016.

Grant, Peter. *Communications Law and the Courts in Canada: An Annotated Guide to Judicial Decisions Relating to the Regulation of Communications and Copyright in Canada*. Toronto: McCarthy Tétrault, 2010.

Jin, Dal Yong. "Transformation of the World Television System under Neoliberal Globalization, 1983 to 2003." *Television & New Media* 8, no. 3 (2007): 179–96.

Meehan, Eileen R., and Ellen Riordan, eds. *Sex & Money: Feminism and Political Economy in the Media*. Minneapolis: University of Minnesota Press, 2002.

Raboy, Marc. *Missed Opportunities: The Story of Canada's Broadcasting Policy*. Montreal: McGill-Queen's University Press, 1990.

Roth, Lorna. *Something New in the Air: The Story of First Peoples Television Broadcasting in Canada*. Montreal: McGill-Queen's University Press, 2005.

Salter, Liora, and Felix N.L. Odartey-Wellington. *The CRTC and Broadcasting Regulation in Canada*. Toronto: Carswell, 2008.

Thomas, Eric. "Canadian Broadcasting and Multiculturalism: Attempts to Accommodate Ethnic Minorities." *Canadian Journal of Communication* 17, no. 3 (1992).

# NOTES

1. Robert Armstrong, *Broadcasting Policy in Canada*, 2nd ed. (Toronto: University of Toronto Press, 2016), 3. A more complex definition, and the one used in the Canadian *Broadcasting Act*, will be discussed in Chapter 10.

2. Gabriele Balbi and Juraj Kittler, "One-to-One and One-to-Many Dichotomy: Grand Theories, Periodization, and Historical Narratives in Communication Studies," *International Journal of Communication* 10 (2016): 20.

3. CRTC, "Public Notice CRTC 1999-197: Exemption Order for New Media Broadcasting Undertakings."

4. In 2011, the CRTC revoked the licence from CKLN-FM, a campus radio station at Ryerson University, because the station was not in compliance with regulatory requirements. CKLN-FM had encountered management difficulties and was unable to consistently remain on the air as scheduled. Due to internal disputes, programming had been interrupted, and the station had failed to file annual returns and provide proper logs of their programming. CRTC, "Broadcasting Decision CRTC 2011-56: CKLN-FM Toronto—Revocation of Licence," Decisions, January 28, 2011, https://crtc.gc.ca/eng/archive/2011/2011-56.htm.

5. CRTC, "Broadcasting Decision CRTC 2004-271: CHOI-FM—Non-Renewal of Licence," Decisions, September 20, 2007, https://crtc.gc.ca/eng/archive/2004/db2004-271.htm; Armstrong, 88–92; Anne-Marie Gingras, "Freedom of Expression and Shock Radio: Quebec CHOI-FM as a Case Study," *World Political Science* 4, no. 3 (2008): 2363–4782.

6. *Broadcasting Act*, SC 1991, c 11, s 2 (1); Armstrong, 9.

7. Armstrong, 9.

8. Ibid., 10.

9. Lessig, *The Future of Ideas: The Fate of the Commons in a Connected World* (New York: Vintage Books, 2002), chaps. 5 and 12.

10. For more, see Armstrong, 8–10.

11. Sheryl Hamilton, *Law's Expression: Communication, Law and Media in Canada* (Toronto: LexisNexis, 2009), 7–9.

12. Maurice Charland, "Technological Nationalism," *CTheory* 10, no. 1–2 (1986): 196–220.

13. Eric Thomas, "Canadian Broadcasting and Multiculturalism: Attempts to Accommodate Ethnic Minorities," *Canadian Journal of Communication* 17, no. 3 (1992).

14. Armstrong, 7–8.

15. Marc Raboy, "Media," in *Media Divides: Communication Rights and the Right to Communicate in Canada*, eds. Marc Raboy, William J. McIver, and Jeremy Shtern (Vancouver: UBC Press, 2010), 102–3.

16. *FCC v Pacifica Foundation*, 438 US 726 (1978); Ashley Packard, *Digital Media Law*, 2nd ed. (Malden, MA: Wiley-Blackwell, 2013), 51–54, 63–66.

17. Marc Raboy, William J. McIver, and Jeremy Shtern, *Media Divides: Communication Rights and the Right to Communicate in Canada* (Vancouver: UBC Press, 2010), 100–1.

18. Allan Gregg, "What Canadians Think of the News Media," *Policy Options*, February 10, 2017, http://policyoptions.irpp.org/magazines/february-2017/what-canadians-think-of-the-news-media/.

19. Eugene F. Shaw, "Agenda-Setting and Mass Communication Theory," *Gazette (Leiden, Netherlands)* 25, no. 2 (1979): 96–105.

20. *Broadcasting Act*, SC 1991, c 11, s 3(2); see also Armstrong, 34, 41; David Skinner, "Divided Loyalties: The Early Development of Canada's 'Single' Broadcasting System," *Journal of Radio Studies* 12, no. 1 (2005): 136–55; CRTC, "Canadian Broadcasting 'a Single System': Policy Statement on Canadian Television," Ottawa: Bell Canada, 1971.

21. *Broadcasting Act*, s 2(1).

22. Ibid.

23. Marc Raboy, *Marconi: The Man Who Networked the World* (New York: Oxford University Press, 2016).

24. Armstrong, 23.

25. Royal Commission on Radio Broadcasting and John Aird, *Report of the Royal Commission on Radio Broadcasting* (Ottawa: F.A. Acland, Printer, 1929).

26. Ibid., 6.

27. Ibid.

28. Ibid.

29. Armstrong, 27.

30. Royal Commission on Radio Broadcasting, 12–13; Marc Raboy, *Missed Opportunities: The Story of Canada's Broadcasting Policy* (Montreal: McGill-Queen's University Press, 1990), 29.

31. Mike Gasher, "Invoking Public Support for Public Broadcasting: The Aird Commission Revisited," *Canadian Journal of Communication* 23, no. 2 (1998), para 3; Marc Raboy, "The Role of Public Consultation in Shaping the Canadian Broadcasting System," *Canadian Journal of Political Science/Revue Canadienne de Science Politique* 28, no. 3 (1995): 455–77.

32. *Canadian Radio Broadcasting Act, 1932*, SC 1932, c 51.

33. Mary Vipond, "The Beginnings of Public Broadcasting in Canada: The CRBC, 1932–1936," *Canadian Journal of Communication* 19, no. 2 (1994): 151.

34. Raboy, *Missed Opportunities*, 29.

35. Armstrong, 29.

36. *Canadian Broadcasting Act, 1936*, c 24, 1 Ed VIII, s 22.

37. CBC, "Our History," accessed November 1, 2018, http://www.cbc.radio-canada.ca/en/explore/our-history/.

38. Ibid.

39. Raboy, *Missed Opportunities*, 93.

40. Armstrong, 33–34.

41. Raboy, *Missed Opportunities*, 103.

42. Ibid., 95–108.

43. Ibid., 118.

44. Ibid., 129.

45. Ibid.

46. Ibid., 119–30; Armstrong, 34–35.

47. *Broadcasting Act*, SC 1958, c 22.

48. Armstrong, 36.

49. Ibid.

50. Ibid., 37.

51. Raboy, *Missed Opportunities*, 133–36.

52. Ibid., c. 4.

53. Raboy, McIver, and Shtern, 179; Armstrong, 42; *Broadcasting Act*, 1968, s 2.

54. Armstrong, 42.

55. *Capital Cities Comm. v CRTC*, [1978] 2 SCR 141; *Public Service Board et al v Dionne et al*, [1978] 2 SCR 191; Armstrong, 43.

56. Armstrong, 48–50, chap. 10.

57. Anne F. MacLennan, "Cultural Imperialism of the North? The Expansion of the CBC Northern Service and Community Radio," *Radio Journal: International Studies in Broadcast & Audio Media* 9, no. 1 (2011): 63–81.

58. Ibid.

59. Ibid. For more on radio broadcasting in the North, see Heather E. Hudson, "The Role of Radio in the Canadian North—The Far North," *Journal of Communication* 27, no. 4 (1977): 130–39.

60. MacLennan.

61. Ibid.; Bruce L. Smith and Jerry C. Brigham, "Benchmark: Native Radio Broadcasting in North America: An Overview of Systems in the United States and Canada," *Journal of Broadcasting & Electronic Media* 36, no. 2 (1992): 183–94.

62. MacLennan.

63. *Broadcasting Act*, SC 1991, c 11, s 3(1)(d).

64. *Broadcasting Act*, SC 1991, s 3(1)(o) and (p); see also Skinner.

65. *Broadcasting Act*, SC 1991, s 3(1)(a).

66. For further detail, see Armstrong, chap. 13.

67. Raboy, McIver, and Shtern, 96.

68. CRTC, "Broadcasting Public Notice CRTC 2008-4: Regulatory Policy: Regulatory Policy—Diversity of Voices," Regulatory Policies, January 15, 2008, https://crtc.gc.ca/eng/archive/2008/pb2008-4.htm.

69. Deborah Jones, "CRTC Deals with Media Concentration," J-Source, January 15, 2008, http://j-source.ca/article/crtc-deals-with-media-concentration/.

70. Ibid.

71. Dwayne Winseck, "Media and Internet Concentration in Canada Report 1984–2015," Canadian Media Concentration Research Project, November 22, 2016, http://www.cmcrp.org/media-and-internet-concentration-in-canada-report-1984-2015/.

72. See the Canadian Media Concentration Research Project at http://www.cmcrp.org/. See also David Skinner and Mike Gasher, "So Much by So Few: Media Policy and Ownership in Canada," in *Converging Media, Diverging Politics: A Political Economy of News in the United States and Canada*, eds. David Skinner, Mike Gasher, and James Compton (Lanham, MD: Rowman & Littlefield, 2005), 51–76.

73. CRTC, "Broadcasting Regulatory Policy CRTC 2010-499: Campus and Community Radio Policy" (Gatineau, QC: CRTC, 2010), https://crtc.gc.ca/eng/archive/2010/2010-499.htm; Brian Fauteux, *Music in Range: The Culture of Canadian Campus Radio* (Waterloo, ON: Wilfrid Laurier University Press, 2015).

74. Armstrong, 96–97.

75. Ibid., 104.

76. Ibid.; CRTC, "Broadcasting Regulatory Policy CRTC 2015-86: Let's Talk TV—The Way Forward—Creating Compelling and Diverse Canadian Programming," Regulatory Policies, March 12, 2015, para 193, https://crtc.gc.ca/eng/archive/2015/2015-86.htm.

77. Armstrong, 104.

78. Mary Elizabeth Luka and Catherine Middleton, "Citizen Involvement during the CRTC's Let's Talk TV Consultation," *Canadian Journal of Communication* 42, no. 1 (2017).

79. Armstrong, 101.

80. The CRTC points system is similar to the Canadian Audio-Visual Certification Office (CAVCO) points system, which is used to determine eligibility for federal and provincial tax credits. Programs certified by CAVCO also qualify as Canadian. See Armstrong, 101.

81. CRTC, "So What Makes It Canadian?" accessed November 1, 2018, https://crtc. gc.ca/eng/cancon/c_cdn.htm.

82. CRTC; CRTC, "Public Notice CRTC 2000-42: Certification for Canadian Programs—A Revised Approach," Regulatory Policies, March 17, 2000, https://crtc.gc.ca/eng/ archive/2000/pb2000-42.htm.

83. Ibid.

84. Ibid.

85. CRTC, "Let's Talk TV," para 128.

86. CRTC, "Certification for Canadian Programs."

87. Armstrong, 98; CRTC, "Broadcasting Regulatory Policy CRTC 2010-167: A Group-Based Approach to the Licensing of Private Television Services," Regulatory Policies, March 22, 2010, https://crtc.gc.ca/eng/archive/2010/2010-167.htm; CRTC, "Let's Talk TV."

88. Armstrong, 108–10. The CRTC indicated that it would lift some expenditure requirements for Programs of National Interest (PNI).

89. Armstrong, 98; CRTC, "Canadian Content Requirements for Canadian Music on Radio Stations," accessed November 1, 2018, https://crtc.gc.ca/eng/cancon/r_ cdn.htm.

90. Armstrong, 98; CRTC, "Broadcasting Public Notice CRTC 2006-158: Commercial Radio Policy 2006," Regulatory Policies, December 15, 2006, para 38, https:// crtc.gc.ca/eng/archive/2006/pb2006-158.htm.

91. Armstrong, 99; CRTC, "Introduction to Broadcasting Decisions CRTC 2005-246 to 2005-248," Decisions, September 20, 2007, https://crtc.gc.ca/eng/archive/2005/ pb2005-61.htm; CRTC, "Broadcasting Decision CRTC 2005-247: Satellite Subscription Radio Undertaking," Decisions, September 20, 2007, https://crtc.gc.ca/ eng/archive/2005/db2005-247.htm.

92. CRTC, "Broadcasting Regulatory Policy CRTC 2015-25: Measures to Address Issues Related to Simultaneous Substitution," Regulatory Policies, January 29, 2015, https://crtc.gc.ca/eng/archive/2015/2015-25.htm; CRTC, "Broadcasting Regulatory Policy CRTC 2015-24: Over-the-Air Transmission of Television Signals and Local Programming," Regulatory Policies, January 29, 2015, https://crtc. gc.ca/eng/archive/2015/2015-24.htm.

93.  *Bell Canada v Canada (Attorney General)*, 2016 FCA 217.

94.  Armstrong, 110–12; CRTC, "Measures to Address Issues Related to Simultaneous Substitution"; CRTC, "Over-the-Air Transmission"; CRTC, "Broadcasting Regulatory Policy CRTC 2016-334 and Broadcasting Order CRTC 2016-335: Simultaneous Substitution for the Super Bowl," Regulatory Policies, Orders, August 19, 2016, https://crtc.gc.ca/eng/archive/2016/2016-334.htm.

95.  Christine M. Rubie-Davies, Sabrina Liu, and Kai-Chi Lee, "Watching Each Other: Portrayals of Gender and Ethnicity in Television Advertisements," *The Journal of Social Psychology* 153, no. 2 (2013): 175–95; Nancy Signorielli, "Gender Stereotyping on Television," in *Media Psychology*, eds. Gayle Brewer and Nancy Signorielli (New York: Palgrave Macmillan, 2011), 170–86.

96.  For discussion, see Josh Heuman, "'Integral to the Plot, and in No Way Gratuitous'? Constructing Creative Freedom in the Liberalization of Canadian Content Regulation," *Television & New Media* 12, no. 3 (2011): 248–72. See also Linda Trimble, "Coming Soon to a Station Near You?: The CRTC Policy on Sex-Role Stereotyping," *Canadian Public Policy/Analyse de Politiques*, 1990, 326–38.

97.  CBSC, "Canadian Association of Broadcasters' Equitable Portrayal Code (2008)," accessed November 3, 2018, https://www.cbsc.ca/codes/cab-equitable-portrayal-code/.

98.  *Broadcasting Act*, SC 1991, c 11, s 3(1)(d)(iii)

99.  *Broadcasting Act*, SC 1991, c 11, s 3(1)(o)

100. Truth and Reconciliation Commission of Canada, "Honouring the Truth, Reconciling for the Future: Summary of the Final Report of the Truth and Reconciliation Commission of Canada" (Winnipeg: Truth and Reconciliation Commission of Canada, 2015), 293–94, http://www.trc.ca/.

101. Ibid.

102. Ibid.

103. Rob McMahon, Heather E. Hudson, and Lyle Fabian, "Canada's Northern Communication Policies: The Role of Aboriginal Organizations," *The Shifting Terrain: Public Policy Advocacy in Canada*. 2017: 264–65. See also Valerie Alia, *The New Media Nation: Indigenous Peoples and Global Communication*, volume 2 (New York: Berghahn Books, 2010).

104. Smith and Brigham.

105. The previous Native Broadcasting Policy had focused on northern regions. CRTC, "Public Notice CRTC 1990-89, Native Broadcasting Policy," Notices of Consultation, September 20, 1990, https://crtc.gc.ca/eng/archive/1990/PB90-89.htm.

106. Ibid.

107. CRTC, "Public Notice CRTC 1998-62: Exemption Order Respecting Certain Native Radio Undertakings," Orders, December 17, 1999, https://crtc.gc.ca/eng/

archive/1999/PB99-197.htm; Szwarc, "Indigenous Broadcasting and the CRTC: Lessons from the Licensing of Native Type B Radio" (Gatineau, QC: Canadian Radio-television and Telecommunications Commission, 2018), https://crtc. gc.ca/eng/acrtc/prx/2018szwarc.htm#_tc14.

108. Ibid.

109. Szwarc.

110. Greg Smith, "Aboriginal Broadcasters' Perspectives on Broadcasting Policy: Report to Northern Native Broadcast Access Program (NNBAP) and the Department of Canadian Heritage" (Ottawa: Canadian Heritage, 2004), 3–4. As cited in MacLennan, 69.

111. Szwarc.

112. Ibid.

113. Mostoller, "Awakening the 'Voice of the Forest': Radio Barriere Lake," in *Islands of Resistance: Pirate Radio in Canada*, eds. Andrea Langlois, Ron Sakolsky, and Marian van der Zon (Vancouver: New Star Books, 2010), 75–87.

114. Neskie Manuel, "Secwepemc Radio: Reclamation of Our Common Property," in *Islands of Resistance: Pirate Radio in Canada*, eds. Andrea Langlois, Ron Sakolsky, and Marian van der Zon (Vancouver: New Star Books, 2010), 71.

115. Ibid., 72.

116. Szwarc.

117. Charles Fairchild, "Below the Hamelin Line: CKRZ and Aboriginal Cultural Survival," *Canadian Journal of Communication* 23, no. 2 (1998).

118. Ibid.

119. CRTC, "Decision CRTC 99-42, Summary Television Northern Canada Incorporated," Decisions, September 20, 2007, https://crtc.gc.ca/eng/archive/1999/DB99-42.htm.

120. CRTC, "Public Notice CRTC 1999-70: Order Respecting the Distribution of the Aboriginal Peoples Television Network," Orders, April 21, 1999, https://crtc. gc.ca/eng/archive/1999/PB99-70.htm. See also Armstrong, 156–57.

121. Truth and Reconciliation Commission of Canada, 293–94.

122. Chris Albinati, Geneviève Bonin-Labelle, Kathleen Buddle, John Gagnon, Gretchen King, and Julia Szwarc, "Recommendations for a New Consultation Process and Policy for First Nations, Inuit and Métis Broadcasting—Final Report," 2019; Szwarc.

123. Albinati et al.

124. CRTC, "Co-Development of the Indigenous Broadcasting Policy," June 20, 2019, https://crtc.gc.ca/eng/comm/ppl/index.htm.

125. Ibid.

126. United Nations, *Declaration on the Rights of Indigenous Peoples*, A/RES/61/295, October 2, 2007, https://www.un.org/development/desa/indigenouspeoples/declaration-on-the-rights-of-indigenous-peoples.html. As quoted in Truth and Reconciliation Commission of Canada, 203.

127. CRTC, "Ethnic Broadcasting Policy," Regulatory Policies, July 16, 1999, https://crtc.gc.ca/eng/archive/1999/pb99-117.htm.

128. Ibid., paras 16–17, 29–32.

129. Ibid., paras 18–25.

130. *Broadcasting Act*, SC 1991, c 11, s 3(1)(p).

131. CRTC, "Broadcasting and Telecom Regulatory Policy CRTC 2009-430: Accessibility of Telecommunications and Broadcasting Services," Regulatory Policies, July 21, 2009, https://crtc.gc.ca/eng/archive/2009/2009-430.htm.

132. Ibid., paras 72–101.

133. Ibid., paras 102–29.

134. CRTC, "Broadcasting Decision CRTC 2013-385: AMI-TV—Licence Renewal and Amendment," Decisions, August 8, 2013, https://crtc.gc.ca/eng/archive/2013/2013-385.htm.

135. "Consolidated Federal Laws of Canada, Television Broadcasting Regulations, 1987, SOR/87-49," September 1, 2009, sec 5(1)(b), https://laws-lois.justice.gc.ca/eng/regulations/SOR%2D87%2D49/20090901/P1TT3xt3.html.

136. CRTC, "Broadcasting Decision CRTC 2008-9: Complaint Regarding the Broadcast by the CBC of the Little Mosque on the Prairie Episode 'Traditional Mother,'" Decisions, September 20, 2007, para 42, https://crtc.gc.ca/eng/archive/2008/db2008-9.htm.

137. Ibid., para 29.

138. Raboy, "The Role of Public Consultation."

139. Raboy, *Missed Opportunities*.

140. Bob Hackett, "Taking Back the Media: Notes on the Potential for a Communicative Democracy Movement," *Studies in Political Economy* 63 (Autumn 2000): 63.

141. Szwarc.

142. Raboy, *Missed Opportunities*, 96.

143. Ibid., 109.

144. Tammy Bruce, *The New Thought Police: Inside the Left's Assault on Free Speech and Free Minds* (Roseville, CA: Forum, 2001), 8–9.

145. Dal Yong Jin, "Transformation of the World Television System under Neoliberal Globalization, 1983 to 2003," *Television & New Media* 8, no. 3 (2007): 179–96.

146. Tasneem Chipty, "Vertical Integration, Market Foreclosure, and Consumer Welfare in the Cable Television Industry," *American Economic Review* 91, no. 3 (2001): 428–53.

147. Gregory S. Crawford, Robin S. Lee, Michael D. Whinston, and Ali Yurukoglu, "The Welfare Effects of Vertical Integration in Multichannel Television Markets," *Econometrica* 86, no. 3 (2018): 891–954, https://doi.org/10.3982/ECTA14031.

148. Robert E. Babe, *Telecommunications in Canada: Technology, Industry, and Government* (New York: Routledge, 2018); Robert E. Babe, *Canadian Television Broadcasting Structure, Performance and Regulation* (Ottawa: Economic Council of Canada, 1979); Robert E. Babe, *Communication and the Transformation of Economics: Essays in Information, Public Policy, and Political Economy* (New York: Routledge, 2018); Patricia Mazepa and Vincent Mosco, "A Political Economy Approach to the Internet," in *Handbook on the Economics of the Internet,* eds. Johannes Bauer and Michael Latzer (Cheltenham, UK: Edward Elgar Publishing, 2016), 163–80; Patricia Mazepa, "Manifest Spatialization: Militarizing Communication in Canada," *Global Media Journal* 8, no. 1 (2015): 9; Eileen R. Meehan and Ellen Riordan, eds., *Sex & Money: Feminism and Political Economy in the Media* (Minneapolis: University of Minnesota Press, 2002); Vincent Mosco, *The Political Economy of Communication: Rethinking and Renewal,* 2nd ed. (London: SAGE, 2009); Christine Quail, "Producing Reality: Television Formats and Reality TV in the Canadian Context," *Canadian Journal of Communication* 40, no. 2 (2015); Dallas Smythe, *Dependency Road: Communications, Capitalism, Consciousness, and Canada* (Praeger Pub Text, 1981).

149. Raboy, *Missed Opportunities.*

150. Chipty.

151. Toby Miller, *Cultural Citizenship: Cosmopolitanism, Consumerism, and Television in a Neoliberal Age* (Philadelphia: Temple University Press, 2007).

152. *Broadcasting Act,* s 3 (1) (d) (iii); Suzanne Strutt and Lynne Hissey, "Feminisms and Balance," *Canadian Journal of Communication* 17, no. 1 (1992).

153. Martha M. Lauzen, "Boxed in 2017–18: Women on Screen and Behind the Scenes in Television," Center for the Study of Women in Television & Film, San Diego State University, September 2018, https://womenintvfilm.sdsu.edu/wp-content/uploads/2018/09/2017-18_Boxed_In_Report.pdf.

154. Wendy Cukier, Samantha Jackson, Mohamed A. Elmi, Erin Roach, and Darren Cyr, "Representing Women? Leadership Roles and Women in Canadian Broadcast News," *Gender in Management: An International Journal* 31, no. 5/6 (2016): 376.

155. Stacey Copeland, "Broadcasting Queer Feminisms: Lesbian and Queer Women Programming in Transnational, Local, and Community Radio," *Journal of Radio & Audio Media* 25, no. 2 (2018): 212.

156. Trimble; Strutt and Hissey.

157. Cukier et al.; Mary Lynn Young and Alison Beale, "Canada: The Paradox of Women in News," in *The Palgrave International Handbook of Women and Journalism*, ed. Carolyn M. Byerly (Springer, 2013), 109–21.

158. Strutt and Hissey.

159. Rina Fraticelli, "Women on Screen," *Women in View*, October 2015.

160. Martha M. Lauzen, "The Celluloid Ceiling: Behind-the-Scenes Employment of Women on the Top 100, 250, and 500 Films of 2015," *Center for the Study of Women in Television and Film*, 2016, 1–6.

161. David Hesmondhalgh and Sarah Baker, "Sex, Gender and Work Segregation in the Cultural Industries," *The Sociological Review* 63, no. 1 (2015): 23–36; Leung Wing-Fai, Rosalind Gill, and Keith Randle, "Getting in, Getting on, Getting out? Women as Career Scramblers in the UK Film and Television Industries," *The Sociological Review* 63, no. 1 (2015): 50–65.

162. Rosalind Gill and Shani Orgad, "The Shifting Terrain of Sex and Power," *Sexualities* 21, no. 8 (December 2018): 1313–24, https://doi.org/10.1177/1363460718794647; Meehan and Riordan; Catherine Murray and Alison Beale, "Commentary: Sex, Money, Media: A Tribute and Political Reflection," *Canadian Journal of Communication* 36 (2011): 179–84.

163. Copeland; Phylis Johnson and Michael C. Keith, *Queer Airwaves: The Story of Gay and Lesbian Broadcasting* (Armonk, NY: M.E. Sharpe, 2001).

164. Copeland, 218.

165. Thomas.

166. Thomas; Truth and Reconciliation Commission of Canada, 1.

167. Ibid.

168. MacLennan.

169. Lorna Roth, "The Delicate Acts of 'Colour Balancing': Multiculturalism and Canadian Television Broadcasting Policies and Practices," *Canadian Journal of Communication* 23, no. 4 (1998): 487–506.

170. Ibid., 10.

171. Ibid.

172. Lorna Roth, *Something New in the Air: The Story of First Peoples Television Broadcasting in Canada* (Montreal: McGill-Queen's University Press, 2005).

173. John McMurria, "From Net Neutrality to Net Equality," *International Journal of Communication* 10, no. 2016 (2016): 5931–48.

174. Thomas.

175. McMurria, 5938.

# 10 Internet Regulation

## INTRODUCTION

It may seem impossible to regulate the internet or activities that take place on the internet. In 1996, John Perry Barlow, lyricist for the Grateful Dead, wrote "A Declaration of the Independence of Cyberspace."[1] In it, he declared that governments have "no moral right to rule [internet users]" nor "any methods of enforcement we have true reason to fear"; that the internet "is different"—subject to its own rules, open to all—a place "independent of the tyrannies [governments] seek to impose."[2]

In some ways, Barlow was right. The internet does challenge existing regulations, and it raises difficult problems of enforceability. However, in other ways, Barlow was wrong. Governments, and private organizations, do regulate the internet in a number of ways, sometimes very effectively.

Several different arms of government, as well as non-governmental organizations (NGOs) and private companies, play roles in regulating the internet. The CRTC has claimed jurisdiction over internet broadcasters, though it has largely declined to regulate them. The CRTC also regulates the internet by establishing the rules governing the telecommunications industry, including net neutrality regulations, and it sets regulations intended to facilitate broadband access and competition. As well, criminal law applies to many activities that take place on the internet, including the publishing of obscene content and computer fraud and misuse.

Non-profit organization and NGOs, both in Canada and internationally, oversee the domain name system, making sure that information is properly addressed and transmitted. The Internet Corporation for Assigned Names and Numbers (ICANN) and internet registries like the Canadian Internet Registration Authority (CIRA) play important roles in this regard.

Private corporations like Facebook, Google, and Twitter are also, in a sense, regulators of the content that most people interact with on a day-to-day basis when they use the internet. Through their user agreements, licensing agreements, and roles in copyright enforcement, private companies like these set the rules for what users can and cannot do online.

This chapter will provide an overview of how these three groups (government, NGOs, and private companies) work together (and sometimes at odds with each other) to govern the internet. The first section is about the CRTC and the government's role in regulating the internet. The second section is about NGOs like ICANN and CIRA that administer the addressing system of the internet. The third section is about the way corporations like Facebook and Google regulate the internet. The final section asks, "Whom does internet regulation serve?", drawing on the theories introduced in Chapter 1.

# GOVERNMENT REGULATION OF THE INTERNET

Several branches of government are involved in regulating the internet and activities that take place online. In this section, we first discuss the CRTC's approach to internet broadcasting and some of the controversies and dilemmas that surround CRTC regulation of the internet. Internet broadcasting raises all kinds of questions. Are Netflix, YouTube, Spotify, podcasts, or other online audio and video services broadcasters, as defined under the *Broadcasting Act*? If they are, then it would appear the CRTC has jurisdiction to regulate them. Are the regulatory standards that have been applied to traditional broadcasters appropriate for online broadcasting? Second, we will examine the CRTC's role in regulating the internet as a telecommunications service, including the role of the CRTC in setting rules about net neutrality. Finally, we will examine some of the ways that criminal law applies online.

## The CRTC and Internet Broadcasting

In 1991, researchers at the University of Cambridge developed a program that made a video of their coffee pot available over their internal computer network. That way, researchers in the building could check whether coffee was available before going to get a cup. In 1993, the video program was updated to make the coffee pot video stream available publicly on the internet. The coffee pot livestream became the first public video broadcast to take place over the World Wide Web.[3]

That same year, the first non-profit internet radio station was launched, and the following year, WXYC in North Carolina became the first traditional radio station to broadcast over the internet.[4] Broadcasting had started to take place online, and this would ultimately raise the question: Do the laws and policies that had been developed for traditional broadcasting apply to broadcasting on the internet?

The CRTC first considered the question of whether—or how—to regulate the internet in 1999. It did so in response to calls for clarification as to whether internet broadcasting was subject to CRTC regulation. Its initial policy approach, outlined in the 1999 *Report on New Media*, set the framework the CRTC would use to think about whether and how to regulate broadcasting on the internet.[5] This was followed ten years later by its *Review of Broadcasting in New Media*.[6]

The CRTC is responsible for regulating both telecommunications under the *Telecommunications Act* and broadcasting under the *Broadcasting Act*. Internet access services, such as the internet services provided by Rogers, Telus, Bell, TekSavvy, Shaw, or other companies, are regulated as telecommunications services. As we saw in Chapter 8, telecommunications companies are seen as common carriers that convey content in a neutral manner; thus, content is not regulated. In broadcasting regulation, as we saw in Chapter 9, content is regulated: Codes of conduct such as the Canadian Broadcast Standards Council's *Equitable Portrayal Code* apply, and broadcasters must meet Canadian content requirements. In its 1999 *Report on New Media* and in the 2009 *Review of Broadcasting in New Media*, the CRTC focused on internet broadcasting; it was concerned about the possibility of regulating internet content that fell under its mandate to regulate broadcasting.

### Policy Questions
The questions raised by internet broadcasting in 1999 were:

- Does the CRTC have jurisdiction over broadcasting over the internet?
- Is regulation required to encourage a sufficient presence of Canadian content on the internet?
- Is regulation required to protect the Canadian broadcasting system?
- Is regulation required in order to address offensive or potentially illegal content on the internet?[7]

### What Is New Media?
In 1999, the CRTC used the term *new media* to refer to digital content delivered over networks.[8] This included text, but also includes images, video, and audio.

It included both interactive content and non-interactive content.[9] Some new media fit into the legal definition of *broadcasting*. Other new media did not.

### What Is Broadcasting?

Is new media *broadcasting*? This question is important, because the CRTC has jurisdiction to regulate broadcasting under the *Broadcasting Act*.

In its 1999 *Report on New Media*, the CRTC noted that much internet content did not qualify as broadcasting. The *Broadcasting Act* defines *broadcasting* as:

> any transmission of *programs*, whether or not encrypted, by radio waves or other means of telecommunication for reception by the public by means of broadcasting receiving apparatus, but does not include any such transmission of programs that is made solely for performance or display in a public place.[10]

The *Broadcasting Act* defines *program* as:

> sounds or visual images, or a combination of sounds and visual images, that are intended to inform, enlighten or entertain, but *does not include* visual images, whether or not combined with sounds, that consist predominantly of *alphanumeric text*.[11]

In 1999, most consumers connected to the internet through slow dial-up connections. Audio and video were available on the internet, but in the low-bandwidth environment, most internet content was text-based, including web pages and email. The text-based parts of the internet, the CRTC noted, do not constitute broadcasting and fall outside the broadcasting side of the CRTC's jurisdiction.[12]

However, internet content consisting of "sounds and or visual images ... intended to inform, enlighten or entertain" *does* meet the definition of broadcasting, according to the CRTC. This could include Netflix and YouTube content, Skype or FaceTime video, podcasts, webcasts, emailed videos, and even other user-generated content. The CRTC noted, "speaking in full-motion video through any digital transmission system is potentially subject to the licensing power of the federal government, because it can be defined as 'broadcasting.'"[13] Such content, according to the CRTC's interpretation, falls under the CRTC's jurisdiction under the *Broadcasting Act*, giving the CRTC the potential legal jurisdiction to license and regulate it.

### Exemption Order

The broad potential jurisdiction of the CRTC to license and regulate internet content has alarmed many. To the partial relief of advocates of an internet free of government regulation, the CRTC issued an exemption order, noting that while it had apparent jurisdiction under the *Broadcasting Act* to license and regulate internet audio-video content, it would decline to exercise such power.[14]

In deciding to issue the exemption, the CRTC reasoned that regulation of internet audio-video content was unnecessary for three reasons:

1. There was enough Canadian content available on the internet; Canadian content regulation was not required to encourage the production and availability of Canadian content;
2. The internet was not, in 1999, a significant threat to Canadian broadcasters or the Canadian broadcasting system; and
3. It was not necessary for the CRTC to regulate obscene or potentially illegal content on the internet.

### Promoting Canadian Content

In 1999, the CRTC concluded that there was "a strong Canadian presence" on the internet and that "the circumstances that led to the need for regulation of Canadian content in traditional broadcasting do not currently exist in the internet environment. Market forces are providing a Canadian presence on the internet that is also supported by a strong demand for Canadian new media content."[15]

By 2009, some groups wanted the CRTC to revoke the 1999 exemption order and regulate Canadian content providers on the internet. For example, the Society of Composers, Authors and Music Publishers of Canada (SOCAN), which collects royalties on radio airplay of Canadian music, called on the CRTC to introduce minimum Canadian content requirements for new media broadcasters. This proposal was declined.[16]

In 2009, the CRTC again concluded that "innovative and creative approaches to promote Canadian content on new media platforms" were underway.[17] As it had in 1999, the Commission concluded that no policy measure was needed to ensure the visibility and promotion of Canadian content on the internet.[18]

### Funding Canadian Content

Many stakeholders have called on the CRTC to put in place initiatives for funding Canadian content on the internet. As noted in Chapter 9, traditional broadcasters and broadcast distribution undertakings are required to contribute to meet spending and financial contribution requirements set by the CRTC. Calls for similar contributions by internet service providers (ISPs) grew; by 2009 some parties argued ISPs were becoming an important part of the Canadian broadcasting system and that, similar to broadcasters, ISPs should charge customers a levy, with the proceeds going toward the production of Canadian content.[19]

The CRTC declined to require new media broadcasters to contribute to Canadian media production funds through a levy or otherwise. It noted that funding was already available through the Canada Media Fund and other programs.[20] Further, it was unclear whether the CRTC had the requisite jurisdiction over ISPs to impose such a levy.[21]

### *Internet Broadcasting as a Threat to Traditional Broadcasters*

As Canadians increasingly "cut the cord" and abandon cable and traditional broadcast services, opting instead to watch television and movies on the internet and to access news through websites and podcasts, the business models of traditional broadcasters may be threatened. In 1999, just 20 percent of Canadians had internet access, and internet broadcasting business models were still in development. The internet was seen as an opportunity, rather than a threat, by most traditional broadcasters.[22] At that stage, audiences, advertising, and commerce had not yet shifted significantly to the internet. The CRTC decided not to regulate new media, but to allow business models to evolve and monitor the potential threat. By the time it considered its position on the regulation of new media again in 2009, **broadband internet** was available to 93 percent of Canadian households and almost half of Canadians were broadband subscribers.[23] However, it was only after the 2009 decision that Netflix streaming services were introduced in Canada.[24] Traditional television subscriptions began to slowly decline about two years later.[25]

Should the role of the CRTC be to protect traditional television services? This is a question with which the CRTC has struggled. The *Broadcasting Act* does not mandate the CRTC with protecting traditional business models or traditional broadcasters. It does mandate the CRTC to implement broadcasting policy and to regulate and supervise the broadcasting system "in a flexible manner" that "is readily adaptable to scientific and technological change."[26] In 1999, the Commission was clearly engaged with the question of whether the protection of traditional broadcasting business models was required.[27] Some stakeholders argued internet broadcasting could threaten traditional broadcasters' revenue, and thus their "ability to fulfil their obligations under the *Broadcasting Act*."[28] The Commission did not agree that, at that time, traditional broadcasters' revenue was under immediate threat. In 2009, CRTC Commissioner Timothy Denton argued that protecting traditional broadcasters was not the role of the CRTC, stating, "The relevant issue is freedom of speech, not potential damage to the broadcasting system."[29]

### *The Dangers of CRTC Regulatory Power over the Internet*
One of the most vocal critics of the CRTC's broad potential regulatory power is former CRTC Commissioner Timothy Denton. Prior to heading the Commission in 2008, Denton had worked as legal counsel to the Canadian Association of Internet Providers (CAIP). He objected to the CRTC's assertion of jurisdiction over the internet because it left the door open to potential regulation and government licensing of internet broadcasting. In his view, government licensing of internet broadcasting would amount to a form of censorship. "Several important political revolutions have been fought to ensure freedom of the press and speech; it would be repugnant to nibble away at it in defence of anything as comparatively unimportant as Canadian broadcasting policy," he argued.[30] The idea of licensing internet broadcasters threatens, he suggested, "the essence of the Internet," which is "innovation without permission.[31] Such power, he argued, "should be put permanently beyond the reach of the CRTC."[32] He called for the *Broadcasting Act* to be rewritten to remove the possibility of government licensing of speech on the internet.[33]

## CRTC Reference: Are ISPs Broadcasters?

The CRTC turned to the courts, asking them to resolve the question "Do retail Internet service providers (ISPs) carry on, in whole or in part, 'broadcasting undertakings' subject to the *Broadcasting Act* when, in their role as ISPs, they provide access through the internet to 'broadcasting' requested by end-users?"[34] Some had called for ISPs like Rogers, Bell, and TekSavvy to be treated as broadcasters. ISPs, they argued, now played a significant role in providing access to video, television, and films. Did the CRTC have jurisdiction to regulate ISPs as broadcasters?

The Federal Court of Appeal responded that ISPs, when they provide the means of transmission for content and play no role in selecting or producing the content itself, are not broadcasters and are not subject to the *Broadcasting Act*.[35] The Supreme Court of Canada agreed, holding that "the terms 'broadcasting' and 'broadcasting undertaking,' interpreted in the context of the language and purposes of the *Broadcasting Act*, are not meant to capture entities which merely provide the mode of transmission."[36] Because ISPs' only involvement in broadcasting is to transmit content, they have no control or input over content. They are unable to promote the policy objectives outlined in the *Broadcasting Act*; as such, they are not broadcasters.[37] Furthermore, the *Broadcasting Act* specifically states that it does not apply to telecommunications common carriers acting solely as common carriers.[38]

While the courts have clarified that ISPs that merely provide the means of transmission of content are not broadcasters, the activities of other new media entities that more directly transmit or publish audio or audio-video content over the internet may meet the definition of *broadcasting* under the *Broadcasting Act* and, therefore, may fall under the jurisdiction of the CRTC.

### Reporting Requirements

Until 2009, the CRTC had entirely exempted internet broadcasters from regulation. In 2009, however, the CRTC narrowed this exemption and imposed a seemingly minor requirement on internet broadcasters. The Commission now requires that internet broadcasters like Netflix submit information on their broadcasting activities, or other information the Commission may request from time to time in the process of monitoring internet broadcasting.[39] Netflix, for its part, refuses to comply with this requirement.[40]

## Broadcasting Act Revision

In its 2017 budget, the federal government promised to "review and modernize" the *Broadcasting Act* and the *Telecommunications Act* "to ensure that Canadians continue to benefit from an open and innovative Internet."[41] It reiterated that the two acts would be reviewed in the major statement of its *Creative Canada Policy Framework*, announced in October 2017.[42] The review commenced in June 2018 and issued its report in January 2020. The report's recommendations are, as of this writing, under consideration by the government.[43]

## CRTC Regulation: Net Neutrality

**Net neutrality** is the principle that networks should treat all traffic the same, regardless of its content or origin. The concept of net neutrality is similar to common carriage. As we saw in Chapter 8, common carriage in Canada ensures "No Canadian carrier shall, in relation to the provision of a telecommunications service or the charging of a rate for it, unjustly discriminate or give an undue or unreasonable preference toward any person, including itself, or subject any person to an undue or unreasonable disadvantage." [44]

It is sometimes argued that networks should be "smart": They should put time-sensitive data such as live video or emergency communications in the "fast lane," and other, less time-sensitive data, such as emails, in the "slow lane." [45] Proponents of net neutrality dispute this logic, arguing that advanced network functionality should be kept to the outer layers of the network, like software on your computer, leaving the network core neutral. They argue that anytime the edge needs to ask the centre for permission to do something or for modification or special treatment, innovation can be potentially stalled. New services that require access to the "fast lane" but cannot afford to pay for it or cannot get permission from the network could be stalled. [46]

ISPs might block or slow certain internet traffic for various reasons. Some reasons include:

1. **Attempts to censor political views**: Telus blocked access to its striking union's website. They said the union was posting photos of employees crossing the picket line and advocating jamming Telus phone lines. [47]
2. **Anti-competitive conduct**: There have been cases where ISPs who are cable providers, such as the American company Comcast, have been suspected of degrading competitor Netflix's service. [48]
3. **Legal reasons**: ISPs may block illegal content such as child pornography.
4. **Traffic management**: ISPs may block or slow content in order to manage traffic on its networks, such as by slowing data-intensive services during peak hours. [49]

Some of these reasons are sometimes considered legitimate, such as blocking websites that contain child pornography or traffic management. Censorship and anti-competitive conduct are more broadly considered to be illegitimate reasons for blocking or slowing websites or services.

In 2009, the CRTC established four net neutrality rules:

1. **No blocking**. The CRTC noted that telecommunications companies are prohibited, under the *Telecommunications Act*, from controlling content or influencing the meaning or purpose of content, except where the CRTC approves otherwise. [50] ISPs are therefore prohibited from blocking content, except with prior approval of the CRTC. [51]

2.  **No noticeable slowing.** For the same reason that they are not allowed to block content, ISPs are also prohibited from slowing content in a way that results in "the noticeable degradation of time-sensitive Internet traffic," except with prior approval of the CRTC.[52] The same goes for non-time-sensitive traffic, if that traffic is slowed such that "it amounts to blocking the content."[53]

3.  **No discrimination.** Telecommunications companies are prohibited, under the *Telecommunications Act*, from "unjustly discriminating" and giving "undue or unreasonable preference toward any person, including itself, or subject[ing] any person to an undue or unreasonable disadvantage."[54] The CRTC's policy on net neutrality notes ISPs that "degrade or prefer one application, class of application, or protocol over another" could warrant an investigation by the CRTC.[55] This investigation would be sparked by a complaint.[56]

4.  **Transparency.** The CRTC requires ISPs to disclose information on traffic management practices to their customers by displaying information on their websites.[57]

In 2017, the CRTC further strengthened its net neutrality rules, prohibiting *zero-rating* (offering free access to certain apps or data sources, while access to other data is either paid or counted against a data cap). This practice is also known as *discounting data.*[58]

## CRTC Anti-Spam Regulation

The word *spam* originally referred to a canned meat, and came to be applied to unwanted email messages via a Monty Python sketch in which a chorus of Vikings sing about the meat product so loudly that they drown out everything else.[59] The word now refers mainly to unsolicited (and often unwanted) emails, especially when sent as part of a mass-mailing.[60] It was once feared that email **spam** would virtually drown out legitimate email messages.

*Canada's Anti-Spam Legislation* (CASL) came into force in 2014. Under the law, the CRTC investigates cases of unsolicited mass email messages, while the Competition Bureau examines cases of false or deceptive advertising (as they also do in offline contexts), and the Office of the Privacy Commissioner of Canada investigates cases of personal information (including email) harvesting, spyware, and keystroke logging.[61] Under CASL, the CRTC has the authority to impose large monetary penalties. CASL requires senders of commercial email messages to obtain consent, identify themselves, and provide an unsubscribe mechanism.[62]

## Cybercrime

A number of criminal laws apply to traditional crimes committed via the internet, as well as to new types of crimes involving computers.

### *Traditional Crimes Committed via the Internet*

The *Criminal Code of Canada* prohibits the making and distribution of obscene materials, and the making, distribution, accessing, and possession of child pornography.[63] This includes access and distribution via the internet.[64] Police enforcement efforts are largely focused on online child pornography.[65] Fraud and identity theft are crimes under the *Criminal Code of Canada*.[66] **Fraud** involves the taking of money, property, valuables, or services "by deceit, falsehood or other fraudulent means,"[67] while **identity theft** involves "obtaining or possessing "another person's identity information with intent to use it to commit an indictable offence that includes fraud, deceit or falsehood as an element of the offence."[68] Both crimes are increasingly carried out via the internet. Fraud is often carried out using scareware, phishing, phony websites, and online dating schemes.[69] Identity theft is often conducted through phishing, Trojans, and malware used to collect personal and banking information; stolen mobile phones; or negligent or rogue employees who steal or fail to protect data.[70]

### *Computer Crimes*

While child pornography, fraud, and identity theft all existed before, computers and the internet have given rise to several new misuse crimes. The *Criminal Code* makes destroying or altering data via malware attacks or computer viruses a crime.[71] It also makes the possession of a computer virus or other malware for the purpose of committing mischief a crime.[72] Hacking—gaining access to a computer system without authorization—is a crime under the *Criminal Code*,[73] as is the willful interception of private communication.[74]

# NGO REGULATORS

A number of non-governmental organizations play significant roles in regulating the internet.

## ICANN and TLDs

The Internet Corporation for Assigned Names and Numbers (ICANN) is a non-profit corporation that administers internet (Internet Protocol [IP]) addresses and domain names. In other words, it administers the central address book that allows websites and other internet services to be located on the internet. This central address book allows us to use domain names (such as http://google.ca), rather than numerical IP addresses (such as http://172.217.14.195), to access sites and resources on the internet. The domain name system (DNS) routes requests for the Google website to its numerical IP address.

Without a unitary DNS, the address *www.google.ca* wouldn't work. Entering Google's address in the search bar of your browser might take you to an unexpected website or nowhere at all. If there were multiple DNSs, entering Google's address in the search bar might take you to various different sites, depending on your location and which DNS you were using at the time. Thus, ICANN's DNS function is extremely important to a unified worldwide internet.

ICANN decides what domain names can be registered, what alphabets can be used in domain names, what top-level domains (TLDs; such as .com, .ca, .xxx, or .baby) exist, and how the registration of domain names will be administered by domain name registrars.[75]

### *Who Should Control the Domain Name System?*

With so much power, there are questions about who should regulate the domain name system. The American government has argued that American control over the internet through ICANN ensured the stability and growth of the internet, protecting free flow of information. Critics have argued that American control of ICANN and the DNS has caused American policy to dominate worldwide. Other countries (like Brazil and China) therefore pressed for control to be transferred to an international body, such as the United Nations' International Telecommunication Union. However, some feared that this move could lead to authoritarian governments having input or sway on how the internet is administered. Instead, in 2016, US control of ICANN ended and the organization transitioned to a **multi-stakeholder** model, in which governments, civil society, private businesses, NGOs, experts, and researchers all play a role.[76]

### The Internet Governance Forum

Since there is so much at stake, a forum was established by the United Nations (UN) to discuss many of the political issues involved. The Internet Governance Forum (IGF) has no direct power over the internet, but brings together government, civil society, business, and international community representatives to make policy recommendations.

# PRIVATE REGULATORS

Private companies like Google, Facebook, and Apple, and ISPs like Rogers, Bell, Telus, and Cogeco, play increasingly significant roles in internet regulation. The Terms of Use agreements they have with their customers set the basic ground rules for most people's use of internet services and platforms. These companies have tremendous power to police the internet by retaining information about their customers' identities and web activities, by providing access to such information to law enforcement and national security agencies, and by shutting down user accounts or websites and services.

## Content Blocking

Most major Canadian ISPs block foreign websites containing child pornography.[77] Cleanfeed Canada is an initiative run by the Canadian Centre for Child Protection (C3P), spurred through the Canadian Coalition Against Internet Child Exploitation (CCAICE), a coalition chaired by C3P involving industry, government, non-governmental, and law enforcement. Cleanfeed Canada maintains a list of foreign websites hosting child pornography involving images of pre-pubescent children. Its list is used by most major Canadian ISPs to block foreign websites containing child pornography.

Most initiatives to block websites would require approval by the CRTC under the CRTC's network neutrality policy and under section 36 of the *Telecommunications Act*, which prohibits telecommunication companies from controlling content. However, as discussed in Chapter 3, it is illegal under the *Criminal Code of Canada* to transmit, make available, or distribute child pornography.[78]

Some have raised concerns that internet content blocking systems could expand to other areas. Some have also criticized the growing role of private companies in censoring the internet without due process or transparency.[79] Cleanfeed enjoys substantial support in protecting children from sexual abuse and exploitation.[80] Other proposals to block internet content, such as copyright infringing content or gambling sites, have been far more controversial.[81] A Quebec government proposal to block foreign online gambling sites has been challenged by the CRTC and at the Quebec Superior Court where, as of this writing, it awaits a hearing.[82]

## Architecture and Algorithms

Online platforms like Facebook, Amazon, Netflix, and Google use algorithms to determine what news and updates, recommendations, or search results a user sees.

The power of such algorithms to direct users' attention toward "fake news" and propaganda and to create filter bubbles such that the user sees more stories that affirm their existing beliefs and biases has become more apparent.[83] In attempts to forestall formal government regulation of social media and online platforms, Facebook has responded with various endeavours to appear accountable and responsive to these problems. For example, to combat inauthentic news and pages, Facebook announced plans to require organizations running election-related ad campaigns to confirm their identities; this will allow Facebook to show viewers all the ads run by a particular organization and who paid for them. Facebook will also archive ads, to allow them to be reviewed. Facebook has made it easier to report false news, has hired third-party fact-checkers who flag false stories, has adjusted its algorithm, and has hired safety and security personnel.[84] Many ask whether all of this is enough to combat the difficulties of social media and their implications for communication and democracy.

## Search Engine Regulation

Search engines can also play significant roles in regulating the internet. Google regulates the content that users see when they search for things on the internet using Google's search engine through fine-tuning its search algorithm and through its SafeSearch feature, which removes pornography and other offensive content from search results. As discussed in Chapter 5, some countries have also implemented a right to be forgotten, which requires search engines to delist content that is "inadequate, irrelevant or no longer relevant, or excessive in relation to the purposes for which they were processed."[85] Search engines also come under pressure for producing racist or allegedly biased search results.[86] Such concerns about search engines and their role in regulating speech have led, in turn, to calls for regulation.[87]

# WHOM DOES INTERNET REGULATION SERVE?

## The Public Interest?

### *Pluralism*

Internet governance has often been viewed through the lens of pluralism. Many scholars have noted that a diversity of groups, including civil society groups, private corporations such as Google and IBM, and governments are involved in internet governance. Some scholars and observers view the involvement of multiple groups in internet governance, and in the Internet Governance Forum in particular, as a democratizing force. Civil society groups and private corporations, along with states, have a voice in governance processes. This positive view of the involvement of multiple stakeholders is called multi-stakeholderism.[88]

## Bureaucracy and Bureaucrats?

### Neoliberalism

Internet governance has been, to a great extent, based on neoliberal principles of individual freedom, economic freedom, and the protection of private property.[89] Market-based competition and concepts of property have been incorporated into the internet's domain name system. Domain names can be bought and sold on a competitive basis.[90] Intellectual property is recognized in the domain name system; registrants for generic TDLs must warrant that the names they propose to register do not infringe trademark rights.[91] An arbitration process to resolve trademark disputes has also been incorporated into the domain name system.[92] The rise of neoliberalism in the 1980s, communication scholars Marc Raboy and Normand Landry argue, fed a utopian vision of a global information society that led to the rise of multi-stakeholder governance, permitting private companies to be accredited at international telecommunication decision-making bodies and to have a seat at the table, alongside governments and civil society representatives, at the Internet Governance Forum.[93]

Many scholars note that the American "internet freedom" foreign policy agenda favours the international business interests of American technology companies such as Google, Facebook, Apple, Microsoft, and IBM over domestic policy priorities, local content controls, and domestic businesses. The private provision of internet services and domain names follows the neoliberal economic model in communication services provision.[94] Weak regulation of the internet, including weak privacy protection and weak competition laws, has permitted the commodification of personal data and the global domination of a few American giants like Facebook, Amazon, and Google.[95]

### Libertarian Theory

Libertarian theory, as applied to the internet, is known as **cyberlibertarianism**: "the belief that individuals—acting in whatever capacity they choose (as citizens, consumers, companies, or collectives)—should be at liberty to pursue their own tastes and interests online."[96] In his famous "Declaration of the Independence of Cyberspace," cyberlibertarian John Perry Barlow declared, "Your legal concepts of property, expression, identity, movement, and context do not apply to us. They are all based on matter, and there is no matter here."[97] Cyberlibertarians support a vision of the free flow of information and ideas on the internet, unimpeded by intellectual property rights. They envision a radically reduced role for the state in the internet and in human affairs, where interactions would be managed between autonomous individuals as mediated by the network, with minimal or no regulation of internet content or technologies.[98] Cyberlibertarians are typically highly optimistic and enthusiastic about technologically mediated life and the freedoms such technologies as the internet can bring if left largely unregulated.

## The Privileged?

### *Critical Political Economy*

Critics of the liberal pluralist view of internet governance, and of multi-stakeholderism, argue that internet governance is dominated by a powerful few. They argue that a group of elites, formed through the co-option of civil society leaders by powerful states and corporations—neither a true plurality of diverse actors, nor a network of individuals made equal through technological mediation—governs the internet.[99] In this view, both the liberal pluralist view of internet governance as drawing on democratic diversity and voices and the cyberlibertarian view of the internet as a technologically mediated space of freedom and equality are mirages that veil the dominance of powerful states and corporations in internet governance, content, and design.

Critical scholars cast doubt on many of the neoliberal and libertarian ideas that have been influential in internet governance. Richard Barbrook and Andy Cameron dubbed the set of ideals popular in the California tech sector the *Californian ideology*.[100] The Californian ideology combines neoliberal emphases on market freedom with appeals to direct democracy, sexual egalitarianism, and environmentalism. The Californian ideology, however, is a false ideology, in that it masks the truth: Computer and networking technologies were developed with massive government subsidies, not through economic free markets; and the networked society has reproduced massive inequality, racism, poverty, and environmental problems, rather than creating a new virtual world of egalitarianism.[101] Under high-tech capitalism, they argue, "the relationship between masters and slaves endures in a new form."[102] New worlds of virtual reality and communicative freedom are likely only to benefit the high-tech few, while their construction is dependent on poorly paid labourers and massive inequalities structured by racialization, class, and international divides.[103]

Critical political economists study the power relations that govern the "production, distribution, and consumption" of the internet as a resource.[104] They have noted that the history of internet technologies tends toward monopolistic, or oligopolistic, corporate ownership, which tends to reproduce social, class, gender, race, and other inequalities, skewing "public access and participation away from those who can least afford it."[105] The "wealth of networks" can also be seen, Patricia Mazepa and Vincent Mosco quip, as networks of wealth.[106] Many critical political economists of the internet therefore study and take part in social movements to democratize access to the internet and the political processes that surround it.[107]

### Feminist and Queer Studies

Feminists have noted that many internet governance processes, including those that take place under the World Summit on the Information Society, the Internet Governance Forum, or the Internet Association for Assigned Names and Numbers (ICANN), are male-dominated, especially at higher levels.[108] This has meant that internet governance processes have been insensitive to gender inequalities and have not adequately taken up concerns about gender imbalance in internet-related employment and education.[109] For example, reducing the digital divide for men does not necessarily equate to reducing the digital divide for women, who may access the internet differently from men.[110] Women sometimes have greater or different privacy concerns than do men, as they may face threats of harassment online or internet-facilitated controlling behaviour.[111] Women may be confronted with filtering technologies in libraries and schools that limit access to information on reproductive rights.[112] These issues are not always recognized or may not fit in to the world view of the male-dominated internet governance forums.[113] At the same time, feminists have been successful in establishing gender-sensitive indicators to track the use of and need for information and communication technologies.[114]

In Canada, gender has been integrated into internet policy to varying degrees.[115] The Canadian government has made numerous commitments to bridging gender divides in internet access, and it played a role in calling attention to gendered dimensions of the internet at the World Summit on the Information Society in 2003 and 2005.[116] While some initiatives for women's digital inclusion went into decline during the tenure of the Conservative government from 2006 to 2015, gender has once again been highlighted under the Liberal government since 2015.[117]

Internet governance also has implications for queer people. Some countries, like Russia, prohibit queer expression online or install filters in libraries and public schools to censor queer content.[118] The approval of the .gay and .lgbt domain names was contentious, as is the question of what type of organizations should be permitted to own such domains; who represents the gay or LGBT communities?[119]

### Critical Race Theory

Internet technologies and architecture embed racism. Critical race theorists like Safiya Noble and Ruha Benjamin have demonstrated that many of the technologies and algorithms used to govern the internet reinforce oppressive social relationships, embedding racism and colonialism in the technologies and code that define our online experiences.[120] Because the people who design these technologies, the culture in which they are based, and the corpuses of text and information that machine learning is based on are steeped in assumptions embedded in culture, racism and neocolonialism become part of the technologies themselves. For example, until 2012, a Google search on "black girls" yielded pornography sites as the top results, and the same was true for other girls and women of colour.[121] The search engine had learned the racism of internet users. Targeted online advertisements have been used to exclude people of colour from seeing housing advertisements[122] and to suppress African American votes and stoke racial divides for electoral advantage.[123] Online hate is a huge problem, and the architecture and governance of platforms and the internet make hateful content difficult to take down.[124] Platform and internet architectures make possible and facilitate race-based online surveillance by governments (see Chapter 6) and private entities.[125]

The structures of internet and platform regulation have, to date, been inadequate to addressing the problems of online hate, racism, and race-based surveillance. This is due in large part to the ways in which race and racism infuse culture and private and state governance structures. Internet libertarians and cyberutopians have suggested that the online environment could liberate users from offline identities and racism, but this has proven untrue.[126] Internet and platform technologies learn, embed, and are used to facilitate racism.

When techno-regulatory structures purport to be *neutral* or *colourblind*, they can fail to address racial inequalities. For example, the principle of net neutrality may, on the one hand, prevent internet service providers from interfering with the internet content and access of organizers of protests against police brutality. On the other hand, some critical race theorists and multicultural advocacy organizations have argued that net neutrality could prevent internet service providers from providing low-cost access to internet services for low-income users by charging more to high-volume users like Netflix.[127] Critical race theorists call not for "colourblind" policies on platform and internet regulation but for policies that confront and contribute to ending racism and inequality.[128]

Self-regulation of internet companies, technological approaches, and **technological solutionism**—or the idea that problems have technological solutions (as opposed to requiring political, economic, or social change)—along with the failure of state regulation to adequately address racism, are some of the deep challenges to internet regulation and governance.[129]

### Critical Disability Studies

People with disabilities have been pioneer users of the internet, making innovative uses of new technologies to overcome barriers. Internet architecture can be enabling and empowering or exclusionary. People with disabilities have advocated successfully, in many cases, to put accessibility on the agenda of digital policymaking.[130] Web and internet development must take greater account of people's variations and varying needs to foster digital inclusion.[131]

### Indigenous and Postcolonial Analysis

For Indigenous peoples, the internet and information and communication technologies present enormous opportunities for self-representation, economic development, political organization, and the preservation and creation of culture through websites, digitization projects, and online alternative media.[132] At the same time, Indigenous peoples often wish to lead and control the appropriate dissemination of their culture online.[133] Indigenous peoples' potential to control their digital cultures and internet resources, Millar notes, comes up against "the glaring whiteness of digital culture" and the often false promise that digital technologies are liberating:

> Digital ideology retains significant elements of western imperialism. In fact, it seems that the globalization advocated by digital ideology involves less an exchange of cultural knowledge (or information) than a self-interested extraction and commodification of subordinate culture.... A lack of respect is shown for the integrity of the world's diverse cultures in digital ideology ... the glaring whiteness of digital culture is reinvented as the white box of the Macintosh or PC computer and deployed as a civilizing force of the information age.... Like the civilizing mission of the colonial period, new digital technologies are sold to the world as a new liberating "truth" in a crusade embarked upon in the name of development.[134]

Syed Mustafa Ali argues that "the expansionist outreach of ubiquitous or pervasive computing (ubicomp) is driven by and exemplifies a 'colonial impulse.'"[135] The "civilizing mission" attached to this "colonial impulse" is sometimes reproduced in policy documents that portray "First Nations as helpless and dependent on government and telecom industry intervention."[136] To counter this manufactured dependency—one Duncan Philpot, Brian Beaton, and Tim Whiteduck argue is supported by the federal government's ties to telecommunications companies and policies that create neocolonial relationships of dependency between telecom providers and First Nations—some First Nations have worked to support locally owned and managed telecommunications and internet broadband services.[137] Indigenous peoples have, in fact, been leaders in digital innovation and services.[138] This approach—also driven by past failures of the Canadian federal government to establish an overarching broadband plan in consultation with Indigenous peoples—allows Indigenous peoples to establish their own forms of digital self-determination.[139] This work builds on Indigenous peoples' histories of building communications infrastructures, from telecommunications to broadcasting to broadband.[140]

### Governmentality and Networked Governance

A complex network of actors is involved in regulating the internet at national and international levels. No single actor is in control; control is shared by a complex network of private, public, and technological actors and institutions.[141] While it is important to focus beyond the state to look at technological and private actors, especially in the realm of internet governance, it may be that the door has opened to a greater role for states in governing transnational platforms to establish forms of national digital sovereignty. States are under greater pressure to respond to the crises of funding in traditional media, to privacy abuses by transnational platforms, and to platform monopolies.[142]

### Technology and Geography

The rise of platforms like Netflix has shifted regulatory power away from traditional regulators and toward private platforms. For such platforms, former policy questions that revolved around nationalistic sentiment and shoring up a sense of Canadian identity have less importance.[143] As Canadian communications scholar Ira Wagman notes:

> The result of all of this is the effective withering away of the kinds of cultural nationalism that supported the creation and maintenance of the policy

frameworks that have structured the cultural industries—particularly in the audiovisual sector—for much of Canada's experience with mass media technologies. The forms of discourse that once supported assertive and elaborate policy interventions are largely ineffective in an era where media are presented as representative of individual or community identity as much as they are as expressions of national sovereignty.[144]

While internet regulation is a domain of policymaking, technologies and software codes, along with the politics and cultures associated with technology-making, also play a tremendous role in the regulation of the internet. While the policies of the CRTC are significant in determining what can be done on the internet, so are the algorithms used by network technology designers.[145] These operate "under the hood," both being influenced by the regulatory systems with which their operators must comply, but also influencing the range of possibilities available to policymakers, and the interpretation and implementation of policies relating to internet governance. Algorithms, codes, and the material form of network architecture can have huge political consequences, affecting the course of innovation and determining who can—and who cannot—access the network resources necessary for innovation and networked forms of communication.[146]

## FURTHER READING

Chakravartty, Paula. "Who Speaks for the Governed? World Summit on Information Society, Civil Society and the Limits of Multistakeholderism'." *Economic and Political Weekly*, 2006, 250–57.

DeNardis, Laura. *The Global War for Internet Governance*. New Haven, CT: Yale University Press, 2014.

DeNardis, Laura, and Andrea M. Hackl. "Internet Governance by Social Media Platforms." *Telecommunications Policy* 39, no. 9 (2015): 761–70.

Goggin, Gerard. "Communication Rights and Disability Online: Policy and Technology after the World Summit on the Information Society." *Information, Communication & Society* 18, no. 3 (2015): 327–41.

Jin, Dal Yong. *Digital Platforms, Imperialism and Political Culture*. New York: Routledge, 2015.

Mansell, Robin, and Marc Raboy. *The Handbook of Global Media and Communication Policy*. West Sussex, UK: Wiley-Blackwell, 2011.

Mazepa, Patricia, and Vincent Mosco. "A Political Economy Approach to the Internet." In *Handbook on the Economics of the Internet*, edited by Johannes Bauer and Michael Latzer, 163–80. Cheltenham, UK: Edward Elgar Publishing, 2016.

McChesney, Robert Waterman. *Digital Disconnect: How Capitalism Is Turning the Internet against Democracy.* New York: The New Press, 2013.

McChesney, Robert Waterman, and John Nichols. *People Get Ready: The Fight against a Jobless Economy and a Citizenless Democracy.* New York: Nation Books, 2016.

McMurria, John. "From Net Neutrality to Net Equality." *International Journal of Communication* 10, no. 2016 (2016): 5931–48.

Powers, Shawn M., and Michael Jablonski. *The Real Cyber War: The Political Economy of Internet Freedom.* Urbana: University of Illinois Press, 2015.

Shade, Leslie Regan. "Gender and Digital Policy: From Global Information Infrastructure to Internet Governance." In *The Routledge Companion to Media & Gender*, 240–50. Routledge, 2013.

Wagman, Ira. "Talking to Netflix with a Canadian Accent: On Digital Platforms and National Media Policies." In *Reconceptualising Film Policies*, 205–21. London: Routledge, 2017.

Wu, Tim. "Network Neutrality, Broadband Discrimination." *Journal on Telecommunications & High Technology Law* 2, no. 2003 (2003): 141–76.

Wu, Tim, and Christopher Yoo. "Keeping the Internet Neutral?: Tim Wu and Christopher Yoo Debate." *Federal Communications Law Journal* 59, no. 3 (2007): 575–92.

# NOTES

1.  Barlow wrote in protest of the US 1996 *Communications Decency Act*, which pro-hibited internet users from using the internet to communicate material that, un-der contemporary community standards, would be deemed patently offensive to minors under 18.

2.  John Perry Barlow, "A Declaration of the Independence of Cyberspace," Elec-tronic Frontier Foundation, January 20, 2016, https://www.eff.org/cyberspace-independence.

3.  Andrew Murray, *The Regulation of Cyberspace: Control in the Online Environment* (Abingdon, UK: Routledge-Cavendish, 2007), 3–4.

4.  Gordon Bathgate, *Voices from the Ether: The History of Radio* (Morrisville, NC: Lulu.com, 2012), 156.

5.  CRTC, "Public Notice CRTC 1999-84: New Media," Regulatory Policies, May 17, 1999, https://crtc.gc.ca/eng/archive/1999/PB99-84.htm.

6. CRTC, "Broadcasting Regulatory Policy CRTC 2009-329: Review of Broadcasting in New Media," Regulatory Policies, June 4, 2009, https://crtc.gc.ca/eng/archive/2009/2009-329.htm.

7. CRTC, "New Media."

8. The CRTC defined new media as follows: "New media can be described as encompassing, singly or in combination, and whether interactive or not, services and products that make use of video, audio, graphics and alphanumeric text; and involving, along with other, more traditional means of distribution, digital delivery over networks interconnected on a local or global scale." Ibid., para 14.

9. Ibid.

10. *Broadcasting Act*, SC 1991, c 11 s 2(1), emphasis added.

11. Ibid., emphasis added.

12. CRTC, "New Media," para 35.

13. CRTC, "Broadcasting Regulatory Policy CRTC 2009-329: Review of Broadcasting in New Media. Concurring Opinion of Timothy Denton," Regulatory Policies, June 4, 2009, sec 6, https://crtc.gc.ca/eng/archive/2009/2009-329.htm.

14. CRTC, "New Media"; CRTC, "Public Notice CRTC 1999-197: Exemption Order for New Media Broadcasting Undertakings," Orders, December 17, 1999, https://crtc.gc.ca/eng/archive/1999/PB99-197.htm.

15. CRTC, "New Media," paras 68–69.

16. Society of Canadian Authors and Composers (SOCAN), "C. Paul Spurgeon, Vice-President Legal Services & General Counsel, SOCAN to Robert A. Morin, Secretary General, CRTC, 10 July 2008," May 13, 2016, https://services.crtc.gc.ca/Pub/ListeInterventionList/Documents.aspx?ID=72066&en=pb2008-44&dt=c&Lang=e.

17. CRTC, "Review of Broadcasting in New Media," para 48.

18. CRTC, "New Media," paras 67, 71; CRTC, "Review of Broadcasting in New Media," para 48.

19. CRTC, "Review of Broadcasting in New Media," para 67.

20. CRTC, "New Media," paras 76–89; CRTC, "Review of Broadcasting in New Media," paras 42–43.

21. CRTC, "Review of Broadcasting in New Media," paras 38, 66–70.

22. CRTC, "Review of Broadcasting in New Media," para 13; CRTC, "New Media," para 90.

23. CRTC, "Review of Broadcasting in New Media," para 11.

24. Peter Nowak, "Netflix Launches Canadian Movie Service," *CBC News*, September 22, 2010, https://www.cbc.ca/news/technology/netflix-launches-canadian-movie-service-1.872505.

25. Armstrong, *Broadcasting Policy in Canada*, 60.

26. *Broadcasting Act*, SC 1991, c 11, s 5(1), 5(2), and 5(2)(c).

27. CRTC, "New Media," paras 90–116.

28. Ibid., para 90.

29. CRTC, "Review of Broadcasting in New Media: Concurring Opinion of Commissioner Timothy Denton," sec 5.

30. Ibid.

31. Ibid., sec 4.

32. Ibid., sec 1.

33. Ibid., sec 8.

34. CRTC, "Review of Broadcasting in New Media," para 67; CRTC, "Broadcasting Order CRTC 2009-452: Reference to the Federal Court of Appeal—Applicability of the Broadcasting Act to Internet Service Providers," Orders, July 28, 2009, https://crtc.gc.ca/eng/archive/2009/2009-452.htm.

35. *Canadian Radio-television and Telecommunications Commission (Re)*, 2010 FCA 178.

36. *Reference Re: Broadcasting Act*, 2012 SCC 4 at 3; Armstrong, 185.

37. *Reference Re: Broadcasting Act*.

38. *Broadcasting Act*, SC 1991, s 4(4).

39. CRTC, "Broadcasting Order CRTC 2009-660: Amendments to the Exemption Order for New Media Broadcasting Undertakings (Appendix A to Public Notice CRTC 1999-197); Revocation of the Exemption Order for Mobile Television Broadcasting Undertakings," Orders, October 22, 2009, https://crtc.gc.ca/eng/archive/2009/2009-660.htm; CRTC, "Broadcasting Regulatory Policy CRTC 2010-582: Reporting Requirements for New Media Broadcasting Undertakings," Regulatory Policies, August 13, 2010, https://crtc.gc.ca/eng/archive/2010/2010-582.htm; CRTC, "Broadcasting Order CRTC 2012-409: Amendments to the Exemption Order for New Media Broadcasting Undertakings (Now Known as the Exemption Order for Digital Media Broadcasting Undertakings)"; CRTC, "Broadcasting Procedural Letter Addressed to Corie Wright (Netflix)," February 2, 2018, https://crtc.gc.ca/eng/archive/2018/1b180202m.htm; CRTC, "Broadcasting Commission Letter Addressed to the Distribution List," March 28, 2019, https://crtc.gc.ca/eng/archive/2019/lb190328.htm.

40. Laura Armstrong, "Netflix Refuses CRTC Demand for Confidential Data," *The Toronto Star*, September 22, 2014, https://www.thestar.com/news/gta/2014/09/22/netflix_refuses_crtc_demand_for_confidential_data.html.

41. William Francis Morneau, "Building a Strong Middle Class: Budget 2017" (Ottawa: Minister of Finance, March 22, 2017), 106.

42. Canada and Canadian Heritage, *Creative Canada Policy Framework*, 2017, 106, https://www.canada.ca/en/canadian-heritage/campaigns/creative-canada/framework.html.

43. Canadian Heritage, "Broadcasting and Telecommunications Legislative Review," June 5, 2018, https://www.canada.ca/en/canadian-heritage/news/2018/06/government-of-canada-launches-review-of-telecommunications-and-broadcasting-acts.html.

44. *Telecommunications Act*, SC 1993, c 38, s 27(2).

45. Pablo Bello and Juan Jung, "Net Neutrality," *Global Commission on Internet Governance Paper Series*, May 6, 2015, https://www.cigionline.org/publications/net-neutrality-reflections-current-debate.

46. Mark A. Lemley and Lawrence Lessig, "The End of End-to-End: Preserving the Architecture of the Internet in the Broadband Era," *UCLA Law Review* 48 (2000): 925–72. See also Tim Wu, "Network Neutrality, Broadband Discrimination," *Journal on Telecommunications & High Technology Law* 2, (2003): 141; Tim Wu and Christopher Yoo, "Keeping the Internet Neutral?: Tim Wu and Christopher Yoo Debate," *Federal Communications Law Journal* 59, no. 3 (2007): 575–92.

47. Telus, "Press Release: Alberta Court Grants Interim Injunction against Posting TELUS Employee Photos," July 28, 2005, http://test-about.telus.com/cgi-bin/media_news_viewer.cgi?news_id=605&mode=2&news_year=2005.

48. Julio Ojeda-Zapata, "Netflix Members Who Use Comcast Face Streaming Hiccups," *Pioneer Press*, February 11, 2014, https://www.twincities.com/2014/02/11/netflix-members-who-use-comcast-face-streaming-hiccups/; Public Knowledge, "Net Neutrality," accessed November 3, 2018, https://www.publicknowledge.org/issues/net-neutrality; Brian Fung, "Verizon Denies Using Net Neutrality Victory to Sabotage Netflix, Amazon," *Washington Post*, February 5, 2014, https://www.washingtonpost.com/news/the-switch/wp/2014/02/05/verizon-denies-using-net-neutrality-victory-to-sabotage-netflix-amazon/.

49. Claims that an ISP is slowing traffic to preserve bandwidth can mask its competitive reasons for slowing content. For example, an ISP might slow or block a video streaming service that competes with its own video services.

50. *Telecommunications Act*, s 36.

51. CRTC, "Telecom Regulatory Policy CRTC 2009-657: Review of the Internet Traffic Management Practices of Internet Service Providers," Regulatory Policies, October 21, 2009, paras 121–22, https://crtc.gc.ca/eng/archive/2009/2009-657.htm. See also Marc Raboy, William J. McIver, and Jeremy Shtern, eds., *Media Divides: Communication Rights and the Right to Communicate in Canada* (Vancouver: UBC Press, 2010), 145–74.

52. CRTC, "Review of the Internet Traffic Management Practices," para 126; see also paras 123–27.

53. Ibid., para 127; see also paras 123–27.

54. *Telecommunications Act*, SC 1993, c 38, s 27(2).

55. CRTC, "Review of the Internet Traffic Management Practices," para 40; see also paras 38–45.

56. ISPs who implement traffic management practices that discriminate or give preference to a person (or their content) would be required to:

> demonstrate that the ITMP is designed to address the need and achieve the purpose and effect in question, and nothing else; establish that the ITMP results in discrimination or preference as little as reasonably possible; demonstrate that any harm to a secondary ISP, end-user, or any other person is as little as reasonably possible; and explain why, in the case of a technical ITMP, network investment or economic approaches alone would not reasonably address the need and effectively achieve the same purpose as the ITMP. (Ibid., para 43)

57. Ibid., paras 50–67.

58. CRTC, "Strengthening Net Neutrality in Canada," Consumer Information, September 26, 2016, https://crtc.gc.ca/eng/internet/diff.htm. See also CRTC, "Telecom Decision CRTC 2017-105: Complaints against Quebecor Media Inc., Videotron Ltd., and Videotron G.P. Alleging Undue and Unreasonable Preference and Disadvantage Regarding the Unlimited Music Program," Decisions, April 20, 2017, https://crtc.gc.ca/eng/archive/2017/2017-105.htm; CRTC, "Broadcasting and Telecom Decision CRTC 2015-26: Complaint against Bell Mobility Inc. and Quebecor Media Inc., Videotron Ltd. and Videotron G.P. Alleging Undue and Unreasonable Preference and Disadvantage in Regard to the Billing Practices for Their Mobile TV Services Bell Mobile TV and Illico.TV," Decisions, January 29, 2015, https://crtc.gc.ca/eng/archive/2015/2015-26.htm.

59. Sara M. Smyth, *Cybercrime in Canadian Criminal Law* (Toronto: Carswell Thomson Reuters, 2015), 203.

60. *OED Online*, s.v. "spam, n. 1," accessed August 19, 2019.

61. Smyth, 211–17.

62. Ibid., 212.

63. *Criminal Code*, RSC 1985, c C-46, ss163 and 163.1.

64. These provisions are discussed in greater detail in Chapter 3. Criminal cases relating to the distribution of obscene materials other than child pornography via the internet are now relatively rare, and many of the charges that have been brought since 1998 have been unsuccessful.

65. Janine Benedet, "The Paper Tigress: Canadian Obscenity Law 20 Years after *R v Butler*," *The Canadian Bar Review* 93, no. 1 (2015): 1–37; Smyth, 87–138.

66. *Criminal Code*, ss 342.01 (credit card fraud), 342.1 (unauthorized use of a computer), 342.2, and 380 (fraud).

67. *Criminal Code*, s 380(1).

68. *Criminal Code*, s 402.2(1); Smyth, 47.

69. Smyth, 45–86.

70. Ibid.

71. *Criminal Code*, s 430; Smyth, 180.

72. *Criminal Code*, s 342.2; Smyth, 181.

73. *Criminal Code*, ss 342.1 and 342.2; Smyth, 198.

74. *Criminal Code*, s 184(1); Smyth, 198.

75. For further history, see Daniel J. Paré, *Internet Governance in Transition: Who Is the Master of This Domain?* (Lanham, MD: Rowman & Littlefield, 2003).

76. ICANN, "Stewardship of IANA Functions Transitions to Global Internet Community as Contract with U.S. Government Ends," October 1, 2016, https://www.icann.org/news/announcement-2016-10-01-en.

77. "Cleanfeed Canada," accessed October 30, 2018, https://cybertip.ca/app/en/projects-cleanfeed.

78. *Criminal Code*, s 163.1(3).

79. Lilian Edwards, "From Child Porn to China, in One Cleanfeed," SSRN Scholarly Paper (Rochester, NY: Social Science Research Network, May 3, 2008), 174–75, https://papers.ssrn.com/abstract=1128062.

80. Michael Geist, "Project Cleanfeed Canada," November 24, 2006, http://www.michaelgeist.ca/2006/11/project-cleanfeed-canada/.

81. Sophia Harris, "'Slippery Slope': Opposition Mounts to Canadian Media's Plan to Block Piracy Websites," *CBC News*, February 18, 2018, https://www.cbc.ca/news/business/fairplay-piracy-website-blocking-crtc-1.4539566.

82. CRTC, "Telecom Decision CRTC 2016-479: Public Interest Advocacy Centre—Application for Relief Regarding Section 12 of the Quebec Budget Act," Decisions, December 9, 2016, https://crtc.gc.ca/eng/archive/2016/2016-479.htm.

83. Nicholas W. Jankowski, "Researching Fake News: A Selective Examination of Empirical Studies," *Javnost—The Public* 25, no. 1–2 (April 3, 2018): 248–55, https://doi.org/10.1080/13183222.2018.1418964; Eli Pariser, *The Filter Bubble: How the New Personalized Web Is Changing What We Read and How We Think* (London: Penguin Books, 2012); Safiya Umoja Noble, *Algorithms of Oppression: How Search Engines Reinforce Racism* (New York: Oxford University Press, 2018); Taina Bucher, *If ... Then: Algorithmic Power and Politics* (New York: Oxford University Press, 2018).

84. Samidh Chakrabarti, "Hard Questions: What Effect Does Social Media Have on Democracy?" *Facebook Newsroom* (blog), January 22, 2018, https://newsroom.fb.com/news/2018/01/effect-social-media-democracy/.

85. *Google Spain SL and Google Inc. v Agencia Española de Protección de Datos (AEPD) and Mario Costeja González*, case C-131/12, http://curia.europa.eu/juris/document/document.jsf?docid=163494&mode=req&pageIndex=1&dir=&occ=-first&part=1&text=&doclang=EN&cid=863577.

86. Noble; Bucher.

87. Oren Bracha and Frank Pasquale, "Federal Search Commission—Access, Fairness, and Accountability in the Law of Search," *Cornell Law Review* 93, no. 6 (September 2008): 1149–1210.

88. Jeremy Malcolm, *Multi-Stakeholder Governance and the Internet Governance Forum* (Perth: Terminus Press, 2008); Jeremy Malcolm, "Criteria of Meaningful Stakeholder Inclusion in Internet Governance," *Internet Policy Review* 4, no. 4 (2015): 1–14; Mark Raymond and Laura DeNardis, "Multistakeholderism: Anatomy of an Inchoate Global Institution," *International Theory* 7, no. 3 (2015): 572–616; Marc Raboy, Normand Landry, and Jeremy Shtern, *Digital Solidarities, Communication Policy and Multi-Stakeholder Global Governance: The Legacy of the World Summit on the Information Society* (New York: Peter Lang, 2010).

89. Jean-Marie Chenou, "From Cyber-Libertarianism to Neoliberalism: Internet Exceptionalism, Multi-Stakeholderism, and the Institutionalisation of Internet Governance in the 1990s," *Globalizations* 11, no. 2 (March 4, 2014): 212–13, https://doi.org/10.1080/14747731.2014.887387.

90. Samantha Bradshaw and Laura DeNardis, "The Politicization of the Internet's Domain Name System: Implications for Internet Security, Universality, and Freedom," *New Media & Society* 20, no. 1 (January 2018): 337–38, https://doi.org/10.1177/1461444816662932.

91. Ibid.

92. Ibid.

93. Raboy, Landry, and Shtern, 130.

94. Shawn M. Powers and Michael Jablonski, *The Real Cyber War: The Political Economy of Internet Freedom* (Urbana: University of Illinois Press, 2015), 61.

95. Monika Zalnieriute, "The Anatomy of Neoliberal Internet Governance: A Queer Critical Political Economy Perspective," in *Queering International Law: Possibilities, Alliances, Complicities, Risks*, ed. Dianne Otto (Abingdon, UK: Routledge, 2018), 63; Powers and Jablonski, 23.

96. Adam Thierer and Berin Szoka, "CyberLibertarianism: The Case for Real Internet Freedom," *The Technology Liberation Front* (blog), August 12, 2009, https://techliberation.com/2009/08/12/cyber-libertarianism-the-case-for-real-internet-freedom/.

97. Barlow.

98.  David Golumbia, "Talk: Cyberlibertarianism: The Extremist Foundations of Digital Freedom,'" accessed November 3, 2018, http://www.uncomputing.org/?p=276.

99.  Jean-Marie Chenou, "Is Internet Governance a Democratic Process? Multistake-holderism and Transnational Elites," in *ECPR General Conference*, 25–27, 2011.

100.  Barbrook and Cameron, "The Californian Ideology," 45, 54; Streeter, "That Deep Romantic Chasm': Libertarianism, Neoliberalism, and the Computer Culture."

101.  Richard Barbrook and Andy Cameron, "The Californian Ideology," *Science as Culture* 6, no. 1 (January 1996): 45, 54, https://doi.org/10.1080/09505439609526455.

102.  Ibid., 61.

103.  Ibid., 61–63.

104.  Patricia Mazepa and Vincent Mosco, "A Political Economy Approach to the Internet," in *Handbook on the Economics of the Internet*, ed. Johannes Bauer and Michael Latzer (Cheltenham, UK: Edward Elgar Publishing, 2016), 163–64.

105.  Ibid., 165. See also Fuchs, "A Contribution to the Critique of the Political Economy of Google"; Christian Fuchs, "Dallas Smythe Today—The Audience Commodity, the Digital Labour Debate, Marxist Political Economy and Critical Theory," *TripleC: Communication, Capitalism & Critique* 10, no. 2 (2012): 692–740.; Christian Fuchs, "Wikinomics: How Mass Collaboration Changes Everything—by Don Tapscott & Anthony D. Williams," *Journal of Communication* 58, no. 2 (2008): 402–3; Christian Fuchs, *Foundations of Critical Media and Information Studies* (New York: Routledge, 2011); Dwayne Winseck, "Reconstructing the Political Economy of Communication for the Digital Media Age," *The Political Economy of Communication* 4, no. 2 (2017); Dwyane Winseck, "Information Operations 'Blowback,'" *International Communication Gazette* 70, no. 6 (December 2008): 419–41, https://doi.org/10.1177/1748048508096141; Robert Waterman McChesney and John Nichols, *People Get Ready: The Fight against a Jobless Economy and a Citizenless Democracy* (New York: Nation Books, 2016); Robert Waterman McChesney, *Digital Disconnect: How Capitalism Is Turning the Internet against Democracy* (New York: The New Press, 2013); Dal Yong Jin, *Digital Platforms, Imperialism and Political Culture* (New York: Routledge, 2015).

106.  Mazepa and Mosco, 165.

107.  Ibid., 165–68.

108.  Paula Chakravartty, "Who Speaks for the Governed? World Summit on Information Society, Civil Society and the Limits of 'Multistakeholderism,'" *Economic and Political Weekly*, 2006: 256; Avri Doria, "Internet Governance and Gender Issues," in *Critically Absent: Women's Rights in Internet Governance* (Melville, South Africa: Association for Progressive Communication, 2012), 14.

109. Chakravartty, 256.

110. Molly Dragiewicz, Delanie Woodlock, Bridget Harris, and Claire Reid, "Technology-Facilitated Coercive Control," in *The Routledge International Handbook of Violence Studies* (New York: Routledge, 2018), 266–275; Doria, 12.

111. Ibid.

112. Ibid.

113. Doria, 14.

114. Chakravartty, 256.

115. Leslie Regan Shade, "Missing in Action: Gender in Canada's Digital Economy Agenda," *Signs: Journal of Women in Culture and Society* 39, no. 4 (Summer 2014): 888–96; Leslie Regan Shade, "Integrating Gender into Canadian Internet Policy: From the Information Highway to the Digital Economy," *Journal of Information Policy* 6 (2016): 338–70.

116. Leslie Regan Shade, "Gender and Digital Policy: From Global Information Infrastructure to Internet Governance," in *The Routledge Companion to Media & Gender* (New York: Routledge, 2013), 240–50.

117. Ibid.

118. Zalnieriute.

119. Mark Naimark, "In the Fight Over .gay and .lgbt, the Cyberpowers That Be Are Redefining Our Community," *Slate*, May 7, 2014, https://slate.com/human-interest/2014/05/icann-and-the-fight-for-gay-and-lgbt-does-the-gay-community-even-exist.html.

120. Noble; Ruha Benjamin, *Race after Technology: Abolitionist Tools for the New Jim Code.* Hoboken, NJ: John Wiley & Sons, 2019.

121. Ibid., 3–4.

122. Julia Angwin, Ariana Tobin, and Madeline Varner, "Facebook (Still) Letting Housing Advertisers Exclude Users by Race," *ProPublica*, November 21, 2017.

123. Ibid.; Devin Coldewey, "Bannon and Cambridge Analytica Planned Suppression of Black Voters, Whistleblower Tells Senate," *TechCrunch* (blog), May 16, 2018, https://techcrunch.com/2018/05/16/bannon-and-cambridge-analytica-planned-suppression-of-black-voters-whistleblower-tells-senate/.

124. Richard Delgado and Jean Stefancic, "Hate Speech in Cyberspace," *Wake Forest Law Review* 49 (2014): 319; Craig Timberg, Drew Harwell, Hamza Shaban, Andrew Ba Tran, and Brian Fung, "The New Zealand Shooting Shows How YouTube and Facebook Spread Hate and Violent Images—Yet Again," *Washington Post* (blog), March 15, 2019, https://www.washingtonpost.com/technology/2019/03/15/facebook-youtube-twitter-amplified-video-christchurch-mosque-shooting/.

125. Steven Malcic, "Proteus Online: Digital Identity and the Internet Governance Industry," *Convergence* 24, no. 2 (2018): 209.

126. Ibid., 207; Lisa Nakamura, *Cybertypes: Race, Ethnicity, and Identity on the Internet* (New York: Routledge, 2013).

127. John McMurria, "From Net Neutrality to Net Equality," *International Journal of Communication* 10, no. 2016 (2016): 5936 and 5943; Rachel E. Moran and Matthew N. Bui, "Race, Ethnicity, and Telecommunications Policy Issues of Access and Representation: Centering Communities of Color and Their Concerns," *Telecommunications Policy* 43, no. 5 (2019): 461–73.

128. McMurria, 5938.

129. Rob Kitchin, *The Data Revolution: Big Data, Open Data, Data Infrastructures and Their Consequences* (London: SAGE, 2014), 181.

130. Gerard Goggin, "Communication Rights and Disability Online: Policy and Technology after the World Summit on the Information Society," *Information, Communication & Society* 18, no. 3 (2015): 327–41; Elizabeth Ellcessor, "Bridging Disability Divides: A Critical History of Web Content Accessibility through 2001," *Information, Communication & Society* 13, no. 3 (2010): 289–308.

131. Lareen Newman, Kathryn Browne-Yung, Parimala Raghavendra, Denise Wood, and Emma Grace, "Applying a Critical Approach to Investigate Barriers to Digital Inclusion and Online Social Networking among Young People with Disabilities," *Information Systems Journal* 27, no. 5 (2017): 559–88; Sarah Lewthwaite, "Web Accessibility Standards and Disability: Developing Critical Perspectives on Accessibility," *Disability and Rehabilitation* 36, no. 16 (2014): 1375–83.

132. Cynthia J. Alexander, "Wiring the Nation! Including First Nations? Aboriginal Canadians and Federal e-Government Initiatives," *Journal of Canadian Studies* 35, no. 4 (2001): 277–96.

133. Jeremy de Beer and Daniel Dylan, "Traditional Knowledge Governance Challenges in Canada," in *Indigenous Intellectual Property*, ed. Matthew Rimmer (Cheltenham, UK: Edward Elgar, 2015), https://doi.org/10.4337/9781781955901.00035.

134. Melanie Stewart Millar, *Cracking the Gender Code: Who Rules the Wired World?* (Toronto: Second Story Press, 1998), 151–52. As quoted in Alexander, 282.

135. Syed Mustafa Ali, "A Brief Introduction to Decolonial Computing," *XRDS: Crossroads, The ACM Magazine for Students* 22 no. 4 (June 13, 2016): 18, https://doi.org/10.1145/2930886.

136. Duncan Philpot, Brian Beaton, and Tim Whiteduck, "First Mile Challenges to Last Mile Rhetoric: Exploring the Discourse between Remote and Rural First

Nations and the Telecom Industry," *Journal of Community Informatics* 10, no. 2 (2014).

137. Ibid.

138. B. Bell, P. Budka, and A. Fiser, "'We Were on the Outside Looking in': MyKnet. org–A First Nations Online Social Environment in Northern Ontario," in *Connecting Canadians: Investigations in Community Informatics*, eds. A. Clement, M. Gurstein, G. Longford, M. Moll, and L.R. Shade (2012): 237–54.

139. Rob McMahon, "From Digital Divides to the First Mile: Indigenous Peoples and the Network Society in Canada," *International Journal of Communication* 8 (2014): 25; Rob McMahon, "The Institutional Development of Indigenous Broadband Infrastructure in Canada and the United States: Two Paths to 'Digital Self-Determination,'" *Canadian Journal of Communication* 36, no. 1 (2011): 115–40.

140. McMahon, "The Institutional Development," 121.

141. Robin Mansell and Marc Raboy, "Introduction: Foundations of the Theory and Practice of Global Media and Communication Policy," in *The Handbook of Global Media and Communication Policy* (West Sussex, UK: Wiley-Blackwell, 2011), 4–5.

142. Ibid., 12–13.

143. Ira Wagman, "Talking to Netflix with a Canadian Accent: On Digital Platforms and National Media Policies," in *Reconceptualising Film Policies* (New York: Routledge, 2017), 205–21.

144. Ibid., 217.

145. Fenwick McKelvey, "Ends and Ways: The Algorithmic Politics of Network Neutrality," *Global Media Journal* 3, no. 1 (2010): 51.

146. Lemley and Lessig; Mel Hogan and Tamara Shepherd, "Information Ownership and Materiality in an Age of Big Data Surveillance," *Journal of Information Policy* 5 (2015): 6–31; Alison Powell, "Argument-by-Technology: How Technical Activism Contributes to Internet Governance," in *Research Handbook on Governance of the Internet*, ed. Ian Brown (Cheltenham, UK: Edward Elgar, 2013), 198–220.

# 11 Access to Information

## INTRODUCTION

From tax and income information to statistical information, to law enforcement information and criminal records, to surveillance and intelligence, governments have a tremendous amount of information about individuals. What about the reverse? How do individuals access information about government?

This chapter introduces the right of access to information and related institutions in Canada. It reviews the process for requesting information under access to information law. In the second half, it asks, "Whom does access to information law serve?", drawing on the theories outlined in Chapter 1.

## WHAT IS ACCESS TO INFORMATION?

**Access to information** laws, also known as **freedom of information** laws, give individuals a right of access to records held by government. These laws cover federal, territorial, provincial, and municipal levels of government. With specific exceptions and exemptions, this right applies to records held by government, such as reports, memos, email correspondence, or recordings.

Access to information law, in theory, ensures that citizens can access the information they need to participate in democratic processes and safeguards the democratic values of transparency, accountability, and governance.[1] These laws require governments to provide access to information that members of the public ask for, rather than simply what the government chooses to release. They allow members of the public to track government action throughout the term of government.

There are innumerable examples where these laws have provided access to documents and records that have been important to journalistic reporting, academic research, or other information-gathering. For example, freedom of information requests for government records have led to reporting on and a growing public awareness of police carding, the mental health problems associated with the use of long-term segregation in Canadian prisons, and police use of stingray surveillance devices.[2] They have revealed lavish spending by public officials and Canadian drug companies' failures to report problems with their medications.[3]

At the same time, there are also many examples where access to information law has fallen short, has failed to provide full access to records, or has provided access only after extensive delay. The Office of the Information Commissioner of Canada has investigated cases where emails were deleted to avoid their being subject to an access to information request, where decisions relating to the death of Robert Dziekanski after he was tasered by the RCMP were not documented, and where there were long delays in receiving records relating to the residential school system.[4]

The federal *Access to Information Act* says:

Every person who is

    a.   a Canadian citizen, or
    b.   a permanent resident ...

has a right to and shall, on request, be given access to any record under the control of a government institution.[5]

The right of access to information is not granted under the *Canadian Charter of Rights and Freedoms* and is thus not a "Charter right." However, the right of access has been held to be "quasi-constitutional."[6] The purpose of the right of access is to ensure that citizens are able to access the information necessary to participate meaningfully in democratic processes.[7] The principles inherent in the right to freedom of expression also lie behind the principle of freedom of information. These include the encouragement of free and open discussion, free dissemination of information, the ability to seek and attain truth, and participation in social and political decision-making.

## Information Commissioner

The federal Information Commissioner, and provincial and territorial counterparts, investigates complaints about how access to information requests are handled. Requestors who do not feel their request was appropriately handled can submit a complaint to the relevant Information Commissioner for review. The federal Office of the Information Commissioner monitors government's performance, issues reports, and provides advice to government on access to information law.

The Office of the Information Commissioner publishes reports of its investigations, along with reports of the Commissioner's parliamentary activities and reports, on its website. Provincial and territorial counterparts do the same.

## What Is a Record?

Canadian citizens and residents have a right of access to "any record under the control of a government institution."[8] The definition of a **record** is quite broad; it includes "any documentary material, regardless of medium or form."[9] It includes electronic records, such as emails.

## Exclusions

Certain records are excluded from the scope of the *Access to Information Act*. This includes material that is already publicly available (such as published material or library or museum material).[10] Confidences of the Queen's Privy Council for Canada are also excluded, including "memoranda the purpose of which is to present proposals or recommendations to Council," "discussion papers the purpose of which is to present background explanations, analyses of problems or policy options to Council for consideration by Council in making decisions," records reflecting "communications or discussions between ministers relating to ... decisions or the formulation of government policy," and draft legislation.[11] The purpose of the latter exclusions is, arguably, to permit a sphere of discussion within which ideas, including potentially unpopular ideas, can be freely discussed. While the *Access to Information Act* applies to the CBC, records relating to "journalistic, creative or programming activities" are excluded to preserve press and journalistic freedom.[12]

## Exemptions

Certain records are exempted from release under the *Access to Information Act*. This includes mandatory exemptions (here, the act provides that "the government *shall* refuse to disclose" the record) covering information obtained in confidence from other governments,[13] records relating to some types of investigations and audits,[14] records containing third-party information,[15] and personal information.[16] Personal information is subject to a separate access regime, under which a person may request *their own* personal information.[17]

There are also discretionary exemptions; here, the act provides that "the government *may* refuse to disclose" the record. Discretionary exemptions permit government to refuse to release records whose release would be injurious to federal-provincial affairs, to international affairs and defence,[18] or to the economic interests of Canada;[19] records that could facilitate the commission of an offence;[20] records relating to law enforcement or other types of investigations;[21] records subject to solicitor-client privilege;[22] and records whose disclosure "could reasonably be expected to threaten the safety of individuals."[23] To protect an uninhibited zone of discussion and decision-making, discretionary exemptions also permit government to refuse to release records containing "advice or recommendations developed by government" and accounts "of consultations or deliberations ... by employees of government."[24]

### Request Process

Access to information requests can be submitted directly to the relevant Access to Information Officer of the relevant department, or in some cases, they can be submitted online.[25] Under the federal act, each request costs $5.[26] It is not necessary, under current federal access to information legislation, to disclose the reason for your request.

Under the federal act, government is required to respond to the request within 30 days and may seek an extension for requests that may take more than 30 days to fulfill. Requests that require consultations with other government departments or outside third parties can be time-consuming.

## WHOM DOES ACCESS TO INFORMATION LAW SERVE?

Access to information laws have been put in place by many countries, especially since the 1980s. While the first access to information law was put in place by Sweden in 1766,[27] only a few countries had such laws in the mid-1980s. The United States adopted the *Freedom of Information Act* in 1966,[28] and Canada's *Access to Information Act* came into force in 1983. Between the 1980s and 2016, the number of countries that had access to information laws in place grew to 111, encompassing more than half the countries in the world.[29] Whom do these laws serve?

## The Public Interest?

### *Pluralism*

The right of access to information is an important tool in pluralist societies, as it ensures that groups have adequate access to the information they need to participate meaningfully in political processes. Secrecy, on the other hand, can allow insiders and those who are politically connected to have greater sway in government decision-making.[30] A right of access, along with low request and processing fees, can be important in empowering a broad range of groups to participate in democracy and policymaking. Higher levels of secrecy or higher request and processing fees would tend to permit only those groups with more resources to participate in democratic processes.

The power of access to information law has been reduced by the rise of pluralistic, complex governance systems. Public sector restructuring in the 1980s and 1990s led to a move away from centralized mass government bureaucracies to an increasing reliance on multiple special-purpose government units, specialized agencies, outsourcing, and privatization. On one hand, an increasing number of rival government departments, agencies, and private firms can help to ensure that no one group dominates the policymaking process. On the other hand, the increased turn to private or semi-private provision of public services has moved a number of services outside the ambit of access to information laws.[31] Private firms are generally not subject to access to information laws, though privacy law grants a right of access to personal information held by private companies. Some countries also recognize the right of access as applying to private firms performing public services.[32]

Access to information laws can be viewed as a response to demands from a variety of groups, each with varying resources and power. These include private companies with an interest in access to information related to their properties and businesses. They also include journalists, the media, and researchers. From a pluralist perspective, the right of access to information responds to such groups' interests and demands, while carving out exceptions and limitations for other groups, including government security and policing, bureaucrats, and businesses that deal and contract with government.

## Bureaucracy and Bureaucrats?

### *Bureaucratic Theory*

The dynamics of government bureaucracy have an influence on how access to information laws are implemented. Public servants responsible for implementing access to information laws and responding to requests may be faced with particular reward structures, pressures, and organizational visions that impact on their procedures and responses.[33] Organizational leadership that places an emphasis on norms of transparency and access, emanating from the top of government, is an important factor in full implementation of a right of access.[34]

An organizational culture of secrecy can impede the implementation of access to information laws, particularly under historically more authoritarian governments and under regimes that do not have, or have not had, a culture of journalistic freedom. Under more secretive bureaucratic regimes, information can be held back or leaked selectively against political rivals.[35]

### Neoliberalism

Freedom of information laws have proliferated since the 1980s, which coincides with the rise of neoliberalism. Two factors may help to explain this.

First, neoliberal theory emphasizes the importance of curtailing state power, cutting regulations, and free markets. On one hand, access to information law creates a substantial bureaucracy, with officials being charged with the review and release of records in a system that is often highly bureaucratic. While this does not appear to accord with neoliberalism's emphasis on government downsizing, access to information law is, at the same time, a tool of government oversight that, insofar as it places the power of information in the hands of private actors, transfers power out of the hands of the state and into the hands of private businesses, investors, civil society groups, and individuals.

Second, the importance of a free marketplace of ideas—of businesses' and investors' full access to information—is also emphasized in the neoliberal model. Businesses, which under neoliberalism are fully privatized rather than being integrated with government as they might be under socialist regimes, do not have insider access to government information. A right of access to information to government-held records can provide insight into property and markets; access, here, is a significant ingredient in promoting well-functioning economic markets.[36]

Freedom of information law reflects the general idea, which is also emphasized under the neoliberal "free flow of information" doctrine, that restrictions should not be placed on the flow of information and media content. This American doctrine decried regulation of media and information flow across international borders, bolstering access to foreign markets for American media.[37]

## The Privileged?

### *Critical Political Economy*

Although access to information laws can be used by any group, the reality is that more access to information requests are made by businesses, and not by journalists, academics, and public interest groups.[38] For example, businesses may seek information about properties they own or have another interest in. Such requests may not face the delays and scrutiny that journalists, opposition politicians, and interest groups seem to face.[39] In fact, journalists' requests are often subject to extra processing and scrutiny, delaying or even preventing records' release.[40]

While access to information laws may benefit privileged business actors, they also tremendously benefit civil society actors. Critical political economists, therefore, tend to focus their critique not on the right of access to information itself but on its curtailment.

Some critical commentators have argued that access to information laws are part of a discourse of transparency that masks an underlying neoliberal agenda.[41] Access to information laws may, such critics argue, actually restrict access for the poor, protecting third-party information of corporations, while serving to provide efficient access to corporations and property owners.

### *Indigenous and Postcolonial Analysis*

The United Nations Commission on Human Rights has published a set of principles stating that states must recognize that victims of past human rights violations have a right "to know the truth about what happened to them."[42] "Society at large," the TRC noted, "also has a right to know the truth about what happened in the past."[43] States therefore have an obligation to safeguard knowledge and documentation about the past and to preserve that documentation in records and archives. States must provide ready access to those archives to victims, their families, and researchers.

Canada's Truth and Reconciliation Commission cited this right to truth in noting that access to information can be a key ingredient in reconciliation. They said:

> In many countries, including Canada, the access to, and protection of, historical records have been instrumental in advancing the rights of Indigenous peoples and documenting the state's wrongful actions. In the wake of the South African and other truth commissions, some archivists have come to see themselves not simply as neutral custodians of national history, but also as professionals who are responsible for ensuring that records documenting past injustices are preserved and used to strengthen government accountability and support justice.[44]

Indigenous peoples have archives, often contained in oral histories maintained by Elders and Knowledge Keepers. Settler archives can help to fill in gaps or absences that may appear in Indigenous oral histories.[45] Access to settler archives and records through access to information law is extremely important in establishing Indigenous peoples' rights and land claims. This was noted during the process leading up to 2019 revisions to the *Access to Information Act* under Bill C-58, where the government had proposed measures that would have seriously undermined "the ability of Indigenous communities to access government records and information in support of their claims against the Government of Canada"[46] and "to request records related to residential schools, land claims and other important issues."[47]

The TRC's work was enabled by measures requiring government and churches "to provide all relevant documents in their possession or control to and for the use of the Truth and Reconciliation Commission" in compliance with access to information legislation.[48] At the same time, the TRC faced obstacles in obtaining that access, and questions over who (the Commission, or the staff of the National Archives of Canada) was responsible for identifying and organizing the documents relevant to the Commission.[49] The TRC thus called for work to be done, in collaboration with Indigenous peoples, to ensure that archival policies contribute to reconciliation.[50]

Access to information and archives can be an essential component in processes of reconciliation, but archives have also played significant roles in colonialism. Archives and records are often created and controlled by settler governments. They thus present the perspectives of settler governments and dominant white populations in ways that legitimate, and sometimes produce a sanitized or skewed narrative of, the government and its past.[51]

Access to information law is sometimes used to limit and prohibit access to information sought by Indigenous or racialized groups. Aboriginal activist groups seeking land reclamations, for example, are often the subject of police investigations and treated with a national security framing. This permits the use of law enforcement and national security access to information exemptions that may not apply to information being sought by other groups.[52]

Access to information laws now come as part of the Western legal paradigm and have been associated with the postcolonial development paradigm. Access to information laws, and transparency more generally, has often been associated with, or posed as an ingredient for, socioeconomic "development" and political freedom.[53] Some ask whether economic growth, economic liberalism, and political liberty necessarily go hand in hand. Others argue that transparency is a necessary but not sufficient ingredient of political freedom from authoritarianism.[54] It is less clear that access to information laws have a causal effect more broadly on economic or political "development," though they may have a role to play.[55] Indigenous peoples are, for their part, exploring ways to assert sovereignty through ownership, control, access, and possession (OCAP) over their own information and data.[56]

### Critical Race Theory

There has been little examination of access to information law from a critical race theory perspective. Access to information law has certainly been used to uncover bias and discrimination on the part of government and government agencies. A "Race and Crime" investigation by the *Toronto Star* in 2002, for example, uncovered apparent racial bias in policing by drawing on data requested under freedom of information laws.[57] There are many examples of access laws being used to uncover bias and discrimination; one story drew on a freedom of information request to find that Black people in Halifax were three times more likely to be street checked than whites.[58] At the same time, it is possible that access to information requests that seek to uncover government or police wrongdoing against racialized people are denied for similar reasons to those of Indigenous activist groups discussed above; they may be treated with a national security framing, permitting exemptions that may not apply to information being sought by other groups.[59] Further, as Beutin notes, even where information and evidence is revealed to the public, it may not have the effect of producing change and transformation, due to racist framings, interpretations, and institutional practices that are difficult to dislodge and transform.[60]

### Governmentality and Networked Governance

Access to information law reconfigures the "relationship between state and citizen by specifying how and under what terms politicised knowledge is shared—in other words reconfiguring at least partially the nexus of knowledge and power."[61] The rationalities and mentalities of government (what Michel Foucault called *governmentality*) at work in the access to information regime, and in the information-sharing practices of government more generally, form an important part of the context of the access to information regime.

Willem de Lint and Reem Bahdi describe the ways in which practices, mentalities, and rationalities of information production and disclosure by Canadian law enforcement and security agencies have shifted historically, for example in response to crises such as 9/11. Prior to 9/11, information was shared between law enforcement and security agencies on a "need-to-know" basis, but 9/11 shifted mentalities to favour greater sharing, or a "need-to-share" information regime, among law and security agencies transnationally. This increased sharing, however, was accompanied by a reluctance of law enforcement and security agencies to create records, in efforts to evade the transparency imposed by access to information law. It was also accompanied by the increasing use of discourses designed to exempt law enforcement and security from transparency requirements in the interests of security and Canada's transnational commitments to other security agencies. This increasing emphasis on security at the expense of transparency represents a significant shift in governmentality.[62]

### Technology and Geography

The rise of government transparency initiatives, including the adoption of access to information laws in many countries since the 1980s, has been attributed in part to the growth of information and communication technologies that, theoretically at least, make openness and transparency possible, affecting expectations and cultural attitudes about transparency.[63] Sandra Braman has argued that the rise of information and communication technologies is tied to fundamental changes in the functions and character of the state; the state has transformed from a welfare state in the 1960s to an informational state today, one of whose central purposes is the management and control of information in governance.[64] The institution of access to information laws, she argues, is part of that.[65]

Technological changes play a significant role in the rise of access to information law. Many have argued that the use of information and computer technologies has made possible the kinds of transparency required by access to information laws. Information and communication technologies reduce the potential for corruption in government, allowing the tracking of government activities by citizens, and enable greater transparency, especially in the realms of taxation, government purchasing, and contracting.[66] At the same time, it must be noted that technology such as internet filtering also permits *reductions* in citizens' access to information.[67] Technology alone cannot create a culture of openness; leadership, oversight, and resources are also required.[68]

## FURTHER READING

Craig, Suzanne. "Municipal Access to Information, Delays, and Denials: An Insider's View."
   In *The Unfulfilled Promise of Press Freedom in Canada*, edited by Lisa Taylor and Cara-
   Marie O'Hagan, 167–74. Toronto: University of Toronto Press, 2017.

Darch, Colin, and Peter G. Underwood. *Freedom of Information and the Developing World: The Citizen, the State and Models of Openness.* St. Louis: Elsevier, 2009.

Larsen, Mike. *Access in the Academe: Bringing ATI and FOI to Academic Research.* Vancouver: British Columbia Freedom of Information and Privacy Association, 2014.

Larsen, Mike, and Kevin Walby, eds. *Brokering Access: Power, Politics, and Freedom of Information.* Vancouver: UBC Press, 2012.

Roberts, Alasdair. *Blacked Out: Government Secrecy in the Information Age.* Cambridge: Cambridge University Press, 2006.

Tromp, Stanley. *Fallen Behind: Canada's Access to Information Act in the World Context.* 2008. www3.telus.net/index100/report.pdf.

Vallance-Jones, Fred. "Freedom of Information: How Accountability to the Public Is Denied." In *The Unfulfilled Promise of Press Freedom in Canada*, edited by Lisa Taylor and Cara-Marie O'Hagan, 157–66. Toronto: University of Toronto Press, 2017.

## NOTES

1.  Fred Vallance-Jones, "Freedom of Information: How Accountability to the Public Is Denied," in *The Unfulfilled Promise of Press Freedom in Canada*, eds. Lisa Taylor and Cara-Marie O'Hagan (Toronto: University of Toronto Press, 2017), 157–66; Lisa Taylor and Cara-Marie O'Hagan, eds., *The Unfulfilled Promise of Press Freedom in Canada* (Toronto: University of Toronto Press, 2017); *Dagg v Canada (Minister of Finance)*, [1997] SCJ No 63, [1997] 2 SCR 403.

2.  Jim Rankin and Patty Winsa, "Carding Drops but Proportion of Blacks Stopped by Toronto Police Rises," *Toronto Star*, July 26, 2014, https://www.thestar.com/news/insight/2014/07/26/carding_drops_but_proportion_of_blacks_stopped_by_toronto_police_rises.html; Wendy Gillis and Kate Allen, "Police Admit Using Cellphone Snooper; Toronto Cops Originally Denied Using Controversial 'Stingray' Device That Captures Other Calls Near Target," *Toronto Star*, March 5, 2018; Patrick White, "Disturbed Inmates Caught in Solitary Trap," *The Globe and Mail*, April 25, 2016.

3.  San Grewal, "Fennell's Travel Expenses Sky High; Brampton Mayor Rings Up More than $185,000 over Five Years on First-Class Airline Tickets and Luxury Hotels, Documents Reveal," *Toronto Star*, January 7, 2014; David Bruser and Jesse McLean, "Companies Knew Drugs They Sold Were Defective; U.S. Food and Drug Administration Reports Reveal Canadian Pharmaceutical Firms Changed and Destroyed Test Data Showing Products Were Tainted and Health Canada Kept Inspection Details Secret, Potentially Putting Health of Patients

at Risk," *Toronto Star*, September 11, 2014; CTV News Staff, "Critics Blast Oda's Swanky Hotel Stay, $16 Orange Juice," April 23, 2012, https://www.ctvnews.ca/critics-blast-oda-s-swanky-hotel-stay-16-orange-juice-1.799961.

4. Office of the Information Commissioner of Canada, "Annual Report 2016–2017" (Gatineau, QC: Office of the Information Commissioner of Canada, 2017), http://www.oic-ci.gc.ca/eng/rapport-annuel-annual-report_2017-2018.aspx.

5. *Access to Information Act*, RSC 1985, c A-1, s 4(1).

6. *Canada (Attorney General) v Canada (Information Commissioner)*, 2004 FC 431 at 20 and 194.

7. "The overarching purpose of access to information legislation is to facilitate democracy by helping to ensure that citizens have the information required to participate meaningfully in the democratic process and that politicians and bureaucrats remain accountable to the citizenry." *Dagg v Canada (Minister of Finance)* at 61; [1997] 2 SCR 403 (dissenting judgment).

8. *Access to Information Act*, s 4.

9. Ibid., s. 3.

10. Ibid., s 68.

11. Ibid., s 69(1).

12. Ibid., s 68.1.

13. Ibid., s 13(1).

14. Ibid., ss 16.1–16.2, 16.4–16.6.

15. Ibid., s 20(1).

16. Ibid., s 19.

17. *Privacy Act*, RSC 1985, c P-21, s 12.

18. *Access to Information Act*, ss 14 and 15.

19. Ibid., s 18.

20. Ibid., s 16(2).

21. Ibid., ss 16(1), 16.3, 16.31.

22. Ibid., s 23.

23. Ibid., s 17.

24. Ibid., s 21(1).

25. Government of Canada, "Access to Information and Privacy (ATIP) Online Request," April 9, 2013, https://atip-aiprp.apps.gc.ca/atip/welcome.do.

26. "Access to Information Regulations, SOR/83-507." Additional processing fees have been waived as per a 2016 directive; see Treasury Board of Canada Secretariat, "Interim Directive on the Administration of the Access to Information Act," March 30, 2010, sec 7.5, http://www.tbs-sct.gc.ca/pol/doc-eng.aspx?id=18310. Fees must not be charged for the processing of computerized records; see

Office of the Information Commissioner of Canada, "Advisory Notice on Fees for Electronic Records," accessed November 3, 2018, http://www.oic-ci.gc.ca/eng/droits-pour-documents-electroniques_fees-for-electronic-records.aspx.

27. Juha Mustonen and Gustav Björkstrand, eds., *The World's First Freedom of Information Act: Anders Chydenius' Legacy Today* (Kokkola, Finland: Anders Chydenius Foundation, 2006).

28. Kirsten Douglas, "Access to Information Legislation in Canada and Four Other Countries" (Ottawa: Library of Parliament, April 6, 2006), http://www.publications.gc.ca/site/eng/294638/publication.htm.

29. Access Info Europe, *Statement by European RTI Community on the World's First Official Access to Information Day!* https://www.access-info.org/uncategorized/26216. See also John M. Ackerman and Irma E. Sandoval-Ballesteros, "The Global Explosion of Freedom of Information Laws," *Administrative Law Review* 58, no. 1 (2006): 85–130.

30. Juliet Gill and Sallie Hughes, "Bureaucratic Compliance with Mexico's New Access to Information Law," *Critical Studies in Media Communication* 22, no. 2 (2005): 126.

31. Alasdair Roberts, "Structural Pluralism and the Right to Information," *The University of Toronto Law Journal* 51, no. 3 (2001): 243–71.

32. Ibid., 251–52.

33. Gill and Hughes.

34. Ibid.

35. Ibid.

36. Joanne Bates, "Politics of Open Government Data: A Neo-Gramscian Analysis of the United Kingdom's Open Government Data Initiative" (Manchester: Manchester Metropolitan University, 2012), 53; Tom McClean, "Who Pays the Piper? The Political Economy of Freedom of Information," *Government Information Quarterly* 27, no. 4 (2010): 392–400; Colin Darch and Peter G. Underwood, *Freedom of Information in the Developing World* (Oxford: Chandos, 2010), 4; Daniel Berliner, "The Political Origins of Transparency," *The Journal of Politics* 76, no. 2 (2014): 479–91.

37. Diego Giannone, "The Political and Ideological Dimension of the Measurement of Freedom of Information. Assessing the Interplay between Neoliberalism and the Freedom of the Press Index," *International Communication Gazette* 76, no. 6 (October 2014): 505–27, https://doi.org/10.1177/1748048514538927.

38. Taylor and O'Hagan; Vallance-Jones, 157–66; Sandra Braman, *Change of State: Information, Policy, and Power* (Cambridge, MA: MIT Press, 2009), 506; Suzanne Craig, "Municipal Access to Information, Delays, and Denials: An Insider's View," in *The Unfulfilled Promise of Press Freedom in Canada*, eds. Lisa Taylor and Cara-Marie O'Hagan (Toronto: University of Toronto Press, 2017).

39. Taylor and O'Hagan.

40. Ibid; Craig.

41. Darch and Underwood, 129–30.

42. United Nations, *Updated Set of Principles for the Protection and Promotion of Human Rights through Action to Combat Impunity*, E/CN.4/2005/102/Add.1, February 8, 2005. Cited in Truth and Reconciliation Commission of Canada, "Honouring the Truth, Reconciling for the Future: Summary of the Final Report of the Truth and Reconciliation Commission of Canada" (Winnipeg: Truth and Reconciliation Commission of Canada, 2015), 257, http://www.trc.ca/.

43. Ibid.

44. Truth and Reconciliation Commission of Canada, 257.

45. Lara Fullenwieder and Adam Molnar, "Settler Governance and Privacy: Canada's Indian Residential School Settlement Agreement and the Mediation of State-Based Violence," *International Journal of Communication* 12 (2018): 1346.

46. Indigenous Bar Association, "Submission to the Standing Committee on Access to Information, Privacy & Ethics on Bill C-58." See also Union of BC Indian Chiefs, "Open Letter and Joint Submission on Bill C-58, An Act to Amend the Access to Information Act and the Privacy Act and to Make Consequential Amendments to Other Acts from the National Claims Research Directors" October 13, 2017, http://nationtalk.ca/story/re-submission-standing-committee-access-information-privacy-ethics-bill-c-58-act-amend-access-information-act-privacy-act-make-consequential; "Indigenous Bar Association Warns of C-58," *Two Row Times* (blog), October 18, 2017, https://tworowtimes.com/news/regional/indigenous-bar-association-warns-bill-c-58/.

47. Office of the Information Commissioner of Canada, "Preparing for C-58," October 17, 2018, https://www.oic-ci.gc.ca/ar-ra/2018/Preparing.html.

48. Truth and Reconciliation Commission of Canada, 257.

49. Ibid., 254–58.

50. Ibid., 258.

51. Fullenwieder and Molnar.

52. Tia Dafnos, "Beyond the Blue Line: Researching the Policing of Aboriginal Activism Using Access to Information," in *Brokering Access: Power, Politics, and Freedom of Information*, eds. Mike Larsen and Kevin Walby (Vancouver: UBC Press, 2012), 209–33.

53. Amartya Sen, *Development as Freedom* (New York: Knopf, 2001), 39–40.

54. Darch and Underwood.

55. Ibid.

56. Rob McMahon, Tim LaHache, and Tim Whiteduck, "Digital Data Management as Indigenous Resurgence in Kahnawà: ke," *The International Indigenous Policy Journal* 6, no. 3 (2015): 6.

57. Tia Dafnos, "The Quest for Electronic Data: Where Alice Meets Monty Python Meets Colonel Jessop," in *Brokering Access: Power, Politics, and Freedom of Information*, eds. Mike Larsen and Kevin Walby (Vancouver: UBC Press, 2012), 335–57.

58. CBC News, "Black People 3 Times More Likely to Be Street Checked in Halifax, Police Say," January 9, 2017, https://www.cbc.ca/news/canada/nova-scotia/halifax-black-street-checks-police-race-profiling-1.3925251.

59. Dafnos, "Beyond the Blue Line," 209–33.

60. Lyndsey P. Beutin, "Racialization as a Way of Seeing: The Limits of Counter-Surveillance and Police Reform," *Surveillance & Society* 15, no. 1 (2017): 5–20.

61. Darch and Underwood, 9.

62. Braman; Willem de Lint and Reem Bahdi, "Access to Information in an Age of Intelligencized Governmentality," in *Brokering Access: Power, Politics, and Freedom of Information*, eds. Mike Larsen and Kevin Walby (Vancouver: UBC Press, 2012), 115–41.

63. Bates, 53.

64. Braman, 30.

65. Ibid., 297–98.

66. John C. Bertot, Paul T. Jaeger, and Justin M. Grimes, "Using ICTs to Create a Culture of Transparency: E-Government and Social Media as Openness and Anti-Corruption Tools for Societies," *Government Information Quarterly* 27, no. 3 (July 2010): 264–71, https://doi.org/10.1016/j.giq.2010.03.001.

67. Ibid.

68. Ibid.

# 12 Legal and Policy Research and Citation

## INTRODUCTION

Legal and policy research requires specialized skills and knowledge of legislation, judicial decisions, decisions of administrative tribunals like the CRTC, decisions and reports of independent authorities such as the Privacy Commissioner of Canada, parliamentary proceedings, Orders in Council, government documents, and law reviews. In this chapter, we will learn how to find and how to read these types of documents using, where possible, authoritative free online sources. These include government websites, the Canadian Legal Information Institute (CANLII) and its counterparts in other countries, court websites, the websites of relevant administrative tribunals and independent authorities, and parliamentary websites, including the records of parliamentary debates and proceedings (Hansard). You will also learn how to access relevant government documents and law review articles and commentaries. These can be accessed either through free online sources, including institutional repositories, or using subscription databases, available through university and college libraries.

Legal research is a useful skill in a variety of careers. Lawyers, paralegals, legal assistants, law clerks, administrative assistants, legal researchers, advocates, and activists—whether working at law firms, in government, in administrative agencies, in private businesses, or in civil society, NGO-, and community-based organizations—all require skills in legal research. So do those working in the fields of legal writing, publishing, libraries, and advocacy.

### Legal Research: Current Context

Legal research has changed considerably over the past two decades. Prior to the early 1990s, many legal sources, including judicial decisions and legislation, were available only through library hard-copy reference materials, physical visits to courthouses, and expensive subscription-only access to legal databases. With the spread of access to the internet in the 1990s came the establishment of non-profit institutes providing free online access to legal materials such as judicial decisions and legislation, beginning with Cornell's Legal Information Institute in 1992. LexUM, a Canadian company that began at the University of Montreal, started collaborating with the Supreme Court of Canada in 1993 to publish court decisions online.[1] The Canadian Legal Information Institute (CANLII) was established in 2000 with the services of LexUM.[2] The Free Access to Law Movement (FALM) grew worldwide, seeing the establishment of Legal Information Institutes (LIIs) around the world, dedicated to ensuring that legislation and judicial decisions are freely available online.[3]

## ACCESSING SOURCES

### Legislation

In Canada, as in many countries, most legislation can now be found online through government websites and through non-profit LIIs. CANLII operates an online virtual library of legal information, intended to make Canadian law accessible on the internet.[4] Similar LIIs operate in many countries around the world as part of the worldwide FALM.[5] Governments and courts often work cooperatively with LIIs to ensure that the legal information made available is authoritative.[6] See the table below for authoritative sources of federal, provincial, and territorial legislation. Legislation is also available through paid subscription databases like LexisNexis and Westlaw.

| Canada | |
|---|---|
| Federal | Department of Justice: laws-lois.justice.gc.ca |
| | CANLII: www.canlii.org/en/ |
| Alberta | Legislative Assembly of Alberta: www.assembly.ab.ca/ |
| | CANLII: www.canlii.org/en/ab/ |
| British Columbia | BC Laws: www.bclaws.ca/ |
| | CANLII: www.canlii.org/en/bc/ |

| Manitoba | Manitoba Laws: web2.gov.mb.ca/laws/index.php |
| | CANLII: www.canlii.org/en/mb/ |
| New Brunswick | Office of the Attorney General: www2.gnb.ca/content/gnb/en/ departments/attorney_general/acts_regulations.html |
| | Legislative Assembly of New Brunswick: www.gnb.ca/legis/index-e.asp |
| | CANLII: www.canlii.org/en/nb/ |
| Newfoundland and Labrador | House of Assembly Newfoundland and Labrador: www.assembly.nl.ca/legislation/ |
| | CANLII: www.canlii.org/en/nl/laws/ |
| Northwest Territories | Department of Justice: www.justice.gov.nt.ca/en/legislation/ |
| | CANLII: www.canlii.org/en/nt/ |
| Nova Scotia | House of Assembly Office of the Legislative Council: nslegislature.ca/ legc/ |
| | CANLII: www.canlii.org/en/ns/ |
| Nunavut | Government of Nunavut: www.nunavutlegislation.ca/ |
| | CANLII: www.canlii.org/en/nu/ |
| Ontario | Government of Ontario: www.ontario.ca/laws |
| | CANLII: www.canlii.org/en/on/laws/index.html |
| Prince Edward Island | Prince Edward Island: www.princeedwardisland.ca/en/legislation/ all/all/a |
| | CANLII: www.canlii.org/en/pe/ |
| Quebec | Publications Quebec: www3.publicationsduquebec.gouv.qc.ca/ loisreglements.en.html |
| | CANLII: www.canlii.org/en/qc/ |
| Saskatchewan | Queen's Printer: www.qp.gov.sk.ca/ |
| | CANLII: www.canlii.org/en/sk/ |
| Yukon | Yukon Government: www.gov.yk.ca/legislation/ |
| | Yukon Legislative Assembly: www.legassembly.gov.yk.ca/ |
| | CANLII: www.canlii.org/en/yk/ |
| **United States** | |
| Federal legislation | LII: www.law.cornell.edu/ |
| State legislation | LII: www.law.cornell.edu/states/listing |

## The Canadian Constitution and the Canadian Charter of Rights and Freedoms

The *Constitution of Canada*, including the *Canadian Charter of Rights and Freedoms*, is available on the federal Department of Justice website, on CANLII's website, and in subscription databases such as LexisNexis or Westlaw.

| Canadian Constitution | Department of Justice: laws-lois.justice.gc.ca/eng/const/ |
|---|---|
|  | CANLII: canlii.ca/t/8q7l |
| *Canadian Charter of Rights and Freedoms* | Department of Justice: laws-lois.justice.gc.ca/eng/Const/Const_index.html |
|  | CANLII: canlii.ca/t/8q7l |

## Judicial Decisions

Many Canadian judicial decisions are available through CANLII (www.canlii.org) as well as through court websites (such as the Supreme Court of Canada's website: scc-csc.lexum.com) and private subscription databases such as LexisNexis and Westlaw. These may be available through your library.

The Supreme Court of the United States' decisions are available on its website (www.supremecourt.gov/opinions).

### *Extra Features Offered through Subscription Databases*

Databases like LexisNexis and Westlaw provide tools that allow users to evaluate the importance of a court decision by viewing cases that have followed, overturned, mentioned, explained, or cited it. It is especially important to be aware of whether a judicial decision has been overturned by a higher court, as this may mean that the decision is not in force. To view this information in LexisNexis, for example, click on the link "Citator document" near the top of a judicial decision and scroll to "Summary of Judicial Considerations" to see which cases followed, mention, or explained the judicial decision you are examining. Citator documents are, on occasion, not available. Westlaw offers a similar "Keycite" feature.

### *Law Reporters*

Some judicial decisions appear in law reporters, a type of publication that publishes cases selectively, typically selecting cases that deal with important points of law. These can be very helpful when looking for decisions in a particular field of law.

## Decisions of Administrative Tribunals

As mentioned throughout this text, a number of administrative tribunals play roles in the field of communication policy and law. These include the Canadian Radio-television and Telecommunications Commission (CRTC), the Copyright Board, and the Competition Bureau, which sometimes becomes involved in media- and communications-related competition issues such as media ownership.

### *The Canadian Radio-television and Telecommunications Commission (CRTC)*

CRTC decisions, notices, orders, and regulatory policies can be found on the CRTC website (www.crtc.gc.ca). As of this writing, such documents can be found under the "Business" menu, under the subheading "Decisions, Notices & Orders."

Typically, the CRTC holds a hearing or set of hearings on a policy matter, such as whether and when to require closed captioning on television (a broadcasting decision), whether to approve new radio broadcasting licences (a broadcasting decision), whether to permit the elimination of pay phone booths (a telecommunications decision), or whether to permit zero-rating in cellphone plans (a telecommunications decision touching on internet issues). Once a hearing has been held, the CRTC typically issues a decision or an order, which it publishes on its website. Decisions, notices, orders, and regulatory policies are numbered with the year and a sequential ordinal number; for example, Broadcasting Regulatory Policy 2015-86 ("Let's Talk TV") was the 86th decision, notice, order, or regulatory policy issued in 2015. It set out the CRTC's overarching policy on television broadcasting.[7]

The CRTC's decisions, notices, orders, and regulatory policies are often richly informative—especially when they pertain to broader policy issues (as opposed to decisions on individual telecommunications or broadcasting licences). They often set out the views of various stakeholders on an issue, the CRTC's reflections on those views, and the CRTC's reasoning for the decision, order, or policy it has set out. Later policy documents contain references and citations to earlier documents, allowing researchers to study the full history of the CRTC's broadcasting and telecommunications policies.

### *The Copyright Board*

For students studying copyright (see Chapter 7), publications of the Copyright Board of Canada may be relevant. The Copyright Board sets the royalty rates paid for the use of copyright works by entities like radio stations to collective societies, which collect those royalties on behalf of groups of copyright holders. In the process of setting such royalty rates, the Copyright Board holds public hearings at its offices in Ottawa and later issues its decisions. Such decisions, along with the dates and information pertaining to past and upcoming hearings, are available on the website of the Copyright Board (www.cb-cda.gc.ca).

### The Competition Bureau

The Competition Bureau investigates complaints where there has been an alleged breach of the *Competition Act* and other laws relating to market competition. In some cases, historically, the Competition Bureau has dealt with issues of media ownership, especially when it has involved mergers of broadcasting and/or telecommunication companies in Canada. The Competition Bureau has also recently examined issues relating to the broadband market and intellectual property. Decisions of the Competition Bureau and related information are available on the Competition Bureau's website (www.competitionbureau.gc.ca).

## Independent Commissioners' Decisions and Reports

For students studying privacy (see Chapter 5), the decisions and reports of the Privacy Commissioner of Canada may be helpful. The Privacy Commissioner of Canada oversees compliance with the *Privacy Act* and the *Personal Information Protection and Electronic Documents Act* (PIPEDA). The decisions that the Privacy Commissioner renders in cases of alleged privacy infringements by the federal government or private corporations can be found at its website (www.priv.gc.ca).

Students interested in access to information (see Chapter 11) may wish to examine the decisions and reports of the Information Commissioner of Canada. These decisions and reports, along with information about the right of access to information and complaint processes, may be found on the Office of the Information Commissioner website (www.oic-ci.gc.ca). Provincial and territorial freedom of information and privacy commissioners' sites are also rich sources of information.

## Parliamentary Proceedings and Legislative Information

### Hansard

Following the British tradition, the parliamentary debates at the federal and provincial/territorial levels are recorded and transcribed into texts known as "Hansard," after the first official printer to the British parliament at Westminster, Thomas Curson Hansard. The Canadian federal Hansard is available online from 1994 onwards at ourcommons.ca, as well as at openparliament.ca, where statements made in parliament can be viewed alongside social media postings and can be searched by a variety of useful methods. Hansards prior to 1994 can be found online at the Historical Debates of the Parliament of Canada (parl.Canadiana.ca). Video of federal and provincial/territorial debates, as well as parliamentary committee meetings, can also be often found via parliamentary websites (see parlvu.parl.gc.ca).

### *LegisInfo*

Information about federal bills and their passage through parliament is available at LegisInfo (www.parl.gc.ca/LEGISINFO/). On the LegisInfo site, one can view the text of each bill as introduced, its most recent version if it is amended during the legislative process, the votes held on the bill, major speeches related to the bill, coming into force data, legislative summaries, and government press releases and backgrounders.

## Orders in Council

Federal Orders in Council are available through the Order in Council online database website (https://orders-in-council.canada.ca/). It covers 1990 to the present.

## Government Documents

### *Public Consultation Documents*

Public consultations are conducted regularly on matters relating to communications policy. For example, in 2016, the federal government conducted a consultation titled "Canadian Content in a Digital World," which related to the production and availability of Canadian content. Documents associated with public consultations conducted by the federal government can be found at www1.canada.ca/consultingcanadians/. The documents issued by the government, along with the responses submitted by organizations and individuals, are made available through this website. Such documents can give an excellent sense of the policy questions government is confronting, as well as the various positions of organizations, industries, and publics on such questions.

### *Documents in Government Repositories*

Until March 2014, federal government publications were available in print and/or other physical formats through the Depository Services Program (DSP).

After 2014, all federal government publications have been made available online at publications.gc.ca, replacing the DSP.

### Historical Archives of Government Documents

Students seeking to research historical aspects of communication policy and law might turn to Early Canadiana Online, a subscription database available through some libraries. Early Canadiana Online provides a rich range of historical documents.

The Library and Archives of Canada (LAC) is a further source for researchers wishing to turn to primary sources. Often, a visit to the LAC in Ottawa is necessary, although some archival documents have been digitized and are available through the LAC online catalogue on its website.

## Law Review Articles

Journal articles about legal topics are often found in journals or *law reviews*. Like other journals, some law reviews are published online under open-access licences and are available online through journal websites or online repositories. Others must be accessed through subscription databases such as LexisNexis, HeinOnline, or Westlaw. Check your library to find out what databases you have access to.

## READING JUDICIAL DECISIONS

Judicial decisions must be read carefully because they can contain not just the decision itself but also headnotes and summaries, concurring decisions, and dissenting opinions.

Judicial decisions contain two main elements. First, they contain the *holding* or the actual decision, and second, they contain *dicta* (short for *obiter dicta*), the discussion about the decision, giving context and commentary.

Supreme Court of Canada decisions are made by a court of up to nine judges. Decisions made by multiple judges may be unanimous. A **unanimous decision** is one on which the whole court, or all of the judges on the panel, agrees. A unanimous decision is the strongest and most binding on lower courts as precedent. A unanimous decision may start with the phrase "the judgment of the Court" or "The judgment of the Court was delivered by The Chief Justice."

A majority decision is written by a majority, or more than half, of judges on the panel. On the Supreme Court of Canada, where there are nine judges all present, a decision written by five of the judges constitutes a majority decision. A majority decision creates a strong precedent for other courts to follow. A majority decision, where all nine judges took part in the decision, would include at least five of nine names, beginning, for example, like this: "Per McLachlin C.J. and Deschamps, Abella, Moldaver and Karakatsanis JJ."

In a **plurality decision,** a majority of the judges on the panel agree on the decision, but not on the reasoning for it. They may write different opinions, all arriving at the same final holding but for differing reasons. A plurality decision is still binding on lower courts but may be viewed as less authoritative than a majority or unanimous decision. Here, a separate **concurring decision** may be included with the main decision. The concurring decision is written by a judge or judges who support(s) the main decision, but with different reasons.

A **dissenting opinion** may also be issued, if a judgment is not unanimous. A dissenting opinion is written by a judge or judges who dissent from the majority or plurality decision. A dissenting opinion can normally be found beneath any majority, plurality, and concurring decisions and might begin with a phrase such as "Per Abbott J. dissenting," or, if multiple judges dissent for the same reasons, "Per Hall, Spence and Laskin JJ., dissenting." There can be multiple dissenting decisions in a single case.

## CITATIONS AND BIBLIOGRAPHIES FOR LEGAL AND POLICY SOURCES

Legal citations are often opaque to outsiders. They contain abbreviations and formatting unfamiliar to those who do not work with legal citation on a day-to-day basis. This section is intended to give readers a basic familiarity with citation standards in law and policy, to help in both reading legal citations and in citing legal and policy documents properly.

In Canada, the primary guide to legal citation is the *McGill Law Journal Canadian Guide to Uniform Legal Citation* (known as the *McGill Guide*). In the United States, *The Bluebook: A Uniform System of Citation* is the predominant guide to legal citation. However, other manuals, such as the *Chicago Manual of Style*, the *Publication Manual of the American Psychological Association* (APA), and others are also useful. Students in humanities and social sciences or fields other than law may wish to follow the standards of their field, utilizing a general style manual such as the *Chicago Manual of Style* or the *Publication Manual of the American Psychological Association* (APA) for sources such as books and articles, but switching to the *McGill Guide* format for legal sources such as judicial decisions and legislation.[8] That is the approach adopted in this text. The instructions that follow are simplified from the *McGill Guide* for legal sources. For other types of sources, researchers should consult the style guide of their choice.

## General Rules

### *Italicization*

The *Chicago Manual of Style*, and most other guides, calls for the title of books, journals (but not journal articles), legislation, and case names to be italicized, whether in your bibliography, in citations, or in the main text.[9]

---

EXAMPLES:

The *Copyright Act* underwent a major revision in 2012.

In *CCH Canadian Ltd v Law Society of Upper Canada*, the Court gave a clear indication of its position on fair dealing in copyright law.

---

### *Punctuation*

The *McGill Guide* instructs leaving out periods in abbreviations (in cited legislation or jurisprudence), including in the case name (*style of cause*) and after the "v" in a case name. It also instructs omitting commas, except after the style of cause, in citation of jurisprudence. While many sources still include such punctuation, the current *McGill Guide* style is as follows:

> *Broadcasting Act*, SC 1991, c 11. (**not** *Broadcasting Act*, S.C. 1991, c. 11.)
> *Copyright Act*, RSC 1985, c C-42. (**not** *Copyright Act*, R.S.C. 1985, c. C-42.)
> *R v TELUS Communications Co*, 2013 SCC 16. (**not** *R. v. TELUS Communications Co.*, 2013 S.C.C. 16.)

### *In-Text Citations*

Legal writing usually uses footnotes instead of in-text citations. The *McGill Guide* therefore offers little guidance on in-text citations; other style guides should be consulted if you use an in-text citation system. The *McGill Guide* footnote and bibliography format described in this chapter can be adapted for use in in-text citations; see the examples below and the instructions to follow in the next parts of this chapter.

## EXAMPLES:

According to Canadian law, copyright lasts for 50 years after the death of the author (*Copyright Act*, RSC 1985, c C-42, s 23).

Everyone in Canada has the right to freedom of expression (*Canadian Charter of Rights and Freedoms*, 1982, s 2(b)).

The Court gave a clear indication of its position on fair dealing in copyright law (*CCH Canadian Ltd v Law Society of Upper Canada*).

The Court discussed the meaning of the term *original* in the context of fair dealing in copyright law (*CCH Canadian Ltd v Law Society of Upper Canada* at para 18).

In-text citations should be included in the body of your paper, at the end of the relevant sentence or section. They should be included before the period that ends the sentence, in parentheses.

## Legislation

*Format*
*official short title*, | statute volume abbreviation | year, | chapter | pinpoint (if needed).

## EXAMPLES:

*Radiocommunication Act*, RSC 1985, c R-2.

*Radiocommunication Act*, RSC 1985, c R-2, s 2.

### Short Title
Most legislation has both a short title and a long title. Include the short title in your bibliography. While the long title can be found at the top of the act in the

title space, the short title, which can generally be found in the first section of the act, is the one more often used. For example, the *Copyright Act*'s long title is *"An Act respecting copyright,"* but its short title is *"Copyright Act."* The short title can be found in the very first section of the *Copyright Act*, which says, "This Act may be cited as the *Copyright Act*."[10] The *Privacy Act* has an even longer title: *"An Act to extend the present laws of Canada that protect the privacy of individuals and that provide individuals with a right of access to personal information about themselves,"* found in the title space at the top of the legislation itself. However, we commonly use its short title, as indicated in its first section: "This Act may be cited as the *Privacy Act*."[11] The title of legislation, whether short or long, should be written in italics.

### Statute Volume Abbreviation and Year

Legislation is published in annual volumes of statutes, published each year, and in consolidations published following longer periods. The last time a federal consolidation was published was in 1985. Federal legislation first passed in 1985 or earlier, published in the *Revised Statutes of Canada 1985*, is normally cited based on its place in the *Revised Statutes of Canada* (abbreviated as RSC 1985). For example, the *Radiocommunication Act*, which regulates the use of the radio spectrum, is contained in chapter R-2 of the *Revised Statutes of Canada*. It is cited as:

*Radiocommunication Act*, RSC 1985, c R-2.

Statutes are also published in annual volumes. Federal legislation passed since 1985 is normally cited based on its place in the annual *Statutes of Canada* (SC). For example, the *Broadcasting Act* was first published in 1991. It is cited in the *Statutes of Canada 1991* as:

*Broadcasting Act*, SC 1991, c 11.

The publication information for statutes can normally be found at the top of the legislation itself.

### Chapter

The chapter number where the legislation is located in the published statutes is normally also published at the top of the act itself.

### Pinpoint

Pinpoints, or references to particular sections or paragraphs of a piece of legislation, are normally not included in a bibliography, but should be included in footnotes and in-text citations where you wish to refer to a particular section of legislation (see above, "In-Text Citations"). *Section* is abbreviated as "s" with no period or punctuation following, or "ss" to reference multiple sections. *Paragraph* is abbreviated as "para" with no period or punctuation, or "paras" to reference multiple paragraphs.

## EXAMPLES:

*Radiocommunication Act*, RSC 1985, c R-2, s 2.

*Radiocommunication Act*, RSC 1985, c R-2, ss 2–4.

## The Canadian Constitution and the *Canadian Charter of Rights and Freedoms*

The *Constitution Act* and the *Canadian Charter of Rights and Freedoms* should be cited in bibliographies and footnotes, respectively, as follows:

> *Constitution Act, 1982*, being Schedule B to the *Canada Act 1982* (UK), 1982, c 11.
> *Canadian Charter of Rights and Freedoms*, Part I of the *Constitution Act, 1982*, being Schedule B to the *Canada Act 1982* (UK), 1982, c 11.

## Jurisprudence

### Neutral Citation

A new form of legal citation for judicial decisions was adopted in the late 1990s, and it is the dominant format of citation for decisions rendered since then. Whereas prior to the 1990s, jurisprudence was published by the government or other publishers, with the rise of internet publishing and FALM, the online publication of judicial decisions by CANLII, LexUM, or court websites themselves became standard. A system of **neutral citation** has been adopted referencing not specific publication but the names of the court issuing the decision. This standard was adopted by courts between 1997 and 2006. Neutral citations indicate the year of the decision, an abbreviation for the name of the court (e.g., SCC for Supreme Court of Canada), and a case number. Thus, the neutral citation "2004 SCC 13" refers to the 13th decision issued by the Supreme Court of Canada in 2004.

FORMAT

*Name of case (style of cause),* | year | court (abbreviation) | decision number | pin-point (if needed).

## EXAMPLES:

*Clearbrook Iron Works Ltd v Letourneau,* 2006 FCA 42.

*Clearbrook Iron Works Ltd v Letourneau,* 2006 FCA 42 at para 42.

NAME OF CASE (STYLE OF CAUSE)

The names that were parties to the court case are included in the name of the case (also referred to as the *style of cause*). *R* signifies *Regina* or the Queen. For example, for a criminal case brought by the government on behalf of the Queen, against Jones, the style of cause would be:

*R v Jones*

YEAR

Include the year in which the decision was rendered.

COURT ABBREVIATIONS

Include the abbreviation for the court or tribunal that rendered the decision. See the table for the abbreviations currently in use.

| Court | Abbreviation |
|---|---|
| Supreme Court of Canada | SCC |
| Federal Court | FC |
| Federal Court of Appeal | FCA |
| Tax Court of Canada | TCC |
| Court Martial Appeal Court of Canada | CMAC |
| Competition Tribunal of Canada | CT |
| Canadian Human Rights Tribunal | CHRT |
| Public Service Labour Relations Board | PSLRB |
| Courts Martial | CM |
| Court Martial Appeal Court of Canada | CMAC |
| Court of Appeal (Alberta) | ABCA |

| Court | Abbreviation |
|-------|-------------|
| Court of Queen's Bench (Alberta) | ABQB |
| Provincial Court of Alberta | ABPC |
| Alberta Human Rights Commission | AHRC |
| Office of the Information and Privacy Commissioner (Alberta) | AB OIPC |
| Supreme Court of British Columbia | SCBC |
| Court of Appeal (British Columbia) | BCCA |
| British Columbia Human Rights Tribunal | BCHRT |
| Information and Privacy Commissioner (British Columbia) | BCIPC |
| Court of Queen's Bench (Saskatchewan) | SKQB |
| Court of Appeal for Saskatchewan | SKCA |
| Provincial Court (Saskatchewan) | SKPC |
| Court of Appeal (Manitoba) | MBCA |
| Court of Queen's Bench Manitoba | MBQB |
| Provincial Court of Manitoba | MBPC |
| Ontario Court of Appeal | ONCA |
| Superior Court of Justice (Ontario) | ONSC |
| Ontario Court of Justice | ONCJ |
| Human Rights Tribunal of Ontario | HRTO |
| Information and Privacy Commissioner Ontario (Tribunal) | ONIPC |
| Court of Appeal of Quebec | QCCA |
| Superior Court of Quebec | QCCS |
| Court of Quebec | QCCP |
| Human Rights Tribunal (Quebec) | QCTDP |
| Commission d'accès à l'information du Québec | QCCAI |
| Court of Appeal of New Brunswick | NBCA |
| Court of Queen's Bench of New Brunswick | NBQB |
| Provincial Court (New Brunswick) | NBPC |
| Nova Scotia Court of Appeal | NSCA |
| Supreme Court of Nova Scotia | NSSC |
| Supreme Court of Nova Scotia, Family Division | NSSF |
| Provincial Court of Nova Scotia | NSPC |
| Nova Scotia Human Rights Commission | NS HRC |
| Office of the Information and Privacy Commissioner for Nova Scotia | NSOIPC |
| Supreme Court, Appeal Division (Prince Edward Island) | PESCAD |
| Supreme Court, Trial Division (Prince Edward Island) | PESCTD |

| Court | Abbreviation |
| --- | --- |
| Information and Privacy Commissioner (Prince Edward Island) | PE IPC |
| Prince Edward Island Human Rights Commission | PE HRC |
| Supreme Court of Newfoundland and Labrador, Court of Appeal | NLCA |
| Supreme Court of Newfoundland and Labrador, Trial Division | NLSCTD |
| Provincial Court of Newfoundland and Labrador | NLPC |
| Newfoundland and Labrador Human Rights Commission | NLHRC |
| Information and Privacy Commissioner (Newfoundland and Labrador) | NLIPC |
| Court of Appeal (Yukon Territory) | YKCA |
| Supreme Court of the Yukon Territory | YKSC |
| Territorial Court of Yukon | YKTC |
| Court of Appeal for the Northwest Territories | NWTCA |
| Supreme Court of the Northwest Territories | NWTSC |
| Territorial Court of the Northwest Territories | NWTTC |
| Human Rights Adjudication Panel (Northwest Territories) | NT HRAP |
| Northwest Territories Information and Privacy Commissioner | NWT IPC/NTIPC |
| Nunavut Court of Justice | NUCJ |
| Court of Appeal of Nunavut | NUCA |
| Nunavut Human Rights Tribunal | NHRT |
| Information and Privacy Commissioner (Nunavut) | NUIPC |

DECISION NUMBER

The decision number, assigned by the court, signifies the sequential case number heard by the court. The following case, a criminal case against Telus, was the 16th decision the Supreme Court of Canada (SCC) issued in 2013:

> *R v TELUS Communications Co*, 2013 SCC 16.

### *Non-Neutral Citations (1999 and Prior)*

Prior to the late 1990s, judicial decisions were collected and published by either the government (Queen's Printer), as with the *Supreme Court Reports*, or (for most Canadian courts) by private, for-profit legal publishers in publications known as "law reporters."[12] For example, the *Ontario Reports*, published by the Law Society of Upper Canada through LexisNexis, was the primary publisher of Ontario judicial decisions before such decisions were published online. Citations to those judicial decisions referenced the *Ontario Reports* using the abbreviation *OR*, indicating that one could find the decision in the *Ontario Reports* publication.

Decisions rendered before neutral citations were adopted must be cited using non-neutral citations. The *McGill Guide* recommends parallel citations for non-neutral citations; that is, it recommends the inclusion of at least two citations per judicial decision. This assists a reader who is unable to access the decision as published in the first source (the case as published in the *Ontario Reports*, for example) to find it in a second one.

FORMAT

**Without a parallel citation:**
*Name of case (style of cause),* | year | law reporter volume number | law reporter abbreviation | start page number of law report |, pinpoint (if needed).

**With a parallel citation:**
*Name of case (style of cause),* | year | law reporter volume number | law reporter abbreviation | start page number of law report |, pinpoint (if needed), | law reporter volume number for parallel citation | law reporter abbreviation for parallel citation | start page number of law report for parallel citation |, pinpoint in parallel citation (if needed).

## EXAMPLES WITHOUT PARALLEL CITATION:

*R v Nipawin and District Satellite TV Inc,* [1991] 1 SCR 64.

*S Morgan Smith Co v Sissiboo Pulp and Paper Co,* (1904) 35 SCR 93 at para 50.

## EXAMPLE WITH A PARALLEL CITATION:

*Gordon v Goertz,* [1996] 2 SCR 27 at para 13, 134 DLR (4th) 321.

NAME OF CASE (STYLE OF CAUSE)
As with the neutral citation format, the names that were parties to the court case are included in the name of the case (also referred to as the *style of cause*). In the first example above, *R v Nipawin and District Satellite TV Inc* is the style of cause.

**YEAR AND LAW REPORTER VOLUME NUMBER**

In some cases, law reporters are issued in volumes corresponding by year. In the first example above, the *Supreme Court Reports* (SCR) are contained in volumes numbered by year. The *R v Nipawin* decision was issued in 1991 and included in the first volume of the 1991 *Supreme Court Reports*. Where volumes are issued by year, the year is included in square brackets, as was done in this example.

In other cases, law reporters are issued in volumes that do not correspond with a year. In the second example above, the decision was published in the 35th volume of the *Supreme Court Reports*, which did not correspond with a particular year. Therefore, the year must be added in round brackets.

**LAW REPORTER ABBREVIATION**

The abbreviation for the law reporter is included after the volume number. Common abbreviations include *SCR* for the *Supreme Court Reports*, *OR* for *Ontario Reports*, and *DLR (4th)* for *Dominion Law Reports*. In the case of the *Dominion Law Reports*, *(4th)* signifies the fourth series of *Dominion Law Reports*.

**PAGE NUMBER**

In the first example above, the decision appears starting on page 64 of the first 1991 volume of the *Supreme Court Reports*. Thus, *64* follows the law reporter abbreviation. In the second example above, the decision appears starting on page 93 of the 35th volume of the *Supreme Court Reports*.

**PINPOINT**

Pinpointing specific paragraphs or pages of a decision can be done by including *at* and the page number (without *p*) or paragraph number (prefaced by *para*). In the second example above, the pinpoint references the 50th paragraph of the decision.

## Law Review Articles

Law review articles can be included in bibliographies using standard MLA, APA, Chicago, or other formats. However, the *McGill Guide* offers an alternative format that is commonly used in legal citation.

### *Format*

Author. | "Title of Article" | (year) | volume: | Abbreviation of Journal Title | starting page of the article | pinpoint (if needed) | (electronic service).

> ## EXAMPLE:
>
> *Notes format*:
>
> Ryan Calo, "Digital Market Manipulation" (2013) 82 Geo Wash L Rev 995 at 996.
>
> Deven R Desai & Gerard N Magliocca, "Patents, Meet Napster: 3D Printing and the Digitization of Things" (2013) 102 Geo LJ 1691.
>
> *Bibliography format*:
>
> Calo, Ryan. "Digital Market Manipulation" (2013) 82 Geo Wash L Rev 995.
>
> Desai, Deven R & Gerard N Magliocca. "Patents, Meet Napster: 3D Printing and the Digitization of Things" (2013) 102 Geo LJ 1691.

### AUTHOR(S)

The author's name(s) should be given as presented on the title page of the article. Include multiple authors using an ampersand (&). Put the first name first, except for a bibliographic entry; here, put the last name first for the first author listed.

### TITLE

Include the title of the article in quotation marks, with no punctuation added. In English, capitalize nouns, pronouns, verbs, adverbs, adjectives, and some conjunctions in the title. Do not capitalize minor words such as *and*, *but*, *for*, *or*, *nor*, *as*, and *to*, except when they appear first in the title. Consult a style guide for rules of capitalization.

### YEAR

In some cases, law journals are issued in volumes that do not correspond with a particular year. In the examples above, the *George Washington Law Review* (Geo Wash L Rev) is contained in volumes numbered by year. Here, the year must be added in round brackets. Where volumes are issued by year, the year is included in square brackets.

### ABBREVIATION OF JOURNAL TITLE

In the first example above, the *George Washington Law Review* is abbreviated as "Geo Wash L Rev." The standard abbreviations of journal names can be found through various websites online.

**STARTING PAGE OF THE ARTICLE**

Rather than including the full page range of the journal article, the *McGill* style includes only the page of the first page of the article.

**PINPOINT**

Pinpointing specific pages of an article can be done by including *at* and the page number (without *p*). In the first example above, the pinpoint references page 996 of the article.

---

## FURTHER READING

Greenleaf, Graham, Andrew Mowbray, and Philip Chung. "The Meaning of 'Free Access to Legal Information': A Twenty Year Evolution." *Journal of Open Access to Law* 1, no. 1 (December 18, 2013). https://ojs.law.cornell.edu/index.php/joal/article/view/11.

McGill Law Journal. *Canadian Guide to Uniform Legal Citation.* 9th ed. Montreal: Thomson/Carswell, 2018.

Tjaden, Ted. "Doing Legal Research in Canada." *LLRX: Law and Technology Resources for Legal Professionals* (blog), April 4, 2008. https://www.llrx.com/2008/04/doing-legal-research-in-canada/.

---

## NOTES

1.   Lexum, "Our Company," accessed February 17, 2019, https://lexum.com/en/about-lexum/our-company/.

2.   CanLII, "About CanLII," accessed February 17, 2019, https://www.canlii.org/en/info/about.html.

3.   Graham Greenleaf, Andrew Mowbray, and Philip Chung, "The Meaning of 'Free Access to Legal Information': A Twenty Year Evolution," *Journal of Open Access to Law* 1, no. 1 (December 18, 2013), https://ojs.law.cornell.edu/index.php/joal/article/view/11.

4.   CanLII.

5.   "Australasian Legal Information Institute (AustLII)," accessed February 17, 2019, http://fatlm.org/.

6.   Greenleaf, Mowbray, and Chung.

7.   CRTC, "Broadcasting Regulatory Policy CRTC 2015-86: Let's Talk TV—The Way Forward—Creating Compelling and Diverse Canadian Programming," Regulatory Policies, March 12, 2015, https://crtc.gc.ca/eng/archive/2015/2015-86.htm.

8. The *Chicago Manual of Style* recommends such an approach. Its own guidance for legal sources is based on the American *Bluebook* style. *The Chicago Manual of Style Online,* 17th ed. (Chicago: University of Chicago, 2017), sec 14.269.

9. Ibid., sec 8.2.

10. RSC 1985, c C-42, s 1.

11. RSC 1985, c P-21, s 1.

12. Tom McMahon, "Improving Access to the Law in Canada," Government Information in Canada, March 1999, http://library2.usask.ca/gic/16/mcmahon.html#privatizing.

# CONCLUSION

This book has asked, "Whom does communication policy and law serve?" There is no one right answer to this question. The theories discussed in this book have helped us to explore the various ways that communication policy and law serve the public interest by fostering pluralism and promoting individual freedoms. They have also helped us to explore the ways that Canadian communication policy and law has served the privileged, maintaining and extending inequities and failing to remedy injustices. In some cases, little has changed in the recent past to remedy such failings; in other cases, we see evidence that injustices have begun to be addressed.

## SERVING THE PUBLIC INTEREST: PLURALISM

While some dispute whether "pluralism" is ever an accurate descriptor of politics and policymaking processes, and whether true pluralism is possible given vast economic and social disparities entrenched in our current socioeconomic situation, many would probably agree that pluralism is an important normative ideal. Communications law and policy can play a role in bolstering and fostering pluralism, but it can also threaten pluralism in political participation and policy processes. True pluralism depends on relative equality among groups; both pluralism and equality are threatened by policies and policy processes that entrench some groups' dominance over others.

We have seen throughout this book that the ideal of pluralism acts as a significant reference point for communications law and policy in Canada, and the ideal of pluralism is woven into the foundations of Canadian jurisprudence on freedom of expression. However, we have also seen that many communication policies and laws undermine the realization of the pluralist ideal, acting as a part of a broader economic and social system that embeds and extends inequity just as much as it fosters equality. In almost every area covered in this textbook, communications law and policy are legitimized as fostering pluralism and serving the public interest, while simultaneously permitting, entrenching, and extending various forms of inequity.

While policy processes governed by the CRTC incorporate fairly robust (but imperfect) pluralist dialogue, the growing concentration of Canadian media industries permitted under Canadian broadcast ownership policies, and weakened support for public and community broadcasting, threatens the diversity of voices and media available in the Canadian media ecosystem. The liberalization of telecommunications has expanded a high-tech sector that has become increasingly monopolistic and often blind to cultural differences and differing needs.[1] While internet and online communities have fostered pluralism in ways not seen in traditional media, they have also created filter bubbles, echo chambers, and algorithmic enclaves that often do not approach the ideals of pluralist dialogue.[2] Canadian libel law, more draconian than many of its international comparators, threatens to chill pluralist expression and debate (Chapter 4). Growing levels of surveillance (Chapter 6), both by private companies and governments, may chill the private development and expression of beliefs that is so crucial in pluralist society.[3] The seemingly never-ending extension of intellectual property rights (Chapter 7) further skews the "balance" between groups, extending the intellectual property rights owned by corporations, passing enforcement powers to private platforms, and threatening access to knowledge. Canadian processes of telecommunications, broadcast, and internet regulation take place, in part, in a policy venue—the CRTC—that prizes and provides a format for pluralist discussion (Chapters 8–10). At the same time, the CRTC and other bodies (including ICANN and the Internet Governance Forum), while open to pluralist and multi-stakeholder participation, can sometimes be dominated or even captured by the strongest voices and corporate interests (Chapter 10).

## NEOLIBERALISM AND LIBERTARIANISM

We have seen that neoliberal and libertarian thought has been influential, but not totally dominant, in a number of areas of communication policy and law. Neoliberal and libertarian approaches emphasize the importance of a "marketplace of ideas" in which the best way to counter hateful, harmful, or defamatory speech is with more speech (Chapter 3); and in which ideas (or their expression) can be owned *via* intellectual property law (Chapter 7). Theirs is a vision in which individuals—more than governments—are responsible for protecting individual privacy, and in which surveillance encourages self-regulation (Chapters 5 and 6). It is also a vision of free competition that has fired innovation in telecommunications, broadcast, and internet technologies, as well as growing dominance by large corporations in those sectors (Chapters 8–10).

## CRITICAL POLITICAL ECONOMY

Critical political economists have emphasized that freedom of speech, and the ability to defend oneself from defamatory speech, rely not just on an absence of censorship or a "free market" of ideas but on access to resources of communication that are, under our current political economic arrangements, unevenly distributed (Chapters 3 and 4). While workers who rely on online reviews may turn to defamation law to address false or malicious negative reviews of their products and services, defamation lawsuits may be unaffordable or too slow to address the problems they face (Chapter 4).[4] Laws on privacy (Chapter 5), as well as systems of surveillance (Chapter 6), facilitate the economic exploitation of consumers' personal information while mitigating risks to markets. Intellectual property law grants rights to corporations and often facilitates the exploitation of labourers in the cultural and technology sectors (Chapter 7).[5] Telecommunication, broadcasting, and internet policies all serve large corporate sectors (Chapters 8–10). The liberalization of broadcasting and telecommunications has led to the growth of precarious employment in media and communications industries, and communications policy and law in many cases leave precariously employed workers more vulnerable. The "wealth of networks" can also be seen, Patricia Mazepa and Vincent Mosco have argued, as networks of wealth.[6]

## FEMINISM AND QUEER STUDIES

Many areas of communications policy and law, while appearing neutral, have gendered histories and gendered effects. Defamation law has historically treated women differently from men (Chapter 4); privacy law and norms of privacy in various contexts have made it difficult for women to bring issues such as sexual harassment and assault to light (Chapter 5). Women who are subject to aggression and assault are often just as much under surveillance as are aggressors and perpetrators of violence (Chapter 6).[7] Policies regarding access to information on the internet can be gendered; women may be confronted with filtering technologies in libraries and schools that limit access to information on reproductive rights (Chapter 10).[8] Even the basic concepts that form the foundation of intellectual property law, such as authorship, creativity, and commerce are gendered, as is the science that intellectual property law is meant to encourage (Chapter 7).[9] Gender non-conforming and trans-identified people are subject to increased and disproportionate levels of surveillance in immigration, border, and air travel through increased scrutiny of identity documents and airport X-ray and body scanners (Chapter 6).[10] Mainstream representations still often present queer people in commodified and stereotypical roles, with representations of queer women produced for the heterosexual male gaze (Chapter 9).[11] Internet governance policies, in many cases, fail to foster equality; some countries prohibit queer expression online or install filters to censor queer content.[12] Queer top-level domain names (like .gay and .lgbt) have been the sites of battles over whether such domains should be permitted, what organizations should be permitted to own such domains, and who represents queer communities (Chapter 10).[13]

## CRITICAL RACE THEORY AND INTERSECTIONAL ANALYSIS

Many areas of communication law and policy have fostered or done too little to counter racism in Canadian society. Critical race theorists have been some of the strongest challengers of free speech theory, arguing that freedom of speech may do more to protect racism than to protect racialized minorities (Chapter 3). We have seen that ideas about a "reasonable" or "ordinary" person, "reputation," and respectability are concepts that can introduce racial and other stereotypes and bias in many areas of law, including defamation (Chapter 4), privacy (Chapter 5), and intellectual property (Chapter 7). Systems of surveillance can become a normalized form of racism that can damage both their subjects and the relationships between racialized communities and the state (Chapter 6). Telecommunications, broadcasting, and internet technologies and industries have often served to marginalize racialized and ethnic communities, preserving forms of white dominance that can be difficult to challenge in policymaking forums where the neutrality of technology, policy, and law is often the dominant presumption (Chapters 8–10).

## INDIGENOUS THEORY AND POSTCOLONIAL ANALYSIS

Communications law and policy have been harnessed to colonialism. Surveillance practices of monitoring and managing Indigenous peoples are an integral part of racialization and oppression by settler governments (Chapter 6).[14] At the same time, Indigenous peoples, the expropriation of Indigenous lands, and Indigenous culture, law, and rights are often made invisible in settler law and media.[15] Broadcasting policy, in some cases, masks and perpetuates cultural and racial inequality by failing to acknowledge that "anglophones and franco-phones have ethnicity too" (Chapter 9).[16] Indigenous knowledge, culture, and resources, as we saw in Chapter 7, have been appropriated through laws that fail to recognize Indigenous peoples as owners of intellectual property. As we saw in Chapters 5 and 11, privacy and access to information laws can be mobilized to justify the erasure of the records and testimonials of Indigenous peoples about their experiences under the Indian residential school system, or to restrict access to information about Indigenous peoples, preserving or presenting a sanitized version of history and settler colonialism.[17] The "civilizing mission" of settler governments is often reflected in communications policy documents that portray "First Nations as helpless and dependent on government and telecom industry intervention."[18] Indigenous peoples, in many cases, have worked to reduce rela-tionships of dependency and colonialism by establishing independent telecom-munications and broadband operations.[19]

## CRITICAL DISABILITY THEORY

People with disabilities sometimes effectively lose the protection of freedom of expression when they interact with the psychiatric and mental health systems because their expressive abilities are so constrained and undermined by institu-tional ways of knowing and doing (Chapter 3). Copyright law did not permit, for several years, the circumvention of digital locks to make copyright works accessible, and the intellectual property system, like other areas of law, is based on normative ideas of perception and cognition (Chapter 7). Although broadcast and telecommunications includes requirements to make broadcasts and telecom equipment accessible, such requirements have often been slow or insufficient (Chapters 8 and 10).

## FAILURES

This book has pointed to innumerable examples where communication policy and law fail to foster equality. The underrepresentation and inaccurate representation of women, racialized people, people with disabilities, and LGBTQ2+ people in media and in the media and communication industries more generally remains a huge problem that the *Equitable Portrayal Code* and other CRTC policies have been insufficient to resolve. This issue is compounded online as technologies and algorithms embed racism, sexism, ableism, cissexism, heterosexism, and colonialism in the technologies and code that define our online experiences.[20] Racist, misogynist, transphobic, harassing, and homophobic speech is a significant problem, especially online. While there are legitimate debates about what the most effective approach to combating hate speech is, it is certain that more must be done to fight it. Communications policy, through better monitoring and feedback mechanisms, requirements for more robust codes of conduct, more equitable hiring and remuneration within organizations that create platforms for speech, and improved education programs, could play a role in combating inequity. The explosion of surveillance and privacy-invasive technologies that has accompanied the proliferation of mobile technologies and the internet of things is exacerbating the over-surveillance of Canadians, including people who are poor, working-class, differently abled, racialized, and trans. Privacy law, to date, has been ineffective at countering the expansion of surveillance.

## SUCCESSES

This book's examination of Canadian communication policy and law has shown that, against many of the structural constraints we have seen, several advancements for equity within communication policy and law have been achieved. There have been significant gains for women's equity in Canadian communication policy; the need for fair and equitable portrayal of women in broadcasting has been recognized in the CBSC *Equitable Portrayal Code*. The Canadian government has committed to bridging gender divides in internet access and has played a role in calling attention to gendered dimensions of internet governance.[21] For Canadians with disabilities, accessibility policies have been incorporated into telecommunications and internet designs and policies. For Indigenous peoples, the establishment of the Aboriginal Peoples Television Network and the securing of its carriage on basic cable has affirmed the place of Indigenous peoples and ethnic minorities in the Canadian broadcasting system.[22] For LGBTQ2+ Canadians, recent decades have brought the mainstreaming of queer content both in traditional and new media. While communication policy and law cannot claim to have led this progress (indeed, legalized oppression and censorship in general held back progress of LGBTQ2+ rights for many years), it has been ultimately supportive, particularly since the establishment of the *Canadian Charter of Rights and Freedoms* in 1982. Community and campus radio, supported by CRTC broadcasting policies, have been sites of queer broadcasting in Canada since the 1970s.[23] The establishment of access to information regimes has served many causes, in some cases uncovering discrimination, wrongdoing, and injustice in the interest of furthering equity and justice.[24] The adoption of Gender-based Analysis Plus (GBA+) by the federal government may help to further embed policymaking processes that are more aware, sensitive, and responsive to the intersecting considerations of identity and the systemic barriers to inclusion and accessibility in communications law- and policymaking processes.[25]

## FINAL WORDS

Communication policy and law are as harnessed to economic and social forces that perpetuate inequality and injustice as they are to forces of equality and justice. They are frequently weighed down by such forces, as often leading in the wrong direction as in the right. Too often, communications policy and law serve those who are already privileged, failing to serve those who are underrepresented and oppressed. Nevertheless, there are many instances where communication policy and law have enabled and supported those fighting for representation and equality. Communication law and policymakers must use lenses that allow them to see and measure injustices and inequalities, which often remain hidden behind the idea that law and policy are neutral and "colourblind." Communications law and policy, this book shows, are rarely neutral. Change and reform is needed within communications policy and law, as a part of broader struggles for equality.

## NOTES

1. Dal Yong Jin, *Digital Platforms, Imperialism and Political Culture* (New York: Routledge, 2015); Nick Srnicek, *Platform Capitalism* (Cambridge: Polity, 2017).

2. Eli Pariser, *The Filter Bubble: How the New Personalized Web Is Changing What We Read and How We Think* (London: Penguin Books, 2012); Merlyna Lim, "Freedom to Hate: Social Media, Algorithmic Enclaves, and the Rise of Tribal Nationalism in Indonesia," *Critical Asian Studies* 49, no. 3 (2017): 411–27.

3. Clive Barnett, "Convening Publics: The Parasitical Spaces of Public Action," in *The SAGE Handbook of Political Geography*, eds. Kevin Cox, Murray Low, and Jennifer Robinson (London: SAGE, 2008), 405–6; Judith Squires, "Private Lives, Secluded Places: Privacy as Political Possibility," *Environment and Planning D: Society and Space* 12, no. 4 (1994): 387–401.

4. David S. Ardia, "Reputation in a Networked World: Revisiting the Social Foundations of Defamation Law," *Harvard Civil Rights-Civil Liberties Law Review* 45 (2010): 261.

5. Matt Stahl, "From Seven Years to 360 Degrees: Primitive Accumulation, Recording Contracts, and the Means of Making a (Musical) Living," *TripleC: Cognition, Communication, Co-Operation* 9, no. 2 (2011): 668–88; Christian Fuchs, "A Contribution to the Critique of the Political Economy of Google," *Fast Capitalism* 8, no. 1 (2011): 1–24.

6. Patricia Mazepa and Vincent Mosco, "A Political Economy Approach to the Internet," in *Handbook on the Economics of the Internet*, eds. Johannes Bauer and Michael Latzer (Cheltenham, UK: Edward Elgar Publishing, 2016), 165.

7. Safiya Umoja Noble, *Algorithms of Oppression: How Search Engines Reinforce Racism* (New York: Oxford University Press, 2018), 5.

8. Molly Dragiewicz, Delanie Woodlock, Bridget Harris, and Claire Reid, "Technology-Facilitated Coercive Control." In *The Routledge International Handbook of Violence Studies* (New York: Routledge, 2018), 266–75; Avri Doria, "Internet Governance and Gender Issues," in *Critically Absent: Women's Rights in Internet Governance* (Melville, South Africa: Association for Progressive Communication, 2012), 12.

9. Ann Bartow, "Fair Use and the Fairer Sex: Gender, Feminism, and Copyright Law," *American University Journal of Gender, Social Policy & the Law* 14, no. 3 (2006): 551–84; Debora Halbert, "Feminist Interpretations of Intellectual Property," *Journal of Gender, Social Policy and the Law* 14, no. 3 (2006): 435–37.

10. Toby Beauchamp, "Artful Concealment and Strategic Visibility: Transgender Bodies and US State Surveillance after 9/11," *Surveillance & Society* 6, no. 4 (2009): 356–66.

11. Stacey Copeland, "Broadcasting Queer Feminisms: Lesbian and Queer Women Programming in Transnational, Local, and Community Radio," *Journal of Radio & Audio Media* 25, no. 2 (2018): 218.

12. Monika Zalnieriute, "The Anatomy of Neoliberal Internet Governance: A Queer Critical Political Economy Perspective," in *Queering International Law: Possibilities, Alliances, Complicities, Risks*, ed. Dianne Otto (Abingdon, UK: Routledge, 2018).

13. Marc Naimark, "In the Fight Over .gay and .lgbt, the Cyberpowers That Be Are Redefining Our Community," *Slate*, May 7, 2014, https://slate.com/human-interest/2014/05/icann-and-the-fight-for-gay-and-lgbt-does-the-gay-community-even-exist.html.

14. Andrea Smith, "Not-Seeing: State Surveillance, Settler Colonialism, and Gender Violence," in *Feminist Surveillance Studies*, eds. Rachel E. Dubrofsky and Shoshana Magnet (Durham, NC: Duke University Press, 2015).

15. Ibid.

16. Lorna Roth, "The Delicate Acts of 'Colour Balancing': Multiculturalism and Canadian Television Broadcasting Policies and Practices," *Canadian Journal of Communication* 23, no. 4 (1998): 487–506.

17. Lara Fullenwieder and Adam Molnar, "Settler Governance and Privacy: Canada's Indian Residential School Settlement Agreement and the Mediation of State-Based Violence," *International Journal of Communication* 12 (2018): 1332–49; Tia Dafnos, "Beyond the Blue Line: Researching the Policing of Aboriginal Activism Using Access to Information," in *Brokering Access: Power, Politics, and Freedom of Information*, eds. Mike Larsen and Kevin Walby (Vancouver: UBC Press, 2012), 209–33.

18. Duncan Philpot, Brian Beaton, and Tim Whiteduck, "First Mile Challenges to Last Mile Rhetoric: Exploring the Discourse between Remote and Rural First Nations and the Telecom Industry," *Journal of Community Informatics* 10, no. 2 (2014).

19. Ibid., 13.

20. Noble.

21. Leslie Regan Shade, "Gender and Digital Policy: From Global Information Infrastructure to Internet Governance," in *The Routledge Companion to Media & Gender* (New York: Routledge, 2013), 240–50.

22. Lorna Roth, *Something New in the Air: The Story of First Peoples Television Broadcasting in Canada* (Montreal: McGill-Queen's University Press, 2005).

23. Copeland; Phylis Johnson and Michael C. Keith, *Queer Airwaves: The Story of Gay and Lesbian Broadcasting* (Armonk, NY: M.E. Sharpe, 2001).

24. Dafnos; CBC News, "Black People 3 Times More Likely to Be Street Checked in Halifax, Police Say." January 9, 2017, https://www.cbc.ca/news/canada/nova-scotia/halifax-black-street-checks-police-race-profiling-1.3925251.

25. Treasury Board of Canada Secretariat and Open Government Partnership, *Guide to Gender-based Analysis Plus (GBA+) and Inclusive Open Government* (Washington, DC: Open Government Partnership, 2019), 5, 8.

# GLOSSARY

**ableist:** An adjective used to describe policies, programs, and so on that disadvantage and discriminate against people with disabilities.

**access to information:** Access to information laws, also known as freedom of information laws, give individuals a right of access to records held by government. These laws cover federal, provincial, and municipal levels of government. With specific exceptions and exemptions, this right applies to records held by government, such as reports, memos, email correspondence, or recordings.

**appropriation of personality:** The use of someone's name or likeness without permission to one's own benefit, such as to promote one's own business.

**basic services:** A set of telephone services considered to be "basic" by the CRTC, such as individual touchtone landline service, dial-up internet access, 9-1-1 access, operator and directory assistance, and long-distance calling.

**bijural:** A legal system that consists of both common law and civil law.

**broadband internet:** High-speed internet and digital access services.

**broadcasters:** A person or entity that broadcasts sounds and visual images for reception by the public.

**broadcasting:** A one-to-many form of communication involving the transmission of programming to the public.

**bureaucratic theory:** A theory that critiques the role of bureaucracy in the administration of the state.

**bureaucracy:** A hierarchical form of organization, with officials who have fixed duties, and where authority is carried out in a professional and impersonal manner based on rules and often technical expertise, using standardized processes and written documents.

**Californian ideology:** An ideology that combines neoliberal emphases on market freedom with appeals to direct democracy, sexual egalitarianism, and environmentalism. The Californian ideology is seen as a false ideology, in that it masks or ignores the involvement of government in the creation of computer and networking technologies and the inequalities that are reproduced and amplified by new technologies.

**Canadian content:** Content, including music, film, and broadcast programming, that meets criteria set by the Canadian government and agencies defining content as Canadian.

**CanCon:** Canadian content regulations.

**capital:** Money and assets that are used to make more money. Also, the class of people and businesses who own capital.

**censorship:** The suppression or prohibition of specific materials and communications, especially on political, religious, moral, or public safety grounds.

**cisgender:** Refers to a person whose gender identity matches the gender they were assigned at birth. For example, a person declared a girl at birth who also identifies as a girl or woman.

**civil law:** A form of legal system with roots in the sixth-century Roman Empire, in which all laws are written down and compiled in statutes.

**common carrier:** A person or company that transports goods or passengers on regular routes at set rates, such as on a bus or in an airplane. Also, a telecommunication company that carries all communications without discrimination or editorial discretion.

**common law:** A form of legal system originating in England, now used in England and the former British colonies, including Canada. Under a common law system, laws made by parliament are written down and compiled in statutes. However, there are also additional laws, made by judges.

**concurring decision:** A judicial decision that supports the leading decision, coming to the same conclusion, but for different reasons.

**convergence:** The blurring of lines between telecommunications and broadcast or media companies. Also, the joining of several devices performing multiple functions into a single device.

**copyright:** A set of rights in original literary, dramatic, musical, and artistic works.

**critical disability theory:** Analysis centred on the experiences of people with disabilities and the critique of ableism.

**critical race theory:** The analysis and critique of institutional and systemic racism and white supremacy.

**cyberlibertarian:** A person who believes in cyberlibertarianism.

**cyberlibertarianism:** A theory that takes as its main premise that every person has a right to maximum negative liberty—the right not to be interfered with—in cyberspace. A version of libertarianism.

**de-identified information:** Data that has been anonymized or dissociated from particular users.

**defamation:** The act of damaging a person's reputation—of bringing dishonour or disrepute to a person.

**deregulation:** The reduction or elimination of policies, regulations, and laws.

**dissenting opinion:** A judicial decision that differs from the majority or plurality opinion of the court.

**distinguish:** The act of differentiating, especially in differentiating a legal case from previous judicial decisions that otherwise might have set binding precedent.

**Doctrine of Discovery:** A legal doctrine that permitted the European colonization of lands, including those inhabited by Indigenous peoples, under the false premise that the lands were being newly discovered.

*Equitable Portrayal Code*: A code of conduct administered by the Canadian Broadcast Standards Council (CBSC) that aims to achieve the equitable portrayal of all individuals in Canadian broadcasting.

**executive:** A branch of government whose main role is to enforce and implement the laws and policies made by the other two branches of government. *See also* judiciary

**fair dealing:** Under copyright law, fair dealing exceptions allow people to make use of works without the authorization of the copyright owner.

**feminism:** The analysis and critique of gender inequality in society as well as the social system and ideology that either reproduces or changes gender roles and gender-based stereotypes. Feminist legal theory and activism challenges judicial and legislative gender discrimination and patriarchal power structures.

**fraud:** The taking of money, property, valuables, or services by deceit or falsehood.

**freedom of expression:** A constitutional right to freedom of speech and other expressive acts intended to convey a message.

**freedom of information:** Access to information laws, also known as "freedom of information" laws, give individuals a right of access to records held by government.

**government:** The people and bureaucratic entities that fulfill and carry out the functions of the state.

**governmentality:** Analysis (based on the thinking of Michel Foucault) of the way people are governed by institutions as well as the systems that train people to govern or control themselves.

**Governor in Council:** The Governor General of Canada acting on the advice of Cabinet.

**horizontal integration:** Ownership of multiple companies that perform a similar role in an industry, also called consolidation. *See also* vertical integration

**identity theft:** Knowingly obtaining or possessing another person's identity information to commit an indictable offence.

**ideology:** A frame of reference, or common sense, through which people view the world.

**Indigenous legal theory:** The legal tradition and philosophy of Indigenous peoples and the analysis of the conflict between Canadian legislation, treaty rights, and Indigenous rights.

**intellectual property law:** Law that grants ownership rights of intangible things—in works of the mind, works of creativity, and works of expression.

**intersectional analysis:** An anti-essentialist analysis of identity that acknowledges and seeks to contextualize the multiplicity of identities that create a person's subjectivity.

*intra vires*: A piece of legislation that is within the power of the legislature to enact.

**intrusion upon seclusion:** A tort involving invasion of a person's space or affairs.

**iron law of oligarchy:** The theory that power becomes concentrated at the top in a bureaucracy.

**judiciary:** The judicial branch of government, or the courts, which interprets the written laws of the legislature and creates law through establishing precedents. *See also* executive

*jurisprudence constante*: Legal precedent where similar judicial decisions repeatedly come to consistent decisions.

**law:** A body of rules, whether formal or informal, recognized by a state or community as binding on its members. Laws are generally set and enforced by the state. They are contained in legislative statutes, administrative rules, and court decisions.

**lawful access:** Laws that permit law enforcement and security services to intercept communications. The lawful or legal interception of communications and the lawful search and seizure of information.

**legal formalism:** The school of thought that legal interpretation should be confined to the original intent of the law.

**legal interpretivism:** The school of thought that says judges necessarily use moral principles when interpreting the law.

**legal pluralism:** A body of legal thought calling for the recognition of a greater multiplicity of legal sources and norms.

**legislature:** The body of government that passes statutes serving as the written law of the country, province, or territory.

**LGBT:** Lesbian, gay, bisexual, and trans.

**LGBTQ:** Lesbian, gay, bisexual, trans, and queer.

**LGBTQ2+:** Lesbian, gay, bisexual, trans, queer, Two-Spirited, and other sexual orientations and gender identities.

**libel:** Defamation in print or broadcast form, such as newspaper articles, YouTube videos, blog posts, emails, and other communications that leave a record.

**libertarianism:** Libertarian theory takes as its main premise that every person has a right to maximum negative liberty—the right not to be interfered with. It understands people as having full self-ownership: the right to fully control, use, freely give, and to be compensated for the loss of one's self.

**majority decision:** A judicial decision written by a majority, or more than half, of judges on the panel.

**MAPL:** The MAPL system is used to determine whether music is Canadian. MAPL stands for "music, artist, production, and lyrics."

**market failure:** An occasion where the market fails to optimally produce a product or service.

**mass surveillance:** Surveillance conducted on a large scale such that everyone, or virtually everyone, is potentially a target.

**metadata:** Data about data. In particular, data such as the time, duration, sender, addressee, device identifiers, and location associated with communications by telephone, email, internet, social media, and so on.

**moral rights:** Under copyright law, the right to the integrity of the work (to prevent it from being altered) and the right to be associated with the work as its author.

**mosaic effect:** An effect that occurs when data from one seemingly anonymous data set can be de-anonymized by combining it with other data.

**multi-stakeholder:** A form of governance in which multiple stakeholders, such as governments, civil society, private businesses, NGOs, experts, and researchers, all play a role.

**neoliberal:** A theory that posits that human well-being is best advanced in a framework of strong property rights, free markets, and free trade.

**net neutrality:** The principle and policy that networks should treat all traffic the same, regardless of its content or origin.

**networked governance:** A system in which private, public, and technological actors are all involved in governing or regulating behaviour.

**neutral citation:** A form of legal citation for judicial decisions referencing the names of the court issuing the decision rather than published compilations.

**new media:** A term used by the CRTC to refer to digital content delivered over networks. This includes text, images, video, and audio.

*Oakes* **test:** A test the courts use to determine if freedom of expression has been justifiably restricted.

**oligarchy:** Rule by a few.

**Orders in Council:** Orders made by the Governor in Council and signed by the Governor General.

**patent:** A set of rights in new and useful inventions.

**personal information:** Information relating to an identified or identifiable individual.

**pluralism:** According to the pluralist theory, democracy exists if conflict is institutionalized through political processes that allow competing civil society groups' voices to challenge each other and those in power. *See also* legal pluralism

**plurality decision:** A judicial decision in which a majority of the judges on the panel agree on decision, but not on reasoning for it.

**policy:** A plan or course of action, often made by political parties, bureaucrats, or other governance bodies.

**political economy:** The economic and political organization of society in regard to the distribution of wealth and resources, and the associated field of study.

**postcolonial analysis:** The analysis and critique of the historical legacies of Western imperialism and colonialism.

**precedent:** Judicial decisions that may influence or be followed by subsequent judicial decisions.

**price-cap regulation:** Regulation that limits the price of basic services such as individual touchtone landline service, dial-up internet access, 9-1-1 access, operator and directory assistance, and long-distance calling.

**privacy by design:** Principles that require that organization processes and technologies be designed from the start to prevent privacy risks, and that privacy be the default setting of information systems and business practices.

**private law:** Law dealing not with offences against the public at large, but with relationships between people or organizations. This includes civil cases, which are cases not between the state and an individual, but between two individuals or organizations.

**privilege:** A right of immunity from being sued, especially for defamation.

**public law:** Law dealing with the relationship between individuals and the public as represented by the state. It includes constitutional law, administrative law, and criminal law.

**queer theory:** The analysis and critique of heteronormative (a binary way of understanding male and female identity with an assumption of heterosexual relations) and traditional ideologies of gender and sexuality identities, as well as homophobic and transphobic world views, legislation, and discrimination.

**racialized:** Racialization is the process whereby a person is grouped with other people as a "race," e.g., Black or Asian. Racialization often perpetuates race-based stereotypes.

**record:** Any documentary material in any form, including correspondence, memoranda, maps, plans, drawings, pictures, photographs, audio-visual materials, and emails.

**refer:** The government can *refer* to the court, asking the court to consider any important legal question, especially regarding constitutional interpretation.

**right to be forgotten:** The right of individuals to request that search results be deleted for search terms that include their own name.

**simultaneous substitution:** A policy allowing Canadian broadcasters to request that their own advertising be substituted in place of the American advertising on American channels broadcast in the Canadian market.

**slander:** Defamatory statements made verbally.

**spam:** Unsolicited emails, especially when sent as part of a mass-mailing.

**spectrum:** The range of electromagnetic frequencies (including radio and micro-wave frequencies) used to transmit radio or television broadcasting, or other communications signals, wirelessly.

**spectrum management:** The process of allocating and managing the use of radio spectrum.

**spectrum scarcity:** The limited range of electromagnetic frequencies available for over-the-air wireless communications.

*stare decisis:* The practice of following precedent.

**state:** The political entity from which government derives its authority, the unit of politics recognized at the international level, and the abstract notion of the country or nation as a sovereign political power.

**strategic lawsuits against public participation:** Defamation lawsuits used to attempt to intimidate and silence critics.

**sue:** To bring a civil action in court or initiate legal proceedings against.

**surveillance:** The act of keeping a close watch on someone.

**technological determinism:** The idea that the characteristics of technology are a primary driver of events and history.

**technological nationalism:** A concept that connects Canadian nationalism with technologies of transportation like railways and technologies of communication like broadcast networks—technologies that have been constructed with a nationalist motive to knit the country together and to resist the powerful North-South links that would otherwise bind Canada to the United States.

**technological solutionism:** The idea that problems have technological solutions, as opposed to requiring political, economic, or social change.

**telecommunications services:** Services that permit the transmission of communication—whether voice, images, or data—over a distance by radio or wire. These include mobile phone, landline, data, and internet services.

*terra nullius:* A legal concept that stated lands that were "no man's land" could be seized by European colonial powers. Under this colonial reasoning, Indigenous peoples did not own, but merely occupied, the lands on which they lived, because true ownership came from the agricultural working of the land.

**theory:** A system of ideas used to explain or understand phenomena.

**tort:** An act that leads to someone experiencing a harm for which the perpetuator can be legally and financially responsible to amend.

**trademark:** A set of rights in words, symbols, drawings, shapes, packaging, sound, or colours used to distinguish the goods or services of one person or organization from the goods and services of others.

**Truth and Reconciliation Commission:** Canada's Truth and Reconciliation Commission (TRC) was established in 2008 and concluded in 2015. Its mission was to document the experiences of Indigenous peoples who were taken from their families and placed in the Canadian residential school system, and their families.

**ultra vires:** A piece of legislation that falls outside the power of the legislature to enact.

**unanimous decision:** A judicial decision on which the whole court, or all of the judges on the panel, agrees.

**vertical integration:** Ownership of content, the production of content, and the means of transmitting that content. *See also* horizontal integration

**wholesale access:** The ability of competitors to obtain access to existing incumbent networks.

**wiretapping:** The interception of telecommunications.

# LIST OF ACRONYMS

| | |
|---|---|
| APA | American Psychological Association |
| APTN | Aboriginal Peoples Television Network |
| ASD | Australian Signals Directorate |
| BBG | Board of Broadcast Governors |
| BDUs | Broadcast Distribution Undertakings |
| BMO | Bank of Montreal |
| BRC | Board of Railway Commissioners |
| C3P | Canadian Centre for Child Protection |
| CAB | Canadian Association of Broadcasters |
| CAIP | Canadian Association of Internet Providers |
| CANLII | Canadian Legal Information Institute |
| CASL | *Canada's Anti-Spam Legislation* |
| CBC | Canadian Broadcasting Corporation |
| CBSC | Canadian Broadcast Standards Council |
| CCAICE | Canadian Coalition Against Internet Child Exploitation |
| CIRA | Canadian Internet Registration Authority |
| CNCP | Canadian National Canadian Pacific |
| CRBC | Canadian Radio Broadcasting Commission |
| CRTC | Canadian Radio-television and Telecommunications Commission |
| CSE | Canadian Security Establishment |
| CUSFTA | *Canada–US Free Trade Agreement* |
| DNS | domain name system |
| DSP | Depository Services Program |
| EPIC | Electronic Privacy Information Centre |
| FACTOR | Foundation Assisting Canadian Talent on Recordings |
| FALM | Free Access to Law Movement |
| FCC | Federal Communications Commission (USA) |
| GATS | *General Agreement on Trade in Services* |
| GCHQ | Government Communications Headquarters |
| GCSB | Government Communications Security Bureau |
| ICANN | Internet Corporation for Assigned Names and Numbers |
| IGF | Internet Governance Forum |
| IMF | International Money Fund |
| IP | intellectual property *or* Internet Protocol |

ISP         internet service provider
LAC         Library and Archives of Canada
LII         legal information institute
MAPL        music, artist, production, lyrics
NAFTA       *North American Free Trade Agreement*
NGOs        non-governmental organizations
NSA         National Security Agency (USA)
OCAP        ownership, control, access, and possession
OLG         Ontario Lottery and Gaming Corporation
OTA         over the air
PIPEDA      *Personal Information Protection and Electronic Documents Act*
SCC         Supreme Court of Canada
SLAPP       strategic lawsuits against public participation
SOCAN       Society of Composers, Authors and Music Publishers of Canada
TCTS        TransCanada Telephone System (later Stentor)
TLDs        top-level domains
TRC         Truth and Reconciliation Commission
UNDRIP      *United Nations Declaration on the Rights of Indigenous Peoples*
UNESCO      United Nations Educational, Scientific and Cultural Organization
WTO         World Trade Organization

# BIBLIOGRAPHY

## LEGISLATION

*Aeronautics Act*, RSC, 1985, c A-2.

*Alberta Human Rights Act*, RSA 2000, c A-25.5.

*An Act to amend the Criminal Code (protection of children and other vulnerable persons) and the Canada Evidence Act*, SC 2005, c 32.

*Anti-Terrorism Act*, SC 2015, c 20.

*Broadcasting Act*, SC 1958, c 22.

*Broadcasting Act*, SC 1991, c 11.

*Canadian Broadcasting Act, 1936*, c 24, 1 Ed VIII, s 22.

*Canadian Charter of Rights and Freedoms*, Part I of the *Constitution Act, 1982*, being Schedule B to the *Canada Act 1982* (UK), 1982, c 11.

*Canadian Human Rights Act*, RSC 1985, c H-6.

*Canadian Radio Broadcasting Act, 1932*, SC 1932, c 51.

*Civil Code of Québec*, SQ 1991, c 64.

*Criminal Code of Canada*, RSC 1985, c C-46.

*Economic Action Plan 2014 Act, No 1*, SC 2014, c 20.

*Film Classification Act, 2005*, SO 2005, c17, and O Reg 452/05.

*Human Rights Act*, SNWT 2002, c 18.

*Human Rights Code*, RSBC 1996, c 210.

*Human Rights Code*, RSO 1990, c H.19.

*Indian Act*, RSC 1985, c I-5.

*Libel and Slander Act*, RSO 1970, c 243.

*Personal Information Protection and Electronic Documents Act*, SC 2000, c 5.

*Privacy Act*, RSC, 1985, c P-21.

*Safe Streets Act, 1999*, SO 1999, c 8.

*Saskatchewan Human Rights Code, 2018*, SS 2018, c S-24.2.

*Telecommunications Act, SC 1993*, c 38.

## CASES

*Alberta v Hutterian Brethren of Wilson Colony*, [2009] 2 SCR 567.

*Alberta (Education) v Canadian Copyright Licensing Agency (Access Copyright)*, 2012 SCC 37.

*Alberta (Information and Privacy Commissioner) v United Food and Commercial Workers, Local 401*, 2013 SCC 62.

*Aubry v Éditions Vice-Versa*, 1998 1 SCR 591.

*Baglow v Smith*, 2015 ONSC 1175 at 186.

*Baier v Alberta*, 2007 SCC 31.

*Bell Canada v Canada (Attorney General)*, 2016 FCA 217.

*Bitsie v Walston*, 515 P.2d 659 (NM Ct App 1973).

*BMG Canada Inc v Doe*, 2005 FCA 193.

*Bou Malhab v Diffusion Métromédia CMR Inc*, 2011 SCC 9.

*Bracken v Niagara Parks Police*, 2018 ONCA 261.

*Calgary Airport Authority v Canadian Centre for Bio-Ethical Reform*, 2019 ABQB 29.

*Canada (Attorney General) v Canada (Information Commissioner)*, 2004 FC 431.

*Canada (Human Rights Commission) v Taylor*, 1990 3 SCR 892.

*Canada (Information Commissioner) v Canada (Minister of Industry)*, 2007 FCA 212.

*Canadian Radiotelevision and Telecommunications Commission (Re)*, 2010 FCA 178.

*Capital Cities Comm v CRTC*, [1978] 2 SCR 141.

*Carter v BC Federation of Foster Parents Association*, 2005 BCCA 398.

*Carter v Canada (Attorney General)*, 2015 SCC 5.

*CCH Canadian Ltd v Law Society of Upper Canada*, 2004 SCC 13.

*Cinar Corporation v Robinson*, 2013 SCC 73.

*Citizens United v Federal Election Commission*, 2010 558 US 310.

*Committee for the Commonwealth of Canada v Canada*, [1991] 1 SCR 139.

*Crookes v Newton*, 2011 SCC 47.

*Dagenais v Canadian Broadcasting Corporation*, [1994] 3 SCR 835.

*Dagg v Canada (Minister of Finance)*, [1997] SCJ No 63, [1997] 2 SCR 403.

*Dixon v Powell River (City)*, 2009 BCSC 406.

*Enrietti-Zoppo v Colla*, [2007] OJ No 5183.

*Entertainment Software Association v Society of Composers, Authors and Music Publishers of Canada*, 2012 SCC 34.

*Equustek Solutions Inc v Jack*, 2014 BCSC 1063.

*FCC v Pacifica Foundation*, 438 US 726 (1978).

*Glad Day Bookshop v Deputy Minister of National Revenue for Customs & Excise*, [1992] OJ No 1466.

*Google Inc v Equustek Solutions Inc*, 2017 SCC 34.

*Google Spain SL and Google Inc v Agencia Española de Protección de Datos (AEPD) and Mario Costeja González*, case C-131/12.

*Greater Vancouver Transportation Authority v Canadian Federation of Students*, 2009 SCC 31.

*Halton Hills (Town) v Kerouac*, 80 OR (3d) 577, 270 DLR (4th) 479, [2006] OTC 384, 142 CRR (2d) 285.

*Harper v Canada (Attorney General)*, 2004 SCC 33.

*Hill v Church of Scientology of Toronto*, [1995] 2 SCR 1130, [1995] SCJ No 64.

*Hudspeth v Whatcott*, 2017 ONSC 1708.

*Ingersoll Telephone Co. v Bell Telephone Co. of Canada*, (1916) 53 SCR 583 (Supreme Court of Canada June 24, 1916).

*Irwin Toy Ltd v Quebec (Attorney General)*, [1989] 1 SCR 927, 1989 CanLII 87 (SCC).

*John Doe and Suzie Jones v Her Majesty the Queen*, 2015 FC 916.

*Jones v Tsige*, 2012 ONCA 32.

*JTI MacDonald Corp v Canada (Procureure générale)*, 2007 SCC 30.

*Krouse v Chrysler Canada Ltd*, (1973), 1 OR (2d) 225 (Ont CA).

*Lassonde Inc v Canada (Registrar of Trade-marks)* (2000), 5 CPR (4th) 517, 180 FTR 177 (Fed TD), affirmed (2001), 281 NR 365 (Fed CA).

*Lemire v Canada (Human Rights Commission)*, 2014 FCA 18.

*Little Sisters Book and Art Emporium v Canada (Department of Justice)*, 2000 SCC 69.

*Montague (Township) v Page*, 79 OR (3d) 515, [2006] OJ No 331.

*Native Women's Assn of Canada v Canada*, [1994] 3 SCR 627, [1994] SCJ No 93.

*Ontario (Attorney General) v Langer*, (1995) 123 DLR (4th) 289, 1995 CanLII 7422 (ONSC).

*Public Service Board et al v Dionne et al*, [1978] 2 SCR 191.

*Prud'homme v Prud'homme*, 2002 SCC 85.

*R v Ahenakew*, 2009 SKPC 10.

*R v Banks*, 2007 ONCA 19.

*R v Barabash*, 2015 SCC 29.

*R v Butler*, 1992 1 SCR 452, 1989 CanLII 87 (SCC).

*R v Edwards Books and Art Ltd*, [1986] 2 SCR 713.

*R v Glad Day Bookshops Inc*, 70 OR (3d) 691, [2004] OJ No 1766.

*R v Greenbaum*, [1993] 1 SCR 674, [1993] SCJ No 24.

*R v Keegstra*, [1990] 3 SCR 697.

*R v Khawaja*, [2012] 3 SCR 555.

*R v Krymowski*, 2005 SCC 7.

*R v Le*, 2019 SCC 34.

*R v Lucas*, [1998] 1 SCR 439, [1998] SCJ No 28.

*R v Oakes*, [1986] SCR 103.

*R v Presseault*, 2007 QCCQ 384.

*R v Scythes*, [1993] OJ No 537 (Prov Div)(QL) (1993).

*R v Sears*, 2019 ONCJ 104.

*R v Sharpe*, 2001 SCC 2.

*R v Sharpe*, 2002 BCSC 423.

*R v Whatcott*, 2013 SCC 11.

*Re:Sound v Motion Picture Theatre Associations of Canada*, 2012 SCC 38.

*Reference re Broadcasting Act*, 2012 SCC 4.

*Reference re Secession of Quebec*, [1998] 2 SCR 217.

*Regina v Hicklin*, 1868 LR 3 QB 360.

*RJR-MacDonald v Canada*, 3 SCR 199, [1995] SCJ No 68.

*Rodriguez v British Columbia (Attorney General)*, [1993] 3 SCR 519, 107 DLR (4th) 342.

*Rogers Communications Inc v Society of Composers, Authors and Music Publishers of Canada*, 2012 SCC 35.

*Saskatchewan (Human Rights Commission) v Whatcott*, 2013 SCC 11.

*Smith Kline & French Canada Ltd v Canada Registrar of Trademarks*, [1987] 2 FC 633 (FCTD).

*Society of Composers, Authors and Music Publishers of Canada v Bell Canada*, 2012 SCC 36.

*The Attorney General of Quebec v The Attorney General of Canada and others*, [1932] UKPC 7, [1932] AC 304.

*Théberge v Galerie d'Art du Petit Champlain Inc*, 2002 SCC 34.

*Whitney v California*, 1927 274 US 357.

*WIC Radio Ltd v Simpson*, 2008 SCC 40.

## SECONDARY SOURCES

"5G Wireless Spectrum Auction Nets Ottawa $3.5 Billion." *MarketWatch* (blog), April 11, 2019. www.marketwatch.com/press-release/5g-wireless-spectrum-auction-nets-ottawa-35-billion-2019-04-11-91975053.

"'0832993—TOBLERONE & DESIGN (COLOR),' Canadian Trademarks Database." Report. Accessed October 31, 2018. ic.gc.ca/app/opic-cipo/trdmrks/srch/viewTrademark?id=0832993&lang=eng&tab=reg.

"'1586637—MAC START UP CHIME,' Canadian Trademarks Database." Report. Accessed October 31, 2018. ic.gc.ca/app/opic-cipo/trdmrks/srch/viewTrademark?id=1586637&lang=eng&tab=reg.

Access Info Europe. *Statement by European RTI Community on the World's First Official Access to Information Day!* https://www.access-info.org/uncategorized/26216.

"Access to Information Regulations. SOR/83-507." March 7, 2018. https://laws-lois.justice.gc.ca/eng/regulations/SOR-83-507/page-1.html.

Ackerman, John M., and Irma E. Sandoval-Ballesteros. "The Global Explosion of Freedom of Information Laws." *Administrative Law Review* 58, no. 1 (2006): 85–130.

Albinati, Chris, Geneviève Bonin-Labelle, Kathleen Buddle, John Gagnon, Gretchen King, and Julia Szwarc, eds. "Recommendations for a New Consultation Process and Policy for First Nations, Inuit and Métis Broadcasting—Final Report." March 2019.

Alexander, Cynthia J. "Wiring the Nation! Including First Nations? Aboriginal Canadians and Federal e-Government Initiatives." *Journal of Canadian Studies* 35, no. 4 (2001): 277–96.

Alhassan, Amin. "Telecom Regulation, the Post-Colonial State, and Big Business: The Ghanaian Experience." *West Africa Review* 4, no. 1 (2003).

Ali, Syed Mustafa. "A Brief Introduction to Decolonial Computing." *XRDS: Crossroads, The ACM Magazine for Students* 22 no. 4 (June 13, 2016): 16–21. https://doi.org/10.1145/2930886.

Alia, Valerie. *The New Media Nation: Indigenous Peoples and Global Communication.* Vol. 2. Berghahn Books, 2010.

Allen, Anita L. "Coercing Privacy." *William and Mary Law Review* 40, no. 3 (1999): 723–24.

———. *Uneasy Access: Privacy for Women in a Free Society.* Lanham, MD: Rowman & Littlefield, 1988.

Anderson, Benedict. *Imagined Communities: Reflections on the Origin and Spread of Nationalism.* New York: Verso Books, 2006.

Andrejevic, Mark, and Kelly Gates. "Big Data Surveillance: Introduction." *Surveillance & Society* 12, no. 2 (May 9, 2014): 185–96. https://doi.org/10.24908/ss.v12i2.5242.

Anghie, Antony. "Finding the Peripheries: Sovereignty and Colonialism in Nineteenth-Century International Law." *Harvard International Law Journal* 40, no. 1 (1999): 1–80.

Angwin, Julia, Ariana Tobin, and Madeleine Varner. "Facebook (Still) Letting Housing Advertisers Exclude Users by Race." *ProPublica*, November 21, 2017.

Aquinas, Thomas. *On Law, Morality, and Politics.* Edited by William P. Baumgarth and Richard J. Regan. Translated by Richard J. Regan. Indianapolis: Hackett Publishing, 1988.

Ardia, David S. "Reputation in a Networked World: Revisiting the Social Foundations of Defamation Law." *Harvard Civil Rights-Civil Liberties Law Review* 45 (2010): 261–328.

Armstrong, Laura. "Netflix Refuses CRTC Demand for Confidential Data." *The Toronto Star*, September 22, 2014. https://www.thestar.com/news/gta/2014/09/22/netflix_refuses_crtc_demand_for_confidential_data.html.

Armstrong, Robert. *Broadcasting Policy in Canada*. 2nd ed. Toronto: University of Toronto Press, 2016.

Arneil, Barbara. "Trade, Plantations, and Property: John Locke and the Economic Defense of Colonialism." *Journal of the History of Ideas* 55, no. 4 (1994): 591–609.

Arora, Payal. "Decolonizing Privacy Studies." *Television & New Media* 20, no. 4 (2019): 366–78.

Arora, Payal, and Laura Scheiber. "Slumdog Romance: Facebook Love and Digital Privacy at the Margins." *Media, Culture & Society* 39, no. 3 (2017): 408–22.

Auer, Monica L. "Foreign Ownership in Canadian Telecommunications." In *The Internet Tree: The State of Telecom Policy in Canada 3.0*, edited by Marita Moll, Leslie Regan Shade, and Canadian Centre for Policy Alternatives, 45–59. Ottawa: Canadian Centre for Policy Alternatives, 2011.

Austin, Lisa. "Lawful Illegality: What Snowden Has Taught Us about the Legal Infrastructure of the Surveillance State." In *Law, Privacy and Surveillance in Canada in the Post-Snowden Era*, edited by Michael Geist, 103–25. Ottawa: University of Ottawa Press, 2017.

"Australasian Legal Information Institute (AustLII)." Accessed February 17, 2019. http://fatlm.org/.

Babe, Robert E. *Canadian Television Broadcasting Structure, Performance and Regulation*. Ottawa: Economic Council of Canada, 1979.

———. *Communication and the Transformation of Economics: Essays in Information, Public Policy, and Political Economy*. New York: Routledge, 2018.

———. *Telecommunications in Canada: Technology, Industry, and Government*. Toronto: University of Toronto Press, 1990.

Bagdikian, Ben H. *The New Media Monopoly*. Boston: Beacon Press, 2014.

Baglay, Sasha. *Introduction to the Canadian Legal System*. Toronto: Pearson, 2016.

Bailey, Jane. "Private Regulation and Public Policy: Toward Effective Restriction of Internet Hate Propaganda." *McGill Law Journal* 49 (2004): 59–103.

Baker, C. Edwin. "Hate Speech." In *The Content and Context of Hate Speech*, edited by Michael Herz and Peter Molnar, 57–80. Cambridge: Cambridge University Press, 2012. https://doi.org/10.1017/CBO9781139042871.007.

———. "Scope of the First Amendment Freedom of Speech." *University of California Los Angeles Law Review* 25 (1978): 964–1040.

Balbi, Gabriele, and Juraj Kittler. "One-to-One and One-to-Many Dichotomy: Grand Theories, Periodization, and Historical Narratives in Communication Studies." *International Journal of Communication* 10 (2016): 20.

Balkin, Jack M. "Digital Speech and Democratic Culture: A Theory of Freedom of Expression for the Information Society." *NYU Law Review* 79 (2004): 1–55.

Bannerman, Sara. "Crowdfunding Culture." *Wi: Journal of Mobile Media* 7, no. 01 (2013): 1–30.

———. "Crowdfunding Music and the Democratization of Economic and Social Capital." *Canadian Journal of Communication*, forthcoming.

———. *International Copyright and Access to Knowledge*. Cambridge: Cambridge University Press, 2016.

———. "Relational Privacy and the Networked Governance of the Self." *Information, Communication & Society* 2018: 1–16.

———. *The Struggle for Canadian Copyright: Imperialism to Internationalism, 1842–1971*. Vancouver: UBC Press, 2013.

Barbrook, Richard, and Andy Cameron. "The Californian Ideology." *Science as Culture* 6, no. 1 (January 1996): 44–72. https://doi.org/10.1080/09505439609526455.

Barker, Paul, and Kenneth Kernaghan. *Public Administration in Canada*. Toronto: Thomson Nelson, 2008.

Barlow, John Perry. "A Declaration of the Independence of Cyberspace." Electronic Frontier Foundation, January 20, 2016. https://www.eff.org/cyberspace-independence.

Barnett, Clive. "Convening Publics: The Parasitical Spaces of Public Action." In *The SAGE Handbook of Political Geography*, edited by Kevin Cox, Murray Low, and Jennifer Robinson, 403–18. London: SAGE, 2008.

Barney, Darin. "One Nation Under Google: Citizenship in the Technological Republic." Hart House Lecture. Toronto: Hart House Lecture Committee, 2007. https://darinbarneyresearch.mcgill.ca/Work/One_Nation_Under_Google.pdf.

Barthes, Roland. "The Death of the Author." *Contributions in Philosophy* 83 (2001): 3–8.

Bartow, Ann. "Fair Use and the Fairer Sex: Gender, Feminism, and Copyright Law." *American University Journal of Gender, Social Policy & the Law* 14, no. 3 (2006): 551–84.

Bates, Jo. "The Strategic Importance of Information Policy for the Contemporary Neoliberal State: The Case of Open Government Data in the United Kingdom." *Government Information Quarterly* 31, no. 3 (July 2014): 388–95. https://doi.org/10.1016/j.giq.2014.02.009.

Bates, Joanne. "Politics of Open Government Data: A Neo-Gramscian Analysis of the United Kingdom's Open Government Data Initiative." Manchester: Manchester Metropolitan University, 2012.

Bates, Thomas R. "Gramsci and the Theory of Hegemony." *Journal of the History of Ideas* (1975): 351–66.

Bathgate, Gordon. *Voices from the Ether: The History of Radio*. Morrisville, NC: Lulu.com, 2012.

Battiste, Marie. "Indigenous Knowledge: Foundations for First Nations." *World Indigenous Nations Higher Education Consortium-WINHEC Journal* (2005): 1–12.

Batura, Olga. *Universal Service in WTO and EU Law: Liberalisation and Social Regulation in Telecommunications.* The Hague: Asser Press, 2015.

Bauman, Zygmunt, Didier Bigo, Paulo Esteves, Elspeth Guild, Vivienne Jabri, David Lyon, and Rob B.J. Walker. "After Snowden: Rethinking the Impact of Surveillance." *International Political Sociology* 8, no. 2 (2014): 121–44.

Bayer, Carolin Anne. "Re-Thinking the Common Law of Defamation: Striking a New Balance between Freedom of Expression and the Protection of the Individual's Reputation." LLM Thesis, University of British Columbia, 2001. https://doi.library.ubc.ca/10.14288/1.0077572.

Baynes, Leonard M. "Deregulatory Injustice and Electronic Redlining: The Color of Access to Telecommunications." *Administrative Law Review* 56 (2004): 263–352.

Beaton, Brian, Terence Burnard, and Adi Linden. "Keewaytinook Mobile: An Indigenous Community-Owned Mobile Phone Service in Northern Canada." In *Indigenous People and Mobile Technologies*, edited by Laurel Evelyn Dyson, Stephen Grant, and Max Hendriks, 123–39. New York: Routledge, 2015.

Beauchamp, Toby. "Artful Concealment and Strategic Visibility: Transgender Bodies and US State Surveillance after 9/11." *Surveillance & Society* 6, no. 4 (2009): 356–66.

Beaupert, Fleur. "Freedom of Opinion and Expression: From the Perspective of Psychosocial Disability and Madness." *Laws* 7, no. 1 (2018): 3.

Beer, Jeremy de, and Daniel Dylan. "Traditional Knowledge Governance Challenges in Canada." In *Indigenous Intellectual Property*, edited by Matthew Rimmer. Cheltenham, UK: Edward Elgar, 2015. https://doi.org/10.4337/9781781955901.00035.

Beer, Jeremy de, and Robert Tomkowicz. "Exhaustion of Intellectual Property Rights in Canada." *Canadian Intellectual Property Review* 25 (2009): 3–31.

Bell, B., P. Budka, and A. Fiser. "We Were on the Outside Looking in": MyKnet.org—A First Nations Online Social Environment in Northern Ontario. In *Connecting Canadians: Investigations in Community Informatics*, edited by A. Clement, M. Gurstein, G. Longford, Marita Moll, and Leslie Regan Shade, 237–54. 2012.

Bell, Catherine E., and Val Napoleon, eds. *First Nations Cultural Heritage and Law: Case Studies, Voices, and Perspectives.* Vancouver: UBC Press, 2008.

Bell Jr., Derrick A. "Brown v. Board of Education and the Interest-Convergence Dilemma." *Harvard Law Review* 93 (1980): 518–33.

Bello, Pablo, and Juan Jung. "Net Neutrality: Reflections on the Current Debate." *Global Commission on Internet Governance Paper Series*, May 6, 2015. https://www.cigionline.org/publications/net-neutrality-reflections-current-debate.

Benedet, Janine. "The Paper Tigress: Canadian Obscenity Law 20 Years after *R v Butler*." *The Canadian Bar Review* 93, no. 1 (2015): 1–37.

Benjamin, Ruha. *Race after Technology: Abolitionist Tools for the New Jim Code.* Hoboken, NJ: John Wiley & Sons, 2019.

Bennett, Colin J., and Robin M. Bayley. *Canadian Federal Political Parties and Personal Privacy Protection: A Comparative Analysis.* Ottawa: Office of the Privacy Commissioner of Canada, 2012.

Bennett Jones. "Group Defamation Clarified." Accessed December 13, 2018. https://www.bennettjones.com/Publications-Section/Updates/Group-Defamation-Clarified.

Berliner, Daniel. "The Political Origins of Transparency." *The Journal of Politics* 76, no. 2 (2014): 479–91.

Bertot, John C., Paul T. Jaeger, and Justin M. Grimes. "Using ICTs to Create a Culture of Transparency: E-Government and Social Media as Openness and Anti-Corruption Tools for Societies." *Government Information Quarterly* 27, no. 3 (July 2010): 264–71. https://doi.org/10.1016/j.giq.2010.03.001.

Bertram, Theo, Elie Bursztein, Stephanie Caro, Hubert Chao, Rutledge Chin Feman, Peter Fleischer, Albin Gustafsson, Jess Hemerly, Chris Hibbert, and Luca Invernizzi. "Three Years of the Right to Be Forgotten." Mountain View, CA: Google, 2018. https://drive.google.com/file/d/1H4MKNwf5MgeztG7OnJRnl3ym3gIT3HUK/view.

Bettig, Ronald V. *Copyrighting Culture: The Political Economy of Intellectual Property.* New York: Routledge, 2018.

Beutin, Lyndsey P. "Racialization as a Way of Seeing: The Limits of Counter-Surveillance and Police Reform." *Surveillance & Society* 15, no. 1 (2017): 5–20.

Black, Sharon K. *Telecommunications Law in the Internet Age.* San Francisco: Morgan Kaufmann Publishers, 2002.

Blackstone, William. *Commentaries on the Laws of England: A Facsimile of the First Edition of 1765–1769, with an Introduction by Stanley N. Katz*, vols. 1–4. Chicago: University of Chicago Press, 1979.

Blaiwais, Lauren, and Scott Miller. "Offensive Trademarks: The Canadian and American Perspectives." *Intellectual Property Journal* 30, no. 2 (2018): 205–15.

Block, Walter. "A Libertarian Analysis of Suing for Libel." September 5, 2014. https://www.lewrockwell.com/2014/09/walter-e-block/may-i-sue-the-ny-times/.

————. *Defending the Undefendable*. Auburn, AL: Ludwig von Mises Institute, 2003.

Boldrin, Michele, and David K. Levine. *Against Intellectual Monopoly*. Cambridge: Cambridge University Press, 2008.

Borden, Diane L. "Patterns of Harm: An Analysis of Gender and Defamation." *Communication Law and Policy* 2, no. 1 (1997): 105–41.

————. "Reputational Assault: A Critical and Historical Analysis of Gender and the Law of Defamation." *Journalism & Mass Communication Quarterly* 75, no. 1 (1998): 98–111.

Borrows, John. *Canada's Indigenous Constitution*. Toronto: University of Toronto Press, 2010.

————. *Recovering Canada: The Resurgence of Indigenous Law*. Toronto: University of Toronto Press, 2002.

Boyd, Danah. "Facebook's Privacy Trainwreck: Exposure, Invasion, and Social Convergence." *Convergence* 14, no. 1 (2008): 13–20.

Boykoff, Jules. *The Suppression of Dissent: How the State and Mass Media Squelch USAmerican Social Movements*. New York: Routledge, 2013.

Bracha, Oren, and Frank Pasquale. "Federal Search Commission—Access, Fairness, and Accountability in the Law of Search." *Cornell Law Review* 93, no. 6 (September 2008): 1149–210.

Bradshaw, Samantha, and Laura DeNardis. "The Politicization of the Internet's Domain Name System: Implications for Internet Security, Universality, and Freedom." *New Media & Society* 20, no. 1 (January 2018): 332–50. https://doi.org/10.1177/1461444816662932.

Braithwaite, John, and Peter Drahos. *Global Business Regulation*. Cambridge: Cambridge University Press, 2000.

Braman, Sandra. *Change of State: Information, Policy, and Power*. Cambridge, MA: MIT Press, 2009.

Brayne, Sarah. "Big Data Surveillance: The Case of Policing." *American Sociological Review* 82, no. 5 (2017): 977–1008.

Brean, Joseph. "Can Your Old Boss Badmouth You to a Potential Employer? Absolutely, Says an Ontario Court." *National Post*, April 20, 2017. https://nationalpost.com/news/canada/can-your-old-boss-badmouth-you-to-a-potential-employer-absolutely-says-an-ontario-court.

Brown, Raymond E. *Defamation Law: A Primer*. 2nd ed. Toronto: Carswell, 2013.

Brown, Raymond E., and Jeremy S. Williams. *The Law of Defamation in Canada*. 2nd ed. Scarborough, ON: Carswell, 1994.

Brown, Wendy. "Suffering the Paradoxes of Rights." In *Left Legalism/Left Critique*, edited by Wendy Brown and J. Halley, 420–34. Durham, NC: Duke University Press, 2001.

Browne, Simone. *Dark Matters: On the Surveillance of Blackness*. Durham, NC: Duke University Press, 2015.

Bruce, Tammy. *The New Thought Police: Inside the Left's Assault on Free Speech and Free Minds*. Roseville, CA: Forum, 2001.

Bruser, David, and Jesse McLean. "Companies Knew Drugs They Sold Were Defective; U.S. Food and Drug Administration Reports Reveal Canadian Pharmaceutical Firms Changed and Destroyed Test Data Showing Products Were Tainted and Health Canada Kept Inspection Details Secret, Potentially Putting Health of Patients at Risk." *Toronto Star*, September 11, 2014.

"Bryan Adams Not Canadian?" CBC Archives. Accessed October 3, 2018. https://www.cbc.ca/archives/entry/bryan-adams-not-canadian.

Bucher, Taina. *If...Then: Algorithmic Power and Politics*. New York: Oxford University Press, 2018.

Burman, Tony. "The Real Danger to Press Freedom." In *The Unfulfilled Promise of Press Freedom in Canada*, edited by Lisa Taylor and Cara-Marie O'Hagan, 15–30. Toronto: University of Toronto Press, 2017.

Burnap, Pete, and Matthew L. Williams. "Us and Them: Identifying Cyber Hate on Twitter across Multiple Protected Characteristics." *EPJ Data Science* 5, no. 1 (December 2016). https://doi.org/10.1140/epjds/s13688-016-0072-6.

Caldbick, Mary. "Privacy and Access to Information of Aboriginal Peoples in Canada." LLM Major Research Paper, University of Ottawa, 2007.

Canada, and Canadian Heritage. *Creative Canada Policy Framework*. 2017. https://www.canada.ca/en/canadian-heritage/campaigns/creative-canada/framework.html.

"Canada's Top Court Overstepped, Can't Enforce Google to Delist Search Results in U.S., Judge Rules." *Toronto Star*, November 3, 2017. https://www.thestar.com/business/2017/11/03/canadas-top-court-overstepped-cant-enforce-google-to-delist-search-results-in-us-judge-rules.html.

Canadian Broadcast Standards Council. "Canadian Association of Broadcasters' Equitable Portrayal Code (2008)." Accessed November 3, 2018. https://www.cbsc.ca/codes/cab-equitable-portrayal-code/.

Canadian Heritage. "Broadcasting and Telecommunications Legislative Review." June 5, 2018. https://www.canada.ca/en/canadian-heritage/news/2018/06/government-of-canada-launches-review-of-telecommunications-and-broadcasting-acts.html.

———. "The Government of Canada Wants to Ensure the Right Balance of Investment in Content and in the Ability to Compete." December 12, 2018. https://www.newswire.ca/news-releases/the-government-of-canada-wants-to-ensure-the-right-balance-of-investment-in-content-and-in-the-ability-to-compete-640390183.html.

————. "Rights of LGBTI Persons." October 23, 2017. https://www.canada.ca/en/canadian-heritage/services/rights-lgbti-persons.html.

Canadian Intellectual Property Office (CIPO). "Manual of Patent Office Practice (MOPOP)—Canadian Intellectual Property Office." Accessed October 31, 2018. https://www.ic.gc.ca/eic/site/cipointernet-internetopic.nsf/eng/h_wr00720.html.

Canadian Radio-television and Telecommunications Commission (CRTC). "Broadcasting and Telecom Decision CRTC 2015-26: Complaint against Bell Mobility Inc. and Quebecor Media Inc., Videotron Ltd. and Videotron G.P. Alleging Undue and Unreasonable Preference and Disadvantage in Regard to the Billing Practices for Their Mobile TV Services Bell Mobile TV and Illico.Tv." Decisions, January 29, 2015. https://crtc.gc.ca/eng/archive/2015/2015-26.htm.

————. "Broadcasting and Telecom Regulatory Policy CRTC 2009-430: Accessibility of Telecommunications and Broadcasting Services." Regulatory Policies, July 21, 2009. https://crtc.gc.ca/eng/archive/2009/2009-430.htm.

————. "Broadcasting Commission Letter Addressed to the Distribution List." March 28, 2019. https://crtc.gc.ca/eng/archive/2019/lb190328.htm.

————. "Broadcasting Decision CRTC 2004-271: CHOI-FM—Non-Renewal of Licence." Decisions, September 20, 2007. https://crtc.gc.ca/eng/archive/2004/db2004-271.htm.

————. "Broadcasting Decision CRTC 2005-247: Satellite Subscription Radio Undertaking." Decisions, September 20, 2007. https://crtc.gc.ca/eng/archive/2005/db2005-247.htm.

————. "Broadcasting Decision CRTC 2008-9: Complaint Regarding the Broadcast by the CBC of the Little Mosque on the Prairie Episode 'Traditional Mother.'" Decisions, September 20, 2007. https://crtc.gc.ca/eng/archive/2008/db2008-9.htm.

————. "Broadcasting Decision CRTC 2011-56: CKLN-FM Toronto—Revocation of Licence." Decisions, January 28, 2011. https://crtc.gc.ca/eng/archive/2011/2011-56.htm.

————. "Broadcasting Decision CRTC 2013-385: AMI-TV—Licence Renewal and Amendment." Decisions, August 8, 2013. https://crtc.gc.ca/eng/archive/2013/2013-385.htm.

————. "Broadcasting Order CRTC 2009-452: Reference to the Federal Court of Appeal—Applicability of the Broadcasting Act to Internet Service Providers." Orders, July 28, 2009. https://crtc.gc.ca/eng/archive/2009/2009-452.htm.

————. "Broadcasting Order CRTC 2009-660: Amendments to the Exemption Order for New Media Broadcasting Undertakings (Appendix A to Public Notice CRTC 1999-197); Revocation of the Exemption Order for Mobile Television

Broadcasting Undertakings." Orders, October 22, 2009. https://crtc.gc.ca/eng/archive/2009/2009-660.htm.

———. "Broadcasting Order CRTC 2012-409: Amendments to the Exemption Order for New Media Broadcasting Undertakings (Now Known as the Exemption Order for Digital Media Broadcasting Undertakings)." July 26, 2012. https://crtc.gc.ca/eng/archive/2012/2012-409.htm.

———. "Broadcasting Procedural Letter Addressed to Corie Wright (Netflix)." February 2, 2018. https://crtc.gc.ca/eng/archive/2018/1b180202m.htm.

———. "Broadcasting Public Notice CRTC 2006-158: Commercial Radio Policy 2006." Regulatory Policies, December 15, 2006. https://crtc.gc.ca/eng/archive/2006/pb2006-158.htm.

———. "Broadcasting Public Notice CRTC 2008-4: Regulatory Policy—Diversity of Voices." Regulatory Policies, January 15, 2008. https://crtc.gc.ca/eng/archive/2008/pb2008-4.htm.

———. "Broadcasting Regulatory Policy CRTC 2009-329: Review of Broadcasting in New Media." Regulatory Policies, June 4, 2009. https://crtc.gc.ca/eng/archive/2009/2009-329.htm.

———. "Broadcasting Regulatory Policy CRTC 2009-329: Review of Broadcasting in New Media. Concurring Opinion of Timothy Denton." Regulatory Policies, June 4, 2009. https://crtc.gc.ca/eng/archive/2009/2009-329.htm.

———. "Broadcasting Regulatory Policy CRTC 2010-167: A Group-Based Approach to the Licensing of Private Television Services." Regulatory Policies, March 22, 2010. https://crtc.gc.ca/eng/archive/2010/2010-167.htm.

———. "Broadcasting Regulatory Policy CRTC 2010-499: Campus and Community Radio Policy." https://crtc.gc.ca/eng/archive/2010/2010-499.htm.

———. "Broadcasting Regulatory Policy CRTC 2010-582: Reporting Requirements for New Media Broadcasting Undertakings." Regulatory Policies, August 13, 2010. https://crtc.gc.ca/eng/archive/2010/2010-582.htm.

———. "Broadcasting Regulatory Policy CRTC 2015-24: Over-the-Air Transmission of Television Signals and Local Programming." Regulatory Policies, January 29, 2015. https://crtc.gc.ca/eng/archive/2015/2015-24.htm.

———. "Broadcasting Regulatory Policy CRTC 2015-25: Measures to Address Issues Related to Simultaneous Substitution." Regulatory Policies, January 29, 2015. https://crtc.gc.ca/eng/archive/2015/2015-25.htm.

———. "Broadcasting Regulatory Policy CRTC 2015-86: Let's Talk TV—The Way Forward—Creating Compelling and Diverse Canadian Programming." Regulatory Policies, March 12, 2015. https://crtc.gc.ca/eng/archive/2015/2015-86.htm.

————. "Broadcasting Regulatory Policy CRTC 2016-334 and Broadcasting Order CRTC 2016-335: Simultaneous Substitution for the Super Bowl." Regulatory Policies, Orders, August 19, 2016. https://crtc.gc.ca/eng/archive/2016/2016-334.htm.

————. "Canadian Broadcasting 'a Single System': Policy Statement on Canadian Television." Ottawa: Bell Canada, 1971.

————. "Canadian Content Requirements for Canadian Music on Radio Stations." Accessed November 1, 2018. https://crtc.gc.ca/eng/cancon/r_cdn.htm.

————. "Co-Development of the Indigenous Broadcasting Policy." June 20, 2019. https://crtc.gc.ca/eng/comm/ppl/index.htm.

————. "CRTC Origins: History and Chronology." December 20, 2013. http://web.archive.org/web/20131220213318/http://www.crtc.gc.ca/eng/backgrnd/brochures/b19903.htm.

————. "CRTC, Telecom Decision CRTC 97-9: Price Cap Regulation and Related Issues." Decisions, May 1, 1997. https://crtc.gc.ca/eng/archive/1997/DT97-9.htm.

————. "Decision CRTC 99-42, Summary Television Northern Canada Incorporated." Decisions, September 20, 2007. https://crtc.gc.ca/eng/archive/1999/DB99-42.htm.

————. "Ethnic Broadcasting Policy." Regulatory Policies, July 16, 1999. https://crtc.gc.ca/eng/archive/1999/pb99-117.htm.

————. "Introduction to Broadcasting Decisions CRTC 2005-246 to 2005-248: Licensing of New Satellite and Terrestrial Subscription Radio Undertakings." Decisions, September 20, 2007. https://crtc.gc.ca/eng/archive/2005/pb2005-61.htm.

————. "Public Notice CRTC 1990-89, Native Broadcasting Policy." Notices of Consultation, September 20, 1990. https://crtc.gc.ca/eng/archive/1990/PB90-89.htm.

————. "Public Notice CRTC 1998-62: Exemption Order Respecting Certain Native Radio Undertakings." July 9, 1998. https://crtc.gc.ca/eng/archive/1998/pb98-62.htm.

————. "Public Notice CRTC 1999-70: Order Respecting the Distribution of the Aboriginal Peoples Television Network." Orders, April 21, 1999. https://crtc.gc.ca/eng/archive/1999/PB99-70.htm.

————. "Public Notice CRTC 1999-84: New Media." Regulatory Policies, May 17, 1999. https://crtc.gc.ca/eng/archive/1999/PB99-84.htm.

————. "Public Notice CRTC 1999-197: Exemption Order for New Media Broadcasting Undertakings." Orders, December 17, 1999. https://crtc.gc.ca/eng/archive/1999/PB99-197.htm.

————. "Public Notice CRTC 2000-42: Certification for Canadian Programs—A Revised Approach." Regulatory Policies, March 17, 2000. https://crtc.gc.ca/eng/archive/2000/pb2000-42.htm.

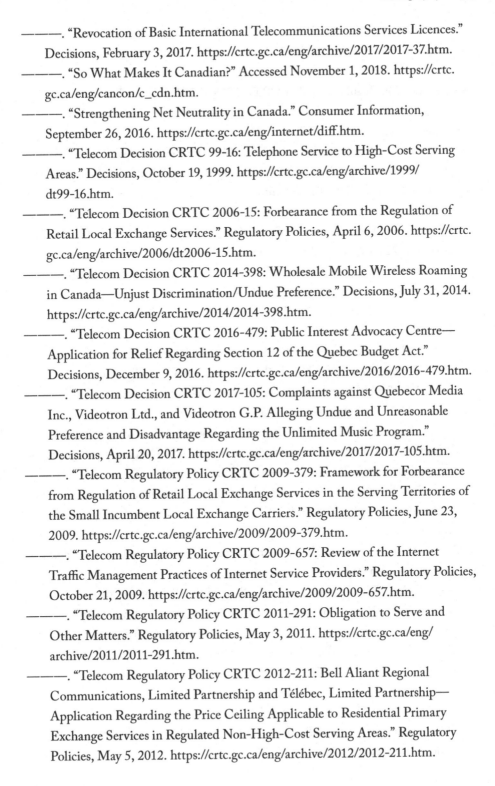

———. "Revocation of Basic International Telecommunications Services Licences." Decisions, February 3, 2017. https://crtc.gc.ca/eng/archive/2017/2017-37.htm.

———. "So What Makes It Canadian?" Accessed November 1, 2018. https://crtc.gc.ca/eng/cancon/c_cdn.htm.

———. "Strengthening Net Neutrality in Canada." Consumer Information, September 26, 2016. https://crtc.gc.ca/eng/internet/diff.htm.

———. "Telecom Decision CRTC 99-16: Telephone Service to High-Cost Serving Areas." Decisions, October 19, 1999. https://crtc.gc.ca/eng/archive/1999/dt99-16.htm.

———. "Telecom Decision CRTC 2006-15: Forbearance from the Regulation of Retail Local Exchange Services." Regulatory Policies, April 6, 2006. https://crtc.gc.ca/eng/archive/2006/dt2006-15.htm.

———. "Telecom Decision CRTC 2014-398: Wholesale Mobile Wireless Roaming in Canada—Unjust Discrimination/Undue Preference." Decisions, July 31, 2014. https://crtc.gc.ca/eng/archive/2014/2014-398.htm.

———. "Telecom Decision CRTC 2016-479: Public Interest Advocacy Centre—Application for Relief Regarding Section 12 of the Quebec Budget Act." Decisions, December 9, 2016. https://crtc.gc.ca/eng/archive/2016/2016-479.htm.

———. "Telecom Decision CRTC 2017-105: Complaints against Quebecor Media Inc., Videotron Ltd., and Videotron G.P. Alleging Undue and Unreasonable Preference and Disadvantage Regarding the Unlimited Music Program." Decisions, April 20, 2017. https://crtc.gc.ca/eng/archive/2017/2017-105.htm.

———. "Telecom Regulatory Policy CRTC 2009-379: Framework for Forbearance from Regulation of Retail Local Exchange Services in the Serving Territories of the Small Incumbent Local Exchange Carriers." Regulatory Policies, June 23, 2009. https://crtc.gc.ca/eng/archive/2009/2009-379.htm.

———. "Telecom Regulatory Policy CRTC 2009-657: Review of the Internet Traffic Management Practices of Internet Service Providers." Regulatory Policies, October 21, 2009. https://crtc.gc.ca/eng/archive/2009/2009-657.htm.

———. "Telecom Regulatory Policy CRTC 2011-291: Obligation to Serve and Other Matters." Regulatory Policies, May 3, 2011. https://crtc.gc.ca/eng/archive/2011/2011-291.htm.

———. "Telecom Regulatory Policy CRTC 2012-211: Bell Aliant Regional Communications, Limited Partnership and Télébec, Limited Partnership—Application Regarding the Price Ceiling Applicable to Residential Primary Exchange Services in Regulated Non-High-Cost Serving Areas." Regulatory Policies, May 5, 2012. https://crtc.gc.ca/eng/archive/2012/2012-211.htm.

———. "Telecom Regulatory Policy CRTC 2013-271: The Wireless Code." Regulatory Policies, June 3, 2013. https://crtc.gc.ca/eng/archive/2013/2013-271.htm.

———. "Telecom Regulatory Policy CRTC 2015-177: Regulatory Framework for Wholesale Mobile Wireless Services." Regulatory Policies, May 5, 2015. https://crtc.gc.ca/eng/archive/2015/2015-177.htm.

———. "Telecom Regulatory Policy CRTC 2015-326: Review of Wholesale Wireline Services and Associated Policies." Regulatory Policies, July 22, 2015. https://crtc.gc.ca/eng/archive/2015/2015-326.htm.

———. "Telecom Regulatory Policy CRTC 2016-496: Modern Telecommunications Services—The Path Forward for Canada's Digital Economy." Regulatory Policies, December 21, 2016. https://crtc.gc.ca/eng/archive/2016/2016-496.htm.

———. "The Wireless Code, Simplified." Consumer Information, June 3, 2013. https://crtc.gc.ca/eng/phone/mobile/codesimpl.htm.

CanLII. "About CanLII." Accessed February 17, 2019. https://www.canlii.org/en/info/about.html.

Carmichael, Harold. "Out-of-Town Crown Dropped Charges vs Sudbury Man." *Sudbury Star*, December 30, 2015. https://www.thesudburystar.com/2015/12/31/out-of-town-crown-dropped-charges-vs-sudbury-man/wcm/9b90e126-4220-e0da-9e3e-afb5e4a414db.

Cavoukian, Ann. "A Primer on Metadata: Separating Fact from Fiction." Toronto: Information and Privacy Commissioner of Ontario, 2013. https://www.ipc.on.ca/wp-content/uploads/Resources/metadata.pdf.

———. "The 7 Foundational Principles." Toronto: Information and Privacy Commissioner of Ontario, 2011. https://www.ipc.on.ca/wp-content/uploads/Resources/7foundationalprinciples.pdf.

CBC. "Our History." Accessed November 1, 2018. http://www.cbc.radio-canada.ca/en/explore/our-history/.

———. "Trudeau: 'There's No Place for the State in the Bedrooms of the Nation.'" CBC Digital Archives, n.d. https://www.cbc.ca/archives/entry/omnibus-bill-theres-no-place-for-the-state-in-the-bedrooms-of-the-nation.

*CBC News*. "Black People 3 Times More Likely to Be Street Checked in Halifax, Police Say." January 9, 2017. https://www.cbc.ca/news/canada/nova-scotia/halifax-black-street-checks-police-race-profiling-1.3925251.

Ceyhan, Ayse. "Surveillance as Biopower." In *Routledge Handbook of Surveillance Studies*, edited by Kirstie Ball, Kevin Haggarty, and David Lyon, 2nd ed., 38–45. London: Routledge, 2012.

Chakrabarti, Samidh. "Hard Questions: What Effect Does Social Media Have on Democracy?" *Facebook Newsroom* (blog), January 22, 2018. https://newsroom. fb.com/news/2018/01/effect-social-media-democracy/.

Chakravartty, Paula. "Telecom, National Development and the Indian State: A Postcolonial Critique." *Media, Culture & Society* 26, no. 2 (2004): 227–49.

———. "Who Speaks for the Governed? World Summit on Information Society, Civil Society and the Limits of 'Multistakeholderism.'" *Economic and Political Weekly*, 2006: 250–57.

Chakravartty, Paula, and Katharine Sarikakis. *Media Policy and Globalization.* Edinburgh: Edinburgh University Press, 2006. http://dx.doi. org/10.1007/978-1-137-09876-4.

Chang, Ha-Joon. *Kicking Away the Ladder: Development Strategy in Historical Perspective.* London: Anthem Press, 2002.

Charland, Maurice. "Technological Nationalism." *CTheory* 10, no. 1–2 (1986): 196–220.

Chenou, Jean-Marie. "From Cyber-Libertarianism to Neoliberalism: Internet Exceptionalism, Multi-Stakeholderism, and the Institutionalisation of Internet Governance in the 1990s." *Globalizations* 11, no. 2 (March 4, 2014): 205–23. https://doi.org/10.1080/14747731.2014.887387.

———. "Is Internet Governance a Democratic Process? Multistakeholderism and Transnational Elites." In *ECPR General Conference*, 25–27, 2011.

*The Chicago Manual of Style Online.* 17th ed. Chicago: University of Chicago, 2017.

Chipty, Tasneem. "Vertical Integration, Market Foreclosure, and Consumer Welfare in the Cable Television Industry." *American Economic Review* 91, no. 3 (2001): 428–53.

Chon, Margaret. "Intellectual Property and the Development Divide." *Cardozo Law Review* 27, no. 6 (2005): 2821–912.

Chu, Rong-Xuan, and Chih-Tung Huang. "Indigenous Peoples in Public Media: A Critical Discourse Analysis of the Human Zoo Case." *Discourse & Society* 30, no. 4 (2019): 395–411.

Citron, Danielle Keats, and Helen Norton. "Intermediaries and Hate Speech: Fostering Digital Citizenship for Our Information Age." *Boston University Law Review* 91 (2011): 1435–84.

"Cleanfeed Canada." Accessed October 30, 2018. https://cybertip.ca/app/en/ projects-cleanfeed.

Clement, Andrew. "Limits to Secrecy: What Are the Communications Security Establishment's (CSE) Capabilities for Intercepting Canadians' Internet Communications?" In *National Security Intelligence and Surveillance in a Big Data*

*Age*, edited by David Lyon and David Murakami Wood. Vancouver: UBC Press, forthcoming.

Coldewey, Devin. "Bannon and Cambridge Analytica Planned Suppression of Black Voters, Whistleblower Tells Senate." *TechCrunch* (blog), May 16, 2018. https://techcrunch.com/2018/05/16/bannon-and-cambridge-analytica-planned-suppression-of-black-voters-whistleblower-tells-senate/.

Collins, Patricia Hill, and Sirma Bilge. *Intersectionality.* Hoboken, NJ: John Wiley & Sons, 2016.

Committee to Protect Journalists. "Critics Are Not Criminals: Comparative Study of Criminal Defamation Laws in the Americas." 2016. https://cpj.org/reports/2016/03/critics-are-not-criminals.php.

Connolly, William E. *Pluralism.* Durham, NC: Duke University Press, 2005.

"Consolidated Federal Laws of Canada, Television Broadcasting Regulations, 1987, SOR/87-49." September 1, 2009. https://laws-lois.justice.gc.ca/eng/regulations/SOR%2D87%2D49/20090901/P1TT3xt3.html.

Coombe, Rosemary J., and Andrew Herman. "Rhetorical Virtues: Property, Speech, and the Commons on the World-Wide Web." *Anthropological Quarterly* 77, no. 3 (2004): 559–74.

Copeland, Stacey. "Broadcasting Queer Feminisms: Lesbian and Queer Women Programming in Transnational, Local, and Community Radio." *Journal of Radio & Audio Media* 25, no. 2 (2018): 209–23.

Cossman, Brenda. "Censor, Resist, Repeat: A History of Censorship of Gay and Lesbian Sexual Representation in Canada." *Duke Journal of Gender Law & Policy* 21 (Fall 2014): 45–66.

———. *Censorship and the Arts: Law, Controversy, Debate, Facts.* Toronto: Ontario Association of Art Galleries, 1995.

———. "Gender Identity, Gender Pronouns, and Freedom of Expression: Bill C-16 and the Traction of Specious Legal Claims." *University of Toronto Law Journal* 68, no. 1 (2018): 37–79.

Cossman, Brenda, Shannon Bell, Lise Gotell, and Becki Ross. *Bad Attitude/s on Trial: Pornography, Feminism, and the Butler Decision.* Toronto: University of Toronto Press, 1997.

Coughlan, Stephen Gerard, Catherine Cotter, and John A. Yogis. *Canadian Law Dictionary.* 7th ed. Hauppauge, NY: Barrons Educational Series, 2013.

Craig, Carys J. "Reconstructing the Author-Self: Some Feminist Lessons for Copyright Law." *Journal of Gender, Social Policy and the Law* 15, no. 2 (2007): 207–68.

Craig, Suzanne. "Municipal Access to Information, Delays, and Denials: An Insider's View." In *The Unfulfilled Promise of Press Freedom in Canada*, edited by Lisa Taylor and Cara-Marie O'Hagan. Toronto: University of Toronto Press, 2017.

Cram, Ian. "Hate Speech and Disabled People: Some Comparative Constitutional Thoughts." *Disability Rights in Europe: From Theory to Practice* (2005): 65–86.

Crawford, Gregory S., Robin S. Lee, Michael D. Whinston, and Ali Yurukoglu. "The Welfare Effects of Vertical Integration in Multichannel Television Markets." *Econometrica* 86, no. 3 (2018): 891–954. https://doi.org/10.3982/ECTA14031.

Crenshaw, Kimberlé. "Mapping the Margins: Identity Politics, Intersectionality, and Violence against Women." *Stanford Law Review* 43, no. 6 (1991): 1241–99.

Crow, Barbara, and Graham Longford. "Digital Restructuring: Gender, Class and Citizenship in the Information Society in Canada." *Citizenship Studies* 4, no. 2 (2000): 207–30.

Crow, Barbara, and Kim Sawchuk. "The Spectral Politics of Mobile Communication Technologies: Gender, Infrastructure and International Policy." *Feminist Interventions in International Communication: Minding the Gap*, edited by Katharine Sarikakis and Leslie Regan Shade, 90–106. Toronto: Rowman & Littlefield, 2008.

CTV News Staff. "Critics Blast Oda's Swanky Hotel Stay, $16 Orange Juice." April 23, 2012. https://www.ctvnews.ca/critics-blast-oda-s-swanky-hotel-stay-16-orange-juice-1.799961.

Cukier, Wendy, Samantha Jackson, Mohamed A. Elmi, Erin Roach, and Darren Cyr. "Representing Women? Leadership Roles and Women in Canadian Broadcast News." *Gender in Management: An International Journal* 31, no. 5/6 (2016): 374–95.

Culhane, Dara. *The Pleasure of the Crown: Anthropology, Law, and First Nations*. Victoria, BC: Talonbooks, 2014.

Currie, Tim. "Process Journalism and Responsible Communication." In *The Unfulfilled Promise of Press Freedom in Canada*, edited by Lisa Taylor and Cara-Marie O'Hagan, 66–83. Toronto: University of Toronto Press, 2017.

Dafnos, Tia. "Beyond the Blue Line: Researching the Policing of Aboriginal Activism Using Access to Information." In *Brokering Access: Power, Politics, and Freedom of Information*, edited by Mike Larsen and Kevin Walby, 209–33. Vancouver: UBC Press, 2012.

———. "The Quest for Electronic Data: Where Alice Meets Monty Python Meets Colonel Jessop." In *Brokering Access: Power, Politics, and Freedom of Information*, edited by Mike Larsen and Kevin Walby, 335–57. Vancouver: UBC Press, 2012.

Dahl, Robert A. *Who Governs?: Democracy and Power in an American City*. New Haven, CT: Yale University Press, 2005.

Dakroury, Aliaa, and Julia Hoffmann. "Communication as a Human Right: A Blind Spot in Communication Research?" *International Communication Gazette* 72, no. 4–5 (2010): 315–22.

Darch, Colin, and Peter G. Underwood. *Freedom of Information in the Developing World: The Citizen, the State and Models of Openness*. Oxford: Chandos, 2010.

Davies, Margaret. "Queer Property, Queer Persons: Self-Ownership and Beyond." *Social & Legal Studies* 8, no. 3 (September 1999): 327–52. https://doi.org/10.1177/096466399900800303.

Davis, Lennard J. "Introduction: Normality, Power, and Culture." In *The Disability Studies Reader*, 4th ed., 1–14. New York: Routledge, 2016.

Dean, Mitchell M. *Governmentality: Power and Rule in Modern Society*. London: SAGE, 1999.

"Decisions." *Columbia Law Review* XL, no. 7 (1940): 1241–87.

Deibert, Ron. "The Geopolitics of Cyberspace after Snowden." *Current History* 114, no. 768 (2015): 9.

Delgado, Richard. "Campus Antiracism Rules: Constitutional Narratives in Collision." *Northwestern University Law Review* 85 (1990): 343–87.

———. "Words That Wound: A Tort Action for Racial Insults, Epithets, and Name-Calling." *Harvard Civil Liberties Law Review* 17 (1982): 133–81.

Delgado, Richard, and Jean Stefancic. "Hate Speech in Cyberspace." *Wake Forest Law Review* 49 (2014): 319.

———. "Images of the Outsider in American Law and Culture: Can Free Expression Remedy Systemic Social Ills." *Cornell Law Review* 77 (1991): 1258–97.

Demaske, Chris. "Modern Power and the First Amendment: Reassessing Hate Speech." *Communication Law and Policy* 9, no. 3 (2004): 273–316.

DeNardis, Laura. *The Global War for Internet Governance*. New Haven, CT: Yale University Press, 2015.

DeNardis, Laura, and A.M. Hackl. "Internet Governance by Social Media Platforms." *Telecommunications Policy* 39, no. 9 (October 2015): 761–70.

Dent, Chris. "Copyright, Governmentality and Problematisation: An Exploration." *Griffith Law Review* 18, no. 1 (January 2009): 129–50. https://doi.org/10.1080/10383441.2009.10854633.

Department of Justice. "Civil and Criminal Cases." October 16, 2017. https://www.justice.gc.ca/eng/csj-sjc/just/08.html.

Devlin, Richard F., and Dianne Pothier. "Introduction: Toward a Critical Theory of Dis-Citizenship." In *Critical Disability Theory: Essays in Philosophy, Politics, Policy, and Law*, edited by Richard F. Devlin and Dianne Pothier. Vancouver: UBC Press, 2006.

Dewey, John, and Melvin L. Rogers. *The Public and Its Problems: An Essay in Political Inquiry*. University Park, PA: Penn State Press, 2012.

Doria, Avri. "Internet Governance and Gender Issues." In *Critically Absent: Women's Rights in Internet Governance*, 10–15. Melville, South Africa: Association for Progressive Communication, 2012.

Douglas, Kristen. "Access to Information Legislation in Canada and Four Other Countries." Ottawa: Library of Parliament, April 6, 2006. http://www.publications.gc.ca/site/eng/294638/publication.html.

Dragiewicz, Molly, Delanie Woodlock, Bridget Harris, and Claire Reid. "Technology-Facilitated Coercive Control." In *The Routledge International Handbook of Violence Studies*, 266–75. New York: Routledge, 2018.

Drahos, Peter. *Intellectual Property, Indigenous People and Their Knowledge*. Cambridge: Cambridge University Press, 2014.

———. "Six Minutes to Midnight: Can Intellectual Property Save the World?" In *Emerging Challenges in Intellectual Property*, edited Kathy Bowrey, Michael Handler, and Dianne Nicol. Oxford: Oxford University Press, 2011.

Drahos, Peter, and John Braithwaite. *Information Feudalism: Who Owns the Knowledge Economy?* New York: Routledge, 2017.

Dubrofsky, Rachel E., and Shoshana Magnet, eds. *Feminist Surveillance Studies*. Durham, NC: Duke University Press, 2015.

Duclos, Nitya. "Disappearing Women: Racial Minority Women in Human Rights Cases." *Canadian Journal of Women and the Law* 6, no. 1 (1993): 25–51.

Duff, Andrew. "Defamation of Blogger Was 'Fair Comment,' Judge Rules." Canadian Justice Review Board, March 4, 2015. https://www.canadianjusticereviewboard.ca/articles-caselaw/articles/defamation-of-blogger-was-%e2%80%98fair-comment,%e2%80%99-judge-rules.

Dye, Thomas R. *Understanding Public Policy*. 5th ed. Englewood Cliffs, NJ: Prentice-Hall, 1992.

Edwards, Lilian. "From Child Porn to China, in One Cleanfeed." SSRN Scholarly Paper. Rochester, NY: Social Science Research Network, May 3, 2008. https://papers.ssrn.com/abstract=1128062.

Eko, Lyombe. "Globalization and the Diffusion of Media Policy in Africa: The Case of Defamation of Public Officials." *Africa Policy Journal* 12 (2017/2016): 17–44.

Ellcessor, Elizabeth. "Bridging Disability Divides: A Critical History of Web Content Accessibility through 2001." *Information, Communication & Society* 13, no. 3 (2010): 289–308.

Ellis, Katie, and Mike Kent. *Disability and New Media*. New York: Routledge, 2011.

Eng, David L. *The Feeling of Kinship: Queer Liberalism and the Racialization of Intimacy.* Durham, NC: Duke University Press, 2010.

Escobar, Arturo. *Encountering Development: The Making and Unmaking of the Third World.* Princeton, NJ: Princeton University Press, 2011.

Eubanks, Virginia. *Automating Inequality: How High-Tech Tools Profile, Police, and Punish the Poor.* New York, NY: St. Martin's Press, 2018.

———. *Digital Dead End: Fighting for Social Justice in the Information Age.* Cambridge, MA: MIT Press, 2011.

———. "Want to Predict the Future of Surveillance? Ask Poor Communities." *The American Prospect*, January 15, 2014. https://prospect.org/article/ want-predict-future-surveillance-ask-poor-communities.

Ewart, Jacqui. "The Scabsuckers: Regional Journalists' Representation of Indigenous Australians." *Asia Pacific Media Educator* 1, no. 3 (1997): 108–17.

Fairchild, Charles. "Below the Hamelin Line: CKRZ and Aboriginal Cultural Survival." *Canadian Journal of Communication* 23, no. 2 (1998).

Fauteux, Brian. *Music in Range: The Culture of Canadian Campus Radio.* Wilfrid Laurier University Press, 2015.

Feasby, Jonathon T. "Who Was That Masked Man? Online Defamation, Freedom of Expression, and the Right to Speak Anonymously." *Canadian Journal of Law and Technology* 1, no. 1 (2002).

Felesky, Leigh. "Exploring How Emerging Digital Business Models and Journalistic Innovation May Influence Freedom of the Press." In *The Unfulfilled Promise of Press Freedom in Canada*, edited by Lisa Taylor and Cara-Marie O'Hagan, 31–46. Toronto: University of Toronto Press, 2017.

Ferguson, Kathy E. *The Feminist Case against Bureaucracy.* Philadelphia: Temple University Press, 1984.

Finnis, John. *Natural Law and Natural Rights.* Oxford: Oxford University Press, 1980.

Fitzgerald, Oonagh, and Risa Schwartz, eds. *UNDRIP Implementation: Braiding International, Domestic and Indigenous Laws.* Waterloo, ON: Centre for International Governance Innovation, 2017.

Flagg, Barbara J. *Was Blind, but Now I See: White Race Consciousness & the Law.* New York: NYU Press, 1998.

Flew, Terry. "Six Theories of Neoliberalism." *Thesis Eleven* 122, no. 1 (2014): 49–71.

Forcese, Craig, and Kent Roach. "Delete: Criminalizing and Censoring Extremist Speech." In *False Security: The Radicalization of Canadian Anti-Terrorism.* Toronto: Irwin Law, 2015.

———. *False Security: The Radicalization of Canadian Anti-Terrorism.* Toronto: Irwin Law, 2015.

Foucault, Michel. *Discipline and Punish: The Birth of the Prison*. New York: Vintage Books, 1995.

———. *Power/Knowledge: Selected Interviews and Other Writings, 1972–1977*. Edited by Colin Gordon. New York: Pantheon Books, 1980.

———. "What Is an Author?" *Screen* 20, no. 1 (March 1, 1979): 13–34. https://doi.org/10.1093/screen/20.1.13.

Fraser, Nancy. "Rethinking the Public Sphere: A Contribution to the Critique of Actually Existing Democracy." *Social Text*, no. 25/26 (1990): 56–80.

———. "Rethinking the Public Sphere: A Contribution to the Critique of Actually Existing Democracy." In *Habermas and the Public Sphere*, edited by Craig J. Calhoun, 109–42. Cambridge, MA: MIT Press, 1992.

Fraser, Nancy, and Axel Honneth. *Redistribution or Recognition? A Political-Philosophical Exchange*. London: Verso, 2003.

Fraticelli, Rina. "Women on Screen." *Women in View*, October 2015.

Friedland, Hadley. "Reflective Frameworks: Methods for Accessing, Understanding and Applying Indigenous Laws." *Indigenous Law Journal* 11, no. 1 (2012): 1–40.

Froc, Kerri A. "Multidimensionality and the Matrix: Identifying Charter Violations in Cases of Complex Subordination." *Canadian Journal of Law & Society* 25, no. 1 (2010): 21–49.

Fuchs, Christian. "A Contribution to the Critique of the Political Economy of Google." *Fast Capitalism* 8, no. 1 (2011): 1–24.

———. "Dallas Smythe Today—The Audience Commodity, the Digital Labour Debate, Marxist Political Economy and Critical Theory." *TripleC: Communication, Capitalism & Critique* 10, no. 2 (2012): 692–740.

———. *Foundations of Critical Media and Information Studies*. New York: Routledge, 2011.

———. "Wikinomics: How Mass Collaboration Changes Everything—by Don Tapscott & Anthony D. Williams." *Journal of Communication* 58, no. 2 (2008): 402–3.

Fullenwieder, Lara, and Adam Molnar. "Settler Governance and Privacy: Canada's Indian Residential School Settlement Agreement and the Mediation of State-Based Violence." *International Journal of Communication* 12 (2018): 1332–49.

Fung, Brian. "Verizon Denies Using Net Neutrality Victory to Sabotage Netflix, Amazon." *Washington Post*, February 5, 2014. https://www.washingtonpost.com/news/the-switch/wp/2014/02/05/verizon-denies-using-net-neutrality-victory-to-sabotage-netflix-amazon/.

Gall, Gerald L. *The Canadian Legal System*. 5th ed. Toronto: Thomson/Carswell, 2008.

Gandy, Oscar. "Inequality: You Don't Even Notice after a While." In *Telecommunications and Equity: Policy Research Issues Proceedings of the Thirteenth*

*Annual Telecommunications Policy Research Conference, Airlie House, Airlie, Virginia, USA, April 21–24, 1985*, edited by James Miller, 9–20. Amsterdam: North-Holland, 1986.

Gangadharan, Seeta Peña. "The Downside of Digital Inclusion: Expectations and Experiences of Privacy and Surveillance among Marginal Internet Users." *New Media & Society* 19, no. 4 (2017): 597–615.

Gasher, Mike. "Invoking Public Support for Public Broadcasting: The Aird Commission Revisited." *Canadian Journal of Communication* 23, no. 2 (1998).

Geist, Michael, ed. *Law, Privacy, and Surveillance in Canada in the Post-Snowden Era.* Ottawa: University of Ottawa Press, 2015.

———. "Project Cleanfeed Canada." November 24, 2006. http://www.michaelgeist.ca/2006/11/project-cleanfeed-canada/.

Ghanea, Nazila. "Intersectionality and the Spectrum of Racist Hate Speech: Proposals to the UN Committee on the Elimination of Racial Discrimination." *Human Rights Quarterly* 35, no. 4 (2013): 935–54.

Giannone, Diego. "The Political and Ideological Dimension of the Measurement of Freedom of Information. Assessing the Interplay between Neoliberalism and the Freedom of the Press Index." *International Communication Gazette* 76, no. 6 (October 2014): 505–27. https://doi.org/10.1177/1748048514538927.

Gill, Juliet, and Sallie Hughes. "Bureaucratic Compliance with Mexico's New Access to Information Law." *Critical Studies in Media Communication* 22, no. 2 (2005): 121–37.

Gill, Rosalind, and Shani Orgad. "The Shifting Terrain of Sex and Power: From the 'Sexualization of Culture' to #MeToo." *Sexualities* 21, no. 8 (December 2018): 1313–24. https://doi.org/10.1177/1363460718794647.

Gillis, Wendy, and Kate Allen. "Police Admit Using Cellphone Snooper; Toronto Cops Originally Denied Using Controversial 'Stingray' Device That Captures Other Calls near Target." *Toronto Star*, March 5, 2018.

Gingras, Anne-Marie. "Freedom of Expression and Shock Radio: Quebec CHOI-FM as a Case Study." *World Political Science* 4, no. 3 (2008): 2363–4782.

Girard, Daniel. "CRTC Drops NFL Content Case against Bell Canada." *Toronto Star*, March 1, 2012. https://www.thestar.com/sports/2012/03/01/crtc_drops_nfl_content_case_against_bell_canada.html.

Globe Staff. "Trans Mountain, Trudeau and First Nations: A Guide to the Political Saga so Far." *The Globe and Mail*, April 18, 2018. https://www.theglobeandmail.com/politics/article-trans-mountain-kinder-morgan-pipeline-bc-alberta-explainer/.

Goggin, Gerard. "Communication Rights and Disability Online: Policy and Technology after the World Summit on the Information Society." *Information, Communication & Society* 18, no. 3 (2015): 327–41.

Goggin, Gerard, and Christopher Newell. *Digital Disability: The Social Construction of Disability in New Media*. Lanham, MD: Rowman & Littlefield, 2003.

Goldfarb, Sally F. "Violence against Women and the Persistence of Privacy." *Ohio State Law Journal* 61, no. 1 (2000): 1–87.

Golumbia, David. "Talk: 'Cyberlibertarianism: The Extremist Foundations of 'Digital Freedom.'" Accessed November 3, 2018. http://www.uncomputing.org/?p=276.

Goodon, Roxanne. "An Update on Disparaging Marks." Intellectual Property Institute of Canada, February 8, 2018. https://ipic.ca/english/blog/an-update-on-disparaging-marks-2018-02-08.htm.

Google. "EU Privacy Removal." Accessed October 31, 2018. https://www.google.com/webmasters/tools/legal-removal-request?complaint_type=rtbf&visit_id=636765972026970240-3559955740&rd=1.

"*Google v. Equustek*." Electronic Frontier Foundation, October 24, 2016. https://www.eff.org/cases/google-v-equustek.

Government of Canada. "Access to Information and Privacy (ATIP) Online Request." April 9, 2013. https://atip-aiprp.apps.gc.ca/atip/welcome.do.

Grant, Peter S. *Communications Law and the Courts in Canada 2014: An Annotated Guide to Judicial Decisions Relating to the Regulation of Communications and Copyright in Canada*. 2nd ed. Toronto: McCarthy Tetrault, 2014.

Gratton, Eloïse, and Jules Polonetsky. "Submission: Privacy above All Other Fundamental Rights? Challenges with the Implementation of a Right to Be Forgotten in Canada—August 2016." https://fpf.org/wp-content/uploads/2016/04/PolonetskyGratton_RTBFpaper_FINAL.pdf.

Green, Leslie. "Legal Positivism." Accessed October 2, 2018. https://plato.stanford.edu/archives/fall2009/entries/legal-positivism/.

Green, Lezlie L. "Gender Hate Propaganda and Sexual Violence in the Rwandan Genocide: An Argument for Intersectionality in International Law." *Columbia Human Rights Law Review* 33 (2001): 733–76.

Greene, Ian. *The Charter of Rights and Freedoms: 30+ Years of Decisions That Shape Canadian Life*. Toronto: James Lorimer & Company, 2014.

Greenleaf, Graham, Andrew Mowbray, and Philip Chung. "The Meaning of 'Free Access to Legal Information': A Twenty Year Evolution." *Journal of Open Access to Law* 1, no. 1 (December 18, 2013). https://ojs.law.cornell.edu/index.php/joal/article/view/11.

Greenwald, Glenn. *Transcript of "Why Privacy Matters."* 2014. https://www.ted.com/talks/glenn_greenwald_why_privacy_matters/transcript.

Greer, Edward. "Antonio Gramsci and Legal Hegemony." In *The Politics of Law: A Progressive Critique*, edited by David Kairys, 304–8. New York: Pantheon Books, 1982.

Gregg, Allan. "What Canadians Think of the News Media." *Policy Options*, February 10, 2017. http://policyoptions.irpp.org/magazines/february-2017/what-canadians-think-of-the-news-media/.

Grewal, San. "Fennell's Travel Expenses Sky High; Brampton Mayor Rings up More than $185,000 over Five Years on First-Class Airline Tickets and Luxury Hotels, Documents Reveal." *Toronto Star*, January 7, 2014.

Ha, Tu Thanh. "Holocaust Denier and Former Alberta Teacher Jim Keegstra Dead at 80." *The Globe and Mail*, June 13, 2014. https://www.theglobeandmail.com/news/national/holocaust-denier-and-former-alberta-teacher-jim-keegstra-dead-at-the-age-of-80/article19155171/.

Habermas, Jürgen. *The Structural Transformation of the Public Sphere: An Inquiry into a Category of Bourgeois Society.* Cambridge, MA: MIT Press, 1989.

Hackett, Bob. "Taking Back the Media: Notes on the Potential for a Communicative Democracy Movement." *Studies in Political Economy* 63 (Autumn 2000): 61–86.

Hackett, Bob, and Richard Gruneau. "Is Canada's Press Censored?" In *The Missing News: Filters and Blind Spots in Canada's Media*, 22–51. Ottawa: Canadian Centre for Policy Alternatives, 2000.

Hacking, Ian. *The Taming of Chance.* Cambridge: Cambridge University Press, 1990.

Halbert, Debora. "Feminist Interpretations of Intellectual Property." *Journal of Gender, Social Policy and the Law* 14, no. 3 (2006): 431–60.

Hamelink, Cees, and Julia Hoffmann. "The State of the Right to Communicate." *Global Media Journal* 7, no. 13 (2008): 1–16.

Hamilton, Sheryl. *Law's Expression: Communication, Law and Media in Canada.* Toronto: LexisNexis, 2009.

Hamilton, Wawmeesh. "Treaties Are No Guarantee of Freedom of the Press, but There's Little Media Coverage of First Nations Anyway." *Policy Options*, December 1, 2016. https://policyoptions.irpp.org/magazines/december-2016/in-first-nations-freedom-of-the-press-is-unclear/.

Hancock, Ange-Marie. *Intersectionality: An Intellectual History.* Oxford: Oxford University Press, 2016.

Hanna, Alan. "Spaces for Sharing: Searching for Indigenous Law on the Canadian Legal Landscape." *UBC Law Review* 51, no. 1 (2017): 105–59.

Haraway, Donna. "Situated Knowledges: The Science Question in Feminism and the Privilege of Partial Perspective." *Feminist Studies* 14, no. 3 (1988): 575–99.

Haraway, Donna Jeanne. *The Haraway Reader.* London: Routledge, 2003.

Harding, Sandra. "Rethinking Standpoint Epistemology: What Is 'Strong Objectivity?'" *The Centennial Review* 36, no. 3 (1992): 437–70.

———. *The Feminist Standpoint Theory Reader: Intellectual and Political Controversies.* London: Routledge, 2003.

Hardy, Jonathan. *Critical Political Economy of the Media: An Introduction.* London: Taylor & Francis Group, 2014.

Harris, Sophia. "'Slippery Slope': Opposition Mounts to Canadian Media's Plan to Block Piracy Websites." *CBC News*, February 18, 2018. https://www.cbc.ca/news/business/fairplay-piracy-website-blocking-crtc-1.4539566.

Hartsock, Nancy C.M. *The Feminist Standpoint Revisited and Other Essays.* New York: Basic Books, 1999.

Harvey, David. *A Brief History of Neoliberalism.* Oxford: Oxford University Press, 2007.

"'Hate Speech' No Longer Part of Canada's Human Rights Act." *National Post*, June 27, 2013. https://nationalpost.com/news/politics/hate-speech-no-longer-part-of-canadas-human-rights-act.

Hesmondhalgh, David, and Sarah Baker. "Sex, Gender and Work Segregation in the Cultural Industries." *The Sociological Review* 63, no. 1 (2015): 23–36.

Hettinger, Edwin C. "Justifying Intellectual Property." *Philosophy & Public Affairs* (1989): 31–52.

Heuman, Josh. "'Integral to the Plot, and in No Way Gratuitous'? Constructing Creative Freedom in the Liberalization of Canadian Content Regulation." *Television & New Media* 12, no. 3 (2011): 248–72.

Hewitt, Steve. "Chapter II. Forgotten Surveillance: Covert Human Intelligence Sources in Canada in a Post-9/11 World." In *Law, Privacy and Surveillance in Canada in the Post-Snowden Era*, edited by Michael Geist, 45–67. Ottawa: University of Ottawa Press, 2017.

Himma, Kenneth Einar. "Natural Law." *Internet Encyclopedia of Philosophy*, n.d. http://www.iep.utm.edu/natlaw/.

Hirsh, Elizabeth, Gary A. Olson, and Sandra Harding. "Starting from Marginalized Lives: A Conversation with Sandra Harding." *JAC* 15, no. 2 (1995): 193–225.

Hogan, Mél, and Tamara Shepherd. "Information Ownership and Materiality in an Age of Big Data Surveillance." *Journal of Information Policy* 5 (2015): 6–31.

Holvast, Jan. "History of Privacy." In *The Future of Identity in the Information Society*, edited by Vashek Matyáš, Simone Fischer-Hübner, Daniel Cvrček, and Petr Švenda, 13–42. Berlin: Springer, 2009.

Horkheimer, Max, and Theodor W. Adorno. "The Culture Industry: Enlightenment as Mass Deception." In *Dialectic of Enlightenment: Philosophical Fragments*, edited by

Gunzelin Schmid Noerr, translated by Edmund Jephcott, 94–136. Stanford, CA: Stanford University Press, 2002.

House of Commons Standing Committee on Access to Information, Privacy, and Ethics. "Addressing Digital Privacy Vulnerabilities and Potential Threats to Canada's Democratic Electoral Process." Ottawa: House of Commons, June 2018.

———. "Democracy Under Threat: Risks and Solutions in the Era of Disinformation and Data Monopoly." Ottawa: House of Commons, December 2018.

———. "Towards Privacy by Design: Review of the Personal Information Protection and Electronic Documents Act." Ottawa: House of Commons, February 2018.

"How Do You Fight Back against Online Defamation?" *CBC News*, May 7, 2013. https://www.cbc.ca/news/technology/ how-do-you-fight-back-against-online-defamation-1.1314609.

Howard, Philip, Laura Busch, and Penelope Sheets. "Comparing Digital Divides: Internet Access and Social Inequality in Canada and the United States." *Canadian Journal of Communication* 35, no. 1 (2010).

Hrynyshyn, Derek. *The Limits of the Digital Revolution: How Mass Media Culture Endures in a Social Media World*. Santa Barbara, CA: Praeger, 2017.

Hudson, Heather E. "The Role of Radio in the Canadian North—The Far North." *Journal of Communication* 27, no. 4 (1977): 130–39.

Hughes, Eric. "A Cypherpunk's Manifesto." Accessed February 15, 2019. https:// www.activism.net/cypherpunk/manifesto.html.

Hunt, Alan. "Foucault's Expulsion of Law. Toward a Retrieval." *Law & Social Inquiry* 17, no. 1 (1992): 1–38.

———. "Marxist Theory of Law." In *A Companion to Philosophy of Law and Legal Theory*, edited by Dennis Patterson, 2nd ed., 350–60. Malden, MA: Blackwell, 2010.

Hunt, Chris D.L. "The Common Law's Hodgepodge Protection of Privacy." *University of New Brunswick Law Journal* 66 (2015): 161–84.

Ibbitson, John. "Canada Shows Leadership in Advancing Human Rights." *The Globe and Mail*, June 15, 2017. https://www.theglobeandmail.com/news/politics/ with-gender-identity-bill-canada-shows-leadership-in-advancing-humanrights/ article35323583/.

ICANN. "Stewardship of IANA Functions Transitions to Global Internet Community as Contract with U.S. Government Ends." October 1, 2016. https:// www.icann.org/news/announcement-2016-10-01-en.

Iljazi, Michi. "TPA Submits Comments to FCC on Broadband Privacy Rule." Taxpayers Protection Alliance, March 8, 2017. https://www.protectingtaxpayers. org/blog/a/view/tpa-submits-comments-to-fcc-on-broadband-privacy-rule.

Indigenous Bar Association. "Submission to the Standing Committee on Access to Information, Privacy & Ethics on Bill C-58." October 13, 2017. http://nationtalk. ca/story/re-submission-standing-committee-access-information-privacy-ethics-bill-c-58-act-amend-access-information-act-privacy-act-make-consequential.

"Indigenous Bar Association Warns of C-58." *Two Row Times* (blog), October 18, 2017. https://tworowtimes.com/news/regional/indigenous-bar-association-warns-bill-c-58/.

Industry Canada. "Government Opts for More Competition in the Wireless Sector." 2007. https://www.canada.ca/en/news/archive/2007/11/government-opts-more-competition-wireless-sector.html.

Innis, Harold A. *The Bias of Communication*. 2nd ed. Toronto: University of Toronto Press, 2008.

Innovation, Science and Economic Development Canada. "Government Orders the CRTC to Investigate High-Pressure Telecom Sales Practices." June 14, 2018. https://www.newswire.ca/news-releases/government-orders-the-crtc-to-investigate-high-pressure-telecom-sales-practices-685582231.html.

International Telecommunications Union. "ICT Statistics Database." https://www. google.com/publicdata/explore?ds=emi9ik86jcuic_&ctype=l&strail=false&bcs= d&nselm=h&met_y=i91&scale_y=lin&ind_y=false&rdim=country&idim= country:IN:CA&ifdim=country&hl=en_US&dl=en&ind=false&icfg.

Iseke-Barnes, Judy M., and Deborah Danard. "Indigenous Knowledges and Worldview: Representations and the Internet." In *Information Technology and Indigenous People*, 27–29. IGI Global, 2007.

Jankowski, Nicholas W. "Researching Fake News: A Selective Examination of Empirical Studies." *Javnost—The Public* 25, no. 1–2 (April 3, 2018): 248–55. https://doi.org/10.1080/13183222.2018.1418964.

Jin, Dal Yong. *Digital Platforms, Imperialism and Political Culture*. New York: Routledge, 2015.

———. "Transformation of the World Television System under Neoliberal Globalization, 1983 to 2003." *Television & New Media* 8, no. 3 (2007): 179–96.

Jobb, Dean. "The Responsible Communication Defence: What's in It for Journalists?" J-Source, December 23, 2009. http://j-source.ca/article/the-responsible-communication-defence-whats-in-it-for-journalists/.

Johns, Adrian. *Piracy: The Intellectual Property Wars from Gutenberg to Gates*. Chicago: University of Chicago Press, 2010.

Johnson, Eric E. "Intellectual Property's Need for a Disability Perspective." *George Mason University Civil Rights Law Journal* 20 (2009): 181–208.

Johnson, Kirsten. *Undressing the Canadian State: The Politics of Pornography from Hicklin to Butler.* Halifax: Fernwood, 1995.

Johnson, Phylis, and Michael C. Keith. *Queer Airwaves: The Story of Gay and Lesbian Broadcasting.* Armonk, NY: M.E. Sharpe, 2001.

Jones, Bernie D. "Critical Race Theory: New Strategies for Civil Rights in the New Millennium." *Harvard Black Letter Law Journal* 18 (2002): 1–90.

Jones, Deborah. "CRTC Deals with Media Concentration." J-Source, January 15, 2008. http://j-source.ca/article/crtc-deals-with-media-concentration/.

Joseph, Kris. "Analysis of Canadian Wireless Spectrum Auctions: Licence Ownership and Deployment in the 700 MHz, 2500 MHz and 3500 MHz Frequency Ranges." Gatineau, QC: Canadian Radio-television and Telecommunications Commission, 2018. https://crtc.gc.ca/eng/acrtc/prx/2018joseph.htm.

Judge, Elizabeth Frances, and Daniel J. Gervais. *Intellectual Property: The Law in Canada.* 2nd ed. Toronto: Carswell, 2011.

Karaian, Lara, and Dillon Brady. "Revisiting the 'Private Use Exception' to Canada's Child Pornography Laws: Teenage Sexting, Sex-Positivity, Pleasure, and Control in the Digital Age." *Osgoode Hall Law Journal* 56 (forthcoming).

Kary, Joseph. "The Constitutionalization of Quebec Libel Law, 1848–2004." *Osgoode Hall Law Journal* 42, no. 2 (2004): 229–70.

Kealey, Gregory S. *Spying on Canadians: The Royal Canadian Mounted Police Security Service and the Origins of the Long Cold War.* Toronto: University of Toronto Press, 2017.

Kendall, Christopher N. *Gay Male Pornography: An Issue of Sex Discrimination.* Vancouver: UBC Press, 2005.

Kernaghan, Kenneth, and David Siegel. *Public Administration in Canada: A Text.* 4th ed. Toronto: ITP Nelson, 1999.

Kinsella, N. Stephan. "Against Intellectual Property." *Journal of Libertarian Studies* 15, no. 2; SEAS SPR (2001): 1–54.

———. "Intellectual Property and Libertarianism." *Liberty* 23, no. 11 (2009): 27–46.

Kitchin, Rob. *The Data Revolution: Big Data, Open Data, Data Infrastructures and Their Consequences.* London: SAGE, 2014.

Kosbie, Jeffrey. "(No) State Interests in Regulating Gender: How Suppression of Gender Nonconformity Violates Freedom of Speech." *William and Mary Journal of Women and the Law* 19 (2012): 187–254.

Kratz, Martin P.J. *Canada's Intellectual Property Law in a Nutshell.* 2nd ed. Toronto: Carswell, 2010.

Krause, Jason. "Cyber-Libertarians: A Legal Group Formed to Defend Civil Liberties on the Web Gears Up to Fight the USA Patriot Act." *ABA Journal* 89, no. 11 (2003): 50–56.

Ku, Melissa. "Walking the Tightrope between National Security and Freedom of Expression: A Constitutional Analysis of the New Advocating and Promoting Terrorism Offence." *Appeal: Review of Current Law and Law Reform* 21 (2016): 83–98.

Kuhner, Timothy K. "Citizens United as Neoliberal Jurisprudence: The Resurgence of Economic Theory." *Virginia Journal of Social Policy and the Law* 18, no. 3 (2011): 395–468.

Kutis, Robert. "Bitcoin: Light at the End of the Tunnel for Cyberlibertarians?" *Masaryk University Journal of Law and Technology* 8, no. 2. Accessed February 15, 2019. https://journals.muni.cz/mujlt/article/viewFile/2656/2220.

Landry, Normand. "Strategic Lawsuits against Public Participation and Freedom of the Press in Canada." In *The Unfulfilled Promise of Press Freedom in Canada*, edited by Lisa Taylor and Cara-Marie O'Hagan, 47–65. Toronto: University of Toronto Press, 2017.

———. *Threatening Democracy: SLAPPs and the Judicial Repression of Political Discourse.* Translated by Howard Scott. Black Point, NS: Fernwood, 2014.

Latour, Bruno. *Science in Action: How to Follow Scientists and Engineers through Society.* Cambridge, MA: Harvard University Press, 1987.

———. "The Powers of Association." *The Sociological Review* 32, no. 1 (May 1984): 264–80. https://doi.org/10.1111/j.1467-954X.1984.tb00115.x.

Lauzen, Martha M. "Boxed in 2017–18: Women on Screen and Behind the Scenes in Television." Center for the Study of Women in Television & Film, San Diego State University, September 2018. https://womenintvfilm.sdsu.edu/wp-content/uploads/2018/09/2017-18_Boxed_In_Report.pdf.

———. "The Celluloid Ceiling: Behind-the-Scenes Employment of Women on the Top 100, 250, and 500 Films of 2015." *Center for the Study of Women in Television and Film*, 2016, 1–6.

Lee, Micky. "UNESCO's Conceptualization of Women and Telecommunications 1970–2000." *Gazette (Leiden, Netherlands)* 66, no. 6 (2004): 533–52.

Lemley, Mark A., and Lawrence Lessig. "The End of End-to-End: Preserving the Architecture of the Internet in the Broadband Era." *UCLA Law Review* 48 (2000): 925–72.

Lessig, Lawrence. *Code.* Version 2.0. New York: Basic Books, 2006.

———. *Free Culture: How Big Media Uses Technology and the Law to Lock Down Culture and Control Creativity.* New York: Penguin, 2004.

————. *The Future of Ideas: The Fate of the Commons in a Connected World.* New York: Vintage Books, 2002.

Lester, Toni. "Blurred Lines—Where Copyright Ends and Cultural Appropriation Begins—The Case of Robin Thicke versus Bridgeport Music, and the Estate of Marvin Gaye." *Hastings Communications and Entertainment Law Journal* 36, no. 2 (2014): 217–42.

————. "Oprah, Beyonce, and the Girls Who Run the World—Are Black Female Cultural Producers Gaining Ground in Intellectual Property Law?" *Wake Forest Journal of Business & Intellectual Property Law* 15 (2014): 537.

Lewthwaite, Sarah. "Web Accessibility Standards and Disability: Developing Critical Perspectives on Accessibility." *Disability and Rehabilitation* 36, no. 16 (2014): 1375–83.

Lexum. "Our Company." Accessed February 17, 2019. https://lexum.com/en/about-lexum/our-company/.

Liberal Party of Canada. "Real Change: A Fair and Open Government." August 2015. https://www.liberal.ca/wp-content/uploads/2015/08/a-fair-and-open-government.pdf.

Lim, Merlyna. "Freedom to Hate: Social Media, Algorithmic Enclaves, and the Rise of Tribal Nationalism in Indonesia." *Critical Asian Studies* 49, no. 3 (2017): 411–27.

Lint, Willem de, and Reem Bahdi. "Access to Information in an Age of Intelligencized Governmentality." In *Brokering Access: Power, Politics, and Freedom of Information*, edited by Mike Larsen and Kevin Walby, 115–41. Vancouver: UBC Press, 2012.

Lippmann, Walter. "The Phantom Public." 1925.

Lipset, Seymour Martin. "The Social Requisites of Democracy Revisited: 1993 Presidential Address." *American Sociological Review* 59, no. 1 (1994): 1–22.

Locke, John. *Second Treatise of Government: An Essay Concerning the True Original, Extent and End of Civil Government.* Edited by Richard H. Cox. Hoboken, NJ: John Wiley & Sons, 2014.

Luka, Mary Elizabeth, and Catherine Middleton. "Citizen Involvement during the CRTC's Let's Talk TV Consultation." *Canadian Journal of Communication* 42, no. 1 (2017).

Lyon, David. *The Electronic Eye: The Rise of Surveillance Society.* Minneapolis: University of Minnesota Press, 1994.

————. *Surveillance after Snowden.* Malden, MA: Polity Press, 2015.

Macdonell, Dave. "How to Use the TM and R Symbols—Trademark Registration." *The Trademark Group—Trademark Registration* (blog), September 18, 2012. https://trademarkshop.ca/trademark-symbols/.

MacLennan, Anne F. "Cultural Imperialism of the North? The Expansion of the CBC Northern Service and Community Radio." *Radio Journal: International Studies in Broadcast & Audio Media* 9, no. 1 (2011): 63–81.

Magnet, Shoshana. *When Biometrics Fail: Gender, Race, and the Technology of Identity.* Durham, NC: Duke University Press, 2011.

Maki, Krystle. "Neoliberal Deviants and Surveillance: Welfare Recipients under the Watchful Eye of Ontario Works." *Surveillance & Society* 9, no. 1/2 (November 30, 2011): 47–63. https://doi.org/10.24908/ss.v9i1/2.4098.

Makin, Kirk. "How Canada's Sex-Assault Laws Violate Rape Victims." *The Globe and Mail*, October 5, 2013. https://www.theglobeandmail.com/news/national/how-canadas-sex-assault-laws-violate-rape-victims/article14705289/.

Malcic, Steven. "Proteus Online: Digital Identity and the Internet Governance Industry." *Convergence* 24, no. 2 (2018): 205–25.

Malcolm, Jeremy. "Criteria of Meaningful Stakeholder Inclusion in Internet Governance." *Internet Policy Review* 4, no. 4 (2015): 1–14.

———. *Multi-Stakeholder Governance and the Internet Governance Forum.* Perth: Terminus Press, 2008.

Mansell, Robin, and Marc Raboy. "Introduction: Foundations of the Theory and Practice of Global Media and Communication Policy." In *The Handbook of Global Media and Communication Policy*, 1–20. West Sussex, UK: Wiley-Blackwell, 2011.

Manuel, Neskie. "Secwepemc Radio: Reclamation of Our Common Property." In *Islands of Resistance: Pirate Radio in Canada*, edited by Andrea Langlois, Ron Sakolsky, and Marian van der Zon, 71–72. Vancouver: New Star Books, 2010.

Marchand, Ross. "Pai and Ohlhausen Lead FCC and FTC's Fight Against Misguided Rules." Taxpayers Protection Alliance, April 21, 2017. https://www.protectingtaxpayers.org/blog/a/view/pai-and-ohlhausen-lead-fcc-and-ftcs-fight-against-misguided-rules.

Maréchal, Nathalie. "First They Came for the Poor: Surveillance of Welfare Recipients as an Uncontested Practice." *Media and Communication* 3, no. 3 (2015): 56–67.

Marmor, Andrei, and Alexander Sarch. "The Nature of Law." In *The Stanford Encyclopedia of Philosophy*, edited by Edward N. Zalta, Fall 2015. https://plato.stanford.edu/archives/fall2015/entries/lawphil-nature/.

Martin, Brian. "Against Intellectual Property." *Philosophy and Social Action* 21 (1995): 7–22.

Martin, Michèle. *"Hello, Central?": Gender, Technology, and Culture in the Formation of Telephone Systems.* Montreal: McGill-Queen's University Press, 1991.

Matsuda, Mari J. *Words That Wound: Critical Race Theory, Assaultive Speech, and the First Amendment.* New York: Routledge, 2018.

May, Christopher. *The Global Political Economy of Intellectual Property Rights: The New Enclosures*. New York: Routledge, 2015.

Mazepa, Patricia. "Manifest Spatialization: Militarizing Communication in Canada." *Global Media Journal* 8, no. 1 (2015): 9.

Mazepa, Patricia, and Vincent Mosco. "A Political Economy Approach to the Internet." In *Handbook on the Economics of the Internet*, edited by Johannes Bauer and Michael Latzer, 163–80. Cheltenham, UK: Edward Elgar Publishing, 2016.

McChesney, Robert Waterman. *Digital Disconnect: How Capitalism Is Turning the Internet against Democracy*. New York: The New Press, 2013.

McChesney, Robert Waterman, and John Nichols. *People Get Ready: The Fight against a Jobless Economy and a Citizenless Democracy*. New York: Nation Books, 2016.

McClean, Tom. "Who Pays the Piper? The Political Economy of Freedom of Information." *Government Information Quarterly* 27, no. 4 (2010): 392–400.

McElroy, Wendy. "A Feminist Defense of Pornography." *Free Inquiry* 17, no. 4 (1997): 14–17.

———. *XXX: A Woman's Right to Pornography*. New York: St. Martin's Press, 1995.

McKelvey, Fenwick. "Ends and Ways: The Algorithmic Politics of Network Neutrality." *Global Media Journal* 3, no. 1 (2010): 51.

McMahon, Rob. "From Digital Divides to the First Mile: Indigenous Peoples and the Network Society in Canada." *International Journal of Communication* 8 (2014): 25.

———. "Indigenous Regulatory Advocacy in Canada's Far North: Mobilizing the First Mile Connectivity Consortium." *Journal of Information Policy* 4 (2014): 228–49.

———. "The Institutional Development of Indigenous Broadband Infrastructure in Canada and the United States: Two Paths to 'Digital Self-Determination.'" *Canadian Journal of Communication* 36, no. 1 (2011): 115–40.

McMahon, Rob, Amanda Almond, Greg Whistance-Smith, Diana Steinhauer, Stewart Steinhauer, and Diane P. Janes. "Sweetgrass AR: Exploring Augmented Reality as a Resource for Indigenous–Settler Relations." *International Journal of Communication* 13 (2019): 4530–52.

McMahon, Rob, Heather E. Hudson, and Lyle Fabian. "Canada's Northern Communication Policies: The Role of Aboriginal Organizations." *The Shifting Terrain: Public Policy Advocacy in Canada* (2017): 259–92.

McMahon, Tom, "Improving Access to the Law in Canada." Government Information in Canada, March 1999. http://library2.usask.ca/gic/16/mcmahon.html#privatizing.

McMurria, John. "From Net Neutrality to Net Equality." *International Journal of Communication* 10, no. 2016 (2016): 5931–48.

McNamara, Luke. "Negotiating the Contours of Unlawful Hate Speech: Regulation under Provincial Human Rights Laws in Canada." *UBC Law Review* 38, no. 1 (2005): 1–82.

McStay, Andrew. *Privacy and the Media*. New York: SAGE, 2017.

Medeiros, Ben. "Right to Be Forgotten or Right to Not Be Talked About? Public and Private Speech Regulation and the Panic about Critical Speech on the Interactive Web." University of California San Diego, 2016.

Meehan, Eileen R., and Ellen Riordan, eds. *Sex & Money: Feminism and Political Economy in the Media*. Minneapolis: University of Minnesota Press, 2002.

Meese, James. *Authors, Users, and Pirates: Copyright Law and Subjectivity*. Cambridge, MA: MIT Press, 2018.

Meldrum, Tim. "Domestic Service, Privacy and the Eighteenth-Century Metropolitan Household." *Urban History* 26, no. 1 (1999): 27–39.

Melody, William H. "On the Meaning and Importance of 'Independence' in Telecom Reform." *Telecommunications Policy* 21, no. 3 (1997): 195–99.

Mendes, Kaitlynn. *SlutWalk: Feminism, Activism and Media*. Springer, 2015.

Merry, Sally Engle. "Legal Pluralism." *Law and Society Review* 22, no. 5 (1988): 869–96.

Michels, Robert. *Political Parties: A Sociological Study of the Oligarchical Tendencies of Modern Democracy*. New York: Hearst's International Library Company, 1915.

Middleton, Catherine. "An Introduction to Telecommunications Policy in Canada." *Journal of Telecommunications and the Digital Economy* 5, no. 4 (2017): 97–124.

———. "Structural and Functional Separation in Broadband Networks: An Insufficient Remedy to Competitive Woes in the Canadian Broadband Market." In *The Internet Tree: The State of Telecom Policy in Canada*, edited by Marita Moll and Leslie Regan Shade, 61–72. Ottawa: Canadian Centre for Policy Alternatives, 2011.

Miles, Kathleen. "Glenn Greenwald on Why Privacy Is Vital, Even If You 'Have Nothing to Hide.'" June 20, 2014. https://www.huffingtonpost.ca/entry/glenn-greenwald-privacy_n_5509704.

Miller, Toby. *Cultural Citizenship: Cosmopolitanism, Consumerism, and Television in a Neoliberal Age*. Philadelphia: Temple University Press, 2007.

Milloy, John S. *Indian Act Colonialism: A Century of Dishonour, 1869–1969*. National Centre for First Nations Governance, 2008.

Ministry of the Attorney General. "Protection of Public Participation Act." October 28, 2015. https://news.ontario.ca/mag/en/2015/10/protection-of-public-participation-act.html.

Moll, Marita. "Trading Sovereignty for Surveillance in the Telecommunications Sector." In *The Internet Tree: The State of Telecom Policy in Canada 3.0*, edited by

Marita Moll and Leslie Regan Shade, 93–99. Ottawa: Canadian Centre for Policy Alternatives, 2011.

Moll, Marita, and Leslie Regan Shade, eds. *For Sale to the Highest Bidder: Telecom Policy in Canada*. Ottawa: Canadian Centre for Policy Alternatives, 2008.

Moon, Richard. "Hate Speech Regulations in Canada." *Florida State University Law Review* 36, no. 1 (2008): 79–97.

———. "Report to the Canadian Human Rights Commission Concerning Section 13 of the Canadian Human Rights Act and the Regulation of Hate Speech on the Internet: Report to the Canadian Human Rights Commission." October 2008. https://papers.ssrn.com/sol3/papers.cfm?abstract_id=1865282.

———. *The Constitutional Protection of Freedom of Expression*. Toronto: University of Toronto Press, 2000.

Moran, Rachel E., and Matthew N. Bui. "Race, Ethnicity, and Telecommunications Policy Issues of Access and Representation: Centering Communities of Color and Their Concerns." *Telecommunications Policy* 43, no. 5 (2019): 461–73.

Morneau, William Francis. "Building a Strong Middle Class: Budget 2017." Ottawa: Minister of Finance, March 22, 2017.

Mosco, Vincent. "Changing Telecommunications Policy in Canada." In *Telecommunications and Equity: Policy Research Issues Proceedings of the Thirteenth Annual Telecommunications Policy Research Conference, Airlie House, Airlie, Virginia, USA, April 21–24, 1985*, edited by James Miller, 189–95. Amsterdam: North-Holland, 1986.

———. *The Political Economy of Communication: Rethinking and Renewal*. 2nd ed. London: SAGE, 2009.

Mostoller, Charles. "Awakening the 'Voice of the Forest': Radio Barriere Lake." In *Islands of Resistance: Pirate Radio in Canada*, edited by Andrea Langlois, Ron Sakolsky, and Marian van der Zon, 75–87. Vancouver: New Star Books, 2010.

Murakami Wood, David. "What Is Global Surveillance? Towards a Relational Political Economy of the Global Surveillant Assemblage." *Geoforum* 49 (October 2013): 317–26. https://doi.org/10.1016/j.geoforum.2013.07.001.

Murphy, Mike. "Google Patented Building Robots with Personalities." *Quartz*, March 31, 2015. https://qz.com/373658/google-patented-building-robots-with-personalities/.

Murray, Andrew D. *The Regulation of Cyberspace: Control in the Online Environment*. Abingdon, UK: Routledge-Cavendish, 2007.

Murray, Catherine, and Alison Beale. "Commentary: Sex, Money, Media: A Tribute and Political Reflection." *Canadian Journal of Communication* 36 (2011): 179–84.

Murray, Laura. "Protecting Ourselves to Death: Canada, Copyright, and the Internet." *First Monday* 9, no. 10 (2004).

Mussio, Laurence B. *Telecom Nation: Telecommunications, Computers, and Governments in Canada*. Montreal: McGill-Queen's University Press, 2001.

Mustonen, Juha, and Gustav Björkstrand, eds. *The World's First Freedom of Information Act: Anders Chydenius' Legacy Today*. Kokkola, Finland: Anders Chydenius Foundation, 2006.

Naimark, Marc. "In the Fight Over .gay and .lgbt, the Cyberpowers That Be Are Redefining Our Community." *Slate*, May 7, 2014. https://slate.com/human-interest/2014/05/icann-and-the-fight-for-gay-and-lgbt-does-the-gay-community-even-exist.html.

Nakamura, Lisa. *Cybertypes: Race, Ethnicity, and Identity on the Internet*. New York: Routledge, 2013.

Napoleon, Val. "*Delgamuukw*: A Legal Straightjacket for Oral Histories?" *Canadian Journal of Law & Society/La Revue Canadienne Droit et Société* 20, no. 2 (2005): 123–55.

———. "Extinction by Number: Colonialism Made Easy." *Canadian Journal of Law & Society* 16, no. 1 (2001): 113–45.

———. "Thinking about Indigenous Legal Orders." In *Dialogues on Human Rights and Legal Pluralism*, 229–45. Dordrecht, Netherlands: Springer, 2013.

Napoli, Philip M. "What If More Speech Is No Longer the Solution: First Amendment Theory Meets Fake News and the Filter Bubble." *Federal Communications Law Journal* 70, no. 1 (2018): 55–104.

Newman, Lareen, Kathryn Browne-Yung, Parimala Raghavendra, Denise Wood, and Emma Grace. "Applying a Critical Approach to Investigate Barriers to Digital Inclusion and Online Social Networking among Young People with Disabilities." *Information Systems Journal* 27, no. 5 (2017): 559–88.

Noble, Safiya Umoja. *Algorithms of Oppression: How Search Engines Reinforce Racism*. New York: Oxford University Press, 2018.

Nowak, Peter. "Netflix Launches Canadian Movie Service." *CBC News*, September 22, 2010. https://www.cbc.ca/news/technology/netflix-launches-canadian-movie-service-1.872505.

Nuechterlein, Jonathan E., and Philip J. Weiser. *Digital Crossroads: Telecommunications Law and Policy in the Internet Age*. 2nd ed. Cambridge, MA: MIT Press, 2013.

Obar, Jonathan A., and Anne Oeldorf-Hirsch. "The Biggest Lie on the Internet: Ignoring the Privacy Policies and Terms of Service Policies of Social Networking Services." *Information, Communication & Society* (2018): 1–20.

OECD. *The OECD Privacy Framework*. Paris: OECD, 2013.

————. "OECD Guidelines on the Protection of Privacy and Transborder Flows of Personal Data." Accessed October 31, 2018. http://www.oecd.org/sti/ieconomy/oecdguidelinesontheprotectionofprivacyandtransborderflowsofpersonaldata.htm.

Office of the Information and Privacy Commissioner of British Columbia. "Full Disclosure: Political Parties, Campaign Data, and Voter Consent." February 6. Vancouver: Office of the Information and Privacy Commissioner of British Columbia, 2019. https://www.oipc.bc.ca/investigation-reports/2278.

Office of the Information Commissioner of Canada. "Advisory Notice on Fees for Electronic Records." Accessed November 3, 2018. http://www.oic-ci.gc.ca/eng/droits-pour-documents-electroniques_fees-for-electronic-records.aspx.

————. "Annual Report 2016–2017." Gatineau, QC: Office of the Information Commissioner of Canada, 2017. http://www.oic-ci.gc.ca/eng/rapport-annuel-annual-report_2017-2018.aspx.

————. "Preparing for C-58." October 17, 2018. https://www.oic-ci.gc.ca/ar-ra/2018/Preparing.html.

Office of the Privacy Commissioner of Canada. "About the OPC." September 14, 2016. https://www.priv.gc.ca/en/about-the-opc/.

————. "Data Brokers: A Look at the Canadian and American Landscape—September 2014." October 10, 2014. https://www.priv.gc.ca/en/opc-actions-and-decisions/research/explore-privacy-research/2014/db_201409/.

————. "Federal Court Applications under the *Privacy Act*." September 2016. https://www.priv.gc.ca/en/privacy-topics/privacy-laws-in-canada/the-privacy-act/federal-court-applications-under-the-privacy-act/.

————. "How to Apply for a Federal Court Hearing under PIPEDA." September 2016. https://www.priv.gc.ca/en/privacy-topics/privacy-laws-in-canada/the-personal-information-protection-and-electronic-documents-act-pipeda/pipeda-complaints-and-enforcement-process/federal-court-applications-under-pipeda/.

————. "PIPEDA Fair Information Principles." September 16, 2011. https://www.priv.gc.ca/en/privacy-topics/privacy-laws-in-canada/the-personal-information-protection-and-electronic-documents-act-pipeda/p_principle/.

————. "Privacy Commissioner Seeks Federal Court Determination on Key Issue for Canadians' Online Reputation." October 10, 2018. https://www.priv.gc.ca/en/opc-news/news-and-announcements/2018/an_181010/.

————. "Provincial and Territorial Privacy Laws and Oversight." Accessed February 16, 2019. https://www.priv.gc.ca/en/about-the-opc/what-we-do/provincial-and-territorial-collaboration/provincial-and-territorial-privacy-laws-and-oversight/.

———. "Summary of Privacy Laws in Canada." May 15, 2014. https://www.priv. gc.ca/en/privacy-topics/privacy-laws-in-canada/02_05_d_15/.

Oguamanam, Chidi. *International Law and Indigenous Knowledge: Intellectual Property, Plant Biodiversity, and Traditional Medicine.* Toronto: University of Toronto Press, 2006.

Ojeda-Zapata, Julio. "Netflix Members Who Use Comcast Face Streaming Hiccups." *Pioneer Press,* February 11, 2014. https://www.twincities.com/2014/02/11/ netflix-members-who-use-comcast-face-streaming-hiccups/.

Okediji, Ruth L. "The International Relations of Intellectual Property: Narratives of Developing Country Participation in the Global Intellectual Property System." *Singapore Journal of International & Comparative Law* 7 (2003): 315.

OLG. "OLG PlaySmart—Gambling Facts, Tools and Advice." Accessed October 31, 2018. https://www.playsmart.ca/#FacialRecognition.

OpenCanada. "How the Marrakesh Treaty Makes the Intellectual Property System More Inclusive." Accessed February 17, 2019. https://www.opencanada.org/ features/how-marrakesh-treaty-makes-intellectual-property-system-more-inclusive/.

"Order Issuing a Direction to the CRTC on Implementing the Canadian Telecommunications Policy Objectives." December 14, 2006. https://laws-lois. justice.gc.ca/eng/regulations/SOR-2006-355/FullText.html.

O'Riordan, Kate, and David J. Phillips, eds. *Queer Online: Media Technology & Sexuality.* New York: Peter Lang, 2007.

Osler, Hoskin & Harcourt LLP. "Court Approves US-Style Group Claim for Hate Speech." Accessed December 13, 2018. http://www.osler.com/en/blogs/ classactions/april-2017/court-approves-us-style-group-claim-for-hate-speec.

Packard, Ashley. *Digital Media Law.* 2nd ed. Malden, MA: Wiley-Blackwell, 2013.

Pagliery, Jose. "Criminals Use IRS Website to Steal Data on 104,000 People." *CNN Money,* May 26, 2015. https://money.cnn.com/2015/05/26/pf/taxes/irs-website-data-hack/index.html.

Paré, Daniel J. *Internet Governance in Transition: Who Is the Master of This Domain?* Lanham, MD: Rowman & Littlefield, 2003.

Pariser, Eli. *The Filter Bubble: How the New Personalized Web Is Changing What We Read and How We Think.* London: Penguin Books, 2012.

"Parliament's Authority." UK Parliament. Accessed October 17, 2018. https://www. parliament.uk/about/how/sovereignty/.

Parsons, Christopher. "Beyond Privacy: Articulating the Broader Harms of Pervasive Mass Surveillance." *Media and Communication* 3, no. 3 (2015): 1–11. https://doi. org/10.17645/mac.v3i3.263.

———. "Law Enforcement and Security Agency Surveillance in Canada: The Growth of Digitally-Enabled Surveillance and Atrophy of Accountability." 2018. https://papers.ssrn.com/sol3/papers.cfm?abstract_id=3130240.

———. "Stuck on the Agenda: Drawing Lessons from the Stagnation of 'Lawful Access' Legislation in Canada." In *Law, Privacy and Surveillance in Canada in the Post-Snowden Era*, edited by Michael Geist, 257–83. Ottawa: University of Ottawa Press, 2017.

Passavant, Paul. *No Escape: Freedom of Speech and the Paradox of Rights.* New York: NYU Press, 2002.

Patel, Tina Girishbhai. "Surveillance, Suspicion and Stigma: Brown Bodies in a Terror-Panic Climate." *Surveillance & Society* 10, no. 3/4 (2012): 215–34.

Perez, Caroline Criado. *Invisible Women: Data Bias in a World Designed for Men.* New York: Abrams, 2019.

Perkel, Colin. "Editor Found Guilty of Peddling Hate Says Your Ward News Gave 'Angry Men' a Voice." April 26, 2019. https://nationalpost.com/news/canada/crown-seeks-one-year-jail-term-against-editor-convicted-of-promoting-hate.

———. "James Sears Fires Lawyer; Sentencing for Your Ward News Delayed." *680 News* (blog), May 30, 2019. https://www.680news.com/2019/05/30/james-sears-fires-lawyer-sentencing-for-your-ward-news-delayed/.

Philpot, Duncan, Brian Beaton, and Tim Whiteduck. "First Mile Challenges to Last Mile Rhetoric: Exploring the Discourse between Remote and Rural First Nations and the Telecom Industry." *Journal of Community Informatics* 10, no. 2 (2014).

Posner, Richard A. "The Economics of Privacy." *The American Economic Review* 71, no. 2 (1981): 405–9.

———. "The Right of Privacy." *Georgia Law Review.* 12 (1977): 393.

Powell, Alison. "Argument-by-Technology: How Technical Activism Contributes to Internet Governance." In *Research Handbook on Governance of the Internet*, edited by Ian Brown, 198–220. Cheltenham, UK: Edward Elgar, 2013.

Powers, Shawn M., and Michael Jablonski. *The Real Cyber War: The Political Economy of Internet Freedom.* Urbana: University of Illinois Press, 2015.

Prasad, Kiran. "Gender-sensitive Communication Policies for Women's Development: Issues and Challenges." *Feminist Interventions in International Communication: Minding the Gap*, edited by Katharine Sarikakis and Leslie Regan Shade, 74–89. Toronto: Rowman & Littlefield, 2008.

"Press Release: CRTC Takes Action to Ensure a Wide Choice of Television Programming on All Platforms." *Canada News Wire*, September 21, 2011. https://www.newswire.ca/news-releases/crtc-takes-action-to-ensure-a-wide-choice-of-television-programming-on-all-platforms-521676221.html.

Pribetic, Antonin I., and Marc Randazza. "'War of the Words': Differing Canadian and American Approaches to Internet Defamation." In *Annual Review of Civil Litigation*, edited by Todd L. Archibald, 403. Toronto: Carswell Thomson Reuters, 2015.

Price, Monroe E. *Free Expression, Globalism, and the New Strategic Communication*. New York: Cambridge University Press, 2015.

Pritchard, David, and Lisa Taylor. "In Canada, We Criminalize Public-Interest Speech." *The Globe and Mail*, April 3, 2018. https://www.theglobeandmail.com/opinion/article-in-canada-we-criminalize-public-interest-speech/?utm_medium=Referrer:+Social+Network+/+Media&utm_campaign=Shared+Web+Article+Links.

"Privacy by Design Strong Privacy Protection—Now, and Well into the Future." 33rd International Conference of Data Protection and Privacy Commissioners, 2011. https://www.ipc.on.ca/wp-content/uploads/Resources/PbDReport.pdf.

Proceviat, Steve. "Evening Update: U.S. Senators Urge Trudeau to Block Huawei; Belinda Stronach Offered to Settle Dispute Weeks before Father's Lawsuit." Accessed November 29, 2018. https://www.theglobeandmail.com/canada/article-evening-update-us-senators-urge-trudeau-to-block-huawei-belinda/.

Prosser, William L. *Law of Torts*. St. Paul: West Publishing Company, 1971.

———. "Privacy." *California Law Review* 48, no. 3 (1960): 383–422. https://doi.org/10.15779/z383j3c.

Prunty, John J. "Signposts for a Critical Educational Policy Analysis." *Australian Journal of Education* 29, no. 2 (1985): 133–40.

Public Knowledge. "Net Neutrality." Accessed November 3, 2018. https://www.publicknowledge.org/issues/net-neutrality.

Quail, Christine. "Producing Reality: Television Formats and Reality TV in the Canadian Context." *Canadian Journal of Communication* 40, no. 2 (2015).

Raboy, Marc. *Marconi: The Man Who Networked the World*. New York: Oxford University Press, 2016.

———. "Media." In *Media Divides: Communication Rights and the Right to Communicate in Canada*, edited by Marc Raboy, William J. McIver, and Jeremy Shtern. Vancouver: UBC Press, 2010.

———. *Missed Opportunities: The Story of Canada's Broadcasting Policy*. Montreal: McGill-Queen's University Press, 1990.

———. "The Role of Public Consultation in Shaping the Canadian Broadcasting System." *Canadian Journal of Political Science/Revue Canadienne de Science Politique* 28, no. 3 (1995): 455–77.

Raboy, Marc, and Normand Landry. *Civil Society, Communication, and Global Governance: Issues from the World Summit on the Information Society.* New York: Peter Lang, 2005.

Raboy, Marc, Normand Landry, and Jeremy Shtern. *Digital Solidarities, Communication Policy and Multi-Stakeholder Global Governance: The Legacy of the World Summit on the Information Society.* New York: Peter Lang, 2010.

Raboy, Marc, William J. McIver, and Jeremy Shtern, eds. *Media Divides: Communication Rights and the Right to Communicate in Canada.* Vancouver: UBC Press, 2010.

"Racist Webmaster Gets 6 Months for Hate Propaganda." *CBC News.* January 23, 2007. https://www.cbc.ca/news/canada/montreal/ racist-webmaster-gets-6-months-for-hate-propaganda-1.662779.

Rahmatian, Andreas. "Neo-Colonial Aspects of Global Intellectual Property Protection." *The Journal of World Intellectual Property* 12, no. 1 (2009): 40–74.

Rajabiun, Reza, and Catherine Middleton. "Public Interest in the Regulation of Competition: Evidence from Wholesale Internet Access Consultations in Canada." *Journal of Information Policy* 5 (2015): 32–66.

Rand, Ayn. *Capitalism: The Unknown Ideal.* Centennial ed., 38. New York: Signet Books, 2007.

Rankin, Jim, and Patty Winsa. "Carding Drops but Proportion of Blacks Stopped by Toronto Police Rises." *Toronto Star,* July 26, 2014. https://www.thestar.com/ news/insight/2014/07/26/carding_drops_but_proportion_of_blacks_stopped_by_ toronto_police_rises.html.

Raymond, Mark, and Laura DeNardis. "Multistakeholderism: Anatomy of an Inchoate Global Institution." *International Theory* 7, no. 3 (2015): 572–616.

*Report of the Royal Commission on Aboriginal Peoples.* Ottawa: Canada Communication Group, 1996.

"Resolution on Privacy by Design." Israel: 32nd International Conference of Data Protection and Privacy Commissioners, 2010. https://edps.europa.eu/sites/edp/ files/publication/10-10-27_jerusalem_resolutionon_privacybydesign_en.pdf.

Rideout, Vanda. *Continentalizing Canadian Telecommunications: The Politics of Regulatory Reform.* Montreal: McGill-Queen's University Press; Combined Academic, 2004.

Roberts, Alasdair. *Blacked Out: Government Secrecy in the Information Age.* Cambridge: Cambridge University Press, 2006.

———. "Structural Pluralism and the Right to Information." *The University of Toronto Law Journal* 51, no. 3 (2001): 243–71.

Robinson, Edward Heath. "The Distinction between State and Government." *Geography Compass* 7, no. 8 (2013): 556–66.

Rosenberg, Norman. "Taking a Look at the Distorted Shape of an Ugly Tree: Efforts at Policy-Surgery on the Law of Libel during the Decade of the 1940s." *Northern Kentucky Law Review* 15 (1988): 11–56.

Rosenberg, Norman L. *Protecting the Best Men: An Interpretive History of the Law of Libel.* Chapel Hill: University of North Carolina Press, 1986.

Rosenwald, Michael. "Your iPhone's Secret Past: How Cadaver Ears and a Talking Dog Led to the Telephone." *Washington Post*, November 3, 2017. https://www.washingtonpost.com/news/retropolis/wp/2017/11/03/how-alexander-graham-bells-talking-dog-led-to-the-iphone-x/.

Roth, Gunther. "Introduction." In *Economy and Society: An Outline of Interpretive Sociology*, by Max Weber. Los Angeles: University of California Press, 1978.

Roth, Lorna. *Something New in the Air: The Story of First Peoples Television Broadcasting in Canada.* Montreal: McGill-Queen's University Press, 2005.

———. "The Delicate Acts of 'Colour Balancing': Multiculturalism and Canadian Television Broadcasting Policies and Practices." *Canadian Journal of Communication* 23, no. 4 (1998): 487–506.

Rothbard, Murray Newton. *The Ethics of Liberty.* New York: New York University Press, 2002.

Rottenberg, Catherine. "The Rise of Neoliberal Feminism." *Cultural Studies* 28, no. 3 (2014): 418–37.

Royal Commission on Radio Broadcasting and John Aird. *Report of the Royal Commission on Radio Broadcasting.* Ottawa: F.A. Acland, Printer, 1929.

Rubenstein, William B. "Since When Is the Fourteenth Amendment Our Route to Equality: Some Reflections on the Construction of the Hate Speech Debate from a Lesbian/Gay Perspective." *Law & Sexuality: A Review of Lesbian & Gay Legal Issues* 2, no. 19 (1992): 19–27.

Rubie-Davies, Christine M., Sabrina Liu, and Kai-Chi Katie Lee. "Watching Each Other: Portrayals of Gender and Ethnicity in Television Advertisements." *The Journal of Social Psychology* 153, no. 2 (2013): 175–95.

Rury, Abigail A. "He's So Gay—Not That There's Anything Wrong with That: Using a Community Standard to Homogenize the Measure of Reputational Damage in Homosexual Defamation Cases." *Cardozo Journal of Law & Gender* 17 (2011): 655–82.

Rush, Stacy, Giselle Chin, and Andrew Kaikai. "Software Patent Eligibility in Canada: IP Year in Review." *Canadian Lawyer Mag*, December 29, 2016.

https://www.canadianlawyermag.com/article/software-patent-eligibility-in-canada-ip-year-in-review-3474/.

Rusk, James. "Municipalities Can't Sue for Libel, Judges Say." *The Globe and Mail*, April 18, 2006. https://www.theglobeandmail.com/news/national/municipalities-cant-sue-for-libel-judges-say/article18160475/.

Ryder, Bruce. "The Harms of Child Pornography Law." *University of British Columbia Law Review* 36, no. 1 (2003): 101–35.

———. "Undercover Censorship: Exploring the History of the Regulation of Publications in Canada." In *Interpreting Censorship in Canada*, edited by K. Petersen and A.C. Hutchinson, 129–56. Toronto: University of Toronto Press, 1999.

Salter, Liora, and Felix N.L. Odartey-Wellington. *The CRTC and Broadcasting Regulation in Canada*. Toronto: Carswell, 2013.

Sawchuk, Kim. "Impaired." In *The Routledge Handbook of Mobilities*, edited by Peter Adey, David Bissell, Kevin Hannam, Peter Merriman, and Mimi Sheller, 409–20. New York: Routledge, 2014.

Sawchuk, Kim, and Barbara Crow. "Into the Grey Zone: Seniors, Cell Phones and Milieus That Matter." In *Observing the Mobile User Experience*, 17, 2010.

Scales, Ann. "Avoiding Constitutional Depression: Bad Attitudes and the Fate of Butler." *Canadian Journal of Women and the Law* 7 (1994): 349–92.

Scassa, Teresa. "Journalistic Purposes and Private Sector Data Protection Legislation: Blogs, Tweets, and Information Maps." *Queen's Law Journal* 35 (2010): 733–81.

———. "Right to Be Forgotten Reference to Federal Court Attracts Media Concern." April 17, 2019. https://www.teresascassa.ca/index.php?option=com_k2&view=item&id=305:right-to-be-forgotten-reference-to-federal-court-attracts-media-concern&Itemid=80.

Schneider, Elizabeth M. "The Violence of Privacy." *Connecticut Law Review* 23 (1990): 973–99.

Schultz, David. "The Case for a Democratic Theory of American Election Law." *University of Pennsylvania Law Review Online* 164, no. 2 (2016): 259–68.

Sedgwick, Eve Kosofsky. *Tendencies*. London: Taylor & Francis, 2004.

Sen, Amartya. *Development as Freedom*. New York: Knopf, 2001.

Shade, Leslie Regan. "Gender and Digital Policy: From Global Information Infrastructure to Internet Governance." In *The Routledge Companion to Media & Gender*, 240–50. New York: Routledge, 2013.

———. "Integrating Gender into Canadian Internet Policy: From the Information Highway to the Digital Economy." *Journal of Information Policy* 6 (2016): 338–70.

———. "Missing in Action: Gender in Canada's Digital Economy Agenda." *Signs: Journal of Women in Culture and Society* 39, no. 4 (Summer 2014): 888–96.

Shaffer, Butler. *A Libertarian Critique of Intellectual Property*. Auburn, AL: Mises Institute, 2013. https://mises.org/library/libertarian-critique-intellectual-property.

Shaw, Eugene F. "Agenda-Setting and Mass Communication Theory." *Gazette (Leiden, Netherlands)* 25, no. 2 (1979): 96–105.

Shepherd, Tamara, Gregory Taylor, and Catherine Middleton. "A Tale of Two Regulators: Telecom Policy Participation in Canada." *Journal of Information Policy* 4 (2014): 1–22.

Sherman, Brad. "From the Non-Original to the Ab-Original: A History." In *Of Authors and Origins*, edited by Brad Sherman and Alain Strowel. New York: Oxford University Press, 1994.

Signorielli, Nancy. "Gender Stereotyping on Television." In *Media Psychology*, edited by Gayle Brewer and Nancy Signorielli, 170–86. New York: Palgrave Macmillan, 2011.

Silbey, Jessica. *The Eureka Myth: Creators, Innovators, and Everyday Intellectual Property*. Stanford: Stanford University Press, 2014.

Simpson, Leanne. *Dancing on Our Turtle's Back: Stories of Nishnaabeg Re-creation, Resurgence and a New Emergence*. Winnipeg: Arbeiter Ring, 2011.

Skinner, David. "Broadcasting in Canada." In *Television and Public Policy: Change and Continuity in an Era of Liberation*, edited by David Ward and Anthony McNicholas, 3–26. Mahwah, NJ: Lawrence Erlbaum and Associates, 2008.

———. "Divided Loyalties: The Early Development of Canada's 'Single' Broadcasting System." *Journal of Radio Studies* 12, no. 1 (2005): 136–55.

Skinner, David, and Mike Gasher. "So Much by So Few: Media Policy and Ownership in Canada." In *Converging Media, Diverging Politics: A Political Economy of News in the United States and Canada*, edited by David Skinner, Mike Gasher, and James Compton, 51–76. Lanham, MD: Rowman & Littlefield, 2005.

Smeltzer, Sandra, and Alison Hearn. "Student Rights in an Age of Austerity? 'Security,' Freedom of Expression and the Neoliberal University." *Social Movement Studies* 14, no. 3 (May 4, 2015): 352–58. https://doi.org/10.1080/14742837.2014.945077.

Smiers, Joost, and Marieke van Schijndel. *Imagine There Is No Copyright and No Cultural Conglomerates Too: An Essay*. Vol. 4. Morrisville, NC: Lulu.com, 2009.

Smith, Andrea. "Not-Seeing: State Surveillance, Settler Colonialism, and Gender Violence." In *Feminist Surveillance Studies*, edited by Rachel E. Dubrofsky and Shoshana Magnet, 21–38. Durham, NC: Duke University Press, 2015.

Smith, Bruce L., and Jerry C. Brigham. "Benchmark: Native Radio Broadcasting in North America: An Overview of Systems in the United States and Canada." *Journal of Broadcasting & Electronic Media* 36, no. 2 (1992): 183–94.

Smith, Greg. "Aboriginal Broadcasters' Perspectives on Broadcasting Policy: Report to Northern Native Broadcast Access Program (NNBAP) and the Department of Canadian Heritage." Ottawa: Canadian Heritage, 2004.

Smyth, Sara M. *Cybercrime in Canadian Criminal Law.* Toronto: Carswell Thomson Reuters, 2015.

Smythe, Dallas. *Dependency Road: Communications, Capitalism, Consciousness, and Canada.* Praeger Pub Text, 1981.

————. "National Policy on Public and Private Sectors." In *Telecommunications and Equity: Policy Research Issues Proceedings of the Thirteenth Annual Telecommunications Policy Research Conference, Airlie House, Airlie, Virginia, USA, April 21–24, 1985,* edited by James Miller, 21–30. Amsterdam: North-Holland, 1986.

Society of Canadian Authors and Composers (SOCAN). "C. Paul Spurgeon, Vice-President Legal Services & General Counsel, SOCAN to Robert A. Morin, Secretary General, CRTC, 10 July 2008." May 13, 2016. https://services.crtc.gc.ca/Pub/ListeInterventionList/Documents. aspx?ID=72066&en=pb2008-44&dt=c&Lang=e.

Soos, Gabor. "Smart Decentralization? The Radical Anti-Establishment Worldview of Blockchain Initiatives." *Smart Cities and Regional Development (SCRD) Journal* 2, no. 2 (2018): 35–49.

Spivak, Gayatri Chakravorty. "Can the Subaltern Speak?" In *Can the Subaltern Speak? Reflections on the History of an Idea,* edited by Rosalind C. Morris (New York: Columbia University Press, 2010), 21–78.

Squires, Judith. "Private Lives, Secluded Places: Privacy as Political Possibility." *Environment and Planning D: Society and Space* 12, no. 4 (1994): 387–401.

Srnicek, Nick. *Platform Capitalism.* Cambridge: Polity, 2017.

Stahl, Matt. "From Seven Years to 360 Degrees: Primitive Accumulation, Recording Contracts, and the Means of Making a (Musical) Living." *TripleC: Cognition, Communication, Co-Operation* 9, no. 2 (2011): 668–88.

Stavropoulos, Nicos. "Legal Interpretivism." October 14, 2003. https://plato.stanford. edu/archives/sum2014/entries/law-interpretivist/.

Stewart Millar, Melanie. *Cracking the Gender Code: Who Rules the Wired World?* Toronto: Second Story Press, 1998.

Stewart, Robert Scott. "Is Feminist Porn Possible?" *Sexuality & Culture* (2018): 1–17.

Stigler, George J. "An Introduction to Privacy in Economics and Politics." *The Journal of Legal Studies* 9, no. 4 (1980): 623–44.

Story, Alan. "'Balanced' Copyright: Not a Magic Solving Word." *Intellectual Property Watch* (blog), February 27, 2012. www.ip-watch.org/2012/02/27/%e2%80%98bala nced%e2%80%99-copyright-not-a-magic-solving-word/.

Streckfuss, David. *Truth on Trial in Thailand: Defamation, Treason, and Lèse-Majesté.* New York: Routledge, 2010.

Streeter, Thomas. "Beyond Freedom of Speech and the Public Interest: The Relevance of Critical Legal Studies to Communications Policy." *Journal of Communication* 40, no. 2 (1990): 43–63.

———. "Policy, Politics, and Discourse." *Communication, Culture & Critique* 6, no. 4 (2013): 488–501.

———. "'That Deep Romantic Chasm': Libertarianism, Neoliberalism, and the Computer Culture." *Communication, Citizenship, and Social Policy: Re-Thinking the Limits of the Welfare State*, 1999, 49–64.

Strutt, Suzanne, and Lynne Hissey. "Feminisms and Balance." *Canadian Journal of Communication* 17, no. 1 (1992).

Stychin, Carl F. "Exploring the Limits: Feminism and the Legal Regulation of Gay Male Pornography." *Vermont Law Review* 16 (1991): 857–900.

Sullivan, Rebecca, and Alan McKee. *Pornography: Structures, Agency and Performance.* John Wiley & Sons, 2015.

Sumner, Wayne. "Hate Speech and the Law: A Canadian Perspective." In *Pluralism and Law*, edited by Arend Soeteman, 37–53. Dordrecht: Springer Netherlands, 2001. https://doi.org/10.1007/978-94-017-2702-0_3.

Sumner, Leonard Wayne. *The Hateful and the Obscene: Studies in the Limits of Free Expression.* Toronto: University of Toronto Press, 2004.

Sunder, Madhavi. "The Invention of Traditional Knowledge." *Law and Contemporary Problems* 70, no. 2 (2007): 97–124.

Supreme Court of Canada. "The Canadian Judicial System." February 15, 2018. https://www.scc-csc.ca/court-cour/sys-eng.aspx.

Szwarc, Julia. "Indigenous Broadcasting and the CRTC: Lessons from the Licensing of Native Type B Radio." Gatineau, QC: Canadian Radio-television and Telecommunications Commission, 2018. https://crtc.gc.ca/eng/acrtc/prx/2018szwarc.htm#_tc14.

Tang, Kwong-leung. "Rape Law Reform in Canada: The Success and Limits of Legislation." *International Journal of Offender Therapy and Comparative Criminology* 42, no. 3 (1998): 258–70.

Tawfik, Myra J. "The Supreme Court of Canada and the Fair Dealing Trilogy: Elaborating a Doctrine of User Rights under Canadian Copyright Law." *Alberta Law Review* 51 (2013): 191.

Taylor, Gregory. "Oil in the Ether: A Critical History of Spectrum Auctions in Canada." *Canadian Journal of Communication* 38 (2013): 121–37.

———. "Spectrum Policy in Canada." *IEEE Wireless Communications* 22, no. 6 (2015): 8–9.

Taylor, Lisa, and Cara-Marie O'Hagan, eds. *The Unfulfilled Promise of Press Freedom in Canada*. Toronto: University of Toronto Press, 2017.

Taylor, Lisa, and David Pritchard. "The Process Is the Punishment: Criminal Libel and Political Speech in Canada." *Communication Law and Policy* 23, no. 3 (2018): 243–66. https://doi.org/10.1080/10811680.2018.1467155.

Taylor, Susan R. "Gay and Lesbian Pornography and the Obscenity Laws in Canada." *Dalhousie Journal of Legal Studies* 8 (1999): 94–129.

Telus. "Press Release: Alberta Court Grants Interim Injunction against Posting TELUS Employee Photos." July 28, 2005. https://web.archive.org/web/20110727034812/http://about.telus.com/cgi-bin/news_viewer.cgi?news_id=605&mode=2&news_year=2005.

Thierer, Adam, and Berin Szoka. "CyberLibertarianism: The Case for Real Internet Freedom." *The Technology Liberation Front* (blog), August 12, 2009. https://techliberation.com/2009/08/12/cyber-libertarianism-the-case-for-real-internet-freedom/.

"This Day in 1985—Former Teacher Jim Keegstra Fined for Promoting Hatred against Jews." *Calgary Herald* (blog), July 20, 2012. https://calgaryherald.com/news/local-news/this-day-in-1985.

Thomas, Eric. "Canadian Broadcasting and Multiculturalism: Attempts to Accommodate Ethnic Minorities." *Canadian Journal of Communication* 17, no. 3 (1992).

Thomas, Pradip, and F. Nyamnjoh. "Intellectual Property Challenges in Africa: Indigenous Knowledge Systems and the Fate of Connected Worlds." *Indigenous Knowledge Systems and Intellectual Property in the Twenty-First Century: Perspectives from Southern Africa*, 2007, 12.

"Through Deaf Eyes. Deaf Life. Signing, Alexander Graham Bell and the NAD." PBS.org. Accessed February 17, 2019. https://www.pbs.org/weta/throughdeafeyes/deaflife/bell_nad.html.

Timberg, Craig, Drew Harwell, Hamza Shaban, Andrew Ba Tran, and Brian Fung. "The New Zealand Shooting Shows How YouTube and Facebook Spread Hate and Violent Images—Yet Again." *Washington Post* (blog), March 15, 2019. https://www.washingtonpost.com/technology/2019/03/15/facebook-youtube-twitter-amplified-video-christchurch-mosque-shooting/.

Tjaden, Ted. "Doing Legal Research in Canada." *LLRX: Law and Technology Resources for Legal Professionals* (blog), April 4, 2008. https://www.llrx.com/2008/04/doing-legal-research-in-canada/.

Treasury Board of Canada Secretariat. *Canada's 2018–2020 National Action Plan on Open Government*. Ottawa: Treasury Board Secretariat, 2018.

———. "Interim Directive on the Administration of the Access to Information Act." March 30, 2010. http://www.tbs-sct.gc.ca/pol/doc-eng.aspx?id=18310.

———. "Standard on Web Accessibility." August 2, 2011. http://www.tbs-sct.gc.ca/pol/doc-eng.aspx?id=23601.

Treasury Board of Canada Secretariat and Open Government Partnership. *Guide to Gender-based Analysis Plus (GBA+) and Inclusive Open Government*. Washington DC: Open Government Partnership, 2019. https://www.opengovpartnership.org/wp-content/uploads/2019/05/Guide-GBAandInclusive-Open-Government.pdf.

Tribe, Laura. "Canadian Internet Traffic Is Travelling through the U.S.—Making Canadians Even More Vulnerable to NSA Surveillance." *OpenMedia*. December 16, 2015. https://openmedia.org/en/canadian-internet-traffic-travelling-through-us-making-canadians-even-more-vulnerable-nsa.

Trimble, Linda. "Coming Soon to a Station Near You?: The CRTC Policy on Sex-Role Stereotyping." *Canadian Public Policy/Analyse de Politiques*, 1990, 326–38.

Tromp, Stanley L. *Fallen Behind: Canada's Access to Information Act in the World Context*. Privately published, 2008.

Trubek, David M. "Max Weber's Tragic Modernism and the Study of Law in Society." *Law & Society Review* 20, no. 4 (1986): 573–98.

Trudel, Pierre. "Inhibition Collatérale [Chilling Effect]." *Le Devoir*, March 26, 2019.

Truth and Reconciliation Commission of Canada. "Honouring the Truth, Reconciling for the Future: Summary of the Final Report of the Truth and Reconciliation Commission of Canada." Winnipeg: Truth and Reconciliation Commission of Canada, 2015. http://www.trc.ca/.

Turner, Anne. "Wiretapping Smart Phones with Rotary-Dial Phones' Law: How Canada's Wiretap Law Is in Desperate Need of Updating." *Manitoba Law Journal* 40 (2017): 249–98.

Tusikov, Natasha. *Chokepoints: Global Private Regulation on the Internet*. Berkeley: University of California Press, 2016.

Tutton, Michael. "Advocates for Minority Supreme Court Judge Disappointed by Trudeau's Pick." *The Toronto Star*, October 18, 2016. https://www.thestar.com/news/canada/2016/10/18/advocates-for-minority-supreme-court-judge-disappointed-by-trudeaus-pick.html.

Union of BC Indian Chiefs. "Open Letter and Joint Submission on Bill C-58, An Act to Amend the Access to Information Act and the Privacy Act and to Make Consequential Amendments to Other Acts from the National Claims Research Directors." October 16, 2017. https://www.ubcic.bc.ca/nobillc58.

United Nations. *Declaration on the Rights of Indigenous Peoples*. A/RES/61/295. October 2, 2007. https://www.un.org/development/desa/indigenouspeoples/declaration-on-the-rights-of-indigenous-peoples.html.

United Nations. *Updated Set of Principles for the Protection and Promotion of Human Rights through Action to Combat Impunity*. E/CN.4/2005/102/Add.1. February 8, 2005.

Valdes, Francisco. "Afterword & Prologue: Queer Legal Theory." *California Law Review* 83 (1995): 344–77.

Vallance-Jones, Fred. "Freedom of Information: How Accountability to the Public Is Denied." In *The Unfulfilled Promise of Press Freedom in Canada*, edited by Lisa Taylor and Cara-Marie O'Hagan, 157–66. Toronto: University of Toronto Press, 2017.

Van der Meulen, Emily, and Robert Heynen, eds. *Expanding the Gaze: Gender and the Politics of Surveillance*. Toronto: University of Toronto Press, 2016.

Vats, Anjali, and Deidre A. Keller. "Critical Race IP." *Cardozo Arts & Entertainment Law Journal* 36, no. 3 (2018): 735–95.

Vipond, Mary. "The Beginnings of Public Broadcasting in Canada: The CRBC, 1932–1936." *Canadian Journal of Communication* 19, no. 2 (1994).

Vossen, Bas van der, and Peter Vallentyne. "Libertarianism." In *The Stanford Encyclopedia of Philosophy*, edited by Edward N. Zalta, Fall 2018. https://plato.stanford.edu/archives/fall2018/entries/libertarianism/.

Wagman, Ira. "Talking to Netflix with a Canadian Accent: On Digital Platforms and National Media Policies." In *Reconceptualising Film Policies*, 205–21. New York: Routledge, 2017.

Weatherby, Danielle. "From Jack to Jill: Gender Expression as Protected Speech in the Modern Schoolhouse." *NYU Review of Law & Social Change* 39 (2015): 89–132.

Weber, Max. *Economy and Society: An Outline of Interpretive Sociology*. Los Angeles: University of California Press, 1978.

Weinberg, Lindsay. "Rethinking Privacy: A Feminist Approach to Privacy Rights after Snowden." *Westminster Papers in Communication and Culture* 12, no. 3 (2017).

Wenders, John. "Equity and Politics in the US Telecommunications Industry." In *Telecommunications and Equity: Policy Research Issues Proceedings of the Thirteenth Annual Telecommunications Policy Research Conference, Airlie House, Airlie, Virginia, USA, April 21–24, 1985*, edited by James Miller, 53–60. Amsterdam: North-Holland, 1986.

West, Edwin George. "The Political Economy of Alienation: Karl Marx and Adam Smith." *Oxford Economic Papers* 21, no. 1 (1969): 1–23.

Westin, Alan F. "Science, Privacy, and Freedom: Issues and Proposals for the 1970's. Part I—The Current Impact of Surveillance on Privacy." *Columbia Law Review* 66, no. 6 (1966): 1003–50.

White, Julie. *Losing Canadian Culture: The Danger of Foreign Ownership of Telecom.* Ottawa: Canadian Centre for Policy Alternatives, 2005.

White, Patrick. "Disturbed Inmates Caught in Solitary Trap." *The Globe and Mail,* April 25, 2016.

Williams, Patricia. "In-Laws and Outlaws." *Arizona Law Review* 46 (2004): 199–212.

Williams, Susan H. "Feminist Theory and Freedom of Speech." *Indiana Law Journal* 84 (2009): 999–1013.

Winegust, Tamara Céline, Noelle Engle-Hardy, and Susan J. Keri. "Redskins, Eskimos, and Indians: The Canadian Approach to Disparaging Trademarks." *Trademark Reporter* 105 (2015): 938.

Wing-Fai, Leung, Rosalind Gill, and Keith Randle. "Getting in, Getting on, Getting out? Women as Career Scramblers in the UK Film and Television Industries." *The Sociological Review* 63, no. 1 (2015): 50–65.

Winseck, Dwayne. "Information Operations 'Blowback': Communication, Propaganda and Surveillance in the Global War on Terrorism." *International Communication Gazette* 70, no. 6 (December 2008): 419–41. https://doi.org/10.1177/1748048508096141.

———. "Media and Internet Concentration in Canada Report 1984–2015." Canadian Media Concentration Research Project, November 22, 2016. http://www.cmcrp.org/media-and-internet-concentration-in-canada-report-1984-2015/.

———. "Reconstructing the Political Economy of Communication for the Digital Media Age." *The Political Economy of Communication* 4, no. 2 (2017).

———. *Reconvergence: A Political Economy of Telecommunications in Canada.* Cressville, NJ: Hampton Press, 1998.

Wirtén, Eva Hemmungs. *Terms of Use: Negotiating the Jungle of the Intellectual Commons.* Toronto: University of Toronto Press, 2008.

Wollaston, Paul. "When Will They Ever Get It Right—A Gay Analysis of *R. v. Butler.*" *Dalhousie Journal of Legal Studies* 2 (1993): 251–64.

Woodmansee, Martha, and Peter Jaszi, eds. *The Construction of Authorship: Textual Appropriation in Law and Literature.* Durham, NC: Duke University Press, 1994.

Wu, Tim. "Network Neutrality, Broadband Discrimination." *Journal on Telecommunications & High Technology Law* 2, (2003): 141–76.

Wu, Tim, and Christopher Yoo. "Keeping the Internet Neutral?: Tim Wu and Christopher Yoo Debate." *Federal Communications Law Journal* 59, no. 3 (2007): 575–92.

Yanchukova, Elena. "Criminal Defamation and Insult Laws: An Infringement on the Freedom of Expression in European and Post-Communist Jurisdictions." *Columbia Journal of Transnational Law* 41 (2002): 861–94.

Young, Alyson Leigh, and Anabel Quan-Haase. "Privacy Protection Strategies on Facebook: The Internet Privacy Paradox Revisited." *Information, Communication & Society* 16, no. 4 (2013): 479–500.

Young, Hilary. "Why Canada Shouldn't Let Businesses Sue for Defamation." *The Toronto Star*, September 16, 2012. https://www.thestar.com/opinion/editorialopinion/2012/09/16/why_canada_shouldnt_let_businesses_sue_for_defamation.html.

Young, Mary Lynn, and Alison Beale. "Canada: The Paradox of Women in News." In *The Palgrave International Handbook of Women and Journalism*, edited by Carolyn M. Byerly, 109–21. Springer, 2013.

Zalnieriute, Monika. "The Anatomy of Neoliberal Internet Governance: A Queer Critical Political Economy Perspective." In *Queering International Law: Possibilities, Alliances, Complicities, Risks*, edited by Dianne Otto, 53–74. Abingdon, UK: Routledge, 2018.

Zetter, Kim. "Hackers Finally Post Stolen Ashley Madison Data." *Wired*, August 18, 2015. https://www.wired.com/2015/08/happened-hackers-posted-stolen-ashley-madison-data/.

Zimmer, Michael. "'But the Data Is Already Public': On the Ethics of Research in Facebook." *Ethics and Information Technology* 12, no. 4 (2010): 313–25.

Zingo, Martha T. *Sex/Gender Outsiders, Hate Speech, and Freedom of Expression: Can They Say That about Me?* Westport, CT: Greenwood Publishing Group, 1998.

Zvulony, Gil. "What Is Defamation in Ontario Law." Accessed October 31, 2018. https://zvulony.ca/2010/articles/defamation-articles/definition-defamation/.

# INDEX